Seeing the Future Through New Eyes

Seeing the Future Through New Eyes

Essays published in conjunction with the World
Future Society's annual meeting, WorldFuture 2008:
Seeing the Future Through New Eyes

edited by Cynthia G. Wagner

published by the World Future Society, www.wfs.org

World Future Society Conference Volume Team

Editor: Cynthia G. Wagner, cwagner@wfs.org
Editorial Production: Aaron M. Cohen, Rick Docksai
Business Manager: Jeff Cornish
Art Director: Lisa Mathias
Consulting Editors: Edward Cornish, Susan Echard,
Timothy C. Mack, Patrick Tucker

Published by:
World Future Society
7910 Woodmont Avenue, Suite 450
Bethesda, Maryland 20814, U.S.A.
www.wfs.org

ISBN: 0-930242-65-3
Printed in the United States of America.

Contents

Preface

When I learned that the theme of the World Future Society's 2008 conference would be "Seeing the Future Through New Eyes," I jumped at the chance to help set the stage by assembling this volume of essays. I felt very confident that our longtime contributors would rise to the occasion, and indeed they have. But I was especially delighted to welcome so many new contributors to the conference volume series. Together, these thirty-two authors offer a multitude of unique perspectives. At minimum, any one of these essays could provide the "new eyes" through which a reader might see a different kind of future.

What I did not anticipate, however, was the panoramic vistas that our contributors would provide. The pages of this book will take you on a long, eye-opening journey, from a visit with the oracles living thousands of years ago ("The Ancient Oracles Still Speak" by Barton Kunstler) all the way to a time up ahead—perhaps not so far away—when we take all the wisdom of our years and collective experiences to forge a new path to the stars ("Expansion for the Good of Humanity" by Francis R. Stabler).

Nor did I anticipate the fascinating stories that some of our contributors came here to tell! One of our protagonists, for instance, strove to democratize religion by creating a Bible that everyone could read—challenging the Church's authority and offering a lesson for future generations about the power of communications technology (see "Worldwide Wipeout" by Seth Kaufman). Other heroes and heroines are brought to these pages to illustrate the importance of acting on our visions of the future ("The Future Is All Around Us" by Clifton Anderson). And in a scenario focusing on education, we adopt a fictional teenage daughter,

"Elena," who walks us through the curriculum of "High Schools of the Future" (by Arthur Shostak).

Here is a quick overview of the volume's thematic structure.

Part 1: Perspectives and Prospects illustrates how our points of view are shaped by a wide range of factors. In order to examine the validity of our perspectives (and alternatives), we must also focus on the influencing factors, such as our political or cultural milieu.

Part 2: Tools and Applications assesses the instruments necessary for seeing the future. The authors analyze and recalibrate futures tools, such as paradigms and strategic analysis, and show how they may be applied to our visioning tasks.

Part 3: Problems and Opportunities confronts several key issues requiring our improved perception and perspective, such as global crime, energy, sustainable development, the financial system, and academia.

Part 4: Inspiration and Action: Moving Forward strives to answer the key question, What now? Even when we see the future clearly—or think we do—we must also be able to find our way there.

So off you go; I hope you enjoy the journey ahead with this outstanding cadre of visionary companions.

cgw, Bethesda, June 2008

Executive Summaries

The Ancient Oracles Still Speak: Recasting Forecasting for the 21st Century

by Barton Kunstler

Forecasting, futurism, and fortune-telling have been a central concern of human life throughout history, whose many foresight techniques are, at the least, rich cultural artifacts containing insight into other societies' views of time, fate, the mind, strategic planning, and epistemology. Two ancient oracles in particular have maintained a strong presence in the modern era: the oracle of Apollo at Delphi and the Chinese *I Ching,* or *Book of Changes.* It is especially important to understand the approach to forecasting of ancient societies because we can no longer rely on the rationalistic, mechanistic modes of foresight that currently dominate the field. Archaic people very likely experienced the mind and time differently from us, and in exploring what lay behind ancient eyes we stand a good chance of refreshing our own future sight.

Delphi played a powerful role for centuries in ancient Greece, much of it akin to that of organizational managers and consultants today. It also embraced even more ancient traditions than the Apollonian one. A full consideration of the Delphi's traditions illuminates in surprising ways the daunting challenges that futurists and forecasters face today. The *I Ching* presents us with an approach to both time and management that serves as an alternative to present-day modes of thinking about the future. Between the two oracles, we discover that science, technology, and futurist speculation are converging to validate the perspectives of the archaic world, and that the latter provides, in turn, inspiration and validation for the most cutting-edge approaches to forecasting in the twenty-first century.

Worldwide Wipeout: The Greatest Publishing Story Never Told, Jihad, and the Unintended Consequences of the Internet's Killer App

by Seth Kaufman

This essay investigates the future of the Web and the world by examining the previous revolutions set in motion by that old "new media," the printing press—a platform that unwittingly helped launch the Protestant Reformation. The essay examines a host of parallels between the issues facing William Tyndale, the brilliant evangelist who defied the church and Henry VIII by fleeing to Europe and translating the Bible into English, and hot-button issues involving the Web—control of publishing, property rights, piracy, religious revolution, censorship, propaganda. Tyndale's journey, fueled by his religious fervor, led to enormous geopolitical change. There are echoes of his story line in the radical Islamist movements of today—like Tyndale, they have a powerful new media platform to appeal to the disenfranchised and essentially put their means of salvation in the hands of the proletariat. Of course Tyndale wasn't a Jihadi (he loved the monarchy, but hated the church), but his story and its subsequent reverberations are worth studying. This essay investigates whether the Web is a platform that can be controlled and how governments can and cannot dictate the flow of information, and then even delves into the future of radical Islam.

Toward an Anthropology of the Future

by Alexandra Chciuk-Celt

Oversimplifying grossly, anthropologists distinguish between two main types of society: hunter-gatherer (low population density, challenge viewed as an opportunity, children raised to be self-reliant) and peasant (high density, challenge viewed as a threat, children raised to be obedient). Americans think like hunter-gatherers, who move to a new location when resources become scarce; when they run out of places to go, they generally turn on each other (infanticide, warfare, etc.), ensuring the survival of the nastiest. It is hoped that a change in attitude can help plan a less destructive future.

Technological Evolution

by José Luis Cordeiro

Since the Big Bang, the universe has been in constant evolution and continuous transformation. First there were physical and chemical processes, then biological evolution, and finally now technological evolution. As we begin to ride the wave into human redesign, the destination is still largely unknown, but the opportunities are almost limitless.

Biological evolution continues, but it is too slow to achieve the goals now possible thanks to technological evolution. Natural selection with trial and error can now be substituted by technical selection with engineering design. Humanity's monopoly as the only advanced sentient life-form on the planet will soon come to an end, supplemented by a number of posthuman incarnations. Moreover, how we reengineer ourselves could fundamentally change the ways in which our society functions and raise crucial questions about our identities and moral status as human beings.

The Evolution and Future Direction of Marriage

by Tom Lombardo and Jeanne Belisle Lombardo

In this paper we trace the evolution of marriage from prehistoric to contemporary times. We then examine the main controversies and issues regarding modern marriage in the West. From there we turn to future possibilities connected with cultural and technological changes.

Finally, we outline a vision of the preferable marriage of the future, one that is broad and general enough to accommodate the diverse modes of marriage that have emerged in contemporary times, but also one that is psychologically and ethically informed. We outline a vision based on the notion of the mutual practice and pursuit of character virtues by both partners in the marriage.

Through New Eyes: Transcending Culture-Based Assumptions

by Dave Stein

For several reasons — the challenges that humankind is facing, the accelerating pace of change, growing interest in the future itself, the increased interaction among various peoples and cultures, and the ever-increasing willingness to question the ways and assumptions of the past — the need for "new eyes" has never been greater. At the individual level, the interplay of peoples and cultures (including modern techno-business culture) can have profound consequences, for example, to lifestyles, values, identity, and outlooks on life. A key question is whether humanity is headed toward cultural plurality with alternative "operating systems" or toward a more monolithic world with "no place to hide" for those who ill-adjust.

To futurists and policy analysts, "new eyes" can help one transcend culture-based assumptions and identify alternatives to "plug and play" ways forward. One might even ask how various cultures, present and past, would have addressed various contemporary challenges and how they have approached the future itself. The cultures and peoples of the world offer valuable perspectives for meeting present and forthcoming challenges — perspectives that may be lost if not given audience.

For educators, the "through new eyes" theme ushers in the next frontier in interdisciplinary and liberal education — specifically, true cross-cultural learning among students of diverse backgrounds — in a foundational way.

With the "new eyes" imperative established, this paper helps set the stage.

PART 2: TOOLS AND APPLICATIONS

The Quadrate: A Paradigm for Conflicting Civilizations and Global Futures

by Jitendra G. Borpujari

The proposed quadrate suggests a paradigm shift for a grip on global futures at stake in the ongoing conflict of civilizations. Civilizations may be classified as exclusive or inclusive and as religious or secular. The rival global futures at stake in the conflict of civilizations may be therefore represented in a quadrate comprising a comprehensive and unique classification of the various ways of life: "religious-exclusive," "secular-exclusive," "religious-inclusive," and "secular-inclusive." Allowing for the limitations of such a broad tagging of cultures, the new paradigm provides a fresh perspective to review the past and anticipate the future as an outcome of rival civilizations vying to prevail within a quadrate of possible global futures.

Seeing Newly, Differently, and Futuristically with the Scenario

by Irving H. Buchen

The scenario, which is a more manageable and less sensational version of science fiction, can be an effective lens by which to see and to help others envision a future that may be both reassuring and unnerving. In particular, the scenario — unlike standard forecasts — is not so much a planning but a decisions document that spells out and tests the known and unknown consequences of solutions to problems. Reformulated to incorporate systems analysis and the imaginative power of science fiction, the scenario in the hands of futurists can be one of most effective ways not only of projecting but also of persuading others to see futures that are new, different, and futuristic.

Backcasting from the Future: Predict the Future by Creating It

by Don Mizaur

Planners accuse futurists of being "blue sky" and "out in the ozone." Futurists accuse planners of being unimaginative and didactic. This troublesome chasm between futurists and planners may be best bridged by employing a powerful concept called *backcasting.*

Forecasting is the traditional methodology for stating what the future will look like. When people are asked to make plans for the future, they tend to extrapolate from the past and the present. The past and the present are the time frames where they exist when asked to engage in a futures planning process. For the process to be truly effective, planners must be transported to the future and be allowed to imagine a vastly different environment without being encumbered by the current and past realities. Transporting them to that unencumbered future better state is the first step in using the backcasting approach. Once that future is envisioned, the planners can then backcast from that state and delineate the critical success factors and action plans needed to make that future state a reality.

Forecasting the Next Industrial Revolution: A Structural Perspective from Evolutionary Economics

by Denis L. Balaguer

The essential nature of capitalism is its dynamics and its propensity to change, and the evolutionary kernel of economic change under the capitalist regime — the one element that sets the pace — is technological innovation. This change of the techno-economic paradigm is historically represented by industrial revolutions. So, the systematic forecasting of the structures that determine industrial revolution is an important issue, both for firms and governments. Since forecasting about probabilities understands the forces that will shape the convergence toward the future, it is necessary to build up a conceptual scheme, in order to build a relevant model of the system analyzed. Considering the system "Industrial Revolution," one important contribution comes from evolutionary economics, especially by providing the key variables that describe the system. Using these variables, it is possible to build a framework to objectively analyze the state of the paradigm change in order to support a forecasting study.

Macrotechnology Analysis

by Paul Crabtree

Technology is described as a space matrix with three dimensions. Technological change is defined as a change in the dimensions of the space matrix, with technological progress defined as a net increase in the overall dimensions of the space matrix. Factors governing changes in each of the dimensions of the space matrix are analyzed, and a number of general conclusions follow from the analysis. [Author's note: An earlier version of this essay was published in *The Innovation Journal* (May 2006), www.innovation.cc.]

The Failure of Strategic Planning and Corporate Performance

by Romulo Werran Gayoso

In an effort to see the future through new eyes, it is important for business futurists to come to terms with which sets of future methodology tools would still be able to bring about novel ideas and help forecasters break apart from old paradigms. Business decisions are often made in situations where there is no perfect information. Thus, operating under uncertainty leads companies to attempt several different strategies in order to mitigate risks. Scenario planning, a commonly used strategic-planning tool, is often implemented as a way to manage business and environmental uncertainty, even though some question its usefulness. The objective of this paper is to consider the impact of environmental risks on strategic planning and evaluate the effectiveness of scenario planning in yielding better corporate performance, and thus remaining as a premier analytical vehicle to help business leaders and professional futurists envision the future.

Visionary Concept: Combining Scenario Methodology with Concept Development

by Sami Leppimäki, Jukka Laitinen, Tarja Meristö, and Hanna Tuohimaa

In a world of continuous changes, both individual companies and industries as a whole face the demand of renewal and improvement. In this article we argue that the challenges of the future should be incorporated into strategic considerations, the innovation process, R&D planning, and product development of the companies by combining scenario thinking into concept development. This is done by assessing product needs in different future scenarios and generating product concepts that suit the differing future circumstances. These visionary concepts may then be used to enhance the directing and correct timing of the R&D projects in the long time range.

A Scientific Approach to Collaborative Innovation and Strategic Foresight: Connecting the "Dots" Outside the "Box"

by Howard S. Rasheed

Identifying, creating, and distributing knowledge within an

organizational knowledge network to stimulate awareness and learning may be the most important competency of the future for creating and sustaining competitive advantages in the new global economy. To create competitive advantage, organizations spend tremendous resources on perfecting systems throughout their value chain process—from production to customer service. Most organizations do not invest in developing a system for new idea creation, innovation, and strategic foresight.

So how do we provide a systematic approach to innovation? Traditional brainstorming sessions, where bright people gather in a room and throw thoughts and ideas around, have been the futurist and business world's traditional approach to collaborative innovation. This paper offers a methodology for creating a sustainable innovation value chain using a six-step process entitled "Six Steps to Collective Genius," which is scientifically supported and replicable in many organizations.

This methodology provides a design for a collaborative innovation network—a cyberteam of self-motivated people with a collective vision, enabled by the Web to collaborate in achieving a common goal by systematically stimulating ideation. The result is ideation that exceeds the value creation potential of traditional strategic planning and knowledge management paradigms. This interactive system provides a road map to ignite the collective genius in an organization. Using a neuroscience-based approach to ideation, this paper identifies infinite possibilities through systematically focused attention on "connecting the dots outside the box." Executives and futurists will learn transferable visionary and strategic leadership skills for anticipating future scenarios, breakthrough innovation, and emerging business opportunities.

humankind. Global warming, pollution, transportation, high energy costs, and terrorist attacks are all prime challenges. None of these will be easily tamed by conventional techniques or solutions of the past. We need a fresh way forward. If we begin to see the future through the lens of "telegeography," we can change our world for the better.

Viewing Economics through the Prism of Sustainable Development and Self-Sufficiency

by Bruce E. Tonn

This paper argues that over the long term major aspects of sustainable development and economic theory and policy are incongruent. Sustainable development policies seek to reduce consumption, promote self-sustainability, and require major investments not only in natural capital but also in other programs to sustain life on Earth. If successful, these policies will lead to technical reductions in gross domestic product, require a smaller money supply, boost the share of government spending in the national economy, increase the role of nonprofit organizations in the economy, and decrease the role of the private sector in the economy. Economic theory and policy instruments are ill-suited to respond to these trends and, in the near term, would tend to work against the goals of sustainable development. A new view of economics is needed to support sustainable development over the long term.

Faster, Larger, Riskier: Investing in the Future Global Stock Exchange

by Joan E. Foltz

The globalization of the world's stock exchanges is causing structural shifts in the financial industry that have long-term implications for equity markets, regional economies, and individual investors. Recent mergers and acquisitions among the exchanges show acceleration along a trajectory based on the adoption rate of market-based governance across the world.

Continuing deregulation accompanies free-market economies, which is enabling a global stock exchange to emerge as a self-organizing system. Risk and rewards will be determined by strategies that look at the market as a system restructuring with changing forces. An understanding of how the stock markets will represent the behavioral patterns of their players and how to recognize fundamental organizational structures will benefit investors in the future.

In Praise of Academic *Dis*engagement
by Michael Bugeja

Since the 1990s, educators have invested in consumer technologies in the name of access, which promised to enfranchise everyone. Now that we have bridged the digital divide, we are concerned about access to education. Cause and effect here correlate as tuition continues to spike beyond the means of many students who own the laptops, iPods, and cell phones that are being used to engage them in the interactive classroom. As such, there is a blurring between entertainment and learning that is as distracting as it is expensive. This essay looks at the cost of engagement in the name of retention, often associated with the National Survey on Student Engagement, even though only four of 100 questions on that survey are related to technology. Financial concerns are as much a factor in falling retention rates as engagement. Thus, the author asks educators to consider the prospect of disengagement. He provides assessment techniques to gauge the effectiveness of consumer technologies associated with social networks and virtual worlds and asks educators what they will be willing to sacrifice to make college affordable again. Finally, he recommends less emphasis on engagement and more on commitment to help prepare students for the environmental, health, water, food, and fuel issues that they will encounter in less than a decade.

PART 4: INSPIRATION AND ACTION: MOVING FORWARD

The Future Is All Around Us

by Clifton Anderson

Today's environmental crises arose because decision makers of the past failed to develop adequate solutions for the problems they faced.

Time and again, an unsolved environmental problem recurs as a crisis (or near-crisis). Our battered planet needs careful, sustained therapy by caregivers who will use ambitious new approaches.

In this essay, eight individuals are cited as dedicated problem solvers. They have the ability to see problems in cultural context. They ask a question many of us have neglected to ask ourselves: How might new patterns of human behavior improve the present environmental situation?

The eight individuals mentioned here resemble today's action-oriented social scientists. Present-day progressive thinkers do want to test theories and measure results, of course, but what sustains their reform efforts is the belief that the work they do is socially valuable.

They are activists, eager to accomplish worthwhile achievements, and (at the same time) they are responsible, intellectually honest individuals — well qualified to see the future through discerning eyes. This is the kind of earnest, persevering help we will need to find solutions for global warming; air, soil, and water pollution; resource depletion; environment-related disease; and other persistent problems of our time.

Leadership as Legacy Work

by Les Wallace and James Trinka

The twenty-first century has signaled a need to think differently about leadership, developing leaders, and leadership impact. The last two decades of research and teaching have provided valuable clarity as to how leadership is learned and, therefore, how to help us learn to become better leaders. The age of heroic leadership is over. The myth of the "great man" or "great woman," leading larger than life and rescuing powerless organizational associates, has been dispelled. Great leadership occurs in a culture of leadership that is expected, developed, and distributed at all levels of the organization where people can display their natural ability to learn, adapt, and lead. Leaders don't create followers. They create other leaders. In this article, we explore several ways in which the twenty-first century appears much different from the last century.

Twenty-first-century leaders are also reminded they are leaving a legacy, whether they like it or not. A legacy is defined by the climate of leadership and the capabilities of the organization we lead to be better when we leave. We encourage leaders to think about making their legacy intentional and boldly suggest five legacies worthy of the twenty-first century and five powerful leadership behaviors that embed legacies.

High Schools of the Future: "Boot Camp"

by Arthur Shostak

In 2015, a teenager, Elena, bicycles off to her green-certified magnet high school of the future. The campus, classrooms, curriculum, and co-curriculum activities stand in exciting contrast to what is common in 2008, as futuristics is the guiding concern of the world's first such high school. Lynn gains a sound education from seventeen required courses (History of Forecasting, Strengths and

Weaknesses of Forecasting, etc.), and a bevy of eclectic electives. Better still, she has an opportunity to decide if a career as a professional futurist is her calling. America gets an overdue boost to its need for a supply of well-educated forecasters, and the world gets a model of a farsighted high school that belongs in almost every major city everywhere.

Paid Volunteerism: Is There an Oxymoron in Our Future?

by Jay Herson

A *New York Times* article in 2007 indicated a trend among recent retirees who seek to volunteer their services to nonprofit organizations (dot-orgs) but who prefer to be paid a nominal hourly wage ($10–$15). The term paid volunteer arises from this phenomenon. There is a feeling among baby boomers that volunteer efforts are not taken seriously when there is no compensation. This is particularly an issue for baby boomers bringing professional-type skills to the dot-orgs—legal, Internet, computer network administration, etc. Some dot-orgs feel that they can better rely on volunteers to show up regularly and use them more efficiently if they are paid. An industry is developing on the Internet to match retirees to paid volunteer opportunities.

This article examines the future of paid volunteers by presenting macro-level and operating-level drivers of change (demographic, economic, and societal values), followed by three future scenarios. Scenario 1 is extrapolative and describes the consequences of the continuation of the current trend. Scenario 2 examines the challenging times ahead as this trend moves to the extreme. Scenario 3 presents a paradigm shift toward idealism and commitment toward paying back society. Finally, a normative most-likely scenario is presented, along with useful signposts to watch for development of this trend.

Expansion for the Good of Humanity

by Francis R. Stabler

    Humans have been migrating to new areas for many thousands of years. Most of these moves have added to the quality of civilization and increased the ability of the human species to survive disasters. Humans now have the ability to migrate off of our home planet. This vast new frontier will bring untold advances to Earth while increasing the long-term survivability of the human race. The resources available from space will effectively end the limits of growth for the human race. Access to a new frontier will spur education and lift people's eyes from short-term difficulties to long-term potential. The only limits of growth are those we place on ourselves. The universe offers us unlimited space and resources if we are willing to put forth the effort to accept them. The next destinations for humanity are the Moon, our solar system, our galaxy, and the universe.

Part 1

Perspectives and Prospects

The Ancient Oracles Still Speak

Recasting Forecasting for the 21st Century

Barton Kunstler

Fortune-telling, futurism, foresight, forecasting—all refer to what may truly be the world's oldest profession: anticipating and averting risk and maximizing gain. The very idea of foresight is intrinsic to the mind itself, for the engine that drives humans to extend the range of thought is the desire to predict, to understand where we are going, to anticipate what lies ahead. To that end, human beings have employed a wide range of techniques: astrology, haruspicy (reading entrails), ornithomancy (augury from the flight of birds), casting stones or dregs of wine, trance states, and shamanic journeys. Although some of these methods have been limited by superstition and sloppy methodology, they are all informed by core cultural assumptions about time, space, fate, cosmology, strategy, the limits of human knowledge and effort, uncertainty, and risk. Some, however, are more than just data-rich artifacts of a bygone era. They may well have embodied ways of perceiving, knowing, and thinking very different from our own that we might explore to our benefit.

Barton Kunstler is a consultant and writer. He is the author of *The Hothouse Effect* (Amacom, 2004). E-mail barleeku@comcast.net.

Archaic societies—those we refer to as ancient and primitive—differed greatly from modern civilization, and hence offer insight into regions of mental activity that lie within us as abandoned and forgotten as any mythical lost continent.

The general view of archaic knowledge is skewed by certain modern biases, to wit, that:

- The growth of knowledge has been progressive, using all that was worthwhile in the past and rejecting the past's many misconceptions and superstitions.

- Ancient myths and reflections on the psyche may have "worked well for them," but now we have far superior methodologies for understanding the qualitative aspects of life.

- Such ancient constructs as *fate, time, spirit, soul, space,* and *deities* were clever and often elaborate ways of struggling to understand what is impossible to understand without a materialist, rationalist mind-set.

In other words, now we understand things so much better than we ever have. In many ways, however, our understanding falls short. We fail to see that:

- We simply cannot ascertain what the ancients actually did know, considering all that went up in flames in libraries from Lhasa to Alexandria to Ireland; our lack of knowledge about ancient technology; the loss of oral and contemplative traditions; and the fragmentary nature of archaeological remains.

- Archaic knowledge is associative and qualitative, and thus archaic epistemologies, in effect, require decoding. Freudian psychology and Levi-Strauss's structuralism, for instance, have provided two critical keys, but there are others as well that we have only begun to decipher, and some of which we are likely unaware.

- In terms of the big issues (fate, death, etc.), archaic traditions developed continuously for tens of thousands of years using the empiricism of direct experience distilled through many generations, and they may well comprise very different insights from those of modern epistemologies, which can be as limiting in some areas as they are liberating in others.

- It is possible that archaic minds simply worked differently from ours, due to a variety of factors: lack of conditioning in rationalistic, linear thinking; access to more oxygen and sunlight than we have in the postindustrial era; training in mind- and thought-expanding technologies or "techniques of ecstasy," in Eliade's phrase; dependence upon ways of knowing to which we may apply such terms as gnostic, proprioceptive, and resonant; and growing up in a very different environment with very different demands upon — and opportunities for — the psyche.

This last point seems more likely in light of neuroscience's advances in understanding the brain, which may enable us to stimulate parts of the brain to improve cognitive functioning, or inhibit areas that get in the way. We are already doing that with a host of psychological medications, biofeedback training, and brain-wave programming. These all lend credence to the notion that people in other cultures cultivated other brain regions from those emphasized in our own era.

It is also helpful to recognize the differences between two primary notions of forecasting. The first is the rationalistic, empirical version that we use in strategic planning: trend analysis; algorithms that include data collection, stages of analysis, recommendations, implementation, etc.; scenario building; and so forth. Nor do such methods preclude the use of intuition or imagination. The rational forecaster relies upon pattern recognition, leaps of creative insight, artistic and/or philosophical sensibilities, insofar as they belong to their repertoire. Still, this approach begins with a rational, empirical assessment of a situation and uses data collection, modeling, and causality to derive conclusions.

The second category of foresight is generally consigned to superstition or fable: fortune-telling. This implies the ability to actually see or hear the future as it will actually unfold or key patterns or data-points received using a special gift or method possessed by the reader or oracle. This notion is acausal and does not depend on data collection, analysis, or rational thought. The forecaster becomes a medium for signals emanating from another realm, be it angelic, divine, "higher" levels of reality, the *zeitgeist,* some updated version of the ether, other people's thoughts, or completely separate and co-existing realities. However much justifiable skepticism this purported gift arouses, it is probably wise to adopt an agnostic view concerning its existence in some form. There is, after all, a lot about the mind and its capabilities that we do not understand. It is quite possible that archaic people, with very different environmental conditions and wisdom traditions, had a very different experience of their own mental capacities than we do today of ours. For instance, differences in the archaic perception of time as cyclical and the modern sense of time as linear go beyond a contrast between respective time charts. They refer quite literally to differences in how time and the relationship of events in time are experienced. In turn, this could mean that the relationship of the present moment to future moments may have been experienced differently. Research (De Keyser et al. 1998) has demonstrated the complexity of the brain's construction of duration itself. Ancient philosophers were fascinated with the notion of extension in space as a fundamental principle of ontology. In our post-Einsteinian world, we may have to deconstruct and re-experience the underlying basis of temporal extension in order to align our perceptions and deeper understanding with the new principles of reality that the human intellect has uncovered—or recovered—in the past century.

Quantum mechanics, relativity, and such technologies as holography (Talbot 1991) have inspired alternative models of mind that could accommodate the future sight of the second framework.

David Loye, in the seminal *The Sphinx and the Rainbow* (1983), suggests that the universe is host to multiple realities that coexist within in a vast hologram of interwoven wave patterns—an idea that has become popular among writers who draw upon the seeming paradoxes of matter and energy unearthed by modern physics. These realities include real universes that could become accessible to us when we enter states of higher consciousness. In this view, the path to other dimensions goes through the subatomic world. Thus the relationship between our perceptions and these many-dimensional multiverses is governed by quantum mechanics. In that realm, time flows backward as easily as forward, objects act upon one another simultaneously, quanta move in and out of existence as fluidly as the blinking light of a firefly's lantern, and the observer seems to have a role in bringing subatomic particles into existence. Hence, all past and possible future events exist in holographic form, and our thoughts can move forward as well as backward in time. It has also been suggested that the observer is the crucial figure in bringing the world into existence, that, just as with quanta, things do not exist unless an observer makes them so.

Loye (1983, 114-115) notes physicist Charles Muses's discovery that two precursor electromagnetic waves actually run ahead of the electrical message that carries the signal to shut down a circuit. Muses suggested that, in our world, events send out similar signals that provide a preview of themselves, which could account for future sight. Meanwhile, some physicists think that our four-dimensional world (space plus time) may be embedded in other dimensions, much as a two-dimensional realm, such as a painted landscape, exists inside three-dimensional space.

There is a serious obstacle to such theories, and that is the validity of applying patterns of behavior among quanta to our own physical realm. Even if the brain does work holographically, which may be the approximate case, we cannot assume that the entire universe is a vast hologram in which all that has ever happened has left a trace, or, even more extreme, that all sorts of alternative happenings are also embedded. Even if everything that has occurred or even *will* occur leaves an electromagnetic trace via wave interference patterns, that does not mean we can translate these patterns into a vision of past or future events. Similarly, just because electromagnetic waves send out precursors, it does not mean that events in our own physical dimension send out precursor signals in which events can be "read" ahead of time. Electromagnetic waves may emanate from an individual or from the activity of an event, but are the precursor waves at all interpretable in terms of events at the scale of our observable human world?

I do not mean to deny the implications for philosophy, cosmology, technology, etc., of such discoveries, or the possibility that consciousness may have access to quantum energies, channels, and behaviors. Certainly, their powerful metaphorical impact on how we interpret the mind or human interaction can be the source of fruitful interpretation or investigation. Nor do I think Loye, Talbot, or Muses misdirected in speculating; in fact, such speculations provide a great service to human thought. It is just that, once the speculation has been posed, we — embedded in the modern world among competing technologies and worldviews — require a demonstrable link between the behavior of quanta and the behavior of the physical world apprehensible by our senses. Another aspect of this puzzle is that Loye, Talbot, and Muses may be shown to be correct. The work of physicist Hal Everett (Byrne 2007) positing multiple realities has led to the current frontier of quantum physics. Recent work seeks to unify the quantum and physical worlds and develop a unified field theory in which matter and energy truly are treated as identical forms, which would take us — and our understanding of time and the mind's behavior in relation to it — into unsuspected territory.

A more mundane explanation, however, may also support the

notion of future sight. Looking back, we often see how something simply had to happen. Hindsight recognizes the train of events that led to a seemingly unpredictable act. Some people, though, may unconsciously select from and organize the trillions of data bits that we perceive every day, their minds constructing a mental image that shows the logical conclusion to seemingly disconnected or even chaotic events. After all, every event is the climax of many others, and at some moment it becomes probable, even inevitable, that a given event will occur. At that moment, our "watcher" will be blessed (or cursed) with an image of the future outcome.

In any case, reason-based forecasting, on the one hand, and seeing the actual future, on the other, differ in key ways:

- *The process of selecting data points—including ideas, beliefs, biases, etc.* The selection is likely to be conscious in rationalistic forecasting, although subject to individual and collective biases and habits of thought. In future sight, the selection of data points can be unconscious or conscious. In either case, it occurs under the guidance of an alternative—or altered—state of consciousness from what society accepts as the norm. That is, in the former, one finds and selects data by thinking it through; in the latter, data are revealed to one or are uncovered by seemingly mysterious means.
- *The data selected.* The data accessible to analytic, logical thought will be different from that garnered by "visionary" means.
- *The areas of the brain that make sense of these data points and project their patterns into the future.* There are so many ways the brain can process data that it is hubristic to think that the habits of thought cultivated over the past several hundred years are necessarily the most effective for all tasks.
- *The ability of the mind or consciousness to perceive the flow of time as a substantive dimension.* We use the idea of time as the fourth dimension rather glibly. Is time really a dimension at all?

Is it as palpable and substantive as the other three dimensions? Why does space have three dimensions and time only one? The various models of time's flow may indeed hold the key to how we perceive future events, or they may simply be human constructs that generate the delusion that time can be read in any direction or, indeed, that time even has more than one direction.

- *The ability of the mind to draw upon energies accessible only in a state of heightened awareness.* These could refer to electromagnetic forces or, as Loye and Muses suggest, quantum alterations and their postulated connectivity to events in our own physically manifested sphere of operations. Archaic cultures had their own empiricism; i.e., subjecting propositions and suppositions to trial by generations of experience. It is not really science, but it had the empirical basis that science recognizes, relying on tools adequate to demonstrate that "mystic" aspects of reality are extensions of our own world, subject to laws that we have simply not yet discerned.

In short, we do not know everything we need to fully tap the mind's potential skills at foresight and forecasting. We want to know more because, whichever approach one takes, a clearer view of the future is invaluable to us, especially given the scope of today's challenges. And just as human beings have always been spurred by a desire to clarify what lies ahead, so, too, have we always looked to the past to illuminate the latent potentials of the future. The questions in the title of Gauguin's great masterpiece in Boston's Museum of Fine Arts — "From whence do we come from? Who are we? Where are we going?" — are always intimately bound to one another. This is even implicit in the Sphinx's riddle: What walks on four legs in the morning, two in the afternoon, and three in the evening? Oedipus figured out the answer because he himself was about to confound time by becoming both husband and son to his mother. The answer, of course, is a human being — where we've come from (four legs), who we are (two), where we are going (three). An ancient mantic formula, known to the Greeks and to bardic cultures in general, held that the seer sings of all that has been, all that is, and all that will be. To consider any of Gauguin's three questions is to consider all three at once.

In that spirit, let us look back to where the practice of foresight has come from, focusing on two ancient oracles, one whose home still attracts an endless stream of visitors, and the other that continues to enjoy popularity today: respectively, the oracle of Apollo at Delphi in Greece and the *I Ching,* or *Illustrious Book of Changes,* a gift of Chinese civilization.

First, let us examine the oracle of Apollo at Delphi, revered and renowned throughout the ancient world and a byword in our own era for a futurist orientation, as evidenced by such high-tech corporate names as Oracle, Apollo, and Delphi, or the Delphi forecasting method (which bears no resemblance to the operations of the ancient oracle). We shall find that Delphi itself still has a great deal to tell us, and, as befits an oracle, much of it may prove surprising.

DELPHI

Delphi played a uniquely public role in ancient Greece, especially during the heyday of the *polis,* or city-state, ca. 750-338 BCE. Despite the mystery that attaches to its name, the oracle's purposes were, for the most part, as managerial and pragmatic as those of any business manager or consultant today. The queries posed by emissaries from sovereign states were primarily concerned with religious regulations ("to what god or goddess shall the demos of the Parians sacrifice?"), the best prospective sites for colonies, and political issues (should the Chalcidians ally with Philip of Macedon?). More personal inquiries also involved practical matters: "What is better for him and his sons and daughters to do?" with the response, "Worship Zeus Patroos," etc., or more personal matters (a husband's desire for children). (Fontenrose 1978/1981.)

Greek society in the eighth century BCE was on the threshold of momentous disruptions that placed stress on every aspect of Greek life. No area of life was unaffected: The traditional claims of kinship, the administration of justice, inheritance and property rights, political organization, economic stratification, trade, technology, and intercommunity conflict all were transformed by sharp increases in population, wealth, and connectivity that Greece experienced after four centuries of isolation. This isolation was twofold: In the so-called Greek Dark Ages (ca. 1150-750 BCE), the sea-lanes in the eastern Mediterranean were largely shut down. Greece, whose Bronze Age civilization existed on the fringes of the eastern Mediterranean palace culture, saw its fairly complex Mycenaean society disintegrate during the disturbances of the twelfth century BCE, following the Trojan War. In addition, Greece's many towns and villages were isolated from one another within Hellas, hidden behind the steep mountain crags that define the Greek peninsula and interacting with their neighbors mainly at occasional festivals.

Beginning in the eighth century BCE, Greece was drawn into the orbit of a rejuvenated eastern Mediterranean economy. The impact on Hellas's small communities was far more sudden and dramatic than among the societies of the Near and Middle East. The latter had been much more interconnected and had preserved far more of the Bronze Age culture than had the Greeks. The systemic changes that Greece experienced in the eighth century included the adoption of an alphabet and rediscovery of literacy, the full-scale emergence of a literature of astonishing complexity and beauty, the consolidation of isolated communities into regional city-states, an increase in wealth and population, and a movement from the traditions of village life to the laws of the city-state. Their exposure to external systems was equally dramatic: The mathematics, trade networks, astronomy, time-lines, empires, and technology of Egypt and the East opened the Greek mind almost overnight (by ancient standards) to a systemic complexity that might have overwhelmed another people, but the Greeks had a secret weapon. They had been so isolated for so long that their local traditions had taken deep root. Thus, the Greeks experienced a creative tension between two live-wire systems — one ancient and cosmopolitan, the other immediate and local — a tension that in many respects held the key to their achievements.

The overriding theme to Delphi's pronouncements and its role as chief voice of foresight in the Hellenic world lay in promoting the pan-Hellenic cultural unity of scores of highly competitive and independent Hellenic states. No other entity spoke for the Greek world as Delphi did. Its authority derived in large part from championing the Olympian religion. The Olympian deities — Zeus, Apollo, Hermes, Athena, etc. — did not represent the entirety of Greek religion. In fact, the Olympians were imposed over strata of still-active beliefs, techniques of transcendence, healing practices, and pantheons that can be traced back to the Early Bronze Age and, in some instances, the Neolithic and beyond. The Olympian religion originally was articulated most vividly by the epic poems of Homer and Hesiod, which emerged during the eighth century BCE. These poems established a common language for a Greek world fragmented by numerous dialects. They also created a common religious vocabulary built around the celestial, immortal beings who dwelt atop Mount Olympus. Homer's poems promoted a common ethic geared to the Greek aristocracy for whom the noble quality of *arête* (excellence) formed the basis of their value system, while Hesiod's laid out the case for cosmic order and civic justice that became a central part of Greek thought and society.

In promoting the matrix of values embodied by *arête*, Delphi established ties with the ruling families of the city-states as well as many city governments, most especially that of Sparta. Despite a susceptibility to bribery and favoritism, Delphi managed to retain the loyalty and respect of the city-states in large part because the priests seemed to know the limits of the shrine's agenda. Delphi ruled on political disputes among city-states just as it might advise a peasant to move his land-marker back to its original spot on his neighbor's property. The oracle was committed to maintaining an essential balance in the Greek world while recognizing the inevitable influence of such military powers as Sparta or Athens.

Delphi also probably had the most advanced political intelligence of its day, at least in Greece. That would mean understanding power relations among the city-states, analyzing the consequences of political and military conflicts, being in touch with major political figures, and knowing what areas might be favorable for establishing new colonies. It is thus possible to adopt the rationalistic view that the oracle was a religious authority that also served as political mediator and guide. This would be correct, but nonetheless incomplete.

Several Delphic myths identify deities who presided over the site before Apollo: Gaia, the earth goddess, sometimes in consort with Poseidon; Themis, who embodied law and wisdom; the Titan Phoebe; and Pytho, the serpent that Apollo killed to wrest control of Delphi for Olympus and himself. In ancient times, a shrine often drew its sanctity from its antiquity. Association with the foundation era of a community or culture endowed a site with religious cachet, but even more powerful was association with a primeval time that predated the current inhabitants' history. The string of Delphi's earlier deities speak to such a case. But what was Delphi's oracular role before the city-state era, and did any of it carry over into the historical period (after 750 BCE)?

Legend tells that the answers of the Pythia, the woman of the town of Delphi who served as oracle, were inspired by intoxicating vapors rising from the depths of the earth (Gaia). It was long thought that this was only a fanciful legend, as archaeologists found no evidence of such. In 2001, however, geologists made a stunning discovery: Underground faults did indeed lie beneath Delphi and once emitted "hallucinogenic gases ... preserved within the temple rock" (Hale et al. 2003). It is thus highly likely that the site gained its initial renown from the presence of the gas, identified as ethylene, long before the first known shrine was built there in the eighth century BCE. This psychotropic agent provides a link to older traditions of intoxicated possession, borne out by the fact that in the winter months, even at the height of Delphi's influence, the shrine was consecrated to the wild rites of Dionysus, during which intoxicated women—maenads—raced along the slopes in their ecstatic orgies. But an aspect of Delphic lore dating from the fifth century BCE—the height of the polis era and Delphi's influence—points to a second tradition of visionary foresight in addition to that associated with possession.

One of the greatest Greek poets, Pindar (ca. 522–443 BCE), reportedly had a golden throne reserved for him at Delphi. Pindar is most famous for the victory odes he wrote for winners at the Olympic and other pan-Hellenic games. His odes, however, were more than early sports columns. Victory became the platform from which Pindar launched into profound meditations on origins, fate, change, the limitations of human life, and the metaphysical concerns of Greek philosophy. His poems uphold Delphic values: the importance of excellence and achievement in human affairs; the integrity of noble lineages; the primary role of the Olympians in religious, civic, and cosmological matters; the unity of Greek culture and society; the strict circumscription of human aims and purpose by the boundaries established by the immortal gods; and the sacred nature of Apollonian pursuits, such as music, measure, and dance.

Yet Pindar had another side. His poems occasionally reference shamanic practice, with which Apollo was also associated. Pindar recounts how the spirit of the long-dead seer Alkmaeon prophesies to him while the poet travels to "the *omphalos* (navel-stone) of the earth (Gaia)" located at Delphi, the navel stone signifying the world-center, a traditional destination of shamanic journeys. Elsewhere, he describes a journey to the Hyperboreans, the blessed people of the far north (also a common shamanic destination), associated in Greek myth with psychotropic substances, Apollo, and such Greek shamanic figures as Aristeas and Abaris. In this poem, known as *Pythia X,* dedicated to a winner at the games held at Delphi, Pindar sang of the Hyperboreans sacrificing asses to Apollo, "who looks with laughter at the upright lust of the brutes." This is an astonishingly direct link to shamanic lore, as Siberian shamanism included horse sacrifices at which young men with erect phalluses tied between their legs galloped about on wooden horses. Northern shamanism seems to have been the inspiration for the image of the Hyperboreans among the Greeks (Ruck 1986), and mules with erections in the context of a Hyperborean feast at which Apollo was being honored is unmistakably shamanic. Besides, ribaldry was anathema to Pindar, at least in his poetry, so he was clearly invoking a specific tradition to suit the ode's theme.

It is difficult, though, to determine how shamanism influenced the oracle in the city-state era: whether it was an active but esoteric aspect of Delphi or just dimly understood traces lingering in poetry and legend. Yet the very existence of these older alternative traditions indicates that society demanded that its oracles learn new skills to meet the needs of new conditions. In Delphi's case, that meant abandoning or downplaying both intoxication and shamanism in favor of judicious, sober advice that would guide individuals and communities through the socio-political difficulties of the era.

In fulfilling its role as CFO — Chief Foresight Officer — for an entire culture, Delphi:

- Provided a unifying center for Hellenic identity, symbolized by the famous stone *omphalos,* or navel, that marked Delphi as the center of the world.

- Adjudicated disputes among various contending parties, especially states; other than war, Delphi was the highest authority in conflict management among states.

- Established religious guidelines during an era of religious syncretism, in which overlapping cults were absorbed into the same civic system and new rituals arose.

- Reinforced the primary "vision statement" of ancient Greek civilization, that of the celestially oriented Olympian religion and the aristocratic values associated with it.

- Mediated information as a center of "political intelligence."

- Nurtured the "legacy systems" that kept the Greeks, especially those belonging to the Dorian branch of Hellenic culture, in touch with their earliest traditions.

- Achieved recognition by foreign states as the most authoritative diplomatic voice of the Greek-speaking world, at least during the Archaic and Classical periods (ca. 750-323 BCE). (Part of the political frustration of ancient Greece, and its everlasting charm, was that the most authoritative voice was still rather circumscribed in its influence.)

If we translate these operations into modern terms, we find ourselves in the realm of management rather than long-term futurist planning. Yet, a futurist perspective was implicit in all that Delphi did. On the most obvious level, Delphi's advice exhibited much more rational foresight than the often impulsive political responses of its client states. And while the priests did not ignore their own interests or that of the shrine, and certainly played favorites, Delphi did seem dedicated to a forward-looking vision of balance, regulation, expansion, and cultural identity. Delphi's oracular utterances expressed the vision and mission statements of the culture as, indeed, did all of Greek art, architecture, and literature; it was Delphi, though, that people and communities looked to for explicit guidance.

Just as radically changing conditions generated a "modern" revolution in oracular foresight at Delphi starting in the eighth century BCE, so, too, do today's social, technological, political, and cognitive revolutions require the same from us. In my view, the scale of change that we confront today is not merely dramatic, but potentially catastrophic due to global warming, global ecocide, economic instability and exploitation, the world's saturation with vastly destructive weapons, the emergence of "super germs," and the ongoing disintegration of the nation-state as a source of global security. Rather than moving away from the shamanic and visionary toward the rational, as Delphi did 2,800 years ago, we might try shifting back toward them. However, unlike Delphi, which retained only traces of its visionary past (the intoxicated Pythia, for example, or, possibly, esoteric shamanic traditions taught at the site), we today might dissolve the boundaries between the rational and the visionary. Mechanistic and rationalistic modes of thought are not the same as rational and logical thinking. The mechanized slaughters and relentless economic expansion that mark the past century demonstrate that a highly rationalistic substructure can be used to advance highly irrational ideologies and behaviors; indeed, reason often serves only to concentrate destructive power. If not informed by empathy and emotional intelligence, the rational becomes a uniquely human agent of destruction. But our intellect and rationality will also be emphatically circumscribed if the intuitive, visionary, transcendent, and even ecstatic elements are expunged from our thought processes. Ancient myth credits Apollo and Delphi with reducing the influence and status of these irrational elements. Today, we need to reconcile the sub- and super-conscious minds (the Delphi of intoxicated possession and Hyperborean shamanism, respectively), and the rational managerial approach of the oracle's public expression.

Apollo was not only a god of reason. He also stood for the establishment of super-conscious activities involving music, mathematics, patterning, and visualization that became the basis of Pythagorean and Platonic training. Indeed, Plato's educational program, as sketched out in *The Republic*, is Apollonian, especially if, as seems likely, geometric visualization was a key element. Plato advocated a domain of knowing beyond "normal" thinking whose core processes could be integrated into the "executive" functions of the mind. Shamanism, too, involves a journey to a hyperconscious state in which are revealed the world's governing natural and metaphysical structures and processes. Like Plato's Guardians, shamans return to their communities to bestow the benefits of their insights. Shamanic and Platonic knowledge was gnostic in nature: psychologically internalized, integrated, and transformative, which does not preclude high-level abstract thinking.

These higher Apollonian functions depend on the frontal lobe, which is largely responsible for our ability to plan ahead and envision alternative futures. As David Darling (1993) states, "It is the forebrain, or cerebrum, that is the seat of the mind—and all that elusive thing implies. Not least, the forebrain serves as the brain's 'projection room,' the place where sensory data is transformed and put on display for internal viewing. In our case, we are (or can be) actually aware of someone sitting in the projection room, watching the show." More specifically, several such brain areas, such as the anterior cingulate, seem to govern "the executive attention network" (Posner and Raichle 1994), which both interacts with and distills the brain's visualization function. These areas are also necessary to memory and the ability to recall images fundamental to the construction of meaning. Archaic practices may or may not have explicitly associated thought with specific areas of the brain or body. Certainly in yogic systems—where the chakras are identified with different regions along the spine and within the brain, including an apparent awareness of the importance of the pineal and pituitary glands — one sees evidence of that level of understanding, and it has been suggested that much of ancient myth is indeed a detailed description of the flow of energy and consciousness throughout the body, including the brain (Sansonese 1994). Many archaic people mapped consciousness and mental activity upon the body, not only along its surface but internally as well.

Thus, whether conscious or not, we can view Apollo and Delphi as having presided over a change in neurological patterning and focus that ever since has defined our very notion of higher thought. Of course, humans had fully developed frontal lobes even when Delphi was simply a place for stags and wild boars to drink spiked water and race crazily along the slopes. But to the Greeks, Delphi and Apollo represented this intellectual adventure in a compressed, symbolic, and highly developed form.

Delphi helped set us on a path that we have only just come to exhaust. And an overly rationalistic approach to foresight has perhaps led us to forget that forecasting the future is a highly irrational, even hubristic, act. Yet the development of human consciousness is largely the story of our ability to plan, strategize, and anticipate. Delphi's pivotal role in the intellectual history of civilization demonstrates that far-reaching cultural change requires a change in the foresight function. The following suggestions indicate what such future shifts might entail.

Metaphysical and Cosmological Vision

At the core of Delphic practice was a metaphysical and cosmological vision of balance — not in the ideological sense, but as protoscientific and empirical evaluation of universal laws. This sensitivity to meta-rhythms and mega-cycles is vital for effective forecasting in unsettled times; nor need it presume an ideological bias. Forecasters utilize whatever their belief systems can accommodate, and some will be more influenced by rigid ideology than others. But to be successful, a forecaster must consider the broader "meta" realms the lie behind the situation-specific conditions they are addressing. This concern with the big picture can be distracting and may be mistakenly viewed as an academic exercise. As I have discussed elsewhere, however, a sense of world—and even cosmic—significance in one's work, reinforced by an understanding of the connectivity of the meta-realm to one's own area of focus, can have a profound impact on the level of creativity one applies to a situation (Kunstler 2004).

Justice and Reality

The preeminence of balance as a Delphic principle did not mean Delphi campaigned for political equality among city-states. A strong reality principle complemented its commitment to equitable resolutions. Delphi acknowledged Hellenic *realpolitik,* for instance, the military preeminence of Sparta, but still sought to apply principles of justice that could benefit the weak as well as the strong. This accounting for the relative claims of parties who might otherwise be overwhelmed by power shows a recognition of the importance of weak links and small hubs in a system. Too often, contemporary forecasting and strategic planning focus only on paths to maximum advantage of the primary party—an approach that is ultimately unsustainable. The long view requires a sense of balance too often missing from today's corporate and governmental calculations. Conversely, a stronger reality principle would enable many political and nonprofit groups to employ more tactical sophistication than they often display.

Knew Its Own Limits

Delphi understood the limits not just of its own insight, but also of its ability to sway events. Unlike many other priesthoods throughout history, including those secular priests of the corporate and military domains, the shrine grasped the limits of its own expertise and power. As a general rule, this limiting aspect refines and deepens analysis. Too often, forecasts merely project the client's and/or forecaster's desires and unrealistic assumptions of control over a situation. Awareness of one's limitations is part and parcel of a sensitivity and intuition regarding the unknowns of a complex or chaotic set of conditions, and it is these limitations that bring into focus both what can be known and the boundary conditions of a situation. As basketball legend Bobby Knight (2008) said in a recent interview, "Half of being smart is knowing what you don't know" — a statement in accord with one of Socrates' most famous observations.

Incorporated Legacy Systems and Symbolism

A trip to Delphi was a journey back in time even for those living 2,500 years ago. The ancient legacy represented by the intoxicated Pythia was reinforced by the display of offerings that Homer already mentions in the eighth century BCE and that by the fifth century BCE included treasures of astonishing wealth and beauty. These lined the Sacred Way that wound up the slopes and past the Temple of Apollo and other highlights of the site, and the identity of the donor, the occasion, and their dedication wove into the current moment the diverse and fascinating threads of history and honor accorded the site.

The modern parallel involves understanding the psychological, symbolic, historical, and social forms and language embedded within every situation. Much of the present-day mediocrity of public life — and the superficial, scattershot, and short-term aspect of so much of what passes for strategic planning — is due to an impoverished understanding of the forces that underpin a situation. Of course, one needn't study the liberal arts to be a business success; often, one needn't study anything but the business itself. But at higher levels of forecasting and policy making, the richer the understanding of culture and context, the more profound and on-target the guidance one is likely to provide.

Visioned Globally, Operated Locally

Because the town of Delphi was generally not a contender for power or wealth beyond its attendance upon the oracle, and because of its position as advisor to the entire Greek world, Delphi was afforded the luxury of a global view of events. Yet Delphi was gifted at attending to the most mundane details of anyone who could afford the price of the goat sacrifice that it took to consult the oracle. The dialectic between the cosmopolitan and the local was a central dynamic of Greek civilization. Delphi recognized that the dynamics of change could only unfold through the daily processes of politics and society. Too often, in our own milieus, planning and forecasting fail to acknowledge the inertia of the systems we seek to change; the forces governing this inertia are as critical to engage as the unknowns lying beyond the limits of our influence or knowledge. Plans are easily spun and futures imagined, and goals established and people driven to achieve them, but any forecasting or planning exercise that overrides the intricate realities that bind systems to their present course is doomed to fail.

This is by no means a caution against bold initiatives, but rather a caution to consider tactics and logistics as equals to strategy. Delphi seemed to understand this, which perhaps accounts for its centuries-long influence over Greek life. The very modest price of admission to the oracle's presence — the aforementioned goat — also won respect and support for Delphi among the common people. One of the benefits of operating locally — or, viewed another way, of community service — is that one stays in touch with the currents that feed a society and gains more ready acceptance of the oracle, forecaster, or consulting futurist, which is often viewed with mistrust by a population (or employees) excluded from regular contact with the oracular or strategic function.

Cultivated New Modes of Thinking to Fit Emerging Complexity

It is highly unlikely that Delphi's priests decided one day to reshape Greek thought so the Greeks could cope with rapidly increasing systemic complexity. Delphi evolved along with Greece, influencing its course; to imply that it was pulling the strings of the Hellenic mind is to foment a fairy tale, although we may guess that it was highly sensitive to cultural trends and that the shamanic and psychotropic elements of its traditions point to a long-standing concern with states of consciousness. Today, however, cadres of professionals—futurists, neuroscientists, educators, strategic planners in many fields, psychologists, and more—seek methods for understanding and enhancing thinking. For some, the mission amounts to a desire to revolutionize the cognitive capacities of human beings. And many of these practitioners fuse this pursuit with an explicit desire to shift the course of our future, as they question the viability and sustainability of our current course.

So we tend to be more explicit about the far-reaching cultural results we want the practice and improvement of forecasting skills and cognitive competencies to achieve. We also more directly and explicitly tinker with the mind itself, in large part because our technology has led us to that capability. We are in uncharted waters, in many respects, and many of us believe the stakes for Spaceship Earth are very high. It is my additional belief that our ship can be steadied by understanding forecasting's history, and thus we will now discuss our second oracle, the *I Ching*.

Note on time: The Greeks considered the future as being behind them and the past ahead, the opposite of our own view, which places the future in front of and the past behind us. This implies a different view of the human relationship to time, but we should not automatically assume too much from this contrast. Wherever each culture locates the future, neither claimed to know the future any better than the other. Such formulations also need to be calculated into the culture's view of time as cyclical, linear and open-ended, linear and teleological (with a definitive end in store), spiraline (similar to cyclical but with a progressive tilt), oscillative, or synchronistic, as we will see when we discuss the *I Ching*.

THE *I CHING*

The *I Ching* is well known to modern Westerners, having become popular during the 1960s and 1970s with the Wilhelm translation (1950) and that period's intense interest in Eastern religion. Fascination with the *I Ching* has continued unabated since then, aided, perhaps, by its uncanny resemblance to computer programming languages. Despite its relatively recent upsurge in popularity, the *I Ching* stands on its own as a major text of civilization, a profound encapsulation of Taoist and Confucian thought that also exhibits elements of a prehistoric shamanic past. Despite its philosophical and spiritual pedigree, the *I Ching* was first and foremost an oracle. It developed as such and only accrued its philosophical substance over time (Javary 1997). However, the original shamanic oracular practice involves a metaphysical, psychological, and cosmological worldview no less worthy of respect than the contributions of high Chinese civilization.

The *I Ching*'s predicate assumption is that human events are shaped by broader cosmic, natural, and/or metaphysical energies, on the one hand, and the individual's (hopefully strategic) response to these "atmospheric" conditions on the other. Through the oracle, querents attune themselves to the state of the cosmos at the moment their inquiry is taking place. The *I Ching*, in effect, marshals the collected wisdom of the ages to serve the querent's interests.

We might illuminate this relationship by contrasting the haruspex (reader of entrails) or ornithomantis (forecasting via birds) with the *I Ching*, noting both similarities and differences. These are based on the same principle as the *I Ching:* The state of a sheep's liver or the flight of birds in a certain quarter of the sky reflects, first and foremost, a general environmental or cosmic condition. Such practices recognize that environmental conditions are too vast and complex to "read" directly; instead, the forecaster distills the intrinsic quality of the moment into an easily grasped signal—i.e., the state of a liver or the flight of a bird. (This contrasts with a palm reader, for whom each life- or heart-line is an expression of the life path of the client to whom the palm belongs; that is, the "text" is fixed, embedded in the querent and not in the external environment.)

Such readings can be viewed as naturalistic and scientific, the way one might predict the severity of the oncoming winter by the number of acorns falling from an oak or the busyness of the squirrels in stockpiling them. Thus, a bird in the wrong quarter of the sky may mean the north winds will bring a storm. Or the reading could be based on superstition: "The bird's lost and therefore so are we." Or it could be in between; that is, the priest intuits that something is "off" in the moment and translates that into its correlate in human affairs according to his or her own mix of procedure, knowledge, and bias. All three approaches have probably driven history's oracular practices. J. Nigro Sansonese suggests that, among archaic peoples, a hunter, for example, might draw upon the entire range of his or her perceptions without focusing just on entrails or birds. "His skill depends crucially on a high degree of concentration, amounting to trance." Sansonese compares this state to *samyama,* a state of "frozen awareness" he likens to "grokking" from Robert Heinlein's *Stranger in a Strange Land* (Sansonese 1994, 63). In such a case, the livers or birds may simply serve as the pathway to a state of trance.

The *I Ching* calls upon an even more universal set of variables than Sansonese's hypothetical hunter. Like the occasion-based methods (haruspicy vs. palm reading, for instance), the *I Ching* focuses on the energies that define a given moment. It differs from these others, though, in the complexity with which it engages the cosmos. Whereas other methods focus all their attention on one manifestation of the spirit of the moment or, as in Sansonese's example, the entire, immediately perceivable environment, the *I Ching* draws upon complex and highly sophisticated philosophy, metaphysics, psychology, and cosmology and focuses them onto the present moment.

The *I Ching* purports to read the universals of heaven and earth belonging to any given moment without recourse to the signs that the environment offers to the senses. It follows up this bold claim—to read the moment unadulterated by mediating imagery—with another, more sweeping assertion: that the way it (the *I Ching*) reads cosmic conditions at a given moment can be translated into useful counsel for the conduct of human affairs.

Along with its oracular component, the *I Ching* functions as an ethical and strategic guide subject to scholarship, meditation, contemplation, interpretation, and practical application. Thus, it has a present-oriented function as well as a future-oriented one. At the same time, the two major assumptions upon which it relies beg further address. We can restate the first by saying it assumes that the system of sixty-four hexagrams represents a chart of universal energies and processes and that randomly identifying the one most relevant for a particular situation at a particular time somehow provides an accurate reading of that moment's cosmic attributes.

In the introduction to the Wilhelm translation, Carl Jung identifies the concept of "synchronicity" as a key supporting notion—i.e., that the events of any one moment in time are all connected by being a full expression of that moment. This is an idea we find elaborated in the Mayan notion of time, in which every single day over a fifty-two-year cycle has a specific name that can be related to other days, from other cycles, with the same name. More broadly, in cultures for which time is primarily cyclical, certain key transitions in the cycle—the time of creation, origin, birth, the swing into decline—can be reexperienced during a festival. Thus, in a festival cycle, one does not just celebrate the birth of a god, for example, but is actually *in that moment,* what Mircea Eliade calls in *illo tempore* (in that time) in which the deity was born, or in that moment that the world first took shape, or that consciousness dawned. Ritually, then, one actually returns to *illo tempore* and relives it. Or rather, that special moment becomes the present moment; it is time that catches up with and claims the present via synchronicity with the past.

In contrast, for the *I Ching,* that time can occur at any time and is not bound to a ritualized event such as birth or creation. As Cyrille Javary states, the diviners who contributed to the creation of the *I Ching* "no longer worried about questioning divine beings but were trying to find their way among the different moments that give rhythm to the universe." They considered it "better to question the universe directly" as opposed to having a deity mediate their relationship to the cosmos (Javary 1997, 36). The ritual of the yarrow stalks, through which one identifies the hexagram most suited to the inquirer's question and personal situation, presumably put the inquirer and the oracle in synch with the energies of that moment of cosmic or natural history.

So the first assumption is the connection between the cosmos and the oracle itself. The second critical assumption is that the oracle can correlate a specific, time-dependent cosmic manifestation with an analogous set of events in human affairs. The ancient dictum that governed a large portion of human affairs and provided the underpinnings of archaic thought, ritual, and politics held that "As above, so below." As in heaven, so on earth. If there's a drought, sacrifice the king, as he is the link between cosmic energies and their dispersal over the earth. If the gods are angry up there, we will suffer down here. If something's wrong down here, it means something's wrong up there. From a different viewpoint, whatever makes us suffer can be made into a god, but that is a rationalist's view — or a psychologist's — although it is likely there were those among the ancients who thought this as well.

An important corollary to these two core axioms is that, if both axioms hold, the reading must connect directly to the inquirer and not to another. If I ask the question, the oracle should not give me an answer meant for a young woman in Irkutsk. This is a corollary because, if the two axioms hold, then the legitimacy of the oracle does as well; thrashing out just who is to benefit is important, but not as significant as establishing the basic notion that a foresight process exists. A second corollary is that the oracle will interpret the signs correctly, that it will give me good advice; again, important but not fundamental because, if the two axioms are true, someone is likely to benefit from what it has to tell. The point of view implicit in the axioms and their corollaries are foundational. Without it, no one would ever consult the oracle.

The *I Ching* and other oracles assert that a close relationship exists between the divine realm above and human affairs below. The oracles presume to translate the dynamics of this relationship into terms relevant to human beings, and then actually target it to an inquirer's specific query. And, even more fundamental, it claims that this all comes about because the oracle has access to the spirit of the cosmos at that moment.

Systems and the *I Ching*

The *I Ching* recognizes the complexity of the system of the world far more readily than most modern foresight systems. The notion of fluidity is built into the fabric from the first, given its title, *The Book of Changes*. The hexagrams of the *I Ching* each comprise six stacked lines that are either solid or broken, "yang" or "yin." Each hexagram is composed of two trigrams, one upper and one lower; there are eight possible trigrams, and eight of the hexagrams consist of duplicates of the trigrams. The hexagrams that result from the oracular procedures are inherently unstable; they all have two nuclear or internal trigrams composed of the second-fourth and third-fifth lines of the hexagram, which modulate their meaning.

In addition, any of the six lines may be denoted, during the procedure of producing a hexagram, as "moving" or "strong" (same meaning); that is, the line's yang or yin element is so powerful that it is headed toward becoming its opposite. Occasionally, a hexagram emerges that has no moving lines, but most readings will result in there being between one and six moving lines, which then shift the hexagram into any of the other sixty-three, depending on the combination of moving lines. If no lines move, the hexagram reiterates itself. All of these elements, including the meaning of the strong lines, are built into the interpretation, which, for each line, comprises texts that were added to the book at different periods of Chinese history.

Now it's easily imagined that, with so many variables, an interpretation can be engendered that fits any occasion, but this is to misread the nature of the oracle. The querent is located in a very specific place and time—i.e., the moment of the oracular procedure. That moment is pregnant with possibility and with its own specific nature. Thus, the *I Ching* starts with the present moment. The inquiry, however, addresses the future. In effect, the oracle tells inquirers to first monitor themselves and attend to the conditions in which they and their situation are embedded. It offers suggestions that one can take as straight advice or as guidance for looking more deeply into one's circumstances and the conditions that bound it.

The situation's structural dynamics are interpreted as a function of the structural dynamics of the hexagram. Thus number twenty-three, *Po* (Splitting Apart) is composed of five yin (feminine, dark, yielding aspect of polarity) in the first five places, capped by one yang line (masculine, light, firm, etc.). The idea of splitting apart comes from the internal dynamic of the hexagram. Five yin lines naturally sink downward, pulling apart from the strong yang line at the top, which in one of the hexagram's metaphors represents the roof of a house. The yin line in the fifth place, just below the yang line, is the key, because its proximity to the yang line puts it under its sway, as a lady-in-waiting stands to the queen. The interpretation of the hexagram reflects the instability of its internal structure. The issue is not how to avoid splitting apart, but how to cope with and even make the most of it, as a fruit does when it falls from a tree to disperse its seeds.

Thus, the *I Ching* is designed to illuminate the internal dynamics of a situation or condition, and the hexagrams, skeletal by nature anyway, can be viewed as X-rays of life's conditions. They can be viewed as sixty-four separate conditions, but since each hexagram can be paired with the sixty-three others via the action of the moving lines, and itself (if there are no moving lines), there are actually 64^2 or 4,096 separate conditions that can be described; i.e., number twenty-three with no moving lines, number twenty-three with only the first line moving, with lines two and three moving, etc.

The *I Ching* clearly has points of contact with the advisory function of today's consultants, analysts, managers, and coaches (whose function perhaps comes closest to that of the *I Ching's* oracle, and hence may fall into the following chart's first column in some cases), but there are sharp differences as well, as the chart shows.

One key difference is that the modern practitioner deals with details and specifics while the *I Ching* phrases things in the most general terms. Even in the most general reorganization or culture-change initiative, one still has to say, "This is the way we will pro-

I Ching	Futurist-Oriented Consultant or Manager
Views all systems as complex	Has difficulty coping with complexity
Begins with present conditions	Often focuses on vision, goals
Individual's choices the key focus	Organizational needs override those of individual
External factors built into oracle	Selects specific external factors to focus on
Ethical and operational guidance are inseparable	Ethical concerns separate from operational although they may be addressed
Future a continuum with present moment	Future often breaks from present
Time is synchronistic	Time is linear
Taps cosmic forces and historical legacy	Taps discipline-based expertise
Assumes expertise of the method, not the individual	Assumes expertise of the individual and only then the individual's chosen method
Based on (truly) universal experience	Based on organizational experience and research
Psychology and ethics are universal, intrinsic	Psychology and ethics are situational, applied
Addresses executive functions within mind	Addresses executive functions within organization
Takes the long-term view	Usually takes the short- to mid-term view
Deals largely with generalities	Deals with details and specifics

ceed.... I suggest you do this from now on." The *I Ching* may tell you to visit the great man or "set the calendar in order," but it will not tell you that engineering and sales need to cooperate better. In other respects, though, we might prefer the ancient oracle's approach. The *I Ching* focuses on present conditions; everything else follows from those. Today's modern consultants or managers, who all deal in the currency of foresight in one way or another, often impose prefabricated goals on an organization. The question "where do we want to be (at some future point)" is rife with internal contradictions and is as susceptible to manipulation, bias, and the lure of an advisor's own template for change as any vaguely framed oracular response. The *I Ching* respects systems but always links them inextricably with the individual's intentions and qualities. The modern practitioner often overrides individual concerns for the sake of the system.

FORESIGHT AND SYNCHRONIZATION

Foresight is based on a broadly general notion of synchronization: that conditions frequently return to a prior state. The view of time in today's organizational world is highly linear, measured in short-term results for the most part, and reflecting the broader cultural view of time. Nonetheless, planning does rely upon a knowledge of past patterns as a way of anticipating the future—i.e., three-color sales letters work better than one color; if interest rates go up, our profits will go down; etc. Still, that is only a faint nod in the direction of synchronicity; the past is mainly a database of indications, not a place to which the baseline conditions of existence perpetually return.

For archaic people, the return to *illo tempore* is a matter of synchronizing events in time. Time can be compared to the Enigma code machine used by the Germans in World War II: Both employ a series of circular rotors (in time's case, astronomical orbits that mark the point in a cycle when cosmic energies are synchronized) that, when aligned, reveal an encoded message. For the *I Ching*, however, each moment has the same potential importance as any other. Being in tune with the richness of the moment is what the oracle offers and is the basis of its validity; the querent's job is to synchronize with the moment and understand its implications for both the future and for her or his future actions. The oracle always advises following the true path, which is that action most appropriate to the moment at hand. The "Superior Man" is not a man of high position, but the man or woman who fully understands the moment and acts in full accord with it. Foresight is not forced. The *I Ching* won't say what to do organizationally; it reveals the state of mind that will lead to the best situational response.

Yin and yang are not static or symmetrical, despite their binary character. Their traits can best be described by the verb *become* rather than *is*. That is, yin is not "dark," but a "becoming toward darkness." (Thus, a strong yin line would be one that is in the process of becoming so intensely yin that its valence will soon reverse and start becoming yang). Thus, foresight is intrinsic to the *I Ching* because every line is in a state of becoming, its condition fluid; the same holds for the hexagram itself. Moreover, there is a linear temporal factor in each hexagram: Time progresses from the first line at the bottom to the sixth at the top. Thus, the hexagram exposes a situation sequentially as well as structurally and synchronistically. The meaning of each line—whether it is a "strong" line changing into its opposite or simply that it is "becoming" yin or yang—also contributes to the temporal fluidity of the reading.

This sense of time, and its encapsulation in a system as profound and yet simple as the *I Ching*, is emblematic of archaic thought, where a given mythic image, such as the labyrinth, will accrue layer upon layer of symbolic meaning, each layer resonating with and serving as a commentary upon the other. Thus, the labyrinth represents a journey into the unconscious mind, the path of the sun throughout the year, the birth canal, the chthonic realm of the dead, the epitome of archaic design, the double axe of Minoan culture, a ritual center, the folds of the brain, or the mythological center of the world. Each of these meanings potentially serves as commentary upon one another in any given myth, so that meaning is constantly fluid, synchronistic, and resonant.

The complexity of modern thought tends to be constructed causally and linearly, and is elaborated through ever more complicated branches and offshoots. Modern systems of knowledge generate categories—that's how we think. We move through the realm of knowledge along linear tracks that slide between statements of greater generality (principles, laws, etc.) and those of greater specificity (data, analysis, etc.), and between assertions capable of varying degrees of validation. Time itself is subject to this scheme: We plot threads of time based primarily on the themes and circumstances that link each moment. Thus, 1939-1945 represents World War II; next quarter's projections are based on elaborate charting of sales, cash flow, market conditions; the academic year has its course just as a love affair does, based on the flow of events.

However, where time is cyclical and/or synchronistic, events are subordinate to time. For example, if every origin—birthdays, the founding of a city, the beginning of the world—partakes of the same quality of that time, and occasions the same type of festival, then the specificity of the event is subordinated to its temporal template. Time is felt as a palpable current. Each shift in the seasons, each birth, every kill in the hunt, lunar phase, or astrological sign is viewed as an expression of a recurring moment that always manifests the same qualities of all other such moments that preceded and will follow it. Synchronistic time is a special case of the cyclical. If all origins exist as, and at, the same moment, then one can say that all such moments are called into existence upon the return of any of them. But in the *I Ching,* this synchronicity, as we have seen, does not depend upon a special occasion or specific type of moment; i.e., origins, etc. Any moment contains this potential.

Delphi calls upon us to attend to the scale of change that the twenty-first century CE has brought to us and to adjust our foresight methods accordingly. In Delphic terms, that would mean implementing techniques that call upon the shamanic traditions of higher consciousness, in Willis Harman and Howard Rheingold's term (1984), and the powers of the unconscious, signified at Delphi by the intoxicating techniques of ecstasy fueled by the site's ethylene emanations. The *I Ching* presents us with an enigmatic but highly sophisticated system that resembles one of Turing's early universal computing machines while also doubling as one of civilization's great philosophical and ethical texts. It asks that we see time and the internal relationships of events in fresh ways, and each moment as potentially renewing and alive with creative possibility.

We will not solve today's problems by recourse to the usual tool kit; Toffler's future shock is upon us with a vengeance. The only recourse open to us is the mind, not as it operates in service to limited organizational agendas, but as it can function when drawing upon all its capabilities. As we have noted, technology may offer us such access, but whatever tools we use, the critical step is accepting that foresight is not a purely rationalistic practice. The campy trappings of the fortune-teller may disguise the fact that serious techniques of foresight did in fact exist as a function of a different mode of cognition. If our ancient oracles still have something to tell us, it is perhaps this: In attending to the past and exploring all dimensions of our present, the future may indeed become less opaque. Whether this ability results in better decisions and more fulfilling lives is, however, impossible to foresee, but we can hope.

Author's note: The idea for this article grew out of a suggestion to the author by Dr. Guntram Werther of the Thunderbird School of Global Management that they undertake a project examining historical foresight methods and their implications for modern forecasting. This article is a step in that direction. The content and point of view, and any errors thereof, are strictly those of the author.

REFERENCES

Argüelles, José. 2002. *Time and the Technosphere.* Rochester, VT: Bear and Company.

Byrne, Peter. 2007. "The Many Worlds of Hugh Everett." *Scientific American* (December): 98-105.

Darling, David. 1993. *Equations of Eternity.* New York: MJF Books.

De Keyser, Véronique, Géry d'Ydewalle, and Andre Vandierendonck, eds. 1998. *Time and the Dynamic Control of Behavior.* Seattle: Hogrefe & Huber.

Fontenrole, Joseph [1978] 1981. *The Delphic Oracle.* Berkeley: University of California Press.

Javary, Cyrille. [1989] 1997. *Understanding the* I Ching. Translated by Kirk McElhearn. Boston: Shambhala.

Kunstler, Barton. 2004. *The Hothouse Effect.* New York: Amacom.

Loye, David. 1983. *The Sphinx and the Rainbow.* Boulder, CO, and London: Shambhala.

Posner, Michael I., and Marcus E. Raichle. 1994. *Images of Mind.* New York: Scientific American Library.

Ruck, Carl. "The Offerings from the Hyperboreans." In *Persephone's Quest: Entheogens and the Origins of Religion* by R. Gordon Wasson, Carl Ruck, Stella Kramrisch, and Jonathan Ott, 225-256. New Haven, CT: Yale University Press.

Sansonese, J. Nigro. 1994. *The Body of Myth.* Rochester, VT: Inner Traditions International.

Talbot, Michael. 1991. *The Holographic Universe.* New York: Harper Collins.

Wilhelm, Richard, translator. [1950] 1967. *The I Ching or Book of Changes.* Translated into English by Cary F. Baynes. Foreword by Carl Jung. Princeton, NJ: Princeton University Press.

Worldwide Wipeout

The Greatest Publishing Story Never Told, Jihad, and the Unintended Consequences of the Internet's Killer App

Seth Kaufman

On January 31, 2007, more than fifteen years after English scientist Tim Berniers-Lee and his Belgian counterpart Robert Cailliau unveiled something called the World Wide Web, police in Birmingham, England, announced they had arrested nine suspects in a plot to kidnap a Muslim British soldier. The endgame of the plot, according to initial reports, was to use the World Wide Web as a vehicle for terror: The soldier would be tortured and then beheaded, and the video of this gruesome event would be broadcast on the Web. As the Associated Press reported that day, "the purported style of the conspiracy showed what counterterrorism experts depicted as the central role of the Web in modern insurgencies and conspiracies to broadcast propaganda and spread images."

Berniers-Lee and Cailliau developed the Web while working at CERN, a particle physics laboratory in Switzerland. Together they conceived of the Web as a platform to allow physicists to share

Seth Kaufman is vice president, merchandising, for Barnes&Noble.com (BN.com). E-mail skaufman@gmail.com.

data over the Internet, a communication system built by the U.S. military to transmit information in small, separated packets that could be reassembled at their destination. Until the Web arrived, the Internet could only be navigated through a cumbersome system of computer programming commands. Based on an easy-to-use markup, or layout language, the Web allowed users to navigate with the single click of a mouse. It was, to use what would become a 1990s watchword, user-friendly.

This marvelous invention, coupled with advances in digital technology, has ushered in the greatest publishing revolution since Gutenberg invented the movable type printing press in the mid-fifteenth century. As even the most sheltered technophobe knows by now, anyone with a computer and an Internet connection can publish anything and everything: diary entries, political rants, pornography, sound files, games, and even video footage of British soldiers being tortured and executed. And unless an Internet service provider or the Web publisher decides to block access, anyone else with a computer and an Internet connection can see what's there.

As long as the lanes of the information highway are zooming with innovation, investment, and e-commerce — Google, Yahoo!, eBay, Web mail, 50 million blogs and counting, maps, Craigslist, YouTube, Facebook, public records — the Web is seen as a good and great thing, assuming you steer clear of identity theft, cyberstalking, flame wars, hack attacks, or spam scams.

But publishing and sharing information on the World Wide Web has complicated geopolitical implications that are rarely addressed. Publishing revolutions help fuel other revolutions. Gutenberg's printing press was, as we shall see, a major catalyst for the Protestant Reformation, a movement that spurred more than a century's worth of bloody wars and political battles in England and Europe. Even small publishing revolutions have had social impact.

Carbon paper helped fuel *samizdat* publishing in the Soviet Union. Photocopy machines ratcheted up antigovernment literature in Poland and Czechoslovakia.

So if history is a reliable indicator, the Web will lead us toward dramatic change. While many herald the Web as an inherently democratic and potentially democratizing tool — a not unreasonable stance — it is also a tool for sensationalist propaganda by antidemocratic entities. Currently, fundamentalist Islam is battling both the West and itself, as the sectarian Shiite versus Sunni violence in Iraq attests. Yet, these and other Islamic factions use the Web as the global guerrilla communications arm in the jihad against the West. And why not? This multimedia publishing forum offers a myriad of ways — e-mail, video, discussion forums, chat, telephony, agitprop sites, and news footage — to communicate, to organize, and to transform public opinion. And as horrible as it is to say, beheadings of Westerners and others (numerous video clips of brutal murders have been available on the Web) must rank as excellent content to the naïve, disenfranchised madrassa student inculcated with tales of the Great Satan.

Students of the future and policy pundits interested in how the instant production and distribution of information on the Web can shake up the geopolitical firmament might want to study the story of another Englishman who worked overseas, dedicated to communication. His name was William Tyndale, and he took Gutenberg's printing press, the "killer app" of its time, and harnessed his own must-have content: An English translation of the Bible. It was an act filled with unintended consequences — regime change, war, revolution, piracy, democracy — an act that, centuries later, still reverberates around the world, bouncing off the World Wide Web all the way back to Birmingham. It was an act that suggests a number of insights and responses to the current East–West conflict.

A BIBLE FOR THE MASSES

Before we get to the greatest publish-and-perish story ever told, a little history is in order: From the moment Christianity arrived in England, the New Testament of choice was the Latin Vulgate. In the late 1300s an English theologian named John Wycliffe, working with a few clandestine supporters, translated the Gospel by hand into English. It was widely circulated among his followers, called Lollards (a term probably derived from the Dutch word for mumbler, *lollaert)*, and dozens of copies or snippets of the Wycliffe Bible survive today. The church was not pleased with Wycliffe for a number of reasons—he rejected the pope's supremacy, attacked the church's wealth, and, of course, shared the scriptures with one and all. To say these stances rankled is an understatement; the authorities branded him a heretic thirty-one years after he died, then dug up his bones and burned them. Subsequently, the holy men of England gathered at the 1408 Convocation in Oxford and decreed that translating a single word of the Vulgate into English—or uttering a single prayer in the common tongue—was an act of heresy.

A hundred years passed. The Holy See began to raise money to construct St. Peter's Basilica in Rome. To do it, Pope Leo X authorized churchmen to sell indulgences—pardons for the faithful and the not-so-faithful. This questionable fund-raising approach inspired Martin Luther to post his Ninety-Five Theses on the door of Castle Church in Wittenberg, Germany, and kick off the Reformation.

Some ten years before Luther hammered his ideas to the wall, William Tyndale entered Oxford's Magdalen Collage at about age twelve. There, according to the earliest biographical sketch we have of Tyndale—John Fox's seventeenth-century tribute to Protestant heroes, *Book of Martyrs*—he was "singularly addicted to scriptures" and offered English translations to his fellow students. A linguist of astounding skill—he spoke eight languages—Tyndale read Erasmus, clearly relishing his *Christian Warrior's Handbook,* as well as Luther's writings, including his 1522 translation of German Bible, which was done with a small battalion of assistants.

But it is generally held that Tyndale's biggest influence outside of Erasmus and Luther were the writings of Paul and his message that faith is the only requirement for salvation. Clearly for Tyndale, Paul's words found in Romans 3:21-28 ("For we hold that a person is justified by faith apart from works prescribed by the law") undercut a good deal of the teachings and rituals of the Catholic Church.

Despite leaving Oxford as an ordained priest in 1515, Tyndale did not pursue a church position. Fox's book reports that he went to Cambridge. Scholars have never been able to confirm this point, but it does seem likely he was there; the city was host to a number of Lollards, Luther-sympathizers, soon-to-be heretics, and some of Tyndale's future collaborators. In 1521 he took a position tutoring two sons of Sir John Walsh in Little Sodbury and preached on his days off in nearby Bristol. His preaching reached the ears of the local clergy, and he was brought up on heresy charges. Although Tyndale later complained about being treated "like a dog," he was acquitted. It's worth noting that Lord Walsh's ties to Henry VIII may have influenced the tribunal. (Walsh was knighted as the King's Champion at Henry's coronation, and his sister was a wet nurse for one of Henry's short-lived children.)

Although Tyndale went on to translate many of the most well-known phrases in the English language — "In the beginning was the word," "Seek and ye shall find," "Cast the first stone," "It is easier for camel to go through a needle's eye, than for a rich man to enter into the kingdom of God" — his most famous wholly original line (what corporate America might call his mission statement) was delivered during a dinner party at his employer's manor. According to Fox's *Book of Martyrs,* Tyndale became infuriated by a guest who said he preferred the pope's law to God's law. Enraged, Tyndale decreed, "If God spare my life many more years, I will cause the boy that driveth the plough to know more of Scripture than thou doth."

This was the breakthrough moment. Tyndale's purpose was now clear: Put the means of salvation in the hands of the proletariat. He quit his job, spent a year in London futilely petitioning the church for permission to translate the Gospels, and finally, around 1524, fled to Germany, where he headed to Wittenberg, Luther's hometown. Germany had two things England lacked and Tyndale required: first, a semblance of religious freedom in certain pro-Luther towns, and second, Jews. A rarity since they were banished from England in 1290 by Edward I, Jews were vital to Tyndale's second plan: He needed to learn Hebrew in order to translate the Old Testament.

Around the time Tyndale arrived in Germany, King Henry VIII, already frustrated with Queen Catherine's heir-bearing production (the couple had suffered a slew of miscarriages and infant deaths), fell under the spell of Anne Boleyn. Henry instructed Cardinal Wolsey to obtain a divorce or annulment from Rome. This was a tall order under the best of circumstances, and the possibility that Tyndale was out there—a veritable English Luther attacking the pope—clearly would not have helped Henry's special request. The first in a series of spies was sent to Europe to find Tyndale and stop him.

Tyndale was an elusive quarry. In 1525, aided only by an erratic friar named William Roye, Tyndale finished his first translation of the New Testament. He went to Cologne to finally print the *Good News*. The maiden print run was cut short, however, after one of the printers got drunk and unwittingly bragged to a Henry loyalist that he was printing an "English Luther." As authorities were summoned, Tyndale and Roye grabbed what they could and fled up the river. They set up shop in Worms, where, unimpeded, they printed somewhere between 3,000 and 6,000 copies, and then smuggled them to England hidden in barrels of wheat.

The Tyndale Bible was an immediate best-seller. At the time, books were a luxury item, sold unbound so that buyers could have them covered as they liked, with illustrations, gold leaf, and paintings. Many bookshelves were lined with books spine in, the better to showcase the hand-painted page-edges. According to David Daniell, Tyndale's greatest modern-day biographer, scholar, and champion, the Tyndale Bible sold for the equivalent of half a week's wages for a laborer — the ploughboy, as it were. That was a lot of money. But the book was often treated as communal property, with faithful pooling their money to buy copies.

In his many writings, Daniell has suggested that Tyndale did more for English literacy than Shakespeare. His Bible helped standardize English spelling. It also issued a blow for clarity, as Tyndale strove to deliver his Bible with common language, eschewing the flowery rhetoric that ruled the day.

Interestingly, Tyndale was a victim of the new media that helped him. Northern Europe was filled with book bootleggers. Printers there, some of whom did not speak English, ran off loads of "Tyndale" Bibles with varying degrees of accuracy. Not surprisingly, Tyndale was outraged by bootleg copies, particularly by botched translations. His version was based on painstaking interpretations of the Greek Bible, the Vulgate, and, almost certainly, Luther's translation. These mistakes and errors flew in the face of his second great aim as a translator: to render the teachings of Jesus and the words of the apostles as accurately as possible.

Worse than the bootlegs for Tyndale must have been the ensuing Bible-burning. Thomas More, the man for all seasons who was mayor of London at the time, authorized hunts for the book and led public burnings of the Bible. If that wasn't enough, he supplemented his campaign with pages of bile-filled rants against Tyndale, dubbing his nemesis "a hell-hound in the kennel of the devil" and supplementing that description with language many would deem unbecoming for a future Catholic saint.

"In burning the New Testament," Tyndale wrote, "they did none other thing than I looked for; no more shall they do if they burn me also, if it be God's will it shall so be. Nevertheless in translating the New Testament, I did my duty."

Edward Hall's *Chronicle,* which provides another early Tyndale history, recounts a great, almost comic miscalculation in the battle to stop the English Bible — or perhaps it should be viewed as a great con by Tyndale and a sympathetic trader named Augustine Packington; or, given Tyndale's holy roller solemnity, a fable. Either way, it's a fine example of unintended consequences: Packington approached London's bishop, Cuthbert Tunstall, in Antwerp, and offered to sell him Bibles to burn — at a steeply inflated price. Tunstall agreed to the usurious price, unaware that his payment would go on to fund three times the number of books he had just purchased.

POWER FOR THE PEOPLE

That Bible scam recalls another recent example of unintended consequences involving the Web, digital technology, and the control of information: the slow-motion collision of the music business running smack into the high-speed digital copying revolution. And what is most captivating is the idea that the industry—just like Bishop Tunstall's funding of Tyndale (or, say, the CIA's funding of mujahadeen in Afghanistan)—inadvertently hurt its own cause.

Go back to the age of the long-playing record album: The industry controlled it all. They had cornered distribution, radio (via payola), and billed all expenses back to the band. Then they figured out a way to make even more money with the compact disc. Ultimately, the CD costs less to manufacture and less to ship, and it took up less inventory space — all major boons to anyone looking to improve profit margin. By marketing the CD's supposedly superior

sound quality and inarguably superior portability, record companies impelled fans to buy a second format of their favorite albums
(not to mention a new CD player or a Walkman). Industry captains
had hit a grand slam.

Even long-abused artists benefited from the CD's increased
storage capacity. While vinyl records had a maximum length (about
twenty-five minutes per side), CDs held more than an hour's worth
of music, which meant musicians could put more songs on each release and therefore earn more royalties. Plus, they earned more
money on increased catalog sales. Everybody—even consumers
who considered the CD a superior recording format—was winning.

But industry honchos never envisioned that a CD's digital files
could be copied by users in mere seconds. They never foresaw file
sharing on the World Wide Web or blank discs that cost pennies and
render duplicate albums in the time it takes to play a song. Going
digital, in 20/20 hindsight, created a consumer revolution that now
threatens the business.

Of course, if the music industry hadn't let the digital genie out
of the bottle by launching CDs, there is little doubt hackers and
music lovers would have figured out how to digitize LPs. In fact,
they already have. But digitizing LPs still requires playing them in
real time in order to RIP—that is, encode—an album. So it's a fair
assumption that the so-called plague of file swapping and disc burning that has helped kill the industry would have been considerably
slowed.

Tyndale could not be slowed, either. For a man who lived on
the run, with little money and help, his ten years of translating and
publishing are astounding. He followed up the New Testament with
two books: *The Parable of the Wicked Mammon,* which compared
the pope and his underlings to the Antichrist, and *The Obedience of
the Christian Man,* which, among other things, urged the king to
split from the Vatican. He learned enough Hebrew to translate and

publish the Pentateuch—the first five books of Moses in the Old Testament—and went on to publish a second edition of the New Testament in 1534, complete with commentary.

He also faced one of his stalkers, Stephen Vaughan, a merchant sent by Thomas Cromwell, the King's Chancellor, to find Tyndale and bring him back to England. Aware that Vaughan was looking for him, Tyndale arranged a series of meetings around Antwerp. According to Vaughan's report, Tyndale was moved by Cromwell's opinion that the king would be merciful should Tyndale return. But not moved enough, as his remarkable, martyr-ready response shows: "If it would stand with the king's most gracious pleasure to grant only a bare text of the scripture be put forth among his people ... I shall immediately make faithful promise never to write more, nor abide two days in these parts after the same but ... most humbly submit myself at the feet of his royal majesty, offering my body to suffer what pain or torture, yea, what death his grace will, so this be obtained."

Clearly one to stay on message, Tyndale had planned to finish the Old Testament, but he was finally duped and kidnapped by a ne'er-do-well Englishman named Henry Phillips. To this day, it is not clear who sent Phillips, although suspects include More, who was jailed at the time, and the murderous Bishop Stokesley (who brought back the old-school execution policy of burning heretics while they were still alive). But Phillips wormed his way into Tyndale's trust and then arranged to have him abducted and driven out of the free city of Antwerp to a nearby Belgian prison. One letter written by Tyndale from prison survives. It is a literally chilling missive as Tyndale begs that warmer clothes—clothes he owns—be brought to him; it also speaks to his unmatchable dedication: "But most of all I beg and beseech your clemency ... to have the Hebrew Bible, Hebrew grammar, and Hebrew dictionary that I may pass the time in that study."

A three-man tribunal of clerics sentenced Tyndale to death for heresy. On the day of his execution, Fox tells us, he stepped up to the crowd and said, "Lord, open the eyes of the King of England!" Then he was chained to a stake, choked to death, and finally burned.

Our history and social studies classes rarely, if ever, mention Tyndale. His Bible certainly owes something to Luther's works, but no single book directly shaped the world we know today more than Tyndale's Bible.

The Tyndale Bible was the first attack on the limited theocracy that existed in England at the time. Once the Bible was published in English, the church's big secret—its open source code, to extend the metaphor to the Web—was out there for whoever wanted it. Any man could read it, use it, and understand it. And with it, everyone became a sinner with the same shot at redemption. All were equal under God.

Tyndale's defiant work was never approved by Henry VIII. Eventually, however, the king opened his eyes enough to allow Miles Coverdale, a former Tyndale collaborator, to publish a Bible translated only from the Vulgate. It was a nod to a turning tide—England was awash in English Bibles from smugglers, book bootleggers, and Lollards.

Some seventy years later, in 1611, in an effort to issue a definitive English Bible, a slew of scholars and clergymen issued what is known as the King James Bible. According to Daniell, more than 80 percent of the King James Bible matches Tyndale's work. While that percentage might have irked the perfectionist in Tyndale, he would have been more pleased that the Protestant Revolution in England was in full swing. After King James's son Charles I married a French Catholic and asserted the Divine Right of Kings, religion and parliamentary passion merged: Charles was deposed by devout Protestant army man Oliver Cromwell, who temporarily dismantled the English monarchy. Less than a generation later, Charles II was back in power, but the idea of a monolithic, all-powerful monarchy was over. Charles's death in 1685 was followed by the Glorious Revolution of 1688, which was marked by the removal of Charles's Catholic brother James, the birth of the Bill of Rights, and the assertion of parliamentary and Protestant supremacy. Two years later, John Locke crystallized his theories on government and society, pointing the way toward the ideals of state and democracy as we know it. Underscoring the Bill of Rights, Locke defended private property, majority rule, legislators who grant authority to executors, and administrators. Mix in the evangelism that spurred Tyndale, simmer for another century, and the template for English expansionism was set.

Tyndale embarked on his fatal journey because he believed that the world deserved to know the scriptures and that faith in Christ — not fealty to Catholic doctrine — was the only requirement to enter the pearly gates. As the Empire expanded, so did the missionary fervor that Tyndale personified. Together, English imperialism and the religious call to bring up the white man's burden expanded to Africa, to Asia (including Pakistan and Afghanistan), and to the Middle East and places like Iraq. And that evangelical fervor, that commitment to good works, that burden, helped compel the Empire to open its borders to the people they had colonized.

While many of those who migrated have become successful, integrated English citizens, many have not. Which brings us, sadly, back to Birmingham, terrorists, the World Wide Web, and a far more radical brand of martyrdom than Tyndale's: violent jihad.

INFORMATION VS. EXTREMISM

There is a school of thought that the more information available on the Web, the better. This, after all, is the subtext of Google's mandate: "to organize the world's information and make it universally accessible and useful." Meanwhile, Web inventor Tim Berniers-Lee has remained adamant about not placing content limits on his invention. This is an appealing idea: Freedom of speech and the dissemination of information are building blocks of democracy. When the United States went into Afghanistan in October 2001, a joke went around that the U.S. military forces should simply airdrop pornography; the sexually repressed Taliban would surely surrender immediately.

But the fact is, freedom frightens repressive regimes (not to mention some "permissive" governments in the West). And while the Internet may have been created to ensure that lines of communication stay open, it can, at least temporarily, be stopped. China, for instance, blocks access to sites it doesn't want citizens to see — content devoted to Falun Gong, Tibet, Taiwan, and much more. Other countries, including Saudi Arabia (which has an "access denied" page that requests surfers to submit other URLs to be blocked), Iran, and the United Arab Emirates also ban certain news sites, certain blogs and, of course, all sex sites.

Tyndale's story is, among other things, an epic tale of the battle for free speech. How ironic, then, to discuss his story in terms of wanting to censor violent jihad. But having been attacked by al-Qaeda a number of times — in Kenya, the World Trade Center, and elsewhere — should the West permit virtual town squares where true believers and madrassa students can witness the executions of infidels, the destruction of the towers, and bombs in Nairobi? And where the dispossessed and demented — putty in ideologue hands — can watch powerful snuff propaganda over and over again?

Suppression is, of course, one answer, and probably a bad one. Free speech crackdowns are not the most American of ideals, and such measures probably work more effectively in extremely repressive societies. As the crackdown against Tyndale's Bible teaches us, bans are not always enforceable and often publicize what is being hushed up. In fact, even if governments ban IP addresses, URLs,

and much more, the Web still offers ways to send and receive information (proxy Web sites, encrypted e-mail, and Internet telephony)
that is much harder to monitor and stop. The U.S. government currently works with a company called Anonymizer to offer proxy servers to users in countries with heavy censorship. Theoretically, a
computer user in Mecca can connect to an Anonymizer server (outside Saudi Arabia) and surf to his or her heart's delight for everything from Saudi royal family gossip to Jewish law to porn—all
anonymously.

As Shiites, Sunnis, and Salafists fight for supremacy of the Islamic world, with extremists on all sides talking of a return of the
caliphate—a single Islamic state stretching from Turkey to Pakistan—it is time to examine Tyndale again. The caliphate is frequently portrayed as an enlightened era, one in which—at
times—the Muslim nation was a leader of military, fiscal, and scientific development. This has not been the case for centuries, but it is
a major talking point for Osama bin Laden and other fundamentalist Islamic theoreticians.

As Tyndale, Luther, and everyone in their wake show us, reformation—breaking away from fundamentalism, from theocracy—is
what helped England and Europe take great leaps forward in scientific, military, and fiscal arenas. This is not to denigrate the Catholic
Church or Islam, but strict theocracies do not—or did not—have
the pluralist, social Darwinism that breeds ingenuity and diversity.
The idea that faith alone would get you into heaven was a reassuring
and productive one. On a certain level, there is a "have your cake
and eat it too" structure to the faith-and-salvation doctrine. But that
is not a bad thing. It allowed the West to flourish. Even Catholic nations benefited from the rise of Protestantism; where would *liberté,*
égalité, and *fraternité* be without it?

And so, for the West to cling to the barest hope of maintaining
the geopolitical status quo—something I'm not prepared to bet on

— and for the Middle East to thrive as its oil supply starts to dwindle, the Islamic world needs a reformation; it needs a Tyndale, a non-violent religious warrior.

But perhaps we are already witnessing an Islamic reformation right now, albeit a conservative reformation. To this casual observer — who is not an expert in Islam, the Middle East, or history, for that matter — the Taliban must see themselves as reformers. So, too, must al-Qaeda, the Muslim Brotherhood, and the Salafists. With so much competition among extremist reformers, finding a so-called moderate (Tyndale, remember, hoped to keep the status quo; he loved the Monarchy) is easier said than done. But the opportunity is there.

Instead of the United States combating Hezbollah (Iranian-funded fundamentalist Shiites in Lebanon) by overtly and covertly supporting Sunni-backed fundamentalists, it should be backing a reformer who eschews both factions, one who can find a way to reject Muslim-against-Muslim violence and can appeal to the millions who — judging from their consumption of movies, music, Victoria Secret lingerie, porn, and alcohol — want pop culture now and paradise later. This silent middle-class majority needs a charismatic mullah or scholar who can shape a message to challenge fundamentalism. Let him appeal to the caliphate yet extol the melding of East and West, condemn the cult of the holy warrior, and vilify the Middle East leaders as the crass despots so many of them are. Let him communicate both on and offline, appealing to the impoverished parking boys, illiterate men and women, and subsistence workers on the other side of the digital divide.

Of course, once this reformer is found, a big question remains: How do you get the word out?

Tyndale published something completely banned, something rarely seen that people were thirsting for. It went viral.

Frankly, I have no idea how to make a liberal Islamic reformation viral. But I do know that the Web is only a partial democratic construct and that search results can be influenced by both search engine engineers and by linking behavior on the Web. In other words, one programmer's search relevancy script can be another man's form of censorship. And so it may fall to the International Broadcasting Bureau—the U.S. government's overseas propaganda arm—and engines like Google and Yahoo! to help get the message out. Imagine Web pages being optimized and indexed so that Arabic or Farsi or Urdu speakers (or speakers of any language) would only find moderate visions of Islam on, say, the first 100 search results. Imagine typing in "Islam Fundamentalist Execution Video," and instead of links to executions, you get a passionate Islam-based argument against executions.

That is an extreme, Orwellian use of the Web, and I'm not sure I approve. But the Web already is swarming with Orwellian aspects: Government telecom departments can write a single line of code and deny access to all Web sites from a specific country. "I can wipe out entire cities!" a security guru gleefully told me while demonstrating how he battles the onslaught of spam hitting a Fortune 500 company. Before my eyes, he typed a string of numbers. "There," he said, "I've just blocked every single e-mail from Bangkok, Thailand."

As often happens with the Web, we've wandered a little off track. This essay hoped to examine the lessons of publishing revolutions and to compare Tyndale's story to current religious and political issues amid the reality of the World Wide Web.

When you look at the path I've traced—or, more accurately, leapfrogged—from the Gutenberg press to Luther to Tyndale to Protestantism to the nascent British Empire to democracy to imperialism to terrorism, it's clear that everything is connected. History is a web of unpredictable, long-gestating collisions. And the World Wide Web, the new repository and publisher of everything, offers us future unknown journeys of endless connections. While that's exciting, it's disturbing, too, because the Web, with no up or down, no left or right, no true governing body, seems out of control.

Even the things we may want to stop or control on the Web seem impossible to combat: Piracy abounds. Recently arrested terror suspects in New York allegedly used Google Earth for reconnaissance. Spam, in case you didn't know, is supposed to be illegal.

Thanks to the Web's broadcasting ability, executions—once the provenance of men in power—are now the business of those who want power.

There are saving graces to all this. The Web may be out of control, but spin is impossible to control, too. So as the battles of Islam versus the West continues—no doubt for generations to come—consider a handful of miscalculations, all them intricately planned modern spectacles of death: the 9/11 attack, the shock-and-awe bombings of Baghdad, George W. Bush's "mission accomplished" photo op.

Each of these has backfired to some extent. The 9/11 attacks didn't win much sympathy for al-Qaeda, almost saw its leadership wiped out, and saw the Taliban dismantled (if only temporarily). The aerial bombardment of Baghdad may have played well to the home crowd in the United States, but it's easy to see how this exercise in overkill made Americans look like the bully of the world. Bush's "mission accomplished" bluster must have seemed like a good idea at the time, but how did it play to enraged, newly disenfranchised Sunnis (or antiwar Americans now)? Of course, all of this takes me back to Tyndale's dignified, dramatic behavior at his execution. A gentle man goes to a brutal death thinking of nothing more than furthering the cause that he will now die for. Rather than bolster the church, Tyndale's execution became the stuff of legend, of inspiration.

Who will be the stuff of legend now? A walking human bomb or a brave new prophet redefining Islam or a fanatical conservative?

A scientist who discovers cheap, clean, renewable energy or a visionary Web programmer? Whoever wrests power from the current cultural and political wars will write their story both offline and online, using the Web's potent and easily unbalanced platform to launch healing or dangerous words, images, instructions, and with it all, inevitable, unforeseeable change.

Toward an Anthropology Of the Future

Alexandra Chciuk-Celt

Social scientists are usually chary of making predictions, probably because societies lack the laboratory controls and objective criteria that allow the hard sciences to extrapolate deductions about future behavior. However, I contend that knowledge of the essential mechanisms of the past can support some considered projections of what can reasonably be expected in the future. For instance, my familiarity with the mind-set of the untreated survivors of child abuse led me to visit Russia as soon as the Soviet dictatorship ended, before the people realized they were free and started going haywire. Anthropologists have also noticed that, if a society without a cash economy is suddenly given a chance to earn money, the elders invariably complain that the young people have stopped sharing. As Peter Farb pointed out in *Humankind,* in the absence of money or refrigeration, the best place to store surplus food is in somebody else's belly; that way, when he catches some game, he will share it with you. Money, however, upsets this delicate balance of sharing.

Probably the most important lesson cultural anthropology taught me was that there was a systemic and pervasive difference in mentality between hunter-gatherers and peasants in subsistence (non-money) economies. Hunter-gatherers value initiative and experimentation, think of challenge as an opportunity even in the face

---

Alexandra Chciuk-Celt is a translator, educator, and researcher. E-mail languagelady@juno.com.

of a 90-percent failure rate, are satisfied with being allowed to use (rather than own) resources or territory, have small families (practicing infanticide if need be), and treat their children affectionately, encouraging them to be independent. Peasants value conformity and obedience, think of challenge as a threat, need outright ownership of their resources and territory, have large families, and treat their children like hardware. For hunter-gatherers, envy is an incentive to go out and get their own whatever, while envious peasants try to take the whatever away from its owner, or at least spoil the pleasure for him or her. Hunter-gather bands typically number twenty-five to fifty people, which makes perfect justice easier to achieve (on an asymptotic basis, of course) because everybody knows each other personally; since most of human prehistory involved living in such groups, one can readily understand the phylogenetic longing for community contained in theoretically egalitarian religions such as Christianity, Islam, and Communism. The hunter-gatherer lifestyle is more fun, but also much more wasteful because it is based on selection and consumption of what the environment has to offer, whereas the peasant lifestyle is based on production and planning. On the other hand, peasants have a distinct power advantage because agriculture enables population densities of 400 times as many people in the same amount of space. The intermediate mind-set of pastoralism contains elements of both hunter-gatherer and peasant attitudes and may well be significant in making the transition.

I also learned that the different mentalities carry over into modern societies with a money economy. For instance, Americans think like hunter-gatherers rather than peasants, foraging in the supermarket rather than growing and storing food for their own consumption. According to its June 2000 issue, *National Geographic* takes some 29,000 photographs per article, and by my count uses no more than twenty-nine; raised on the planned scarcity of peasant thinking, Eastern European photojournalists would no doubt be

horrified at the wastefulness of a 99.9 percent rejection rate. Consequently, the American labor market is good example of the wasteful
hunter-gatherer mentality of selection vs. planning. Compared with
European countries and their traditions of apprenticeship, American personnel management is so nonsupportive (probably because
of all those immigrants who arrive pretrained) that it should be
called what it really is: shopping! As a result, I believe the grief that
Americans were surprised to feel for Princess Di is based on their
ability to empathize with her situation: Whether at work or in the
dating circuit, they know what it feels like to be rejected for the silli-
est of non-reasons and considered worthless except as a pop-up doll
in somebody else's coloring book.

Hunter-gatherers think of the economy as nature, warts and
all, including waste, weeds, disorganization, and bullies—anything
goes as it can take care of itself; peasants consider it more of a garden,
where everything needs the gardener's specific permission to exist.
The crisis management of peasants tends to favor rationing and controls; bad times bring out the best in peasants, but the worst in hunter-
gatherers. (See "The Mythfits" [Chciuk-Celt] for the escalation in violence I consider predictable in the United States unless systemic
changes are made.) When hunter-gatherers start running out of resources, they move to another location; once there is nowhere left to
move, they usually turn on each other in combative inward antagonism (infanticide, warfare, even cannibalism), which—unless coun-
tered by a transition to the pastoral or peasant mentality—eliminates
all but the most brutal members of society, limiting population numbers and fostering the survival of the nastiest.

In case you are wondering, the hunter-gatherer mentality is
now the exception rather than the rule, statistically speaking. Most
of the world's people think like peasants, and it is a mistake to ignore
or confuse these disparate mind-sets. For instance, Americans do
not realize that even their imperfect attempt at tolerant multicultur-

alism is a mere pimple, cosmically speaking, upon a planetful of peasants. If they did, they would not have imposed such an inherently unstable multicultural solution upon the Balkans at Dayton or tried to bring democracy to the autocratic Middle East (in any country, the government is the family structure writ large). Furthermore, economists are wearing blinders of their own if they naïvely expect a mere political shift toward a supposed democracy and market economy to turn eastern Europeans (peasants) into astute and adventurous investors (hunter-gatherers) overnight. As an example: When pop star Michael Jackson offered to invest a million dollars in a children's amusement park outside Warsaw, the city fathers declined, claiming that such a project would promote prostitution.

It is easy to overlook the differences between these two mentalities, as when hunter-gatherers are lulled into a false sense of security by peasants using ostensible homology to paper over the divergences. As an example: Just as the Catholic Church co-opted pagan gods and rituals when converting the barbarians of Europe, the Communists during the Cold War intentionally obfuscated cross-cultural differences by giving their organizations such reassuringly homologous names that Westerners were fooled into assuming those institutions to be legitimate counterparts of their own.

Another example would be comparing the academic abuse of Slavic countries to that of the United States: From fraternity hazing to PhD orals, academic abuse in the United States is a derivative of the secret men's clubs of hunter-gatherer societies and stops as soon as the initiate becomes a member; its statistical function is to promote in-group solidarity—anthropologists say that the fiercer the hazing ritual, the greater the subsequent loyalty. (In *Blackberry Winter*, Margaret Mead said that the demise of white supremacy in the wake of the civil rights movement sounded like African-Americans were being accepted into fraternities. I see a similar pattern in the discrimination suffered by the first generation of groups immigrating to the United States; once they are assimilated, the kicks they got are transmitted to the next crop of immigrants.) In places like Poland and Russia, however, the abuse is permanent because it is a derivative of the peasant mentality: The professors are like the nobles of old (who destroy anyone they cannot capture as a satellite), sacred cows who can do no wrong and can mistreat interlopers with impunity until they die. The only way to circumvent their destructiveness is to accomplish something in spite of them and—this is important—let them take credit for what they tried to prevent. The closest equivalent in the United States: Imagine if Hollywood sycophancy had the same kind of transgenerational permanence as the antebellum South, with often self-indulgent landowners lording it over defenseless slaves. (Speaking of lording, men with power sometimes remind me of alpha males in nature programs: They think all the females in their territory belong to them.) See "The Mythfits," "Anglos and Insects," and "The Kom Dynasty" [Chciuk-Celt] for further instances of cross-cultural misunderstandings between hunter-gatherers and peasants and the behavior that can be expected when they are faced with dwindling resources.

POTENTIAL FUTURES FOR HUNTER-GATHERERS AND PEASANTS

Assuming the world continues on its present path instead of making the systemic changes I believe to be urgent, let me hazard the following expectations based on the different mentalities of hunter-gatherers and peasants. Something similarly future-oriented and interdisciplinary has been done before, as documented in Ruth Benedict's *The Chrysanthemum and the Sword:* When the Americans knew they would win World War II against the Japanese, they turned to a highly varied panel of consultants (which included historians, anthropologists, and experts in comparative literature) to advise them how to act as occupiers so as to minimize social damage.

First, since peasant envy tends to make the have-nots try to take away the haves' goodies, or at least poison their enjoyment thereof, I expect the resentful Russians to behave like spoilers and sabotage others' efforts just to prove that they are still a force to be reckoned with. In the foreseeable future, I think they will act like the macrosocial equivalent of the untreated survivors of child abuse, so this pathology should be given greater study by diplomats and others active on the international stage (see "Ruminations on Russia" [Chciuk-Celt]). Suffering alone does not ennoble people; if anything, it makes them bitter and abusive. "The Kom Dynasty," my "Personal Preface" [Chciuk-Celt], and some of the travel articles on East and Southeast Asia document my much grimmer view of what I expect China to do, given its history and the PRC's one-child policy; at the very least, we should stop outsourcing our jobs, thereby financing its military expansionism, which I expect to become a ghastly threat to future generations.

Second, contrary to economists' belief that a prosperous economy generally leads to political liberalism, I expect prosperity in Asia to reinforce tradition and fascism. The respective resources that Latin American gold and Middle Eastern oil contributed to the Spanish empire and the Muslim countries basically enabled the artificial survival of medieval systems, because the people could afford physical and mental luxuries that would otherwise be wildly and prohibitively outdated. India's recent prosperity is actually cementing the caste system, because the newly emergent middle classes can only afford to live like kings on their low wages if they have guaranteed access to cheap, docile labor, an abuse that I fear will culminate in bloodshed. There have been historical precedents for this syndrome: In the postwar United States and in China's Sung Dynasty, prosperity reinforced conservative sexism because men could afford to dismiss women's contribution to the labor force. What the PRC can do with its newfound riches is a particularly horrifying prospect, because China's huge, obedient population and despotic, often ignorant rulership can combine to wreak an ecological havoc that can conceivably culminate in a *Waterworld* scenario (see the Three Gorges project in "The Kom Dynasty" [Chciuk-Celt]). We are already starting to see animal populations becoming extinct because Chinese medicine obsoletely prescribes things like tiger bone and rhinoceros horn, whose ingredients can be found much less destructively in calcium pills and keratin supplements.

Third, when hunter-gatherers start running out of resources, they move to another location; once there is nowhere left to move, they turn on each other in combative inward antagonism. This is starting to happen in the United States, where dwindling resources are making the people more aggressive rather than more efficient. Instead of becoming more entrenched in the behavior of the past ("getting back to basics"), we must realize that the wastefulness of the hunter-gatherer mentality needs to give way to some intelligent planning if we are to give our children a sustainable future; otherwise, it is only a matter of time before aggressive dominance establishes a feudal stranglehold or the army of rejects becomes destructive.

TOWARD A FAIR AND SUSTAINABLE FUTURE

As usual, I hope my predictions are wrong, but I caution that dismissing them will not make them so. I believe we can counter them to a certain extent by encouraging equitable efficiency, discouraging institutionalized brutality, and remembering the intent behind existing laws and principles (the spirit rather than the letter). Unfortunately, legal professionals seem to be going in the opposite direction, probably because simple equity renders them personally less indispensable than do loopholes, technicalities, and procedural formalism.

We could start small, such as by reforming the more destruc-

tive elements of bilingual education and by remembering that
au pairs are mother's-helper teenagers, not professional nannies en-
trusted with household management; if anything, using them for
elder care would teach them more about the local culture than they
could learn from baby-sitting ("Au Pair Means Everybody Wins"
and "Recalibrating Bilingual Education" [Chciuk-Celt]). Similar
principles might be useful for reforming other counterproductive institutions and warped interpretations. Thereafter, perhaps business
and political leaders can be persuaded to stop remaining deliberately difficult of access in their Versailles cocoons and consider including input from people who are neither their clones nor their
cronies.

In terms of brutality: Hospitals should discontinue the savage
practice of thirty-six-hour shifts, which compromises patient care
and whose only conceivable usefulness would be weeding out doc-
tors unfit for combat medicine. The media should also develop some
social responsibility; if violence is consistently shown as entertainment, what can we expect if not more Columbines?

In more formal terms, changes in legislation could also help
avoid exacerbating pointless conflict, preemptive hostility, and rob-
ber-baron predations — e.g., punitive damages for nuisance legal actions, laws preventing CEOs from giving themselves nine-figure
bonuses even in the face of relentlessly mediocre performance, and
the direct election of presidents. The electoral college system was
instituted when people were wearing powdered wigs and white
stockings, the roads were so terrible that it took the electors a month
to reach Washington, and representative democracy had never been
tried on such a scale before. It is senselessly and dangerously outdated in the computer age, as was shown in the 2000 election (cf.
"When Bush Comes to Shove" [Chciuk-Celt]). The relatively recent
phenomenon of vicious and counterproductive partisanship should
be muzzled: Inflammatory rhetoric on the part of politicians was

precisely what triggered Colombia's civil war in 1946.

I also believe the Bill of Rights should be interpreted more in keeping with what the framers had in mind. For instance, since they called anything related to commercial sex "trafficking in hussies," they would not have applied First Amendment protection to pornography and nude dancing—which represent free commerce, not free speech. Similarly, since old-fashioned muskets were virtually the only arms available for bearing at the time, the framers would have looked askance at machine guns, which no hunter can reasonably claim to need unless being attacked by two hundred stags in formation. The Fifth Amendment was obviously designed to outlaw torture, which had theretofore been a rather common method of obtaining confessions, not to allow parties to withhold testimony.

In terms of food production, hunter-gatherer food-acquisition methods such as fishing should be at least partially replaced by more efficient production methods, such as fish farming. PBS programs like Bill Moyers's examination of innovative ecological techniques ("Earth on Edge," aired in June 2001) show that established methodologies can be seriously destructive and that viable alternatives exist.

Once we have dismantled our blinders enough to see how much of the present is wasteful and counterproductive, we can direct our view toward the future, which we can be fairly sure will be radically different. A more complicated future will require more commonsensical legislation and fewer people who believe they are entitled to flout it, as well as a rethinking of the attitude that money equals invincibility.

The essays in my unpublished *Dismantling Blinders: An Invitation to Cross-Cultural Thinking* contain further suggestions for how we need to reorient our mind-set from past to future so as to weather the systemic social changes we will need to, so as to survive as a society in which the pie is much smaller than before and more people are eating from it. An example from history: If the Johnson administration had included the input of Harvard's Whiting and Whiting study, specifically the conclusion linking father absence and the sons' tendency toward violent behavior as a reaction formation to an initial female identification, its welfare program would probably not have unwittingly exacerbated crime by encouraging fatherless households.

If nothing is done, I fear that dwindling resources will cause Americans to turn on each other because, like classic hunter-gatherers, they do not handle deprivation well. I believe the following prefigures such a scenario: Around 1980, there was a mugging spree in New York's Times Square area, which lasted several hours. When the criminals ran out of passersby to victimize, the bigger muggers turned on the smaller muggers and relieved them of their loot.

A good analogy for planning a fairer and more efficient future would be three swimming pools wide enough for swimming eight abreast, identical except for their management philosophies. The first is a hunter-gatherer laneless free-for-all; this sounds like perfect freedom, but since the swimmers typically go back and forth along the same imaginary track, all that wasted space makes the pool feel crowded if there are more than eight people because of the frustration and social friction involved in having to finagle a new opening for every lap. The second (peasants) is dominated by groups; isolated individuals and minorities must either settle for some corner nobody else wants or wait for the dominant groups to leave. It is impossible to swim a straight line because the group members think the tyranny of the majority entitles them to do anything they want; if there is more than one large group, the best that can be hoped for is partition, with everyone scurrying to grab as much territory as possible before the separation. If this sounds like the Balkans, that is by no means a coincidence.

The third type is divided into four lanes (the first for loafing, the others in a speed-graduated manner) in which swimmers keep moving and stay to the right, as though driving a car; this pool can be used comfortably, and with very little conflict, by at least thirty-two people. The interdisciplinary logic I am advocating can similarly smooth our switch to a more logical system.

The transition between the hunter-gatherer and peasant mentalities is lost in the mists of prehistory, but it must have been rather traumatic unless it was quite gradual. We, however, can do a lot better. Modern humanity is adept at systems design (from industrial engineering to packaging-machinery to computer programs) and has enough knowledge to enable planning for a more efficient and equitable future, one that avoids the brutality with which wasteful hunter-gatherers and fascist peasants have traditionally solved the problem of scarce resources.

REFERENCES

Benedict, Ruth. 1934. *Patterns of Culture.* Boston: Houghton Mifflin Company.

Benedict, Ruth. 1946. *The Chrysanthemum and the Sword: Patterns of Japanese Culture.* New York: World Publishing Company.

Chciuk-Celt, Alexandra. *Dismantling Binders: An Invitation to Cross-Cultural Thinking.* Unpublished.

Chua, Amy. 2003. *World on Fire: How Exporting Free Market Democracy Breeds Ethnic Hatred and Global Instability.* New York: Doubleday.

Farb, Peter. 1978. *Humankind.* Boston: Houghton Mifflin Company.

Geertz, Clifford. 2000. *Available Light: Anthropological Reflections on Philosophical Topics.* Princeton: Princeton University Press.

Herrmanns, Mathias. 1949. *Die Nomaden von Tibet. Die sozial-wirtschaftlichen Grundlagen der Hirtenkulturen in A Mdo und von Innerasien.* Vienna: Herold Verlag.

Malefijt, Annemarie de Waal. 1968. *Religion and Culture.* New York: The MacMillan Company.

McClelland, David. 1961. *The Achieving Society.* Princeton: D. Van Nostrand Company Inc.

Mead, Margaret. *Blackberry Winter: My Earlier Years.* 1972. New York: William Morrow Publishing.

York College. 1996. *Understanding Cultural Diversity: An Anthology for Core 101.* City University of New York: Simon & Schuster Custom Publishing.

Zakaria, Fareed. 2003. *The Future of Freedom.* New York: W.W. Norton & Co. Inc.

Technological Evolution

José Luis Cordeiro

The famous astronomer and astrobiologist Carl Sagan popularized the concept of a Cosmic Calendar about three decades ago. In his 1977 book, *The Dragons of Eden: Speculations on the Evolution of Human Intelligence*, Sagan wrote a timeline for the universe, starting with the Big Bang about 15 billion years ago. Today, we think that it all started about 13.7 billion years back, and we keep updating and improving our knowledge of life, the universe, and everything. In his Cosmic Calendar, with each month representing

Table 1: Cosmic Calendar, January/November

Big Bang	January 1
Origin of Milky Way galaxy	May 1
Origin of the solar system	September 9
Formation of the Earth	September 14
Origin of life on Earth	~September 25
Formation of the oldest rocks known on Earth	October 2
Date of oldest fossils (bacteria and blue-green algae)	October 9
Invention of sex (by microorganisms)	~November 1
Oldest fossil photosynthetic plants	November 12
Eukaryotes (first cells with nuclei) flourish	November 15

Source: J. L. Cordeiro based on C. Sagan (1977).

José Luis Cordeiro is co-founder of the Venezuelan Transhumanist Association and chair of the Venezuela Node of the Millennium Project. E-mail jose@cordeiro.org.

slightly over a billion years, Sagan dated the major events during the first eleven months of the cosmic year (see Table 1).

Interestingly enough, most of what we study in biological evolution happened in the last cosmic month. In fact, Sagan wrote that the first worms appeared on December 16, the invertebrates began to flourish on the 17th, the trilobites boomed on the 18th, the first fish and vertebrates appeared on the 19th, plants colonized the land on the 20th, animals colonized the land on the 21st, the first amphibians and first winged insects appeared on the 22nd, the first trees and first reptiles evolved on the 23rd, the first dinosaurs appeared on the 24th, the first mammals evolved on the 26th, the first birds emerged on the 27th, dinosaurs became extinct on the 28th, the first primates appeared on the 29th, and the frontal lobes evolved in the brains of primates and the first hominids appeared on the 30th. Basically, humans are just the new kids in the block, and only evolved late at night on the last day of this Cosmic Calendar (see Table 2).

The previous Cosmic Calendar is an excellent way to visualize the acceleration of change and the continuous evolution of the universe. Other authors have developed similar ideas to try to show the rise of complexity in nature. For example, in 2005, astrophysicist Eric Chaisson published *Epic of Evolution: Seven Ages of the Cosmos*, in which he describes the formation of the universe through the development of seven ages: matter, galaxies, stars, heavy elements, planets, life, complex life, and society. Chaisson presents a valuable survey of these fields and shows how combinations of simpler systems transform into more complex systems, thus giving a glimpse of what the future might bring.

Both Sagan and Chaisson wrote excellent overviews about evolution, from its cosmic beginnings to the recent emergence of humans and technology. However, a more futuristic look is given by engineer and inventor Ray Kurzweil in his 2005 book *The Singular-*

Table 2: Cosmic Calendar, December 31

Origin of *Proconsul* and *Ramapithecus*, probable
ancestors of apes and men .... ˜1:30 p.m.

First humans ,,, ˜10.30 p.m.

Widespread use of stone tools .... 11:00 p.m.

Domestication of fire by Peking man .... 11:46 p.m.

Beginning of most recent glacial period .... 11:56 p.m.

Seafarers settle Australia .... 11:58 p.m.

Extensive cave painting in Europe .... 11:59 p.m.

Invention of agriculture .... 11:59:20 p.m.

Neolithic civilization; first cities .... 11:59:35 p.m.

First dynasties in Sumer, Ebla, and Egypt;
development of astronomy .... 11:59:50 p.m.

Invention of the alphabet; Akkadian Empire .... 11:59:51 p.m.

Hammurabi legal codes in Babylon; Middle
Kingdom in Egypt .... 11:59:52 p.m.

Bronze metallurgy; Mycenaean culture; Trojan
War; Olmec culture; invention of the compass .... 11:59:53 p.m.

Iron metallurgy; First Assyrian Empire; Kingdom
of Israel; founding of Carthage by Phoenicia .... 11:59:54 p.m.

Asokan India; Ch'in Dynasty China; Periclean
Athens; birth of Buddha .... 11:59:55 p.m.

Euclidean geometry; Archimedean physics; Ptolemaic
astronomy; Roman Empire; birth of Christ .... 11:59:56 p.m.

Zero and decimals invented in Indian arithmetic;
Rome falls; Moslem conquests .... 11:59:57 p.m.

Mayan civilization; Sung Dynasty China;
Byzantine empire; Mongol invasion; Crusades .... 11:59:58 p.m.

Renaissance in Europe; voyages of discovery from
Europe and from Ming Dynasty China; emergence
of the experimental method in science .... 11:59:59 p.m.

Widespread development of science and technology;
emergence of global culture; acquisition of the means of
self-destruction of the human species; first steps in spacecraft
planetary exploration and the search of extraterrestrial
intelligence .... Now: The first second of New Year's Day

Source: J. L. Cordeiro based on C. Sagan (1977).

ity Is Near: When Humans Transcend Biology. Kurzweil talks about six epochs with increasing complexity and accumulated information processing (see Table 3).

Table 3: The Six Epochs of the Universe According to Kurzweil

Epoch 1 ....Physics and chemistry (information in atomic structures)

Epoch 2 ... Biology (information in DNA)

Epoch 3 ... Brains (information in neural patterns)

Epoch 4 ... Technology (information in hardware and software designs)

Epoch 5 ... Merger of technology and human intelligence (the methods of biology, including human intelligence, are integrated into the exponentially expanding human technology base)

Epoch 6 ... The universe wakes up (patterns of matter and energy in the universe become saturated with intelligent processes and knowledge)

Source: J. L. Cordeiro based on R. Kurzweil (2005).

According to Kurzweil, we are entering Epoch 5 with an accelerating rate of change. The major event of this merger of technology and human intelligence will be the emergence of a technological Singularity. Kurzweil believes that, within a quarter century, non-biological intelligence will match the range and subtlety of human intelligence. It will then soar past it because of the continuing acceleration of information-based technologies, as well as the ability of machines to instantly share their knowledge. Eventually, intelligent nanorobots will be deeply integrated in our bodies, our brains, and our environment, overcoming pollution and poverty, providing vastly extended longevity, full-immersion virtual reality incorporating all of the senses, and vastly enhanced human intelligence. The result will be an intimate merger between the technology-creating species and the technological evolutionary process it spawned.

Computer scientist and science-fiction writer Vernor Vinge first discussed this idea of a technological Singularity in a now classic 1993 paper, where he predicted:

> Within thirty years, we will have the technological means to create superhuman intelligence. Shortly after, the human era will be ended.

Other authors talk about such technological Singularity as the moment in time when artificial intelligence will overtake human intelligence. Kurzweil has also proposed the Law of Accelerating Returns, a generalization of Moore's law to describe an exponential growth of technological progress. Moore's law deals with an exponential growth pattern in the complexity of integrated semiconductor circuits (see Figure 1).

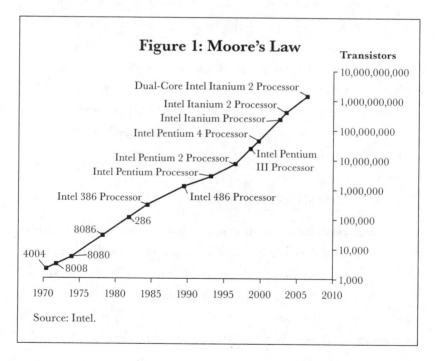

Figure 1: Moore's Law

Source: Intel.

Kurzweil extends Moore's law to include technologies from far before the integrated circuit to future forms of computation. Whenever a technology approaches some kind of a barrier, he writes, a new technology will be invented to allow us to cross that barrier. He predicts that such paradigm shifts will become increasingly common, leading to "technological change so rapid and profound it represents a rupture in the fabric of human history." He believes the Law of Accelerating Returns implies that a technological Singularity will occur around 2045:

> An analysis of the history of technology shows that technological change is exponential, contrary to the common-sense "intuitive linear" view. So we won't experience 100 years of progress in the 21st century — it will be more like 20,000 years of progress (at today's rate). The "returns," such as chip speed and cost-effectiveness, also increase exponentially. There's even exponential growth in the rate of exponential growth. Within a few decades, machine intelligence will surpass human intelligence, leading to the Singularity — technological change so rapid and profound it represents a rupture in the fabric of human history. The implications include the merger of biological and non-biological intelligence, immortal software-based humans, and ultra-high levels of intelligence that expand outward in the universe at the speed of light.

TECHNOLOGICAL CONVERGENCE

Futurists today have diverging views about the Singularity. Some see it as a very likely scenario, while others believe that it is more probable that there will never be any very sudden and dramatic changes due to progress in artificial intelligence. However, most futurists and scientists agree that there is an increasing rate of technological change. In fact, the rapid emergence of new technologies has generated scientific developments never dreamed of before.

The expression "emerging technologies" is used to cover such new and potentially powerful technologies as genetic engineering, artificial intelligence, and nanotechnology. Although the exact denotation of the expression is vague, various writers have identified clusters of such technologies that they consider critical to humanity's future. These proposed technology clusters are typically abbreviated by such combinations of letters as NBIC, which stands for Nanotechnology, Biotechnology, Information technology, and Cognitive science. Various other acronyms have been offered for essentially the same concept, such as GNR (Genetics, Nanotechnology, and Robotics) used by Kurzweil, while others prefer NRG because it sounds similar to "energy." Journalist Joel Garreau in *Radical Evolution* uses GRIN, for Genetic, Robotic, Information, and Nano processes, while author Douglas Mulhall in *Our Molecular Future* uses GRAIN, for Genetics, Robotics, Artificial Intelligence, and Nanotechnology. Another acronym is BANG for Bits, Atoms, Neurons, and Genes.

The first NBIC Conference for Improving Human Performance was organized in 2003 by the National Science Foundation and the U.S. Department of Commerce. Since then, there have been many similar gatherings, in the United States and overseas. The European Union has been working on its own strategy toward converging technologies, as have other countries in Asia, starting with Japan.

The idea of technological convergence is based on the merger of different scientific disciplines thanks to the acceleration of change on all NBIC fields. Nanotechnology deals with atoms and molecules, biotechnology with genes and cells, infotechnology with bits and bytes, and cognitive science with neurons and brains. These four fields are converging thanks to the larger and faster information processing of ever more powerful computers (see Figure 2).

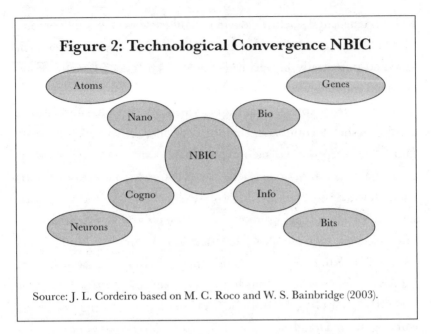

Figure 2: Technological Convergence NBIC

Source: J. L. Cordeiro based on M. C. Roco and W. S. Bainbridge (2003).

Experts from the four NBIC fields agree about the incredible potential of technological evolution finally overtaking and directing biological evolution. Bill Gates of Microsoft has stated:

> I expect to see breathtaking advances in medicine over the next two decades, and biotechnology researchers and companies will be at the center of that progress. I'm a big believer in information technology ... but it is hard to argue that the emerging medical revolution, spearheaded by the biotechnology industry, is any less important to the future of humankind. It, too, will empower people and raise the standard of living.

Larry Ellison of Oracle, Gates's chief rival in the software industry, agrees: "If I were 21 years old, I probably wouldn't go into computing. The computing industry is about to become boring." He explains, "I would go into genetic engineering." Biologist Craig Venter has said that he spent ten years reading the human genome, and now he is planning to write new genomes. He wants to create completely new forms of life, from scratch. Scientist and writer Gregory Stock also believes that cloning, even though a fundamental step in biotechnology, is just too simple and unexciting: "Why copy old life-forms when we can now create new ones?"

Biological evolution allowed the appearance of human beings, and many other species, through millions of years of natural selection based on trials and errors. Now we can control biological evolution, direct it and go beyond it. In fact, why stop evolution with carbon-based life-forms? Why not move into silicon-based life, among many other possibilities? Robotics and artificial intelligence will allow us to do just that.

Scientist Marvin Minsky, one of the fathers of artificial intelligence at MIT, wrote a very famous 1994 article, "Will Robots Inherit the Earth?" in *Scientific American,* where he concludes, "Yes, but they will be our children. We owe our minds to the deaths and lives of all the creatures that were ever engaged in the struggle called Evolution. Our job is to see that all this work shall not end up in meaningless waste." Robotics expert Hans Moravec has written two books about robots and our (their) future: *Mind Children* in 1988 and *Robot* in 1998. Moravec argues that robots will be our rightful descendants, and he explains several ways to "upload" a mind into a robot. In England, cybernetics professor Kevin Warwick has been implanting his own body with several microchip devices and published in 2003 a book explaining his experiments, *I, Cyborg.* Warwick is a cybernetics pioneer who claims that "I was born human. But this was an accident of fate — a condition merely of time and place. I believe it's something we have the power to change.... The future is out there; I am eager to see what it holds. I want to do something with my life: I want to be a cyborg."

As these authors and thinkers suggest, we need to start preparing ourselves for the coming NBIC realities of technological convergence, including robotics and artificial intelligence. Thanks to technological evolution, humans will transcend our biological limitations to become transhumans and eventually posthumans. To ease this transition into a posthuman condition, we must ready ourselves for the distinct possibility that the Earth, and other planets, will be inherited by not just one but several forms of highly intelligent and sentient life-forms. The philosophy of Extropy (see Appendix 1) and Transhumanism (see Appendix 2) explain these boundless possibilities for future generations.

THE HUMAN SEED

Humans are not the end of evolution but just the beginning of a better, conscious and technological evolution. The human body is a good beginning, but we can certainly improve it, upgrade it, and transcend it. Biological evolution through natural selection might be ending, but technological evolution is only accelerating now. Technology, which started to show dominance over biological processes some years ago, is finally overtaking biology as the science of life.

As fuzzy-logic theorist Bart Kosko has said, "biology is not destiny. It was never more than tendency. It was just nature's first quick and dirty way to compute with meat. Chips are destiny." And photo-qubits might come soon after standard silicon-based chips, but even that is only an intermediate means for eternal intelligent life in the universe.

Humans are the first species which is conscious of its own evolution and limitations, and humans will eventually transcend these constraints to become posthumans. It might be a rapid process like caterpillars becoming butterflies, as opposed to the slow evolutionary passage of humans from their pre-hominid ancestors. Future intelligent life-forms might not even resemble human beings at all, and carbon-based organisms will mix with a plethora of other organisms. These posthumans will depend not only on carbon-based systems, but also on silicon and other platforms that might be more convenient for different environments, such as traveling in outer space.

Eventually, all these new sentient life-forms might be connected to become a global brain, a large interplanetary brain, and even a larger intergalactic brain. The ultimate scientific and philosophical queries will continue to be tackled by these posthuman life-forms. Intelligence will keep on evolving and will try to answer the old-age questions of life, the universe, and everything. With ethics and wisdom, humans will become posthumans, as science-fiction writer David Zindell suggested:

"What is a human being, then?"

"A seed."

"A ... seed?"

"An acorn that is unafraid to destroy itself in growing into a tree."

APPENDIX 1: THE PRINCIPLES OF EXTROPY

Perpetual Progress: Extropy means seeking more intelligence, wisdom, and effectiveness, an open-ended life-span, and the removal of political, cultural, biological, and psychological limits to continuing development. Perpetually overcoming constraints on our progress and possibilities as individuals, as organizations, and as a species. Growing in healthy directions without bound.

Self-Transformation: Extropy means affirming continual ethical, intellectual, and physical self-improvement, through critical and creative thinking, perpetual learning, personal responsibility, proactivity, and experimentation. Using technology—in the widest sense to seek physiological and neurological augmentation along with emotional and psychological refinement.

Practical Optimism: Extropy means fueling action with

positive expectations—individuals and organizations being tirelessly proactive. Adopting a rational, action-based optimism or "proaction," in place of both blind faith and stagnant pessimism.

Intelligent Technology: Extropy means designing and managing technologies not as ends in themselves but as effective means for improving life. Applying science and technology creatively and courageously to transcend natural but harmful confining qualities derived from our biological heritage, culture, and environment.

Open Society—information and democracy: Extropy means supporting social orders that foster freedom of communication, freedom of action, experimentation, innovation, questioning, and learning. Opposing authoritarian social control and unnecessary hierarchy and favoring the rule of law and decentralization of power and responsibility. Preferring bargaining over battling, exchange over extortion, and communication over compulsion. Openness to improvement rather than a static utopia. Extropia ("ever-receding stretch goals for society") over utopia ("no place").

Self-Direction: Extropy means valuing independent thinking, individual freedom, personal responsibility, self-direction, self-respect, and a parallel respect for others.

Rational Thinking: Extropy means favoring reason over blind faith and questioning over dogma. It means understanding, experimenting, learning, challenging, and innovating rather than clinging to beliefs.

APPENDIX 2: THE TRANSHUMANIST DECLARATION

(1) Humanity will be radically changed by technology in the future. We foresee the feasibility of redesigning the human condition, including such parameters as the inevitability of aging, limitations on human and artificial intellects, unchosen psychology, suffering, and our confinement to the Planet Earth.

(2) Systematic research should be put into understanding these

coming developments and their long-term consequences.

(3) Transhumanists think that by being generally open and embracing of new technology we have a better chance of turning it to our advantage than if we try to ban or prohibit it.

(4) Transhumanists advocate the moral right for those who so wish to use technology to extend their mental and physical (including reproductive) capacities and to improve their control over their own lives. We seek personal growth beyond our current biological limitations.

(5) In planning for the future, it is mandatory to take into account the prospect of dramatic progress in technological capabilities. It would be tragic if the potential benefits failed to materialize because of technophobia and unnecessary prohibitions. On the other hand, it would also be tragic if intelligent life went extinct because of some disaster or war involving advanced technologies.

(6) We need to create forums where people can rationally debate what needs to be done and a social order where responsible decisions can be implemented.

(7) Transhumanism advocates the well-being of all sentience (whether in artificial intellects, humans, posthumans, or non-human animals) and encompasses many principles of modern humanism. Transhumanism does not support any particular party, politician, or political platform.

REFERENCES

Asimov, Isaac. [1950] 1994. *I, Robot*. New York: Bantam Books.

British Telecom. 2005. *Technology Timeline*. London: British Telecom. http://www.bt.com/technologytimeline.

Chaisson, Eric. 2005. *Epic of Evolution: Seven Ages of the Cosmos*. New York: Columbia University Press.

Clarke, Arthur C. 1984 (revised). *Profiles of the Future: An Inquiry into the Limits of the Possible*. New York: Henry Holt and Company.

Condorcet, Marquis de. 1979. *Sketch for a Historical Picture of the Progress of the Human Mind*. Westport, CT: Greenwood Press.

Cordeiro, José Luis. 1998. *Benesuela vs. Venezuela: El Combate Educativo del Siglo*. Caracas: Cedice. http://www.cordeiro.org.

Drexler, K. Eric. 1987. *Engines of Creation*. New York: Anchor Books. http://www.edrexler.com/d/06/00/EOC/EOC_Cover.html.

Foundation For the Future. 2002. *The Next Thousand Years*. Bellevue, WA: Foundation For the Future. http://www.futurefoundation.org/documents/nty_projdesc.pdf.

Fumento, Michael. 2003. *BioEvolution: How Biotechnology Is Changing the World*. San Francisco: Encounter Books.

Garreau, Joel. 2005. *Radical Evolution: The Promise and Peril of Enhancing Our Minds, Our Bodies—and What It Means to Be Human*. New York: Doubleday.

Glenn, Jerome C., and Theodore Gordon. 2007. *State of the Future 2006*. Washington, DC: The Millennium Project. http://www.stateofthefuture.org.

Haraway, Donna. 1991. "A Cyborg Manifesto." In *Simians, Cyborgs and Women: The Reinvention of Nature*. New York: Routledge.

Hawking, Stephen. 2002. *The Theory of Everything: The Origin and Fate of the Universe*. New York: New Millennium Press.

Joy, Bill. 2000. "Why The Future Doesn't Need Us." In *Wired*. April. http://www.wired.com/wired/archive/8.04/joy.html.

Kurian, George T., and Graham T. T. Molitor. 1996. *Encyclopedia of the Future*. New York: Macmillan.

Kurzweil, Ray. 2005. *The Singularity Is Near: When Humans Transcend Biology*. New York: Viking. http://www.singularity.com.

Kurzweil, Ray. 1999. *The Age of Spiritual Machines*. New York: Penguin Books. http://www.kurzweilai.net.

Minsky, Marvin. 1994. "Will Robots Inherit the Earth?" In *Scientific American*. October. http://www.ai.mit.edu/people/minsky/papers/sciam.inherit.txt.

Minsky, Marvin. 1987. *The Society of Mind*. New York: Simon and Schuster.

Moravec, Hans. 1998. *Robot: Mere Machine to Transcendent Mind*. Oxford: Oxford University Press. http://www.frc.ri.cmu.edu/~hpm/book97.

Moravec, Hans. 1988. *Mind Children*. Boston: Harvard University Press.

More, Max. 2003. *The Principles of Extropy*. The Extropy Institute. http://www.extropy.org/principles.htm.

Mulhall, Douglas. 2002. *Our Molecular Future*. Amherst, NY: Prometheus Books.

Paul, Gregory S., and Earl Cox. 1996. *Beyond Humanity: Cyberevolution and Future Minds*. Hingham, MA: Charles River Media.

Pearson, Ian. 1998. *Atlas of the Future*. New York: Macmillan.

Regis, Edward. 1991. *Great Mambo Chicken and the Transhuman Condition: Science Slightly over the Edge*. New York: Perseus Publishing.

Roco, Mihail C., and William Sims Bainbridge (eds.). 2003. *Converging Technologies for Improving Human Performance*. Dordrecht, Netherlands: Kluwer.

Roco, Mihail C., and Carlo D. Montemagno (eds.). 2004. *The Coevolution of Human Potential and Converging Technologies*. New York: New York Academy of Sciences (*Annals of the New York Academy of Sciences*, volume 1013).

Sagan, Carl. 1977. *The Dragons of Eden: Speculations on the Evolution of Human Intelligence*. New York: Random House.

Stock, Gregory. 2002. *Redesigning Humans: Our Inevitable Genetic Future*. New York: Houghton Mifflin Company.

Teilhard de Chardin, Pierre. 1964. *The Future of Man*. New York: Harper & Row.

Vinge, Vernor. 1993. "The Coming Technological Singularity." In *Whole Earth Review*. Winter.

Warwick, Kevin. 2002. *I, Cyborg*. London: Century.

Wells, H. G. 1902. "The Discovery of the Future." In *Nature*, 65. http://www.geocities.com/yokelcraig/hgwells1.html.

World Transhumanist Association. 2002. *The Transhumanist Declaration*. World Transhumanist Association. http://www.transhumanism.org/declaration.htm.

Zindell, David. 1994. *The Broken God*. New York: Acacia Press.

The Evolution and Future Direction of Marriage

Tom Lombardo and Jeanne Belisle Lombardo

Statistics on marriage since the second half of the twentieth century have not been encouraging. Divorce rates are high. Marriage rates are low. Cohabitation and unwed motherhood have skyrocketed. Responses to the statistics run the usual gamut; in one camp there is a rallying cry for a renewed commitment to marriage, while in another there is a dismissal of marriage as an outdated institution, the usefulness of which has been exhausted in the face of the increasing complexity of society and the demands placed on the individual. Clearly there are arguments to support both positions, but many are based on the too-narrow view of personal experience or ideological orientation. The issue of marriage, and in particular the future of marriage, requires a much larger scope, one that explores the origin, evolution, and current state of marriage and that considers the psychological and ethical dimensions of marriage as well. From this solid footing, one can explore the future possibilities and even preferred direction for an institution that, for better or worse, has long been expected to satisfy a wide range of needs, from intimacy, affection, and sex to domestic stability, family, and eco-

Tom Lombardo is the resident futurist faculty and faculty chair of psychology and philosophy at Rio Salado College, Tempe, Arizona. E-mail tlombardo1@cox.net.

Jeanne Belisle Lombardo is a facilitator in employee and organizational learning at Rio Salado College, Tempe, Arizona. E-mail gknee@cox.net.

nomic partnership.

In this paper we trace the evolution of marriage from prehistoric to contemporary times. We then examine the main controversies and issues regarding modern marriage in the West. From there we turn to future possibilities connected with cultural and technological changes. Finally, we outline a vision of the preferable marriage of the future, one that is broad and general enough to accommodate the diverse modes of marriage that have emerged in contemporary times, but also one that is psychologically and ethically informed. We will outline a vision based on the notion of the mutual practice and pursuit of character virtues by both partners in the marriage.

PREHISTORY AND ANCIENT AND EARLY HISTORY

Marriage is essentially a monogamous arrangement, and there is debate over the point in our evolutionary history at which we developed monogamy as a primary form of male–female bonding. Fossil evidence and comparative biology suggest that mating behavior in our earliest hominid ancestors involved the most powerful and dominant males securing open sexual access to multiple female partners, who being significantly smaller than the males were generally compliant and submissive to the dominant male's wishes.[1] But as sexual dimorphism decreased in later hominids, relative equality and shared responsibilities between the sexes emerged, along with serial monogamy; we also saw the beginnings of romantic love.[2]

There is debate, though, over the primary factors that originally brought our human ancestors together into relatively monogamous and committed relationships. Shlain argues that it was a fundamental negotiation — the female exchanging sex and progeny for meat and protection provided by the male — that was the foundation of marriage among early humans. In fact, this pivotal social negotiation brought with it an enhanced level of future consciousness (making a long-term commitment), social-cognitive evolution (assessing the deep intentions and character of another human being), and self-consciousness and self-control (the female no longer being automatically compliant to the male's overtures).[3] An alternative explanation, provided by Stephanie Coontz, is that the earliest marriages were arranged by the families, perhaps even the tribe, to cement social bonds and contribute to the economic viability of the group; different tribes may have arranged for marriages between their members to create social alliances. The original purpose of marriage was to produce reciprocal obligations and the interlocking of families. Hence, bonding was not a conscious and thoughtful choice, as in Shlain's interpretation, but a social arrangement forced upon the participants.[4] It is this social model and practice that would indeed become the "traditional marriage" in the millennia to follow.

Riane Eisler argues that our earliest civilizations centered around the worship of a mother goddess, though there was usually a male hunter or bull archetypal deity included as well. Eisler describes these goddess societies as partnership (or gylanic) societies, where there was basic equality between the sexes.[5] There appears to have been relative social equality of the sexes in ancient Egypt, for example, where female goddesses had central positions of power.[6] So marriages, up to a certain point in our history, may have involved a relative equality and partnership of male and female, even if the marriages were arranged by parents, family, and the tribe.

By 5000 BCE, however, the rise of urban centers and the emergence of agriculture and farming resulted in a strict division of labor along gender lines. The institution of rigid sexual codes of behavior and the establishment of permanent monogamy as the norm went hand in hand with a decline in women's rights. By 1000 BCE, with the eclipse of the mother goddess, patriarchy emerged as the dominant social system, establishing a double standard that viewed women as chattel. As the main purpose of marriage was procreation, abortions and extramarital sex were not tolerated.[7] In ancient Greece, while we do see some examples of romantic love coupled with marital fidelity with Homer's Hector and Andromache, and Odysseus and Penelope, the darker side of marriage and the relations between the sexes, such as that presented in Greek tragedy, far outweighs such tender views. Thus, when Plato talks about love, his focus is on love between older and younger men, not something strongly connected with marriage. Marriage, in the ancient world, was a social arrangement for consolidating status and resources.[8]

Patriarchy was clearly reinforced in both Judaism and early Christianity. Under Christianity, marriage became the sacrament of matrimony, further buttressing monogamy and lending doctrinal authority to the ban on divorce. By the time of St. Augustine, sexuality, especially when associated with women, came to be seen as evil, thus justifying greater controls on women's freedom. While women's rights did rise and fall throughout the Middle Ages in Europe under the pressure of different cultural norms, economic demands, and social status, it was the spread of urbanization toward the end of the Medieval period that opened up a greater variety of occupations for women, thus affording them greater social power.

This notwithstanding, women were not considered "free and lawful" persons at any time in this period. Reflecting the increasing secularization that accompanied urbanization, however, marriage evolved into a civil contract as well as a religious institution, and, in general, divorce rates remained low throughout the Middle Ages. There remained, though, a deep conceptual gulf between love and marriage, and marriages by and large continued to be arranged and controlled by families or even extended communities.[9]

MODERN HISTORY

In *The Way We Never Were*, Stephanie Coontz argues that the concept of the traditional marriage is, to some degree, a myth. Marriage has changed and evolved, reflective of changes in cultural values and the basic challenges of life. Yet, marriage is generally a human universal across the globe and throughout history, with some set of enforced rights and obligations associated with it.

Moving into the eighteenth century, a real shift in marriage took place, one that reflected a general social-cultural shift in human values and philosophy. The modern Western philosophy of individualism and self-determination probably goes back to the eleventh or twelfth century, but it was with the emergence of the European Enlightenment that freedom, autonomy, and individual rights became the dominant social ideals of the day, impacting all aspects of human life, including marriage. Increasingly, marriage came to be seen as a mutual choice of the couple entering into it, a choice based on love. No longer simply, or primarily, an economic arrangement between families, the expectations of marriage also changed; love, romance, and companionship became important considerations as well.

During the Victorian era, the ideal of love reached new heights; for the first time in Western history, love and marriage were not mutually exclusive. Yet, ironically, it was a love disassociated from sex, at least on the social surface. The ideal woman found her fulfillment in the dual roles of wife and mother; she was seen as pure, asexual, and morally superior (a real shift from the earlier view of the female as morally and spiritually inferior, a suspect being controlled by her lusts). This unrealistic picture of the woman reflected the sexual repressiveness that was, as Freud observed, a key characteristic of the Victorian era. As a major institution of the day, the Victorian marriage perpetuated, if not reinforced, the perceived differences between men and women and locked both into narrowly defined roles in marriage and in life.

The increased emphasis on love as the primary reason for getting married brought with it consequences not entirely unanticipated: The divorce rate shot up. Social commentators of the early twentieth century saw this shift in emphasis toward love and individual choice, and away from social and family control, as a threat to an institution that was, by all conventional standards, in an increasingly precarious position.

The social critics had reason to be alarmed. In the early decades of the twentieth century, with more women working and realizing both economic power and freedom, divorce rates continued to rise. Dating replaced courting, gender segregation in social settings broke down, self-expression was increasingly accepted and encouraged, and by the 1920s the original modern sexual revolution was in full force. The sexual repressiveness of the Victorian era gave way to a new sexual liberalism; sex outside of marriage became more acceptable, and sexual attraction became a key defining criterion for getting married. The party was just starting, though, when it came to a grinding halt. With the Great Depression and then the Second World War, freedom and self-expression as pivotal values took a back seat to social responsibility as the key defining virtue. Divorce rates consequently declined again.

The 1950s were the culmination of the modern individualistic and romantic vision of marriage. Marriage rates surged, and marital stability became the norm. There was a relatively clear division of labor between the husband, identified as the breadwinner, and the wife, in the role of homemaker. Buoyed by the unprecedented economic growth of the postwar years, the nuclear family came into its own. Marital love and family life were strongly connected with self-fulfillment, and devotion to one's spouse was the top priority. Yet, underneath the idealized vision of marriage and family, such as that portrayed in popular television representations,[10] other darker realities simmered; alcoholism and drug abuse, teen pregnancy, psychological problems, and sexual and physical abuse, though kept out of view, reflected the high cost of conforming to the rigid roles prescribed for both men and women.

THE 1960s CULTURAL REVOLUTION, DIVORCE, AND THE DECLINE OF MARRIAGE

Just as the 1950s vision of marriage was the culmination of modern social and philosophical trends centering around freedom, choice, and the centrality of love, the 1960s witnessed the culmination of other trends instigated by many of the same modern ideas, but with an increased emphasis on freedom and individual rights for everyone. Economic and technological factors also came into play. As more and more women went into full-time Jobs, often involving long-term career aspirations, their economic power increased; consequently, their sense of personal identity transcended the singular and limiting image of the housewife. The rise of modern feminism, highlighting the autonomy and equality of women, also contributed to their empowerment.

During this same time, males, too, expressed increasing discontent with the straitjacket stereotyping of men as breadwinners and, in step with women, acted on their desire for more freedom in determining their destiny. Overall, there was a cultural rebellion against conformity — against rigid, socially sanctioned roles — and a rise in the philosophy of being uncommitted as an expression of increased individual freedom. Part of the rejection against conformity and tradition involved a rejection of religious authority and a secularization of values. Postmodernism and relativism further undercut the moral authority of the church, family, and central social institutions; values were increasingly seen as unique and personal choices. How could one judge what was right and wrong regarding love, sex, and marriage? The sexual revolution of the 1960s, which strongly opposed the idea that sex outside of marriage was sinful, for either males or females, enjoyed a real technological boost with the introduction of the Pill, which allowed women increased sexual freedom.

The perhaps not surprising result of all of this freedom was a decoupling of sex and love. In retrospect, some critics have seen the 1960s as an era of narcissism, unconstrained hedonism, irresponsibility, and rampant immorality; the era triggered a dramatic rise again in divorce, a corresponding rise in cohabitation, and a return to the pattern of serial marriage or serial monogamy, which had been much more prevalent in ancient times.[11]

One may interpret the social transformation of the 1960s either as a moral collapse or as a moral evolution, with social mores moving from an authoritarian form of ethics (rules being provided by authorities and universalized social norms) to an individualistic or humanitarian ethics (ethical decisions being determined by individual considerations and choices). Similarly, one could ask whether marriage as an institution began to fall apart in the 1960s or began a new stage in its evolution. Although marriage was supposed to be an individual choice based on love, there was still considerable social pressure in the 1950s to get married and stay married; marriage was for better or worse. In the 1960s, individual choice became more important and more powerful, while social sanctions and rules and regulations became less important. Women especially realized greater equality; if marriage was going to work, it had to be a partnership of equals. All of this points toward moral evolution rather than moral collapse. From contemporary complexity and chaos theory we know that the collapse or disintegration of a system may not be an indication of imminent death, but rather impending evolution; a system has to fall apart—experience some significant chaos — so it can come back together in a transformed and more evolved way. This, we contend, is what happened in the 1960s and 1970s.

CONTEMPORARY TRENDS, ISSUES, AND DEBATES ON MARRIAGE

In 1970, Alvin Toffler announced in *Future Shock* "the death of permanence" and the emergence of "the disposable society," and indeed these expressions seemed to fit modern marriage. Marriage was no longer permanent, and spouses clearly seemed to have become disposable. Not only was sex decoupled from love or marriage, and living together decoupled from marriage, but reproduction and childbirth were increasingly disconnected from marriage as well. The out-of-wedlock birthrate climbed in the 1970s and 1980s along with the divorce rate.[12]

Although divorce rates have leveled off in the last decade, there is still a general concern at a global level over the contemporary crisis in marriage. As Coontz notes, there are numerous and often conflicting explanations and interpretations of the crisis, but there is a widespread belief that marriage is in danger. One issue already raised is whether we are observing a decline (perhaps even extinction) or watching an evolution. Given the moral issues that emerged in the 1960s, such as women's rights and equality and increasing freedom of choice regarding love, marriage, and gender roles, it could be argued that we are witnessing a moral evolution in the institution of marriage; things are getting better, not worse. Although it has been argued that marriage should be abolished, perhaps what in fact is happening is that it is being redefined.

Throughout the ages, the meaning and function of marriage have evolved, beginning with the economic and social cementing of families and tribes, to the religious sacrament and the legally sanctioned contract, and to the personal covenant based on love and devotion. More recently, coincident with the presumed crisis in marriage, the institution has further diversified. In contemporary times, we find delayed marriages (frequently preceded by cohabitation), serial marriages, single-parent households (sometimes in the aftermath of divorce), blended families and stepparents, and cohabitation. But we also find, again breaking out of various social and religious constraints, gay marriages and intercultural and interracial marriages. Part of the concern over marriage as a tradition is based upon a negative reaction to the diversification and loosening up of constraints in marriages and human bonding. As Coontz points out, though, none of these newer forms is really new; all the various arrangements have been tried before — frequently, in fact. What we see now with the emphasis on freedom, equal rights, and nontraditional or nonauthoritarian ethics, is a flowering and proliferation of all the forms simultaneously. And, of special note, there has been a steady increase in solitary living among adults; marriage is no longer seen as an absolute — as the pivotal event in one's adult life — a requirement that everyone must participate in.[13]

There has been a conservative backlash to the perceived collapse of traditional marriage (again, the traditional marriage through most of history was not that of the 1950s nuclear family, but rather the socially arranged marriage). Conservative voices see the decline of marriage as responsible for all our present social ills, and these voices wish to strongly reassert the value of marriage, even creating codes of conduct for how to practice or live a marriage. The conservative concept of the traditional marriage, though, is usually associated with a patriarchal system. Philosophical or moral arguments aside, one perspective on this issue recently put forward is that the patriarchal model will eventually reassert its dominant position in society because people who follow this model are significantly out-reproducing more liberal groups who support more diverse and egalitarian options in love and marriage.

However marriage is defined, the conservative voice has marshaled an array of statistics to support its position on the value of marriage. Interestingly, these positive benefits associated with marriage are also used by more liberal groups, such as gays, as solid reasons for supporting marriage and, in particular, in their case, for demanding the right to marry. Relative to living alone or even in cohabitation, marriage is associated with enhanced mental and physical health, increased longevity, a significant increase in wealth and higher incomes, more personal happiness, higher quality and more frequent sex, greater safety, more peace and contentment, and lower alcohol and drug abuse.[14]

Ironically, given the concerns over the collapse of marriage, the business of marriage, as well as divorce, is booming; the "bridal-industrial complex" generates more revenue than the entertainment industry. People keep getting married and getting divorced and getting married again, spending big bucks on the whole process.

Underneath all the fear and concern over the present condition of marriage, it could be argued that what we are seeing is a "marriage renaissance." More than ever, individuals marry out of choice and mutual consent; they marry for love rather than to participate in a socially sanctioned and reinforced institution; and they marry for mutual benefit and fulfillment. The real value in marriage is marriage itself—the creation of a loving partnership becomes the primary reason to marry. As Coontz observes, our moral standards and personal expectations regarding marriage have actually increased in recent times, making marriage both more fulfilling if it works and more fragile, given the powerful expectations and individual responsibility involved in preserving it.[15]

THE FUTURE POSSIBILITIES OF LOVE, SEX, AND MARRIAGE

If the general historical trends in marriage and bonding have been toward greater individual determination, greater diversity of options and roles, and greater rights within the marriage setting, then what might the future hold for marriage? In Robert Sawyer's *The Neanderthal Parallax*, we encounter the interesting possibility, within an alternative culture, for example, of everyone being bisexual and having both a female and a male mate.[16] Clearly our own cultural evolution could open up new forms of marriage. In fact, the future of marriage is connected with the future of culture, because it has been general cultural trends in the past that have impacted changes in marriage. As one example, globalization is exposing individual cultures to a diversity of practices and options from other cultures; as cultures mix and create new versions and syntheses of different practices, marriage should diversify even further. Of course, it is possible for there to be cultural regressions or historical oscillations, such as tribal marriages or marriages created within matriarchal societies.

Increasing freedom and diversification can instigate counter-reactions emphasizing responsibility, constraint, and uniformity; this can be seen in the recent conservative push back toward so-called traditional marriages. As another example, the increasingly frenetic, fast-paced, and present-oriented modern way of life, which imposes multiple and scattered obligations on all individuals, could further erode the capacity of humans to form intimate, solid, and long-term commitments with each other. Relationships could become increasingly short term and superficial.

Technology will also influence marriage and sex in the future as it has in the past. In the near future, technology will open up all kinds of strange, even outlandish possibilities (relative to our primitive perspective). Transhumanists envision improvement of the species through technology, through the transcendence of our current limitations. Given such a scenario, one can only imagine how what would constitute a fulfilling relationship with another would evolve as well. What would be the romantic or sexual ideals of a techno-logically enhanced or transformed human species? How could we use technology to transform the human psyche to create deeper and more fulfilling marriages?

One can envision virtual spouses, with both partners marry-ing and living in virtual reality, perhaps in addition to or in place of a marriage in "normal" reality. (To some degree, this is happening already on interactive Web sites such as Second Life.) In Charles Stross's *Accelerando*, characters experience multiple identity path-ways with multiple partners through downloading their conscious minds into a computer-supported virtual reality. One can imagine sex and marriage with robots.[17] Marriage could be totally decoupled from both reproduction and parenting. We may enhance, modify, or enrich upon the sexes; who is to say that two sexes are sufficient, especially if sex is disconnected from reproduction. Biotechnology may provide the means for switching back and forth between the sexes so that each partner can be male or female at different times. (This possibility is examined in Ursula LeGuin's *The Left Hand of Darkness*.[18]) Biotechnology, specifically cloning, could offer the op-tion of marrying yourself—of forming a solipsistic marriage with a cloned version of you of the opposite sex. But then, one could just as easily have a homosexual marriage with another version of you of the same sex. Though it involves time travel as an added element, in David Gerrold's *The Man Who Folded Himself*, the main charac-ter, through looping through time, becomes his daughter, his son, his mother, his father, and his wife.[19]

If, as Ray Kurzweil and others have predicted, we are able in the future to download our minds into a computer, then the tradi-tional barrier of separate bodies could be overcome, and distinct minds could engage in a type of conscious fusion where the two re-ally become one. In such a scenario of computer-supported con-scious personalities, marriages could become "eternal" if our conscious minds could be indefinitely supported through advanced technology. As for our physical limitations, both nanotechnology and virtual reality will provide the opportunity for multiple, freely chosen transforming bodies. Based on similar technological powers, it could become possible to recreate conscious minds from the past and reincarnate them in genetically reconstituted bodies; thus, people could opt for marriages with famous people from the past. An example of this is Dan Simmons's *The Fall of Hyperion*, where one of the main characters bonds with a reincarnated John Keats.[20]

If indeed we travel into outer space and contact other forms of intelligence, given our increasing biotechnological powers, we may marry or sexually bond with members of other species. This idea has been quite popular in science fiction; Spock's parents in *Star Trek* are two different species — human and Vulcan — but even earlier in the genre, Philip Jose Farmer achieved great notoriety for envisioning graphic sex and intimate bonding of humans and aliens in *Flesh* and *Strange Relations*.[21]

PARTNERSHIP AND THE PREFERABLE MARRIAGE FOR THE FUTURE

Though the possibilities for the future of marriage may be endless, at this point we want to consider what may be the preferable direction for marriage in the more recognizable future. We will suggest a conceptual framework based on the idea of character virtues — in essence, an ethical framework for the preferable direction for marriage. This vision should be broad and flexible enough to accommodate many diverse possibilities, yet it should be psychologically and historically informed. A "preferable marriage" identifies and describes an ideal partnership or relationship in a way analogous to describing an ideal or preferable individual; it is based on identifying a set of values and character virtues.

We will begin with Riane Eisler's theory of two basic forms of social organization as a way to elucidate the concept of partnership. Eisler distinguishes between dominator and partnership societies. A dominator society has a hierarchical power structure, wherein some members have more power and thus rule over others in the group who have less power and are subordinate. Eisler argues that for most of human history males have occupied a position of domination over women, both in the general public sphere and in interpersonal relationships. Generally, marriages have been patriarchal. Further, Eisler contends that, in male dominator societies, sex was vilified (frequently associated with the temptress nature of the woman who cannot control her erotic impulses). Further, violence was eroticized; sexual violence was socially acceptable, if not condoned under certain circumstances. Finally, male dominator societies adopt a mind–body dualism, clearly separating bodily desires (such as sex) from higher mental and/or spiritual realities. The body is base; the mind or spirit is elevated.

Eisler contends, however, that, prior to the emergence of dominator societies, many societies operated within a partnership mentality under a central female deity, a mother goddess. (In contrast, male dominator societies invariably had a male god at the top of the hierarchy ruling over humanity.) In partnership societies (as well as the marriage relationships within such societies) there was equality of the sexes. Whereas dominator societies motivated the subordinate (women) through fear and pain, in partnership societies, individuals were motivated by pleasure to realize social cohesion. Sexuality was sacred rather than base; hence, there was a rejection of mind–body dualism, and the ideal partnership was a collaboration for mutual benefit.[22]

As a starting point in defining a preferable marriage, partnerships should be founded on equality, on equal power and recognition of the two individual entities, who are both motivated toward collaboration and mutual gain. The core of the relationship should be built upon the desire for pleasure (something positive) rather than the desire to avoid pain (something negative). This distinction corresponds with Neal Miller's psychological distinction between approach and avoidance motivation.[23] Although there is clearly an element of unpleasantness and pain in any human relationship, the primary and psychologically healthy reason for creating and staying in a relationship should be because it is pleasurable, desirable, and positive; the primary reason should not be to avoid something aversive. Also, in keeping with the modern trend toward human rights and equality and the ethics behind it, the ideal partnership and marriage of the future should be founded upon equality, rather than dominance and subordination.

A second key idea in defining the ideal marriage is the yin–yang or reciprocity model of reality. The yin–yang depicts reality as interdependencies and complementarities. Yin and yang are co-dependent. Within such a model, the notion of absolute independence makes no sense. A human relationship is a state of interdependence; both extreme dependence and independence are seen as dysfunctional. Yin and yang also complete each other; neither is fully realized without the other. For humans, full individuality is realized in the context of the other. And when yin and yang are combined together, we get the Tao, a synergistic emergence and co-creation; something new emerges that transcends the parts.[24]

We propose that reality — including human reality — consists of interdependent open systems. No man (or woman) is an island, and as interactive, interdependent social beings, we only realize ourselves fully through relationships with others. An ideal marriage is a reciprocity of interdependent human beings, each giving and receiving from the other. Reciprocity can also be compared to the concepts of justice and fairness; hence, an ideal marriage embodies justice (as opposed to an unjust, lopsided human relationship) and consequently equality. The ideal marriage should be seen as a vehicle toward self-realization and a vehicle for emergent co-creation. We come together to create something that neither of us could create on our own.

We believe it would be a mistake to rigidly stereotype each member of a marriage as possessing certain traits and necessarily carrying certain responsibilities; historically, humans have reacted against such social constraints. What is important is that the areas of strength complement and support each other, regardless of who possesses which qualities. Specifically regarding marriages of men and women, it would be a mistake to view the two sexes as locked into certain distinctive characteristics and abilities. The theory of male–female differences has been used throughout history to subjugate women, based as it is upon the presumed differences between males and females, and the presumed superiority of stereotypical male characteristics over stereotypical female characteristics.

This is not to deny that there may be general statistical differences between men and women.[25] But highlighting the differences between the sexes has a variety of negative consequences. It ignores or minimizes the huge array of commonalities between men and women. (The commonalities and statistical overlap outweigh the differences.[26]) Seeing the "other" as very different from oneself interferes with finding common bonds. Highlighting differences limits our expectations of the other; it sets up barriers and creates an "us" versus "them" mind-set. Further, it limits modes of interaction and intimacy; we don't look for or expect to have common interests, passions, and desires. As noted above, emphasizing irreconcilable differences can create and support an atmosphere of inequality. If one accepts the common sexual stereotypes, it limits one's own individual expression and development; it blinds each of us to opportunities for self-development. Accepting sexual stereotypes of ourselves creates a false sense of security and worth; each human should create self-worth and self-identity through his or her own individual accomplishments, not by identifying with a group. Finally, psychological studies reveal that, as women and men age, they show a convergence of ideals and aspirations, and, in general, women and men of any age tend to agree on fundamental values.

We have considered the issue of stereotyping at length because in adopting the yin–yang model of human relationships we do not mean to assume that women possess one set of qualities (yin qualities such as passivity and nurturance) and men possess a different set of qualities (yang qualities such as activism and detachment). Both men and women can possess either set of qualities in a relationship. The ideal is to realize complementarities, completeness, and balance, but to do so in a context of freedom rather than socially enforced gender rigidity.

In this context, the two members in the relationship need not be a male and a female; there is absolutely no reason we can see why two women or two men could not realize the same level of interdependency, complementarity, intimacy, and resonance of common values and aspirations as a woman and a man. Although at this point in time, members of the same sex cannot, through any simple means, co-create a biological offspring, future biotechnological advances will almost certainly get around this roadblock. Furthermore, co-creation in a marriage should not be limited to making babies together. With the general population living longer, a sustainable and quality marriage must go beyond raising children as its core function. Just as sex goes beyond reproduction — couples make love to realize intimacy — marriage goes beyond raising children.

Returning to Riane Eisler, we would like to next consider the spiritual dimension to an ideal marriage. We distinguish between religion and spirituality, and further we distinguish between spirituality and believing in some particular metaphysical scheme or conception of God. One can be an atheist and spiritual if one has a sense of transcendence and a sense of higher morality and values. Quoting Eisler:

> Spirituality has become the word of the hour. But what is spir-
> ituality? ... Spirituality means feeling at one with that which
> we call the divine. But when I think of the divine I ... think of
> our own most evolved qualities: our profound human capacity
> for empathy, for love, our striving for Justice, our hunger for
> beauty, our yearning to create. ... Spiritual means being ethi-
> cal and, in the true sense of the word, moral.[27]

We would add to this description of spirituality the concept of transcendence, that a person (or a couple) aspires to something higher than themselves (the theist realizes this in the belief in God). Plato found transcendence in the contemplation of "eternal forms"; naturalists may find transcendence in the worship of nature, even the deification of it as a "mother goddess"; scientists can find it in epistemic awe and wonder at the cosmos, at existence; writers like Mihaly Csikszentmihalyi and John Stewart argue that contributing to human evolution should become a central goal in people's lives, and this is another avenue to transcendence. In fact, to return to the topic of children, raising children is clearly a form of transcendence. In general, bequeathing something positive to the future of human-ity is transcendence. We include spirituality, in agreement with Eisler, as a core feature of an ideal marriage because, Just as an in-dividual must realize transcendence and go beyond self-serving ends, a couple must go beyond themselves and serve some greater good as well. Marriages are social units within the broader context of human society; an ideal marriage should contribute to the quality and evolution of humanity as a whole.[28]

But, regarding the connection of spirituality and marriage, and again using Eisler as our inspiration, we also wish to underscore both the sacred quality of marriage and the sacred quality of sexual-ity. Quoting Eisler:

Candles, music, flowers and wine — these we all know are the stuff of romance, of sex and of love. But candles, flowers, music and wine are also the stuff of religious ritual, of our most sacred rites. Why is there this striking, though seldom noted, commonality? Is it Just accidental that passion is the word we use for both sexual and mystical experiences?

Sexuality in ancient times was seen as sacred because of its connection to reproduction; it is the primordial act of biological creation. Yet, sexuality has evolved beyond reproduction; it has become an art and a revelation in beauty, an expression of love and intimacy, a source of intense interpersonal pleasure, and an exceedingly complex (at least in principle) interaction between humans involving a vast array of embellishments and enrichments. As Eisler notes, at an ontological level it is a seeking of oneness. Sexuality is both a cause and a result of human passion, and a marriage without passion is dead. Sexuality brings to the foreground the validity and value of the Romantic vision of the meaning and quality of life. In the Christian West, sex was vilified, and as Eisler points out, it was connected with sin. In the sexual revolutions of the 1920s and the 1960s, this association of sex with the sinful was rejected, but, swinging with the great pendulum of extremes in the opposite direction, sex was trivialized and disconnected from love, intimacy, and personal commitment. Sex and sexuality are both powerful and sacred, as the ancient Greeks who worshipped Eros intuited. Eisler turns, or returns, sexuality from something immoral into something sacred and reaffirms it as an expression of high morality. Sexuality is a deep form of intimacy and a virtue to be cultivated in a marriage. And, in rejection of dualism, sex is not simply physical, but mental and emotional as well.[29]

Marriage should also be seen as a sacred covenant. Marriage embodies a cluster of virtues connected with this covenant between individuals. There is fidelity, trust, loyalty, friendship, commitment, and honesty, to name some of the core virtues. These virtues need not be associated with a particular religion, but they underscore the high importance we should place upon the bonding together of two individuals. It is a covenant that should not be treated lightly, either by those involved in it or by outsiders to the marriage. Seeing marriage as sacred elevates its importance; Just as sex has been trivialized, so has marriage. The contemporary renaissance in marriage is a reassertion of the high significance we should accord this interpersonal reality. It is unquestionably the strongest, deepest connection that two human beings can enter into in their lives.

Helen Fisher, in her book, *Why We Love,* describes some of the most common bits of advice marriage counselors give to couples who come into see them.[30] We are going to summarize these points; the list provides a good introduction into the next section on virtues and the preferable marriage for the future. Many of the items on the list align with the virtues we will subsequently discuss.

To realize a sustainable and romantic marriage, couples should:

- Commit and never give up.
- Listen, ask questions, give answers, identify needs, argue constructively.
- Appreciate, accept, respect.
- Stay attractive, grow intellectually.
- Practice honesty and trust.
- Provide for both space and togetherness.
- Compromise.
- Say "No" to adultery.
- Cultivate romance every day; date.
- Cultivate variety; have multiple common interests.
- Exercise humor.
- Never threaten to leave.
- Forget the past.

THE VIRTUES OF MARRIAGE

We have identified nine clusters of key virtues that form the core of our theory of the preferable marriage for the future. We have already examined some of these virtues.

- **Sexuality, Romance, and Passion.** We see sexuality, romance, and passion as a moral virtue. It is an area of human excellence — something that can be cultivated and developed — and individuals can be better or worse at it. In resonance with the philosophy of Romanticism, passion is critical to a fulfilling and meaningful life, and this is especially true regarding marriage. Sexuality and romance are spiritual — involving body and mind — and produce a unity of spirit and feeling between individuals.

- **Love and Compassion (Gratitude, Forgiveness, Respect, Art of Partnership).** Love coupled with compassion is one of psychologist Martin Seligman's six key character virtues associated with "authentic happiness." Gratitude, forgiveness, and respect are important sub-virtues that contribute to love and support compassionate feelings toward others. As Erik Fromm argued, love is an art — it is an area of excellence, something one learns to do well. Although we may have spontaneous and simple feelings of love, higher love needs cultivation and practice.[31]

- **Transcendence (identification of higher ideal)** and **Spirituality (away from self-centeredness).** Transcendence and spirituality were discussed above.

- **Honesty and Truth.** Intimacy cannot be realized without honesty and truth. Honesty appears on Fisher's list.

- **Fidelity, Loyalty, and Mutual Trust.** Trust also appears on Fisher's list, as well as commitment, which is closely connected with loyalty. Fidelity underscores the sacred quality of sexuality, especially within marriage; it is an expression of a promise of exclusive commitment and togetherness. Adultery destroys marriages and destroys trust; it destroys the self-esteem of those who participate in it. Contrary to the philosophy of being "uncommitted," popular in the 1960s, our argument is that both the sustainability and the quality of marriage clearly depend upon commitment.

- **Justice, Equality, and Reciprocity (mutual gratification).** The importance of these virtues was discussed above.

- **Self-Efficacy, Coupled Responsibility, Co-creativity, Hope, and Optimism.** Without a sense of self-responsibility, and in this case mutual responsibility, and a belief in self-efficacy, none of the other virtues will be cultivated. Virtues are accomplishments and require the belief in one's capacity to improve oneself and one's life.[32] Correspondingly, a married couple needs to believe in its capacity *as a couple* to improve their relationship and their lives. Hope and optimism about the promise of the marriage are absolutely necessary; without these qualities the marriage clearly will not flourish or realize excellence. The marriage will become depressed.

- **Courage and Faith.** Courage is one of Seligman's key virtues. It is important for married couples, as well as individuals. Faith is necessary for optimism. Faith is the belief in something even though one isn't certain. Hence, all beliefs about the future, including the future of one's marriage, involve an element of faith. Faith therefore requires courage — the courage of belief and commitment in the face of uncertainty.

- **Wisdom — Past (Deep) Learning Applied to Betterment of the Future.** Wisdom is another one of Seligman's key virtues and identified by Erik Erikson as the highest human virtue.[33] Although we generally think in terms of wise individuals, we can also imagine wise couples. Wise couples learn and consequently grow. Just as the individual self of the future must be more dynamical and evolutionary, so must the ideal married couple. The couple grows or dies. Wise couples apply what they have learned to improving their lives today and tomorrow. Wise couples have heightened past consciousness and future consciousness. Hence, on this last virtue we would disagree with the item on Fisher's list "Forget the past." As Santayana said, "Those who forget the past are doomed to repeat it." The ideal married couple for the future is reflective, assimilating the lessons of the past and applying these lessons to their ongoing evolutionary transformation.

Wisdom, as a virtue, does not entail always having all the answers to the challenges of life; it involves the capacity to learn from mistakes.[34] The same would be true for the ideal married couple: learning from mistakes rather than being perfect. But also, it means not giving up or throwing in the towel when mistakes happen. Frequently, modern marriages crumble when problems emerge; there is no tenacity in the marriage. The couple would become wiser if they reflected on the problems, blunders, and difficulties and learned from these negative experiences. In the end, the marriage would be strengthened.

SUMMARY AND CONCLUSION

To realize an ideal marriage is not an easy task, but then, as Spinoza noted, "All things excellent are as difficult as they are rare." It is important, though, to envision what kind of marriage would realize the highest levels of human happiness, creativity, and self-expression and that would resonate with the contemporary and future world. Further, in this regard, it is important to learn from history what the evolutionary trajectory of marriage has been: from a socially arranged bonding frequently involving a patriarchal system of control and relatively divorced from love and passion, to a freely chosen covenant and partnership of equals based on sexual attraction, love, and the aspiration for co-creation. The evolution of marriage is a moral evolution in many ways paralleling the moral evolution of human cultures around the world. In this regard, we should envision the marriage of the future as a further moral evolution. Identifying those key virtues, which bring human happiness and both individual and collective fulfillment, will give us a sense of direction for what to aspire toward.

Notes

1. Nicholas Wade, *Before the Dawn: Recovering the Lost History of Our Ancestors* (New York: The Penguin Press, 2006).

2. Helen Fisher, *The Anatomy of Love: A Natural History of Mating, Marriage, and Why We Stray* (New York: Random House, 1992).

3. Leonard Shlain, *Sex, Time, and Power: How Women's Sexuality Shaped Human Evolution* (New York: Viking, 2003); Thomas Lombardo, *The Evolution of Future Consciousness: The Nature and Historical Development of the Human Capacity to Think about the Future* (Bloomington, IN: AuthorHouse, 2006), chapter two.

4. Stephanie Coontz, *Marriage, a History: From Obedience to Intimacy, or How Love Conquered Marriage* (New York: Viking, 2005).

5. Riane Eisler, *The Chalice and the Blade: Our History, Our Future* (San Francisco: Harper and Row, 1987).

6. Leonard Shlain, *The Alphabet Versus the Goddess: The Conflict Between Word and Image* (New York: Penguin Arkana, 1998).

7. Peter Watson, *Ideas: A History of Thought and Invention from Fire to Freud* (New York: HarperCollins Publishers, 2005); Coontz, 2005; Fisher, 1992.

8. Thomas Cahill, *Sailing the Wine-Dark Sea: Why the Greeks Matter* (New York: Anchor Books, 2003); Forrest Baird and Walter Kaufmann (eds.) *Ancient Philosophy,* 5th ed. (Upper Saddle River, NJ:

Prentice Hall, 2008).

9. Shlain, 1998; Coontz, 2005; Fisher, 1992.

10. Stephanie Coontz, *The Way We Never Were: American Families and the Nostalgia Trap* (New York: Basic Books, 1992); Coontz, 2005.

11. Peter Watson, *The Modern Mind: An Intellectual History of the 20th Century* (New York: HarperCollins Perennial, 2001); Coontz, 2005.

12. Alvin Toffler, *Future Shock* (New York: Bantam, 1971); Francis Fukuyama, *The Great Disruption: Human Nature and the Reconstitution of Social Order* (New York: The Free Press, 1999).

13. Harbour Fraser Hodder, "The Future of Marriage: Changing Demographics, Economics, and Laws Alter the Meaning of Matrimony in America" in *Harvard Magazine* (November-December 2004), http://www.harvardmagazine.com/on-line/110491.html; Nancy Cott, *Public Vows: A History of Marriage and the Nation* (Cambridge: Harvard University Press, 2000); "Forms and Meanings of Marriage," in *Magnus Archive for Sexology*, http://www2.huberlin.de/sexology/ATLAS_EN/html/forms_and_meanings_of_marriage.html; Coontz, 2005.

14. Phillip Longman, "The Return of Patriarchy," in *Foreign Policy* (March-April 2006); Michael McManus, "An Overview of Marriage Savers," in *Marriage Savers*, http://www.marriagesavers.org/MarriageSaversOverview.htm; Linda Waite and Maggie Gallagher *The Case for Marriage: Why Married People Are Happier, Healthier, and Better Off Financially* (New York: Doubleday, 2000); "What is the Future of Marriage," in *Voice Box: Toward a More Perfect Union*, http://www.nerve.com/dispatches/voicebox/futureofmarriage/; *Why Marriage Matters: Executive Summary*, http://www.americanvalues.org/pdfs/wmmexsumm.pdf; *Why Marriage Matters: Twenty Six Conclusions from the Social Sciences*, http://www.americanvalues.org/pdfs/wmmsnapshot.pdf; Wade Horn, "Benefits of Healthy Mar-

riages," in *The Healthy Marriage Initiative*, U.S. Department of Health and Human Services, http://www.acf.hhs.gov/healthymarriage/benefits/index.html.

15. Coontz, 2005.

16. Robert J. Sawyer, *Hominids* (New York: Tom Doherty Associates, 2002).

17. Ray Kurzweil, *The Age of Spiritual Machines: When Computers Exceed Human Intelligence* (New York: Penguin Books, 1999); Ray Kurzweil, *The Singularity Is Near: When Humans Transcend Biology* (New York: Viking Press, 2005); Charles Stross, *Accelerando* (New York: Ace Books, 2005); David Levy, *Love and Sex with Robots: The Evolution of Human-Robot Relationships* (New York: Harper, 2007).

18. Ursula LeGuin, *The Left Hand of Darkness* (New York: Ace Books, 1969).

19. David Gerrold, *The Man Who Folded Himself* (New York: Random House, 1973).

20. Dan Simmons, *The Fall of Hyperion* (New York: Bantam Books, 1990).

21. Philip Jose Farmer, *Flesh* (New York: Signet, 1960); Philip Jose Farmer, *Strange Relations* (New York: Avon Books, 1960).

22. Riane Eisler, *Sacred Pleasure: Sex, Myth, and the Politics of the Body* (San Francisco: HarperCollins, 1995).

23. B. R. Hergenhahn and Matthew Olson, *An Introduction to Theories of Personality*, 6th Ed. (Upper Saddle River, NJ: Prentice Hall, 2003).

24. Lombardo, 2006, chapter three.

25. Steven Pinker, *The Blank Slate: The Modern Denial of Human Nature* (New York: Penguin Books, 2002).

26. Carol Wade and Carol Tavris, *Psychology,* 7th Ed. (Upper Saddle River, NJ: Prentice Hall, 2003).

27. Eisler, 1995; Riane Eisler (interviewed by Jerry Snider), "Sacred Pleasure: Sex, Myth, and the Politics of the Body," in *Magical Blend* (January 1996); Riane Eisler, "Spiritual Courage" (1999) http://www.partnershipway.org/html/subpages/articles/spirtitual.htm.

28. Mihaly Csikszentmihalyi, *The Evolving Self: A Psychology for the Third Millennium* (New York: Harper Collins, 1993); John Stewart, *Arrow: The Direction of Evolution and the Future of Humanity* (Canberra, Australia: The Chapman Press, 2000).

29. Eisler, 1995; Eisler, 1996; Eisler, 1999.

30. Helen Fisher, *Why We Love: The Nature and Chemistry of Romantic Love* (New York: Henry Holt, 2004).

31. Martin Seligman, *Authentic Happiness: Using the New Positive Psychology to Realize Your Potential for Lasting Fulfillment* (New York: The Free Press, 2002); Erich Fromm, *The Art of Loving* (New York: Bantam Books, 1956).

32. Thomas Lombardo and Jonathon Richter, "Evolving Future Consciousness through the Pursuit of Virtue," in *Thinking Creatively in Turbulent Times*, ed. Howard F. Didsbury Jr. (Bethesda, MD: World Future Society, 2004).

33. Hergenhahn and Olson, 2003.

34. Thomas Lombardo, "The Pursuit of Wisdom and the Future of Education" in *Creating Global Strategies for Humanity's Future,* ed. Timothy C. Mack (Bethesda, MD: World Future Society, 2006).

Through New Eyes

Transcending Culture-Based Assumptions

Dave Stein

How will you live and work in 2025? Which present-day life-styles will influence this — those of present-day Europe, the United States, or Asia — as various cultures intermingle? For example, will everyday life (for the majority of people) be fast-paced and "worka-holic," or balanced among work, family, and leisure? What about the relative importance of freedom and opportunity versus security? Diversion and stimulation versus introspection? Mastery of nature versus coexistence with it? And, of special interest to futurists, in-stant gratification versus sacrifice and long-range planning? To this list, one might even add the question of reductionist versus holistic thinking and philosophy — with the comparator "versus" itself sug-gesting the former.

This begs a more fundamental question — whether the next two decades will be defined by cultural plurality or cultural hege-mony. Will people have a choice of "operating systems" under which to live, or is humanity headed toward a monolithic, one-size-fits-all world that offers no place to hide for those who are unable to adjust

---

Dave Stein is a physicist, operations research analyst, and retired military officer. He is the current editor-in-chief of *FUTUREtakes*. E-mail editorinchief@ futuretakes.org.

to it? Will business and technology as we know it determine the future — and if so, will it be a future that offers lives of fulfillment or one characterized by alienation and lives of maintenance? Alternatively, will there be a resurgence of interest in various traditions of times past for whatever reason, and with some impact on everyday life?

But the imperative for expanded cross-cultural perspectives does not stop here, as the cultures and peoples of the world offer lessons and perspectives that can be useful, indeed valuable, in this present era of challenge, with such challenges amplified by the ever-increasing pace of change itself. The nature of cross-cultural interaction — be it constructive dialogue or clashes leading to armed strife — will itself influence the future substantially. Futurists, too, can benefit considerably from "new eyes," or a willingness to transcend culture-based assumptions that tend to limit futurist thinking.

THE "ALARM CLOCK CULTURE" — AND OTHERS

To this end, a brief look at the salient distinguishing characteristics of present-day cultures — and ways that they can shape one's thinking — can be useful. (An exhaustive study of cultural values and lifestyles is beyond the present scope.) Let's start with the United States, a land in which liberty, opportunity, and the individual are highly valued, with such value so enshrined in the Declaration of Independence. Traditionally, liberty and opportunity have been valued more than financial security, and arguably this is one underpinning of the workaholic lifestyle. In contrast with various other parts of the world, individual self-reliance is valued over relationships on the average, some well-connected people notwithstanding. Furthermore, while the herd instinct is alive and well, on a relative scale, the United States is not a group-oriented culture.

Furthermore, as in some of the other nations that many associate with "Western civilization," a reductionist or binary way of thinking is commonplace. At least in the United States, people even tend to over-identify with their jobs and professions. Often when people meet for the first time, they ask each other, "What do you do?" (The university equivalent is, "What are you majoring in?") In this way, reductionism manifests as counterpoint-based identity, in which "you know who you are in terms of those who are not like you." For those who are not content with occupational-based identity, self-imposed political and religious labels also serve well. In the United States, there are even those who feel compelled to take a stand on every issue. More fundamentally, this binary way of thinking shapes how people experience the world — as does the holistic way of thinking that prevails elsewhere.

Then there is the instant gratification mind-set that manifests as an emphasis on quarterly earnings statements and their equivalent in politics as well as in everyday life, such as a lack of patience with traffic congestion and long lines (queues). In both politics and business, this mind-set is often counterproductive to long-range planning. In spite of this, a number of political and business leaders do recognize the value of long-range planning and futures studies.

Another salient feature, often disregarded, is the throwaway mind-set. Understandably, during periods of less general affluence, and particularly during the Great Depression, it was common to repair furniture, clothing, and other items. Today, by contrast, it is generally cheaper and/or less time consuming to discard or replace an item when it is broken, torn, or otherwise deemed unserviceable. This need not be surprising, given the confluence of technology enablers and microeconomic imperatives. However, the throwaway mind-set does not stop here. Now one finds disposable employees and even disposable spouses, as evidenced by divorce rates, in which the United States has led the world in recent years (for example, see *The Economist* magazine's *Pocket World in Figures 2005*). This is an interesting counterpoint to parts of Asia that have traditionally placed primacy on relationships both in the workplace and else-where.

Contrast the values and lifestyles of the United States with those of western Europe, where family and leisure time are more balanced, as evidenced by longer vacations, shorter workdays in some places, and even legal restrictions on store hours that would seem tight by U.S. standards. For example, at one time most stores in Germany were required to close by 6 p.m. to enable people to spend more time with their families, and institutionalized uncom-pensated overtime was unheard of. Furthermore, with limited ex-ceptions such as pharmacies, stores were permitted to open Satur-day mornings but only one Saturday afternoon per month. A project that had involved officers from several NATO countries illustrates the differing cultural values quite well. When 5 p.m. came one day and the project was nearly complete, the U.S. officers proposed, "Let's stay another half hour and finish this." However, the officers from various European NATO countries would not hear of it.

Some people have implicated the stress factor and specifically the workaholic lifestyles in the relatively low longevity ranking of the United States (in recent years, thirtieth or lower among industrial-ized nations), during which time several European countries ranked substantially higher. Although any causal relationship is far from clear, the pervasive impacts that cultures can have on living and working patterns mandate that future studies be from a cross-cul-tural vantage point.

For their part, some Asian countries are also known for long workdays but differ profoundly from the United States in several other ways. Traditionally, Asian cultures have valued the group over the individual and are characterized by patience and a longer time horizon than the quarterly earnings statement — a time horizon that figured profoundly in the outcome of the Vietnam War. Age-oriented more than youth-oriented, at least in a traditional sense, some Asian cultures have historically been more auditory and less visual, as evidenced in their languages, in which subtle differences in inflections can radically alter the meanings of words. For this reason, some hearing disorders considered relatively minor in the United States would be regarded as major in China, for example. A salient point of distinction is the holistic approach to matters ranging from medicine to philosophy to warfare. The yin and yang polarities of some Asian traditions notwithstanding, one generally finds less of a binary, "either/or" culture in Asia than in other parts of the world.

Whereas a number of contemporary cultures regard nature as something to be dominated, various Native and Aboriginal peoples have valued coexistence with nature and have traditionally experienced time as an "eternal now," rather than subdivided into past, present, and future. Furthermore, for several reasons, their experience of work and leisure was substantially different from that of many participants in "modern life."

These are but a few comparative descriptors, and one might ask about other ways in which cultures can influence the lifestyles that emerge. For example, in 2025, who will be regarded as celebrities or as the most valued and esteemed people in a culture — or will there be any celebrities at all? Which professions will be most valued in various cultures and among various peoples? Which personality types? How does a given culture view its "challenged" people, its gifted people, and its nonconformists — and with what implications for the future as the world's cultures interact? Will diversity be appreciated? Will cooperation or competition rule the day? Which outlooks on life — for example, self-determination or fatalism (a "discounted future") — will prevail? Will people live lives of fulfillment and positive adventure or lives of maintenance? Will there be opportunities to live and work according to one's full potential? What will be regarded as "prosperity"? Will the economy of the future be growth-based or steady state, and how will it interact with nature?

What will people do for entertainment and leisure? Which family structures will prevail—extended, nuclear, or other? How will leaders emerge, especially considering the salient contrasts in leader emergence between the United States and parts of Asia now? Will learning be valued as an end unto itself, or will it be valued more in a utilitarian sense? How complex will societies of the future be, and will complexity (or simplicity) contribute to fulfillment—or to stress?

More issues to consider: Will we see more transient friendships and business relationships, or will there be more commitment to long-term relationships? A sense of community or a large, impersonal society? Group-based identity (family, ethnicity, religion, nation, socioeconomic class, profession, political party, etc.) or individual-based identity and loose ties? A preponderance of inner-directed people or other-directed people? More of a left-brain culture (analytical and deductive), or a resurgence of the right-brain culture (intuitive, creative)? A propensity for risk taking and adventure, or for risk aversion? A focus on achievement, or not? The same structuring institutions and social support systems to which many people are accustomed (the family, workplace, community, nation-state, tribe, and religious group) or new ones?

In other words, anyone conducting futures work might ask himself or herself, "What aspects of my everyday life am I taking for granted—aspects that may not be universal?" A disregard for questions such as these, and *de facto* buy-in to culture-based assumptions, can limit futurist thinking.

CULTURAL PLURALITY OR CULTURAL HEGEMONY?

Enabled by travel and communications, increased interaction provides an excellent opportunity for the peoples of the world to see through new eyes. For example, the religions, philosophies, and health and wellness practices of Asia are now relatively commonplace in Western nations, while U.S. and European business models are now well rooted in parts of Asia. In health and wellness alone, there are opportunities to develop new therapies and paradigms that combine the best from all cultures. More generally, increased exposure to new traditions and philosophies provides opportunities for individual enrichment—specifically, via transcending hidden assumptions at the personal level that can limit our ability to plan our own future.

However, other developments point to a future that is very different—one that is more monolithic from a cultural vantage point. Television game shows have migrated to Europe, fast-food restaurants appear worldwide (providing an infrastructure to support the possible advent of a fast-paced life in other parts of the world—perhaps even heralding it), and baseball has been exported to Japan. Indeed, one might ask what forms of leisure and entertainment are migrating in the other direction, back to the United States. More generally, one might ask which nations are exporting their cultures and which ones are importing the cultures of other nations and peoples—and whether this trade imbalance will continue or reverse.

There are also signs that the fast-paced, workaholic, stimulation- and diversion-oriented lifestyle is itself becoming the way of the world, with the fast pace driven at least in part by competitive pressures on businesses. As the fast pace takes root in various parts of the world, one must ask how peoples accustomed to a slower pace of life will adapt—or whether countertrends or perhaps "best of all worlds" synergies make alternative scenarios equally likely.

To be sure, the loss of one's ways of life—for example, as a result of military or cultural conquest, or even technology—is nothing new. Native, Aboriginal, and other peoples have been uprooted, many family farms and businesses have given way to larger scale enterprises, and recent years have seen the demise of careers for life, at least for some people. Interestingly, the demise of a career for life may have profound impacts on people's sense of identity as individuals realize that they are more than an executive, a truck driver, a teacher, or a health-care provider, but this issue is best left for another day. In some places, even family and community life have been altered by living and working patterns (i.e., long working hours and lengthy commutes) and by the increasing opportunities for entertainment and pursuit of one's interests, among other factors. In this greater context, and considering the accelerating pace of change, recent developments beg the question, "Which lifestyles will prevail in 2025, and which ones will become marginalized or extinct?" Who will be active participants, and who will be alienated?

"Plug and Play"

But these are matters that extend far beyond academic interest. Futurists study many complex challenges and issues — urbanization (including housing issues, infrastructure, and transportation), environmental issues (dwindling resources, pollution, and loss of biodiversity — with implications for agriculture and food supplies), the economy, socioeconomic polarization, the "social contract," education, health care and wellness, demographic issues, crime and armed strife, aging infrastructure, etc. To this list, one can add other issues — for example, quality of life in a more general sense (including "chronological challenge," that is, not enough hours in the day). Many of these challenges are the focus of policy makers, too. One might ask how other peoples and cultures would have addressed these challenges, what useful insights they can offer, and whether these would have been the challenges that would have arisen had other cultures become dominant in recent decades. Conversely, if the world becomes more culturally homogeneous and the mandate for "new eyes" is not heeded, which useful lessons from various peoples and cultures will be lost?

However, issues and developments of a more immediate nature

point to the need for new eyes, too. Case in point: aid packages, by which several of the world's wealthier nations have brought varying degrees of prosperity to nations and regions that are less developed. Notwithstanding the good intentions and the results that are often favorable (e.g., empowering people, lifting them from poverty, alleviating misery — and above all, offering hope), there is often the underlying assumption that one can "plug and play" prosperity, self-rule, etc. The reverberating question is, "Who defines prosperity?" As a starting point, one might ask whether prosperity is based on a growth economy or a steady-state economy and whether "prosperity" means satisfaction of basic needs, a comfortable lifestyle, a consumerist economy based on a cycle of creating and satiating discontent, or even something else.

"THROUGH NEW EYES" — NEXT STEPS

For several reasons — the challenges that humankind is facing, the accelerating pace of change, growing interest in the future itself, the increased interaction among various peoples and cultures, and the ever-increasing willingness to question the ways, values, and assumptions of the past — the need for cross-cultural dialogue and new eyes has never been greater. To futurists, new eyes provide opportunities to transcend hidden assumptions that tend to limit futurist thinking. More generally, the various cultures and peoples of the world, present and past, offer valuable lessons and perspectives that can be useful in meeting the challenges of the future.

But the imperative for expanded perspectives beyond one's culture extends far beyond academic interest, as various cultures can have pervasive influences on one's values and everyday lifestyles. There is a tendency to take one's values and lifestyles for granted — for example, the alarm clock and commute culture, or notions of prosperity and identity — and these assumptions can limit ways in which people live, work, think, and interact with others. Indeed, futurists do not have a monopoly on interest in lifestyles that might be, can be, or will be. Futurists and non-futurists alike might ask themselves how the world would have been different today if other cultures had prevailed—as indeed they will someday, perhaps sooner than one thinks, given the cyclical nature of history and the accelerating pace of change.

On the education front, the "through new eyes" theme ushers in the next frontier in interdisciplinary and liberal education, specifically, cross-cultural learning among students of diverse backgrounds. The potential educational value of this far eclipses the diversity that several U.S. universities have sought to achieve through their well-intended but controversial admissions policies. This is not a statement of position on the issue—only a statement that the "through new eyes" theme is more foundational, extending beyond tinkering at the margins.

Finally, over-identification with one's culture also tends to limit one's thinking and sense of identity. The fallacy of thinking that all other people are, or should be, like oneself—and the failure to think beyond one's cultural "event horizon"—are largely responsible for cultural clashes today as well as throughout human history. Conversely, seeing through new eyes offers opportunities to expand our notion of identity and thereby achieve our potential, unshackled by hidden culture-based assumptions. We can gain new insights by remaining ever vigilant in questioning those things that we takes for granted. The cultures of the world offer useful counterpoints to hidden assumptions, if we will only observe and study them.

Part 2

Tools and Applications

The Quadrate

A Paradigm for Conflicting Civilizations and Global Futures

Jitendra G. Borpujari

The Cold War narrowed the range of choice in global futures to the sole option to promote or resist the communist vision of a workers' paradise. Across the world, people set aside countless cultural feuds to join the epic struggle. In hindsight, it is hard to believe that so many focused for so long on rivalry of only two visions for a better global future.

The choice is more complex now. The end of the Cold War cued the revival of dormant cultural feuds. The focus of conflicts has shifted from "class" to "civilization." The class conflict paradigm of Marx is no more in vogue. Slogans for crusades, jihads, and ethnic cleansing are now the rage. Samuel P. Huntington saw this coming in 1993 when he wrote in *Foreign Affairs* about a "conflict of civilizations" over "the broadest level of cultural identity people have short of that which distinguishes humans from other species."

For Marx, the global future of a communist paradise was to be the climax in a tale of people making history by waging class conflict to be free first from the mastery of nature and then from all

Jitendra G. Borpujari is a consultant and temporary alternate to executive director for Saudi Arabia on the World Bank executive board. The views expressed here are his own. E-mail jborpujari@gmail.com.

masters.[1] The notion of "conflict of civilizations" offers no such hint of a post-conflict global future. Huntington only outlined an era of endless conflicts with an admonition that each clashing civilization "will have to learn to coexist with the others." The proposed quadrate takes the argument forward by suggesting a paradigm shift for a grip on global futures at stake in the ongoing conflict of civilizations.

A civilization may be defined as a way of life that stands out as distinctly homogeneous despite many levels of subcultural heterogeneity. Conflicts can arise at either the systemic macro level of a civilization or internally among its many subcultures. The Shi'a–Sunni split, for instance, is between subcultures of Islam, which in turn is a part of the broader civilization of everyone sharing the faith of the biblical patriarch Abraham. Jews, Christians, and Muslims differ in many ways and yet comprise a distinct identity for the rest of the world as "Abrahamic."

THE QUADRATE

The Cold War partisans represented classes aspiring for alternate visions of the global future. The conflict of civilizations is similarly a rivalry of competing futures. The challenge is to find a simple yet comprehensive set of tags to mark each civilization by an aspect of its identity that is a given that cannot be changed. Together, the tags will then reveal all visions of the global future in the conflict of civilizations.

The literature on the use of selected attributes for cultural comparisons is considerable. For instance, Thomas McFaul's "Religion in the Future Global Civilization" in *The Futurist*, September-October 2006, suggests a grouping of civilizations by degrees of inclusivism and exclusivism. In the broader literature on cultural comparisons, I refer especially to *Ways of Thinking of Eastern Peoples: India, China, Tibet, Japan* by Hajime Nakamura (1960) and "Transcendence East and West" by David Loy *(Man and World*, 1993). The proposed quadrate paradigm builds on the findings of these works.

As Loy cautions, "cultural typing ... it cannot be emphasized too strongly, is meant to be heuristic." I am also aware of earlier quadrates by Martin Heidegger[2] in philosophy and C. G. Jung in psychology.[3] However, these applications are ahistorical and abstract, if not metaphysical, especially in the case of Heidegger. In comparison, the proposed new paradigm is a rather obvious device for a fresh perspective on history through a comparison of rival global futures at stake in the conflict of civilizations.

Every conflict implies a split of people into rival camps of a "them" and an "us." It is a mistake, however, to treat all civilizations as equally prone to splits. Only exclusive civilizations have a built-in coercion to be confrontational. An Abrahamic, for instance, is divinely enjoined to separate believers from infidels. Being exclusive may also reflect an insular belief in a culture as unique, if not superior, as in the Orient. The Abrahamic and Oriental civilizations are thus naturally exclusive. The inclusive have no coercion to confront. The Indic civilization, discussed below, fits that bill. All rules of exclusion and inclusion are also either religious or secular. For the religious, the rule is transcendent, being directly from the supernatural. To the secular, however, all social rules are from within the world, the will of a temporal authority, be it a king, a dictator, or an elected parliament.

The quadrate follows. No matter how alike cultures may seem, asked if one is "exclusive" or "inclusive," the answer for every person surely must be a "Yes" or a "No." Every social rule to exclude or include also must be either "religious" or "secular," depending on whether its rationale is located beyond or within the world. The potential global futures therefore form a quadrate or fourfold of fault lines tagging civilizations as Religious-Exclusive, Secular-Exclusive,

Religious-Inclusive, or Secular-Inclusive. Each tag is unique, and the four together comprise a comprehensive framework of attributes for all civilizations, the extant and the extinct. Allowing for the limitations of such typecasting, the new paradigm suggests a fresh view of history as an outcome of rival civilizations competing to prevail within a quadrate of possible global futures.

The quadrate reflects the real world closely. Of the four fault lines, the first three define respectively the Abrahamic, Oriental, and Indic that began west, east, and south of the Himalayas. The Religious-Exclusive tag fits the expansive Abrahamic civilization dating back to Old Testament revelations west of the Himalayas in the region now known as Middle East. The Secular-Exclusive label is apt for the insular Oriental civilizations that emerged east of the Himalayas in a mosaic of beliefs, mostly Confucian and Buddhist. The Religious-Inclusive label covers the South Asian Indic vision of nonduality or unity in diversity outlined below. Finally, the Secular-Inclusive residual represents a potpourri of Inclusive Humanist viewpoints opposed to exclusion and religion as defining anchors for a civilization.

More than one-half of the world population of some 6.5 billion is said to be nominally Abrahamic and the rest split in roughly equal shares as Oriental, Indic, and Inclusive Humanist. The Abrahamic population is larger worldwide, except in Oriental and Indic Asia. The estimates, however, can mislead. A rigid slotting makes sense only for extremist fanatics living by one or another of the polarities in the quadrate. In practice, the same person can be nominally in one slot but practically in another. People also move from slot to slot. One may actually adopt or drop a cultural identity at will for exigencies of existential, functional, and physical survival.

The quadrate nonetheless represents a conceptually closed scheme for a comprehensive allocation of the world population in the conflict of civilizations. Although the world is one, everyone in it must choose every moment to be inclusive or exclusive and religious or secular. Paraphrasing Kockelmans's portrayal of Heidegger's quadrate, civilization, even though it is one, is nonetheless also structured; and the structure of all structures is the quadrate of the religious and the secular, the exclusive and the inclusive. In other words, whatever one encounters in history, and however that world in each case may be structured, it can always be understood in terms of the four dimensions of the proposed quadrate.

THE HIMALAYAN SPLIT

The Himalayas are a ready excuse to speculate that geography had a decisive impact in making civilizations exclusive or inclusive. Exclusion of aliens was no doubt vital for mere survival in the harsh and unforgiving Eurasian terrain north of that mostly impassable range of mountains. From the English Channel to the Bering Sea, and from the Arctic Ocean to the Himalayas, the north is a mostly flat and open land where hordes of migrants roamed with hardly any natural cover for hiding. History here is full of preemptive wars launched by powerful warlords. As people huddled for safety, strong leaders fought from within a grim split of the world into a "them" and an "us." Memorials to those wars of exclusion still mark Eurasia with countless martial relics, including most vividly the Great Wall of China.

Notably, coercion to exclude became a sacred duty north of the Himalayas from the Atlantic to the Pacific. However, the sacredness differed between the West and the East. In the West, the sanctity was from a direct divine command that a succession of prophets later confirmed. In the Orient, however, the sanctity was effectively secular, since the coercion to exclude was an indirect exercise of divine will through the regency of a temporal power such as the emperor of Japan. The contrast had a profound impact on the differing histories and prospects of the Occident and the Orient.

Expansive Abrahamic

The Abrahamic is by far the most historic, enduring, and consequential Religious-Exclusive civilization. The culture is naturally expansive, since believers are generally obliged to convert infidels. It is accordingly the most well known and ubiquitous of the ways of life in the quadrate. Its internal fault lines are many and changeable, as the initial split into Jews, Christians, and Muslims has since multiplied into countless doctrinal and sectarian feuds in a complex and changing maze of rival Abrahamic visions of the global future. Yet, despite the many in-house splits, it remains a monolith representing more than half of humanity as Abrahamic.

Insular Oriental

The insular Orient offers a Secular-Exclusive parallel to the Religious-Exclusive Abrahamic Occident. Both exclude aliens and turn to strong rulers for safety. However, God, as it were, steps aside in the Orient for a mortal proxy who acts as regent of heaven to dispense absolute authority without any scope for further recourse to the divine. An Abrahamic looks to heaven as reward for good deeds. An Oriental is content to have the bounties of the earth. Orientals pray to spirits mainly for boons and spells as help in this life. True to that ethos, when exposed to the wisdom of South Asia, the Orient skipped the elaborate Indic metaphysics and adapted only select ethical precepts of the Buddha, who makes no mention of God. Shunning dreams of unseen heaven, the Orient opts for pragmatic actions toward real-time joys.

West to east from Mongolia to Japan and north to south from Korea to the Indian state of Assam, the Orient looked to a mortal autocrat as the ultimate sacred ruler. In Japan, the Emperor is God in Person. In North Korea, power still stems from the ruler's mythical claims of links to God. Farthest south, where the Orient ends and the Indic south begins, the Ahom kings of Assam stand out as the only Indian royalty to rule as God from Heaven. The same pattern fits the imperial regime of divine mandate and Confucian ethics in China, the culture of Samurai loyalty in Japan, and the many blends of Confucian and Buddhist wisdom all over the Orient. The civilization is secular, since its ideas of "good" and "bad" or "right" and "wrong" come from a mortal power. It is also exclusive since the loyalty oath to be for or against the ruling sacred authority splits the world into a "them" and an "us."

Nondualistic Indic

The Indic civilization south of the Himalayas is worlds apart from the Abrahamic and the Oriental on both exclusion and religion.[4] Yet, it has been common to think of the world in terms of East and West. Rudyard Kipling famously wrote in *The Ballad of East and West,* "Oh, East is East, and West is West, and never the twain shall meet." However, as Loy reminds, the Pashtun and English protagonists of the ballad, both being Abrahamic, were joined as Siamese twins in awaiting the biblical promise of a day with God, "Till Earth and Sky stand presently at God's great Judgment Seat." Worse yet, Kipling conflated the Oriental and Indic civilizations, which are diametrically apart. The confusion, however, is natural, since Indic nondualistic thought is relatively unknown. A digression may therefore be useful for a brief account of the Indic approach to life.

Geography is again handy. Mostly walled in from the turbulent north, South Asia was largely free from conflicts raging in the rest of Asia. Wars were fewer in number and smaller in scale, with typically little or no impact on civil life. The relative peace and quiet of the Indic south is evident from the virtual absence here of the memorials to death and destruction so common in the more warlike north. The isolated and restful setting was perfect for emergence of an inclusive parallel to the northern spirit of exclusion. Indeed, the civilization that arose was so inclusive that it had no need for an exclusive name, the default term *Hindu* being a geographic allusion by outsiders to people living near and beyond the river Indus. Significantly, this exotic word does not appear anywhere in the ancient literature of Sanskrit.

The inclusive Indic spirit merges heaven and earth in a unique, nondualistic vision of all beings as cosmic spin-offs from the whim of a pervasive Super-Entity, or God, named *Brahman* (from Sanskrit, *brih,* "to expand") in the Vedas. Once so spun off, every being journeys across cycles of birth, death, and rebirth to gather enough good deeds or karma to qualify for a return to base in the Super-Entity.

The vision does not differentiate among beings, whether human or subhuman, and is free of dualities such as good and bad, believers and infidels, or God and Satan. Any attribute and its opposite, such as good and bad, are the same, being aspects of a single cosmic unity. The vision has no need or means to make converts since it includes all other ways of life as already a part of it. An Indic exalts human life, but only because no other form of life can consciously speed up one's final release from this world of pain. If one fails to reach that goal in this life, then the effort has to go on into the next rebirth and beyond until one is able at last to gain final release from the cycle of karma.

The hierarchy of castes is integral to the Indic order and unrelated to exotic ideas such as "class." The system is usually traced to a lone verse in the Vedas *(Púrushasûkta, Rig-veda,* x, 80) on the mythical origins of priests, warriors, traders, and menials. Notably, castes differ in karma but are otherwise profoundly equal in view of the central Vedic dogma of nonduality or unity in diversity. It seems best, therefore, to view Indic castes in a more comprehensive, four-fold division of the world into Outsiders, Heretics, Brahmins, and Proto-Brahmins. Outsiders would include all who are yet to know the Vedas. Heretics would refer to the likes of the Buddha and the ancient materialist philosopher Carvaka, who rejected the Vedas.[5] Everybody else must be either a believer, who is already a Brahmin at the apex, or a Proto-Brahmin, who is at a lower stage of the climb up the totem pole of karma. The Vedic metaphysics thus reaches well beyond the usual socio-economic interpretations of caste and class.

Inclusive Humanist

The Inclusive Humanist is a residual category comprising all aspirants toward a Secular-Inclusive global future. Inclusive Humanism, despite being secular, has no calling to exclude the religious. The approach also does not seek to impose any prior constraint on the preferred social, economic, political, or philosophical system. The emphasis is most of all on flexibility, as distinct from rigidity of fanatical adherence to the divisive polarities of the quadrate. The flexible approach reflects the basic premise that human beings, by the very nature of their being in the universe, can never be certain enough about any of the great dogmas of either religion or social, economic, political, and philosophical systems. In view of the many universal uncertainties, the only logical response of an individual or a social group is humility and a pledge of tolerance and cooperation as overriding norms for a better global future.

Where is Marxism in the quadrate? Nowhere, and not because Marxism is no more the global force it was in the Cold War. The difficulty is from the basic ambiguities in Marx. He was inclusive in intent yet exclusive in practice, since he trashed religion as "opium of the people." Even so, he went on to base his vision of the global future on the biblical premise of human history moving inexorably forward from an early state of simple and joyous living to an eventual climax of final redemption in a higher state of bliss in heaven. For Marxists, history begins with the initial loss of innocent joys in the Garden of Eden of primitive communism. Next, the sufferings of class conflict mirror tribulations of the fallen Adam. Finally, humanity at last ascends into the communist heaven on earth in the promised kingdom come of a workers' paradise.

The biblical triad of fall, suffering, and eventual redemption is the paradigm and anchor for the system of Marx. His claim to being inclusive also depends crucially on the idealized interpretations of work, human identity, and global unity in the slogan, "Workers of the world, unite!" The secular humanism of Marx thus had religious overtones and was exclusive in practice. Still, despite the reduced global weight now of Marxism, an awareness of its earlier dominance is essential for immunity from mistakes made in the past in the name of secular humanism.

RETROSPECT AND PROSPECT

The quadrate interprets history in a fresh perspective of cultural conflicts shaping the global future. Novel insights emerge from even a cursory glance at the record. Cultures prone to conflicts can become dysfunctional and destructive of the global future. Yet, as Indic history shows, a civilization may degrade despite absence of open conflicts. A candid review of the past could promote a global future of greater tolerance and harmony across the fault lines of the quadrate.

Retrospect

The Abrahamic Occident stands out as the only culture to sanction persecution of infidels and heretics as an act of piety. The results are well known. Religious-Exclusive violence has taken a heavy toll in Abrahamic fratricide. In Europe alone, Abrahamic Europeans have killed their own in amazing numbers that broke earlier records to reach horrendous heights in the last century. Yet, all along, combatants on both sides of battle lines knelt for blessings of the same divinity. At times, the linkage of religion to exclusion became especially grotesque, as in guidelines for exclusion of Jews that Martin Luther detailed in his 1543 treatise, *Jews and Their Lies.*[6] The feuds are also recurrent. Starting some fourteen centuries after Christ, Abrahamic Europe bled from horrors inflicted by the pious in various Inquisitions to suppress heretics. Today, after a similar lapse of time since the dawn of Islam, the world — especially the Middle East — is again in turmoil from feuds raging within the extended household of Abraham. Abrahamic history of Religious-Exclusive dysfunction is too familiar to require further elaboration.

Oriental wars of Secular-Exclusion have been as bloody, albeit not as pervasive or enduring, as the Religious-Exclusive wars of the Occident. Except for the westward conquests of Genghis Khan and the Japanese eastward attack on Pearl Harbor, Oriental warfare focused on the vast region between the Himalayas and the Pacific Ocean. Secular and earthbound, Orientals have gone to war for conquest and control rather than to uphold any high ideal from a transcendent God. The absence of any innate notions of human guilt and divine grace is at once an advantage and a burden. The concentration on material rewards and absence of redeeming universal ideals for the global future can reduce wars of the Orient into guilt-free exercises of raw power. The Abrahamic Occident takes the trouble to rationalize wars as a tribute to values such as freedom, democracy, and redemption of heathen souls. The Orient is yet to show any such urge to justify its wars. Guilt is indeed hardly relevant when the supreme duty is to live by an oath to obey a mortal lord. This may explain why Oriental Japan is yet to match Abrahamic Germany in atoning for the atrocities of World War II. Nakamura provides ample details on how loyalty to mortal mentors has shaped thought and behavior in the Orient.

Indic Asia never descended to the gory depths of ethnic

cleansing and sectarian fratricide. The record is also clear that wars here were tepid affairs relative to those in the Occident and the Orient. Yet, the Indic civilization, too, has a dismal past, since the lofty ideas of cosmic inclusion sank in real life into unspeakable horrors of a *de facto* apartheid. A select few of elite Brahmins were indeed recluses who "never addressed the people, never proselytized, never sought political power, and never cared to emerge from the indolent apathy of a dignified retirement."[7] Mostly, however, the mantra of cosmic inclusion and equality of all beings did nothing to deter the elite from enforcing a caste totem pole valuing people by their social and political proximity to higher castes, especially the Brahmins.

Indic Asia was a land of duress, where less than 5 percent of the populace exuded light of immense learning while the rest wallowed in the utter darkness of poverty, ignorance, and degradation. Heretics such as Buddha and Carvaka developed alternative visions of the global future, but were no match for caste tyrants who shut out all hopes for reform from within. The nightmare lasted more than a thousand years, until rescue came by default from Abrahamic invaders under the flags first of Islam and later of Christianity. Many converted and became Abrahamic, but the main impact was an avalanche of reforms that triggered the renaissance of modern Hinduism.

As for Humanism, the Marxist variant stands out for both the bang of its rise and the whimper of its fall. Marxism claims a secular-humanist outlook. Yet, Marxist ideologues focused on a set of radical certainties that were more akin to religion. The basic opposition to any idea of the divine placed the movement on a collision course with the religious. Since Marxist dogma also held that the global future would inevitably converge to a workers' paradise as a matter of historical necessity, anyone who opposed the communist vision had to be a misguided reactionary who should be condemned for delaying human progress. Effectively, Marxism rationalized institutional persecution and violence in order to exclude all opponents, at least during the period of transition to the promised communist global future. As the faithful waited for a promised global future that never came, persecution became routine, as in the gulags of Stalin.

Prospects

The quadrate shows that history reflects not so much general conflicts of civilizations as micro-level clashes in clash-prone cultures. The record also shows that wars have been more frequent and far-reaching in the Abrahamic Occident. This trend may well persist, since the Abrahamic populace is stronger not only numerically but also in concentration of economic wealth and military technology.

If past is prologue, the global future will likely have more wars of righteous intent for idealist goals, such as the spread of Western freedom and democracy. The mind-set could also remain prone to crusades and jihads for God.

The Orient's Secular-Exclusive past suggests a built-in tendency to remain insular and defensive. Oriental history is not famous for examples of heroes seeking martyrdom in wars for ideals like the spread of freedom and democracy to strangers in distant lands. The Orient thus seems unlikely to emulate the expansive Occidental penchant to reform and reshape the world. Any inspired quest for universal ideals would likely yield to the age-old priority for domestic stability and prosperity.

The insular bent of the Orient would not preclude missions such as the Japanese initiative for a Greater East Asia Co-Prosperity Sphere during World War II. Indeed, the Abrahamic and the Oriental, while differing on idealism, are both upbeat on getting the most in material riches from life on earth. The global future thus seems fraught with dilemmas of face-offs between the expansive idealism of the Abrahamic and the pragmatic insularity of the Oriental in an increasingly integrated global environment of growing economic, political, and military competition.

Already, statements of expansive idealism are common. Stung by critics of future U.S. foreign interventions after the experience in Iraq, Robert D. Kaplan wrote in the *Washington Post* (November 22, 2006), "You'd think—to hear some of them talk—that we're about to emulate China, which seeks only energy sources and advantageous trade agreements and cares nothing at all for the moral improvement of regimes in places such as Zimbabwe, Burma and Uzbekistan." Such idealism can backfire. An Abrahamic idealist invasion to promote personal rights and democracy could easily look more like a stampede of barbarians out to disrupt and destabilize the harmony of the Orient.

The Indic civilization has the advantage of a heritage of inclusion as a guiding spirit. This may explain the absence here of a tradition of wars either against domestic civil society or for military adventures in distant lands. Yet, the Indic culture reached far. Indonesia, for instance, is at home in Indic culture and folklore, although the population is almost entirely Abrahamic. Adaptation, not war, was the channel of choice for spread of Indic culture.

The Indic resembles the Oriental in its lack of any Abrahamic zeal for idealist martyrdom in crusades and jihads. Moreover, the Indic embrace of material riches is ambiguous due to the negative view of the world in the Vedas. An Indic idealizes detachment from wealth, even as material success is lauded as a worthy, albeit fleeting, goal. If the past is any clue, the Indic will remain wary of idealist acts of martyrdom. However, the past Indic circumstance of economic scarcity and widespread material deprivation may be of little help to anticipate a future that is taking shape now in an unfamiliar reality of sustained prosperity in South Asia.

Highlighting the fault lines of civilizations could help to reduce the risks of clashes erupting among nations and national coalitions out of a misunderstanding. However, finding and holding a common ground will not be easy in a world already polarized by proclivities as diverse as the Abrahamic penchant for expansive idealism and martyrdom, the Oriental tradition of loyalty to authority and priority for social stability, the Indic yearning for abstract joys beyond concrete realities of the world, and the Inclusive Humanist impulse for social engineering to improve the living conditions of people everywhere. Risks to the global future have indeed increased, since even the inclusive heritage of Indic Asia is lately under assault in periodic outbreaks of anti-Abrahamic violence.

Epilogue

The global future appears grim if the focus is only on past dysfunctions, return of preemptive attacks, and the widespread use lately of terror as a weapon of war. That, fortunately, is not the only likely eventuality. A spectacular occasion for optimism is the more than half century of progress for the spirit of inclusion to unite the erstwhile warring nations of Europe in the European Union. Inclusion is also taking hold in the Orient, where nations such as China, long isolated as exotic and forbidden, are now major partners in global economic and trading bodies such as the World Trade Organization. Meanwhile, periodic lapses notwithstanding, the Indic worldview of inclusion seems alive and well, as evident in the symbolism and substance of the overwhelming election and continued acceptance of a first-generation Italian immigrant woman of Abrahamic upbringing as leader of the ruling political coalition in India. As for Inclusive Humanists, now that Marx is passé, perhaps fresh visions will emerge for a global future of improvements on a scale more modest and humane than the Marxist quest for systemic perfection in a paradise on earth.

The global future hangs on hopes for a rising spirit of inclusion across the fault lines of civilization. Happily, the time seems more promising now than ever before for the inclusive spirit to grow, since technology is continuing to shrink the world at a rapid pace. The result is a vastly expanded scope for understanding and acceptance of differences within and across diverse ways of life. The rising capacity to process and spread information is continuing to free more and more individuals and communities worldwide from historic isolation and ineffectiveness. This is an especially welcome development for Inclusive Humanists, representing the only cultural identity in the quadrate hamstrung by the absence of a geographical base. As diffuse and international as it has been, Inclusive Humanism retains its syncretic promise for a global future of greater amity and cooperation across the many fault lines of secular and religious exclusion.

NOTES

1. G. A. Cohen, *Karl Marx's Theory of History* (Princeton: Princeton University Press, 1978).

2. Joseph J. Kockelmans, *On the Truth of Being* (Bloomington, IN: Indiana University Press, 1984).

3. C. G. Jung, *Analytical Psychology,* ed. William McGuire (Princeton: Princeton University Press, 1989).

4. Sir Monier Monier-Williams, *Brahmanism and Hinduism; or Religious Thought and Life in India, as Based on the Veda and Other Sacred Books of the Hindus* (London: J. Murray, 1891).

5. K. K. Mittal, *Materialism in Indian Thought* (Delhi: Manshiram, 1974).

6. *Luther's Works,* Vol. 47, *The Christian in Society IV* (Philadelphia: Fortress Press, 1971).

7. Monier Williams, *A Practical Grammar of the Sanskrit Language,*

Arranged With Reference to the Classical Languages of Europe for the Use of English Students (Oxford: Oxford University Press, 1857).

Seeing Newly, Differently, And Futuristically with Scenarios

Irving H. Buchen

Many strategic planners and forecasters find advocates of science fiction suspect. The genre is regarded as too fanciful or far-out to be taken seriously as a forecasting methodology. Indeed, Isaac Asimov conceded its basic escapist nature but then reined it back in by adding mischievously that science fiction was "an escape to reality." It is a teasing paradox. On the one hand, science fiction is powerfully persuasive and inclusive, able to access and portray new and multiple perspectives and populations. On the other hand, it is shaped and urged by a vision that is often so singular or absolute that it reads like the Sermon on the Mount or an ecological manifesto. Still, for some futurists science fiction remains a tantalizingly attractive form of future inquiry. And so for them the question becomes, Is it possible to salvage the mode and make it more manageable and less eccentric — that is, not to throw out the baby with the bathwater?

The answer for many for over the last three decades is Yes — there is the scenario, the cousin of science fiction, its less fanciful alter ego, its more mainstream version. Indeed, scenario planning often accompanied by simulation has become such an attrac-

---

Irving H. Buchen is on the doctoral business faculty of Capella and IMPAC universities. E-mail ibuchen@msn.com.

tive way of both exploring and rendering the future that it is now standard fare of planning workshops and of MBA case studies. But is all well with its use? To be sure, the scenario appears to strike the right balance: preserving the best and avoiding the worst of science fiction. But there is the rub—perhaps the first of many. Selecting the strengths without the weaknesses may turn out finally to be a weakness—preserving the assets and discarding the liabilities may ultimately be a liability. In other words, before automatically recommending and using scenarios to see the future with new eyes, perhaps we need to pause and assess the state of the art, especially its deep and profound ambiguity. Much of the stubborn and complex integrity that scenarios possess stems minimally from a number of paradoxical drivers: the special relationships that the scenario has with the future, the range and often unknown interoperability of its multiple sources, and the way that the future and its inhabitants are rendered.

Although many factors shape the craft of the scenario's difference and power, the following five are critical.

1. Collaborative Relationship with the Future

In many forecasts and plans, the future is positioned predictably and obediently ahead as a target or a goal. The future is asked to sit still while a plan is put in place to get there. But in good scenarios, the future is not that well-behaved or still. Wild cards are often norms. Events and people are autonomous, even willful. They are not just influenced by the future—they already are the future. They embody, sustain, and live a time and place ahead. Most important, then, from the outset is that in the scenario the future is not a passive object but a dynamic partner—not a blank slate, but the handwriting on the wall. Indeed, in all scenarios one can discern two authors—the fictionist and the futurist—often so close that we can't tell where the one begins and the other ends or distinguish what each one contributes. But the final composite has to pass the same test we put on all authentic anticipatory products: namely, is the future there? Is it palpable, threatening, feelable? Finally, has it been made not only more available, but also more definable? Has the future as a co-author left its stamp, signed off finally with his characteristic signature of always being a mixture of the known, unknown, and finally unknowable? Last but not least, are we holding a tiger by the tail?

2. Laws of Fiction

Scenarios have to obey two sets of unwritten laws: those of the future and those of fiction. The surprise is discovering that in many ways they are the same. You direct and are directed, you shape and are shaped, you possess and are possessed. The future is not just ahead, it is alongside — it is at once familiar like your shadow but casts a different likeness. The scenario thus operates under and celebrates the same mysterious dynamics of all imaginative work. You create characters and events, but then they take over and create themselves. Indeed, if they didn't, that would signal that you and your vision are in total control, with little or no room left for them to be autonomous and for your collaborative partner to contribute. That is why the impact of a genuine scenario is always double — it is both familiar and surprising, is easy to follow but then takes an unexpected turn, reads like a daily newspaper and an exotic work of science fiction. It is always and finally an escape to reality.

3. Decision Forecasts

Many planning documents are very busy. They factor in and are animated by a number of megatrends and data patterns. Parameters are put in place to contain the flux. In addition, because the focus is often a moving target or a chancy environment, a monitoring system is put in place. As a result, planning has become increasingly contingency planning. Often that is a mixed blessing. The downside is that it often downgrades all its inputs. Trends are tamed as operating assumptions. Data is often tentative. Outcomes appear on a spreadsheet of options, often displayed without preference or priority. The net result is that everything is conditional. There is a great deal of hemming and hawing. Planners fearful of being found fallible sound the same recurrent qualifying warning, "It all depends." The plan finally loses its value as a basis of decision making and thus invokes the famous observation Werner von Braun made many years ago: "Analysis, analysis — paralysis, paralysis!"

How is the scenario different? It shifts the requirement of being comprehensive from what drives projections to what it means to live such futures — every day, during breakfast, going to work — under different economic conditions and political situations. Moreover, the scenario further can acquire or simulate 360-degree range by playing out multiple impacts — first order, second order, third order, and so on, like the proverbial rock sending out wider and wider ripples in the stream. In other words, the scenario is a test not so much of plans as of the decisions they lead to — not so much of disciplining but of managing discontinuity. It is a futures lab testing the problem of solutions. When future-directed is linked to failure-oriented, every solution is viewed as a livable problem.

4. Diversity as a Norm

Many plans are not good research documents. Sample size is often limited not only by numbers, but also by demographic breadth and depth — the old dilemma of one mile across but only two inches deep. Estimating impacts solely in terms of market research of China excludes the sociology range of the profiles of the Chinese population. Even geographical, like ecological, sampling is often not global. The great advantage of the scenario is summed up by its two most powerful characteristics: cast of characters and dramatic settings.

Like an accordion, it can be expanded to a cast of thousands, its settings even outer space. But it is not enough to see differently. The scenario also compels turnaround—being in turn seen differently. Not only do we perceive with a different set of cultural eyes, but we are perceived by the vision of a different future. In short, the scenario is designed as a series of affirmations and correctives. We look into the diagnostic mirror of the future and ask, "What country or policy or product is the fairest in the world?" We find not a singular or unidirectional answer, but a series of diverse turnarounds in a hall of mirrors.

5. Multidisciplinarity

Scenarios embarrass specialists. They constantly expose the limits of experts' knowledge and the range of their applications. In addition, interoperability tampers with their data. Dennis and Donella Meadows and Jay Forrester discovered in their global model that many of their variables leaked on and turned well-behaved constants into erratic troublemakers—there goes predictability! So the scenario is intensely demanding. It requires what few planners have: the knowledge not only of a great many subject areas and sources, but also of their interfacing knowledge—how they interrelate and interact, sometimes producing wholes greater than the sum of their parts. Above all, scenarios require knowledge of how things work or do not, and generally why or why not. Given such demands for a range of knowledge that is generally not available and sadly often not valued, how are such obstacles overcome? The best crafters of scenarios are those who have learned in various ways to approximate multidisciplinary wholeness.

Who has done that well? Three examples come to mind: science fictionists, systems analysts, and futurists. The discussion of each model serves not only to bring forward in summary fashion all that has been discussed so far, but also to focus now on assessing the epistemology of all three types — not so much what each one knows but how each knows what it knows; not how smart they are, but how they are smart.

Science fictionists are set apart from other fictionists by two distinctions: their knowledge of science and technology and their power to render transformed worlds. They dramatize the supreme leverage of technology to grab center stage and almost overnight dramatically alter the way all things are. But once postulated, what then follows is the drama of adjustment. The imaginative distinction of science fictionists is their unique ability to observe and absorb things whole. People and things are not viewed as separate but of a piece, and always in motion. Process is always give and take. Negotiation, hard and soft, rules all. The science fiction drama is thus always sustained by choice — what decisions have been made and what sadly that has led to, and what readers now being forewarned will decide to do before it is too late. If science fiction scenarios are deficient, it is that they are technology-obsessed and often hysterical or melodramatic.

Systems analysts similarly bring holistics to bear. The special insight of their expertise is connectivity, the principle that all interactions, big and small, are sustained by a complicated chain of both known and unknown interactions, and that finally every organism is a mechanism and every mechanism is an organism. In addition, such systems analysis can be carried over and serve as an analytical overlay of decisions review and the implications of implementations. The downside is being excessively mechanical and lacking verisimilitude.

The expertise of futurists is also 360 but applied exclusively to the future. Over the years they have come to know how the future behaves and misbehaves; they understand that although it is part of a continuum with the past and the present, the future operates under and obeys its own laws. As a result, futurists are often the indispensable critics of the strategic plans of companies and countries. In effect, they point out that the emperor has no clothes and that is not the way the future works. Their great value is to compel engaging the future so that we do not destroy or damage the only common heritage we have. The downsides are functioning excessively as future shock troops of doom and gloom and failing to live up to their own ideal of thinking globally but acting locally.

The obvious conclusion is that each has what the others need. Limiting our focus to futurists, how would their scenarios benefit from those of science fictionists and system analysts? Perhaps in the following ways:

- **Collaborative:** Honoring and blending the co-authors of the probable and the possible, bringing into the fold the minority dissenting forecasts inhabiting the periphery, and finally simulating the whole by speaking not with a singular but a choral voice.

- **Laws of Fiction:** Burdening projections with the messy reality of everyday vulnerable real-time and real-world, and above all earning credibility by profiling the anti-future of self-serving and self-perpetuating politicians and institutions.

- **Decision Forecasting:** Requiring all forecasts to exhibit next steps — following up and spelling out their decision options and alternatives, and recording the multiple impacts of those choices, even unto the biblical span of four generations.

- **Diversity:** Linking and networking nationally and internationally with all other futurists and their organizations, issuing parallel projections in tandem, and preserving cultural diversity as a norm of global futures.

- **Multidisciplinarity:** Becoming increasingly the systems analysts of the future, engaged in the major integrative research project of converging multiple methodologies rather than championing singular approaches.

The argument here is that, if we truly are to see the future, ourselves, and others differently, there is perhaps no better way to do so than with, by, and through the scenario — especially reformulated to include the strengths of its fellow models. Such a reconstituted scenario can be as big and as devious as the world, smart and tough enough to take on the complexity of diversity and the temptation of inertia, shrewd and savvy about the egos of leaders and the lip service of politicians, knowledgeable enough about systems and interoperability to resist the Band-Aids of passing off a half as a whole, and above all a loyal advocate of all people, especially the unborn. Such a reinvented scenario may turn out to be the best and most enduring legacy of futurists and their embracing synthesis of science fiction and system analysis.

Backcasting from the Future

Predict the Future by Creating It

Don Mizaur

Planners accuse futurists of being "blue sky" and "out in the ozone." Futurists accuse planners of being unimaginative and didactic. One doesn't have to look very far to see examples of this conflict. The current presidential campaign provided a poignant example, when Senator Clinton said her opponent, Senator Obama, was providing only speeches, while she was providing solutions. Senator McCain said that Senator Obama was providing eloquent visions of the future, but had no plans for getting there. Back in the 1992 presidential campaign, the incumbent President George H. W. Bush never could incorporate that "vision thing" into his campaign. Meanwhile, his opponent, Bill Clinton, was mesmerizing audiences with his inspiring oratory. This troublesome chasm between futurists and planners may be best bridged by employing a powerful concept, called *backcasting*.

The concept of backcasting was made known in Michael Barzelay's book, *Preparing for the Future*, a study of the history of strategic planning in the U.S. Air Force. In his book, Barzelay recalls a legendary incident in Air Force lore during the mid-1990s when General Ronald Fogleman first became U.S. Air Force chief

Don Mizaur is a senior consultant with Karl Albrecht International.
E-mail don@karlalbrecht.com.

of staff:

> In the course of a briefing on the mission area plan of the Air
> Combat Command, Fogleman asked about plans for a succes-
> sor to the current Airborne Warning and Control System
> (AWACS). The components of this twenty-year old system in-
> cluded a Boeing 707 airframe, sensors housed in a dome
> mounted prominently above the fuselage, data processing
> equipment, and sizable on-board crew. In response to Fogle-
> man's unanticipated question, the briefer volunteered that the
> next-generation system would presumably use a more recent
> model Boeing as a platform, equipped with a dome mounted
> on top. The Chief, in turn, suggested the possibility of perform-
> ing the AWACS mission using space based sensors that trans-
> mitted data to crews situated on the ground and thereby out of
> harm's way. The incident reportedly confirmed Fogleman's
> growing suspicion that the Air Force's legendary innovative
> spirit had somehow been sapped, at least in the modernization
> planning process.

Barzelay further recounts:

> This disappointing incident led Fogleman to coin the phrase
> *backcasting* from the future, conceived as the antitheses of
> forecasting from the present. Rather than project the long-
> range spending consequences of the current planning direc-
> tion, the backcasting principle called for formulating a point of
> view about the future, which would then provide a basis for
> making nearer-term decisions. As Fogleman recalled, partici-
> pants in the planning process were charged to think along the
> following lines:
>
>> "I want to go into low earth orbit in a satellite and you sit
>> up there at 2025, and you look down at the world as it is in

2025 and then you try to figure out what the Air Force should be contributing to national defense. And then look back from that point and see where the pivotal events occur — when we shift from air-breathing to spaced-based AWACS; when we go through a divestiture program and get rid of something we're doing today."

Consider the power of this process. As a result of employing this process, the U.S. Air Force's long-range plans call for the predominant use of unmanned aircraft by the end of the first quarter of the twenty-first century. These plans were largely created by pilots who had advanced to senior leadership. Without the vision-shaping afforded by the backcasting process, these plans would have likely been dominated by manned aircraft. Those involved in the backcasting process admit to being conflicted. Their entire careers have been defined as pilots of manned aircraft. Yet, they were capable of being transported to a future vision by this process, and they recognized what warfare and politics would be like at that future state. Once their vision of the future state was clear, it was easier to identify the critical success factors in achieving it and the necessary steps to get there.

AN OPPORTUNITY LOST?

Forty-five years ago Dr. Martin Luther King gave his inspiring "I have a dream" speech. This speech, on the steps of the Lincoln Memorial, is easily one of the best and most impactful futurist speeches in history. Imagine, however, if after the speech, the leaders of government, and the change agents of that time, had gathered together and decided to plan for making King's dream a reality. King had created a vision and had transported the nation to a future time when the social horrors of 1963 didn't exist.

What if President Kennedy had decided, as General Fogleman had in the U.S. Air Force, to charge the leaders of our nation with backcasting from that future vision and determining the critical success factors and action plans needed to make that future a reality? Wouldn't these leaders have developed a more proactive approach to making King's vision happen sooner and with less violence and injustice? The leadership at that time relied on the normal course of events and let the change happen unassisted. Would it have taken forty-five years before a woman, or a person of color, would be nominated for the presidency, had they assisted in the achievement of King's dream?

President Kennedy did create such a vision when he set the goal to have a man on the Moon before the end of the 1960s. He then asked Congress and the newly formed NASA to "backcast" from this future vision and determine the necessary steps to make this goal a reality.

Too often, inspiring visions of a *future better state* are expressed, but seldom is action taken to explore what it might take to make those visions a reality. Backcasting is a concept that allows for such exploration. Such an exploration will also assess the degree of difficulty, the cost, and the time frame for such an endeavor.

The media and political rhetoric are filled with visions of the United States no longer being dependent on fossil fuels. Why can't we backcast from a future date, determine the critical success factors and action plans required, and make it happen? Sound crazy? Brazil has done it already.

As a nation, Brazil has no fossil fuel reserves and did not want to be dependent on other countries for its energy. Leaders decided on a renewable product with which the country had 400 years of experience: ethanol, made from sugarcane. Brazil's path has taken thirty years of effort, required several billion dollars in incentives, and involved many missteps. Today, Brazil is free of reliance on foreign oil and is now becoming an exporter of its ethanol. The planners probably didn't call it backcasting, but they had to have gone through a similar process to get where they are. Perhaps if they had used a formalized approach, they might have beaten the thirty years it took.

WHAT IS THE BACKCASTING APPROACH?

When people are asked to make plans for the future, they tend to extrapolate from the past and the present. The past and the present are the time frames where they exist when asked to engage in a futures planning process. These planners must be transported to the future and be allowed to imagine a vastly different environment without being encumbered by current and past realities. Transporting them to that unencumbered future better state is the first step in using the backcasting approach. This type of planning approach is best done by a group, preferably composed of the organization's leadership team. This is recommended because the creativity that the group process unleashes is necessary for the optimal results desired from a future planning process. Once the group has been gathered, one effective way to begin to transport the group to a future state is through a headline-writing exercise. This is where the futurists come in: Either bring in a futurist speaker who has relevance to the environment, or at least give the planning group access to such creative insight. A skilled facilitator to conduct the process is also desirable.

Once the planning team is formed, it should be divided into several table groups. Their first assignment is begun by stating that a prestigious and respected business or environmental publication is writing an article about the organization. This proposed article is going to talk about the remarkable positive change in the organization's performance. The planning team's task will be to write the subheadlines for the article that will encapsulate the various elements that would have contributed to this remarkable performance by the organization. The table groups should be encouraged to be creative and relatively unconstrained by resources or current conditions, and to stay within the realistic range of possibility (no colonizing Mars or moving the organization to Honolulu). Each group would report out its ideas.

Once the groups have reported out, it is necessary to achieve consensus around those subheadlines that are the most desirable and doable. Several teams are likely to come up with the same or similar subheadlines. For example, if there are twenty subheadlines total, give each person five votes and have them all select their top five. The scoring usually clusters around a few that are appealing. Engage in some wordsmithing to make the subheadlines believable as likely definitions of the future and its ramifications. Try to achieve consensus around four to six of them.

The planning group has now been transported to a future better state and has a good grasp of what the key elements are that created the remarkable success. They are now poised to backcast from these key elements and to create the plans needed to move the organization aggressively forward, making that future better state a reality.

The remainder of this additional planning involves the use of proven tactics in organizational planning, such as:

- **Identifying the critical success factors to support the subheadlines**. The teams take each subheadline and determine what significant activities or "tricks" (critical success factors) must occur for the subheadline to be written sometime in the future.
- **Developing a work breakdown structure for each critical success factor.** The teams should then address what major elements of resources (labor, capital, and materials) will be needed to achieve the critical success factors. Each team should develop the work breakdown structure for each critical success factor.
- **Taking a SWAG (sophisticated, wild-ass guess) at the resources required for the work breakdown structure.** This is

something that may be done offline, and perhaps by a subcommittee of the leadership team and/or delegated to a qualified group of experts. The magnitude and the required resources are defined to set the organization on a new direction.

- **Recommitting the leadership team to proceed with the new future plans**. This is the moment of truth for the organization. The leadership team has defined a consensus strategy for change and has determined it to be an imperative. The resources required have been estimated. Before proceeding, it is useful to let the team reexamine and recommit (if still committed) and proceed. The team can decide among the following options:
  - Reaffirm the strategy as developed.
  - Determine that the strategy was too ambitious and scale it back.
  - Determine that the strategy was not ambitious enough and expand.
  - Determine what amount of the resources will be funded from new sources.
  - Determine what amount of the resources will be funded from shedding/modifying operations.
  - Abandon the strategy altogether and at least fire the consultant.
- **Conduct a shedding/modifying session with the leadership team.** This exercise will create the organization's "not-to-do list." The backcasting process may yield a plan that will require new resources or that may be redundant to current activities of the organization. Hence, it will be necessary to abandon and/or alter some of the existing activities. In preparation for this shedding/modifying session, the staff should prepare a list of all operations at a digestible level of detail. Each major line item should have an estimated number of resources that may be consumed. Depending on the size of the group and complexity of the operations, a

reasonable process should be determined for making the necessary operational tradeoffs. Affected employees will likely become defensive. The group process and the commitment to the new strategy will serve to ameliorate this behavior. Sacred cows are not easy to kill. It may be necessary for the most senior leadership to make some tough calls. This may best be done offline.

Prolific business author Karl Albrecht wrote a book about organizational strategy called *The Northbound Train*. The "northbound train" is a metaphor for an organization's newly defined direction. Albrecht counsels senior leadership to, at some time, give a "northbound train" speech, define the new direction for the organization, state that this train is going north, say some might find the implications of this new direction uncomfortable, and invite those who do to locate trains going in other directions.

WHERE'S THE BEEF?

For futurists, "Where's the beef?" is often at least implied by the questions and comments that follow their communications. Some of the differences between planners and futurists can be attributed to differing personality types. Those with a "red earth" perspective often cannot relate to those with a "blue sky" perspective, and vice versa. Perhaps the backcasting approach can close the "understanding" gap between them, and cause futurists and planners to shout, "*Vive la différence!*"

Forecasting the Next Industrial Revolution

A Structural Perspective from Evolutionary Economics

Denis L. Balaguer

The essential nature of capitalism is its dynamics and its propensity to change. According to Schumpeter:

> The essential point to grasp is that in dealing with capitalism we are dealing with an evolutionary process. ... Capitalism, then, is by nature a form or method of economic change and not only never is but never can be stationary. And this evolutionary character of the capitalist process is not merely due to the fact that economic life goes on in a social and natural environment which changes and by its change alters the data of economic action (Schumpeter 1984, 82).

The evolutionary kernel of economic change under the capitalist regime, the one element that sets the pace, is technological innovation. More than this, the "one ingredient of modernization that is just about indispensable is technological maturity and the industrialization that goes with it; otherwise one has the trappings with-

---

Denis L. Balaguer is a researcher and technological engineer at Embraer, São Paulo, Brazil. E-mail denis.balaguer@embraer.com.br.

out substance, the pretence without reality" (Landes 1969, 7).

So, in order to improve decision making concerning future moves in the modern capitalist arena, it is necessary to understand the mechanisms of economic change, especially the nature of large technological transitions. Only this way one can try to forecast possible futures.

But it is important to consider that technological forecasting is not about predicting the future. It is about probabilistically understanding the forces that will shape the convergence toward the future (Balaguer 2005). Michel Godet (1999) once stated that the future is multiple, undetermined, and open to a great range of different possible futures.

The work of constructing a vision of possible futures demands an understanding of the objective nature of the system intended to be forecasted, in order to build a model that is simple and representative enough. A model is understood as a useful, simplified representation of essentially important aspects of a real object or situation (Chernoff and Moses 1986, 228).

Considering the need to model economic change, in a macro-aggregation level, it is necessary to deal with complexity. Masini states:

> In Future Studies we are therefore dealing with complex systems that become even more complex in the case of social systems. The situation of uncertainty must thus be examined in relation to complexity. It is important that we detect a situation of risk and uncertainty in a complex present. Even in our normal everyday lives we have accepted risk and uncertainty; we have to face up to them and try to understand them with the tools that are gradually being developed. Futures Studies will never be able to give us certitudes, but they can help us to lower the level of uncertainty through a careful structuring

and analysis of problems (Massini 1993, 36).

To structure the problem of modeling economic change, one good step is to look at economic history and try to systematize its processes and elements. The evolutionary approach to economics does a good job in this intent, especially by taking into account the importance of technological innovation. Freeman and Perez remember:

> It has been argued that a weakness of the most neo-classical and Keynesian theories of technical change and economic growth is that they fail to take account of the specifics of changing technology in each historical period. One reason that economists do not attempt this daunting task is, of course, the sheer complexity of technical change (Freeman and Perez 1988).

The objective of the present work is to propose a general framework that describes the state of "paradigm change" to support the forecasting of large economic changes, based on concepts and structures constructed by the evolutionary economics approach, especially the studies of technological innovation and industrial revolution.

INDUSTRIAL REVOLUTIONS AND TECHNICAL CHANGE

Industrial revolutions, understood as the "complex of technological innovations" (Landes 1969, 1), are a central issue for economic systems.

The importance of industrial revolutions to the wealth of nations is well described by David Landes, when, in the conclusion of his study on the "Technological Change and Industrial Development in Western Europe from 1750 to the Present," he writes:

> Economic history has always been in part the story of interna-

tional competition for wealth. ... The Industrial Revolution gave this competition a new focus—wealth through industrialization—and turned it into a chase. ... To be sure, there are only a few contestants sufficiently endowed to vie for the palm. The rest can at best follow along and make the most of their capacities. But even these are far better off than those who are not running. No one wants to stand still; most are convinced that they dare not. The laggards have good reason to be concerned: the race is getting faster all the time, and the richer get richer while the poor have children (Landes 1968, 578).

Given the importance described, these massive changes have been studied by economists in order to understand their nature, and Joseph A. Schumpeter is a central actor in this search. Schumpeter understood the capitalist system as inherently unstable, and he elaborated the concept of *creative destruction* to describe the process of economic change. According to Schumpeter:

The opening up of new markets, foreign or domestic, and the organizational development from the craft shop and factory ... illustrate the ... process of industrial mutation ... that incessantly revolutionizes the economic structure from within, incessantly destroying the old one, incessantly creating a new one. The process of creative destruction is the essential fact about capitalism (Schumpeter 1984, 83).

The evolutionary tradition that follows Schumpeter, building concepts, is one important indicator of economic change. In order to build a model of this change, one may refer to the taxonomy of innovation built by Christopher Freeman and Carlota Perez (1988):

1. Incremental innovations.
2. Radical innovations.
3. New technology systems.
4. Changes in techno-economic paradigms (technological revolu-

tions).

The latter one is the object of the present work, and Freeman and Perez define "changes in techno-economic paradigms":

> Some changes in technology systems are so far reaching in their effects that they have a major influence on the behaviour of the entire economy. A change of this kind carries with it many clusters of radical and incremental innovations, and may eventually embody a number of new technology systems. A vital characteristic of this fourth type of technical change is that it has *pervasive* effects throughout the economy, i.e. it not only leads to the emergence of a new range of products, services, systems and industries on its own right; it also affects directly or indirectly almost every branch of the economy, i.e. it is a "meta-paradigm" (Freeman and Perez 1988).

In order to understand what kind of changes underpin this type of large-scale transition, several structural analyses are proposed by evolutionary economists.

Schumpeter, in a more general analysis of the mechanisms behind capitalist evolutions, states, "The fundamental impulse that sets and keeps the capitalist engine in motion comes from the new consumers' goods, the new methods of production or transportation, the new markets, the new forms of industrial organization that capitalist enterprise creates" (Schumpeter 1984, 83).

In a more specific analysis of previous industrial revolutions, Landes highlights that the complex of technological innovations that constitute the paradigm change worked by "substituting machines for human skills and inanimate power for human and animal force, brings about a shift from handicraft to manufacture and, doing so, gives birth to modern economy" (Landes 1969, 1).

A more systematic approach is given by Tamás Szmrecsányi. For this author, to conceptually characterize any industrial revolution, it may be useful to start with a simplified scheme of manufacturer production that puts, on the one side, material inputs, and on the other, the final products, and, between both sides, the transformation processes (Szmrecsányi 2001).

More specifically, Szmrecsányi (2001 and 2006) categorizes the technological innovations that constitute an industrial revolution as:

1. New fabrication, transformation, and distribution models.
2. New raw materials.
3. New energetic regimes.
4. New products or services.
5. New markets, before inaccessible or unexplored.
6. New forms of economic organization.

When one or more innovations of these kinds occur on an abrupt and discontinuous way, it may be characterized an industrial revolution.

Complementary to those categories of industrial revolutions, in order to constitute a broad vision useful to support a model building, it is important to understand the scale of change; i.e., how an innovation—which falls under those categories—achieves a critical value that is enough to promote the paradigm shift.

One clue for this critical value measure is given by Freeman and Perez when they describe the process of economic decision making toward revolutionary change. According to them (1988), "the organizing principle of each successive paradigm and the justification for the expression 'techno-economic paradigm' is to be found not only in a new range of products and systems, but most of all in the dynamics of the relative cost structure of all possible inputs to production."

This means that technological innovation must be analyzed under the "relative cost structure of all possible inputs to production."

STRUCTURAL FORECASTING

There are a lot of forecasting approaches. But, considering the complexity of systems (which is the object in the present work), one of the fittest choices is scenarios, because scenario building usually deals with highly complex, nonlinear, and dynamic systems, which have continuous structural changes and an elevated level of uncertainty associated with those changes (Buarque 2003).

One key feature of a scenario-based forecasting is to structure the logic and the dynamics of the reality. This must be done under an analytical referential that indicates which variables that describe the behavior of the system to be modeled.

Consequently, to construct the scenarios, one may start with a mental model (theory) that explains which are the variables and how they interplay, in order to reduce the complexity of the system (Buarque 2003).

Michel Godet et al. (2006) present a scenarios approach with the following stages:

1. Identify the key variables.
2. Analyze the interplay of the actors involved in order to pose key questions about the future.
3. Reduce uncertainty around those key questions and tease out the most probable scenarios based upon, among other things, the input of experts.

For the purpose of the present work, the first stage is the most interesting one, since it's the one that refers to the description of the system in terms of variables.

The "Identify the key variables" step consists of "creating an inventory of variables which characterize the system under study, as well as its internal and external environment" (Godet et al. 2006). The authors also recommend the establishment of a precise definition for each variable.

FRAMEWORK PROPOSAL

Since the logic of the scenarios approach presented above is based on model building, it is important to remember that a model is simply an assemblage of hypotheses about a complex system; it is an attempt to understand some aspect of an infinitely variable world picked from past perceptions and experiences, an assemblage of general observations of the subject's problems (Meadows et al. 1972, 17).

Exploring Godet's approach, one may identify the key variables of the "industrial revolution" system in order to build the forecasting model. Since evolutionary economics provides, as explained above, the best conceptual model for modeling economic change through industrial revolution, the systematization proposed by Szmrecsányi is a good set of key variables.

Using this set of key variables, it is possible to construct a framework for scenario monitoring that allows the analysis of the state of the "paradigm change" (Figure 1). The scale of this frame-

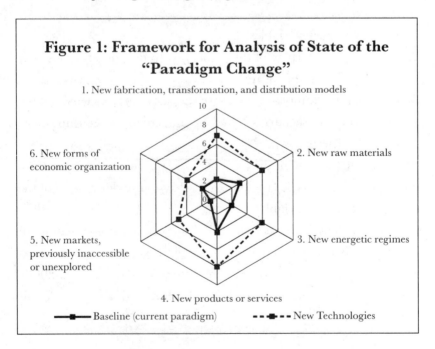

Figure 1: Framework for Analysis of State of the "Paradigm Change"

work may be, as proposed by Freeman and Perez, the relative cost of the new technologies compared with the technologies that constitute the present techno-economic paradigm.

With this framework, it is possible to monitor how the new paradigm is performing compared with the old one. It is especially useful as a base for a forecasting study, because it allows the analysts to understand how change may happen in the system. This is important because, otherwise, the analysis the potential impacts and probability of realization of the new technologies stands on a very subjective basis.

CONCLUSION

The change of the techno-economic paradigm, historically represented by industrial revolutions, constitutes the kernel of economic evolution. So, given this relevance of industrial revolution to economic change, the systematic forecasting of the structures that determine industrial revolution is an important issue, both for firms and governments.

Forecasting techniques demand a conceptual scheme in order to build a relevant model of the system analyzed. Considering the system "industrial revolution," one important contribution is given by evolutionary economics, especially by providing the key variables that describe the system.

Using these variables, it is possible to build a framework to objectively analyze the state of the "paradigm change," in order to support a forecasting study.

REFERENCES

Buarque, Sérgio. 2003. *Metodologias e Técnicas de Construção de Cenários Globais e Regionais*. Brasília: IPEA (Texto para Discussão N. 939).

Chernoff, Herman, and Lincoln E. Moses. 1986. *Elementary Decision Theory*. New York: Dover Publications Inc.

Freeman, Christopher, and Carlota Perez. 1988. *Structural Crisis of Adjustment, Business Cycles and Investment Behaviour.* In *Technical Change and Economic Theory,* Giovanni Dosi et al., eds. Londres: Pinter Publishers.

Godet, Michel, Philippe Durance, and Adam Gerber. 2006. *Strategic Foresight—La Prospective: Problems and Methods.* Paris: LIPSOR; CNAM (Cahiers du LIPSOR - Issue n°20).

Landes, David. 1969. *The Unbound Prometheus: Technological Change and Industrial Development in Western Europe from 1750 to the Present.* Cambridge: Cambridge University Press.

Masini, Eleonora B. 1993. *Why Future Studies?* London: Grey Seal.

Meadows, Dennis, et al. 1972. *The Limits to Growth.* New York: Universe Books.

Schumpeter, Joseph A. 1984. *Capitalism, Socialism and Democracy.* New York: HarperPerennial.

Szmrecsányi, Tamás. 2006. "A Herança Schumpeteriana." In *Economia da Inovação Tecnológica,* Victor Pelaez and Tamás Szmrecsányi. São Paulo: Editora HUCITEC; Ordem dos Economistas do Brasil.

Szmrecsányi, Tamás. 2001. "Esboços de História Econômica da Ciência e da Tecnologia." In *Da Revolução Científica à Big (Business) Science.* Luiz C. Soares. São Paulo: Hucitec; Niterói, RJ: Editora da UFF.

Macrotechnology Analysis

Paul Crabtree

DEFINITION OF TECHNOLOGY ELEMENT

Starting with the proposition that "technology" is a general term for a set of goods, services, or processes used to satisfy human needs, it follows that a specific type of good, service, or process can be thought of as a *technology element*. One might be tempted to think technology might be better defined as a set of inventions. All goods, services, and processes, however, begin as inventions at some point in time, so an "inventions"-based definition of technology reduces to much the same thing, but without providing the same level of specificity and clarity. In this context, inventions not yet translated into goods, services, or processes represent potential technology elements.

Number *(n)*

The aggregate number of different technology elements — the number of types of goods, services, and processes in use at a given time — constitutes the first of three basic facets of a conceptual framework for visualizing and assessing technology change; i.e., the technology space matrix proposed in this paper.

Since the invention of printing and worldwide communication, the number of technology elements available to humankind has been steadily increasing. While modern economies do not now make

Paul Crabtree is retired from the U.S. government, where he held a variety of analytical and managerial positions. E-mail pocrab@wbhsi.net.

much use of cargo sailing ship technology elements, such ships still operate in some parts of the world. Since total extinctions of technology elements are unlikely, short of a worldwide cataclysm, the rate of additions to the inventory of technology elements (n) is likely to be more interesting than the total number.

Diffusion (d)

A society can have a scientific and engineering capability that includes a large repertoire of technology elements, but still be technologically backward. The Soviet Union in the 1950s produced technology elements in such small quantities, particularly consumer-oriented technology elements, that the vast majority of the Soviet population lived as though modern consumer technology did not exist. Even though in a few areas such a restricted technology base could temporarily outpace a more broad-based technology, as the Soviet Union did outpace the West for a time in rockets and space, such a lead was quickly overcome.

Analogous to the way that numbers of units matter in a given technology set, the extent of technology element use is also important. If cell phones are numerous, but no use is made of them, they might as well not exist as far as the technological level of the society is concerned. The number of units of each technology element, together with the average amount of use per unit, represents the extent of diffusion achieved by individual technology elements. Diffusion as used in this paper is analogous to "market penetration" in finance and economics. It constitutes the second facet of the technology space matrix.

Value (v)

Any discussion of the meaning of technology and technological change must take account of the fact that some technology elements are more valuable than others. "More valuable" does not necessarily mean the purchase price of one technology element unit is higher than units of a different technology element, although unit prices of a newly introduced technology element may be a value indicator. Units of the more valuable technology displace or substitute for units of the less valuable technology (as, for example, horseless carriages substituted for and then displaced the horse and buggy).

In some cases of radically new technology elements, it is not immediately obvious what is being substituted for or displaced, but with thought or research one can make such a connection, even if the connection is indirect. What, for instance, did the discovery and provision of electric power substitute for or displace compared to the technology of the late 1800s? The answer is nearly everything—candles or whale oil for lighting, wood and coal for heating, some types of skilled labor, electric trolleys for horse drawn, tooling of all kinds, etc. It is interesting to note that this substitution and displacement of older technologies by electric power occurred in combination with other technology elements, not just through the introduction of electricity alone. Some, perhaps most, technology element units need other technology elements (as well as numbers of units) to be effective and valuable (e.g., an automobile needs numerous gasoline stations and paved roads). Value by technology element unit is the third facet of the technology space matrix.

Based on the preceding discussion, technology at a given point in time can be represented by the number of technology elements present, the extent of the diffusion of those technology elements in the economy and society, and the value contributed by technology element units, either individually or in conjunction with other elements. The verbal description suggests the graphical representation of a three-dimensional *technology space matrix* in Figure 1.

An example of the technology space matrix concept is provided by the introduction and growth of television technology in the 1940s through the 1970s. In the 1940s, practical televisions were

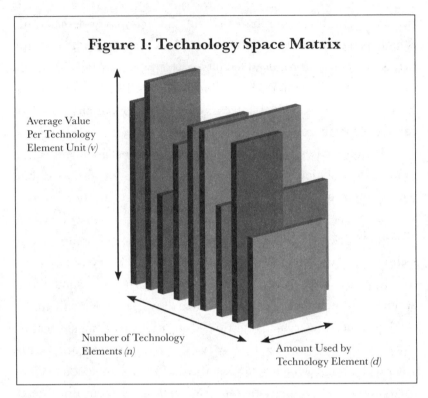

Figure 1: Technology Space Matrix

Average Value Per Technology Element Unit *(v)*

Number of Technology Elements *(n)*

Amount Used by Technology Element *(d)*

introduced to a wide commercial market. Television technology constituted an increase of one in the number of technology elements *(n)* in the technology space matrix. During the period 1940 through 1970, the numbers of television sets in use expanded greatly, as did the average hours of use per household. This constitutes an increase in diffusion *(d)* over the period. Along with the expansion in numbers of television sets and their use, the perceived value *(v)* of television to individuals and society expanded, as indicated by the amount of money spent on television purchases and the willingness to give up time and other pursuits to make way for this technology.

The overall size of the technology space matrix can be taken as a descriptive gauge of the usefulness or power of a technology set. Technology change can be thought of as a change in the dimensions of the technology space matrix. Technological progress can be defined as a net increase in the matrix. In terms of the framework, understanding technological change involves understanding how n, d, and v change (or are made to change) over time.

FACTORS INFLUENCING THE NUMBER OF TECHNOLOGY ELEMENTS (N)

While this is certainly not a complete list, academic research support can be found for each of the following factors in stimulating new technology developments:

1. The quantity and quality of scientific and technical personnel and other resources available for development.
2. Risks and rewards associated with development.
3. Competition between developers.
4. The current state of technology.

Research and historical experience make it a reasonable assumption that more and better scientists and engineers in a field of technology make it more likely that technological advances will occur, or that the speed of innovation will be faster, or both. The proposition that there is a direct correlation between expected technical progress and the number of qualified personnel presupposes, of course, that a corresponding quantity and quality of tools and other material requirements needed to support their work is also available.

Except for the type of risks and rewards, investment in future technology appears to be similar in principle to investing to achieve a greater output of conventional goods and services. An obvious difference between investing in conventional versus new technology is that the new technology generally involves more uncertainty and risk, while accompanied by the potential for a greater than normal return. Technology development incentives can also be negative. Sanctions — the spur of actual or feared adverse consequences if an innovation is not pursued — have historically been important sources of motivation for technical achievements. The U.S. development of the atomic bomb was arguably more due to concern about the consequences of the other side being first with a bomb than any positive incentives for its developers.

Most economists assume that competition plays an important role in the innovation process. If a firm is not performing as efficiently as the competition, it will either lose market share or go out of business in favor of those who are more efficient. If, by accident or design, a technological improvement should take place in any firm that makes it more efficient or its products cheaper or more desirable, its market share would increase, at least temporarily. Competing firms will be under pressure to adopt the same improvement or make equivalent efficiency gains, or risk being driven out. Competition provides an incentive to "break out of the pack" of competitors through the establishment of an innovation-based monopoly or a continuing incentive to innovate in order to sustain a monopoly position against the entry of potential competitors into the market. Over time, such a process leads to continuous technical improvements, even if the individual innovations occur at random. Competition that spurs technological change need not be restricted to economic competition. Harder to quantify but probably equally important are competition for individual and organizational prestige, honors, and psychological rewards.

When a brass device dating from 80 BC was recovered from the sea off Greece in the 1950s, it was determined to be a mechanical calendar with complex gearing; a sort of calculator. It was so lacking in known predecessors in the archaeological record that the discovery was likened to finding a jet plane in a pyramid. The Grecian find (as well as the jet plane comment) makes the implicit point that preexisting technology elements provide essential building blocks for subsequent technology developments. Goods, services, and processes with new or increased capabilities usually result from the employment of older technologies arrayed in new ways. Even revolutionary new developments, such as the transistor seemed to be in 1947, had predecessor devices such as the solid-state diode and the vacuum tube (the vacuum tube performed functions similar to the transistor, albeit in a different way). The larger the effective technology element mass—i.e., numbers of technology elements in a technology space matrix—the greater is the potential that technology developers can find existing technology elements that are suitable for combining, disaggregating, sequencing, or modifying to transmute into new technology elements or provide stepping stones toward new technology elements.

FACTORS GOVERNING CHANGES IN THE DIFFUSION OF TECHNOLOGY ELEMENTS (D)

In microeconomic theory, the number of units of a "good" purchased is determined partly by income and partly by how useful a good is compared with alternatives. There is no apparent reason why we cannot substitute "technology elements" for the "goods" discussed in economic theory. If so, the usefulness to a purchaser of a good (or a technology element) compared with alternatives is revealed in part by the relative proportion of income that purchasers allocate to the different possibilities—i.e., the different technology elements.

The cost of production of a good (or technology element) normally goes down for a while as economies of mass production (i.e., returns to scale) begin to be realized. Cost then begins to rise again as production limits are reached. Technology elements also often grow in usefulness as the number in use increase—if there are more electric cars on the road, more charging stations are likely to be provided and more experienced repairmen made available. These factors can explain the usual "S" curve technology-growth pattern of a slow takeoff followed by rapid growth and then a leveling off in the sales of new technology products and services. The cost-of-production curve and the demand (willingness-to-pay) curve together make it possible to account for changes in the diffusion of technology elements in a similar manner to other competitively priced economic goods.

FACTORS GOVERNING CHANGES IN THE VALUE OF TECHNOLOGY ELEMENTS *(V)*

Demand and supply set the price of a good or a technology element in a market setting. This is true even in the case of a patented product, so long as the patent holder tries to maximize the gain from sales of the technology element and cannot segment the market by individual purchaser. In a monopoly situation, supply will be more limited and the price consequently higher than in a purely competitive market, but demand and supply still set the price. For practically all buyers in a competitive market, however, there is more value gained by purchasers than the market price paid indicates. This excess value is known in economic theory as consumer surplus.

The price of goods and services (i.e., technology elements) tends to drop from the high prices buyers are initially willing to pay down to the unit cost of production due to competition. During the time it takes for competition to bring down the price to the long-run cost of production, innovators may capture much of the potential consumer surplus in the form of monopolistic or semi-monopolistic profits. The end result, however, is that the value of a technology element for most users may eventually be much higher than the market price paid for it.

Technology values, because they are often unintended results of a complex chain of interactions between different technology elements, may not be captured in the market price or consumer surplus of individual technology element units. Neither are they necessarily what the individual user-purchaser would willingly pay for. They may be included in what economics classifies as "external" benefits or economies (or costs, diseconomies). For many analytical purposes, the correct value associated with a technology element unit may be what is known in economics as a shadow price — the price that takes account of all external benefits and costs.

The total technology space matrix value — the number of technology elements *(n)* times the average value per technology element unit *(v)* times amount of use of all technology elements *(d)* equals total economic value. It does not, however, equate to gross domestic product because of the existence of consumer surpluses, shadow prices, imports, etc.

CONCLUSIONS

The technology space matrix framework provides a means of summarizing and evaluating technology-related research in terms of just three fundamental outcomes. The framework provides researchers, managers, and policy makers with a conceptual means to monitor, synthesize, and get a bird's-eye view of the vast array of information on technology change. A summary framework such as technology space matrix can show large-scale relationships that might be missed if seen close up. The technology space matrix framework can also be used as a starting point from which to identify and to "drill down" to more detailed areas of special interest.

Author's note: This paper is a revised and shortened version of a discussion paper first published by *The Innovation Journal: The Public Sector Innovation Journal* in Volume 11, Issue 1, May 2006 as "A Framework For Understanding Technology and Technological Change." *The Innovation Journal* is online at www. innovation.cc, Eleanor Glor, Editor-in-Chief.

The Failure of Strategic Planning and Corporate Performance

Romulo Werran Gayoso

The objective of this paper is to consider the impact of environmental risks on strategic planning and evaluate the effectiveness of scenario planning in yielding better corporate performance. In order to accomplish these goals, this paper will consider a working definition of strategic planning with its benefits and shortcomings. This paper will consider potential sources of environmental risks that could derail formal strategic-planning processes. Then, this paper considers both the benefits and shortcomings of scenario planning as a vehicle to improve corporate performance.

STRATEGIC PLANNING

Although the debate in the literature no longer focuses on why organizations should plan, it is important to note a working definition of strategic planning. In fact, the body of literature (Drucker 1995; Hughes 2005; Mintzberg 1994; Porter 1980; Shapiro 1989) defines it as a set of deliberate actions designed with some specific desired outcome in mind. The set of actions is supported by specific milestones, which, augmented by several techniques, allows management to exert command and control on the organization through

Romulo Werran Gayoso is an economist for Intel Corporation and teaches economics at the University of Phoenix. E-mail romulo.w.gayoso@intel.com.

the creation of a road map. The main function of this road map is to formalize the process and steps the organization will take in order to turn management's goals into a series of actionable items designed to support the mission and corporate objectives. Porter (1980) went so far as to say that not only is the main function of planning to carry out the corporate objectives the way managers envisioned, but it is also the best way to ensure a sharper positioning in the competitive environment. In Porter's (1980) view, the planning process is the ideal formal instrument that organizations use to improve their competitive situation, which in turn helps the organization solve the fundamental management dilemma: how to ensure long-run survival. In essence, planning ensures survival.

Planning Process Mechanics

The literature (Armstrong and Reibstein 1985) describes a basic planning activity as a series of five steps. At the beginning of the process, management sets several desirable outcomes, which both managers and planners use as targets. This planning team then goes through an idea generation phase, when specific actions are designed and communicated throughout the organization.

The next step is often associated with the control function: Managers constantly monitor how the instructions are executed and evaluate how effective the strategy is in terms of producing the desirable results. Management considers the outcomes of each strategy and makes adjustments to ensure greater success rates; it spends most of the time ensuring that the communications process is flowing and that employees are aligned with corporate objectives. This cycle of analyzing a situation, forming ideas to achieve corporate objectives, implementing a set of actions, monitoring results, and communicating with employees is a closed, repetitive loop (Gupta 2004).

Even though it appears that the issue of communications is central to the success of a planning process, the literature (Strandholm 2004) also assigns a great weight to specific leadership characteristics. In fact, Strandholm (2004) very much agrees with Porter (1980) when she advocates that the ability of an organization to change in the face of an environmental threat is key to its survival, but she differs from him when she advocates only organizations whose leaders have some key characteristics will be able to better respond to the environment. In her view, successful organizations have leaders who have a higher uncertainty tolerance, who aspire to create an efficient organization, who focus on consumers' desires, and who have operational experience.

Although it appears that the formal process, combined with selected leadership characteristics, would be sufficient to ensure planning success, the literature and chiefly Mintzberg (1994) argues that the communications process rarely achieves full employee co-operation, and therefore it is difficult to ensure that all resources are committed to full plan implementation. Critics also argue that this formality in the planning process leads to the formation of an official future, itself an artificial construct where the future is predictable with great accuracy. In turn, planning leads to less-flexible organizations, where managers are detached from reality and have great difficulty dealing with unanticipated environmental challenges; in fact, the literature outlines many sources of environmental risk.

Environmental Risks

Challenge of Cognition

Perhaps it is adequate to consider a fundamental aspect of risk perception: In fact, the literature (Stahl and Grigsby 1992) advocates that some of the most serious threats to an organization's plans might not even be perceived as such. The argument is fairly simple: The external environment is so complex, with so many stimuli for one to process, that it becomes virtually impossible for management to capture the essence of the situation. Stahl and Grigsby (1992) argue that education, industry experience, and tenure on the job help managers create a cognitive base, which, supported by one's value set, generates a prism that managers use to confront reality.

Since it is humanly impossible for managers to be everywhere all the time, they actually have a cut-down view of the environment, which, augmented by their selective attention, leads to a very subjective, fractional interpretation of reality. This imperfect view is flushed through the entire organization; Pons-Novell (2003) advocated that this view is communicated, shared, and believed. He contends that this imperfect view crystallizes into the official interpretation, and the entire strategic-planning process is thus contaminated by group-think practices. In essence, the environment is perceived through this imperfect lens, which leads to decision making with incomplete, imperfect, and often faulty information. Thus, it is not unreasonable to encounter situations where apparently obvious environmental threats might take management by complete surprise, since managers' cognition process is faulty and others are more than happy to share the same views that senior management espouses. Perhaps faulty cognition is a serious threat, but not the only one.

Challenge of Technology

Some (Drejer 2004) argue that it is not the cognitive dissonance, but rather the accelerated pace of technological change that makes it difficult for managers to perceive environmental threats, for they often have no clear understanding of the impact of technological change in the environment. In fact, Drejer (2004) says not only is it difficult to gauge the impact of technological change, but also the pace of change is increasing rapidly, which he characterized as the effects of technological turbulence. This environmental uncertainty might be fatal to an unprepared organization, but it might also uncover business opportunities far beyond those anticipated in the strategic-planning process. He does not label technological change as a negative, for every risk is also an opportunity; instead, he advocates that the accelerated pace of change creates a particular kind of challenge often associated with environmental dynamism (Caldart 2006) or hyperactivity (Mintzberg 1994). In this view, the pace of technological change is so rapid, it makes the competitive environment extremely dynamic or hyperactive; in turn, management is unable to comprehend the ever-changing environment, and thus it fails to produce an effective working strategy.

Challenge of Fragmentation

Closely associated with the notion of ever-changing environment is that of an ever-changing consumer preference. In fact, Fletcher (2006) advocates that societal changes lead to a situation where consumers demand increasingly higher degrees of product customization, driven by one's ambivalent desire to be fashionably perceived, as according to the times, while demanding unique product features. Organizations respond by increasing product features, introducing variations in their models, and crowding the product offering with slight variations on a theme. This increased customization leads to an enlarged customization expectation, which in turn results in increasingly fragmented markets. These fragmented markets, says Fletcher (2006), are not only difficult for management to understand, but also for the market research professionals to study; when even research fails to provide insights, it is unreasonable to expect management to develop actionable plans and strategies capable of coping with demand uncertainty.

Challenge of Demand Uncertainty

A significant risk to any strategic-planning process on its own right, it is not too difficult to understand why the literature devotes so much effort to categorize demand uncertainty. McCarthy and Mentzer (2006) conducted a twenty-year longitudinal study of forecasters and found that the increased market fragmentation created so many possible product variations that it became difficult for anyone to keep track of all forecasting targets. The study identified several potential problems, among them management's tendency to believe in forecasts as factual truths rather than merely abstractions of reality. Kotsialos (2005) added that, along with an unreasonable short-term accuracy expectation, managers further demand increasingly longer-term forecasts, which they also view as factual representations of future demand. Although forecasts are often used to augment the planning process, they carry some inherent variability (Kotsialos 2005), which translates into uncertainty about sales volume and average expected price and, in turn, uncertainty about product margin and profit.

Challenge of Regulation

Adding to the debate, Dreyer (2004) and Roney (2003) contend that managers have to deal with yet another source of risk coming from regulatory bodies. They advocate that one of the most important factors of environmental uncertainty is linked to the actions of governments. In fact, very many industries have been caught unprepared to respond to regulatory pressures even when logic dictated that greater pressures were to be expected. One of the most often cited examples is that of the tobacco industry in the United States. Not newcomers to regulation, its members did not fully anticipate how societal pressures led the government to act swiftly and decisively against tobacco interests in recent years.

Summary, Environmental Risks

The survey of literature can be synthesized into four main sources of environmental risks, or situations where the strategic-planning process is most out of synch with the business environment and therefore unable to create a healthy competitive position for the organization. One source is intimately associated with the organization's leadership characteristics, such as its ability to internalize information (cognitive ability), its leaders' attitudes toward uncertainty, and their abilities to communicate well.

Another source is associated with characteristics of the external market, such as the degree of market fragmentation, the level of industry competitiveness, and other variations in demand fluctuations. A different source of risk is associated with the rapid introduction of technological change, combined with shorter product cycles. Lastly, another source of risk is associated with the regulatory environment, where consumer pressure may lead governments to push for increased regulations.

Certainly any one of these sources, often all of them, are present in a typical corporate environment and any one of them can derail strategic-planning efforts. Business reality is often far from the easily predictable future that managers envision, and in fact the corporate reality is characterized by a dynamic, often hypercompetitive environment (Akhter 2003; Mintzberg 1994).

Planning Purpose

Since the sources of risk are so many and so powerful, it is legitimate to ask why bother with planning. Although the literature provided evidence of the many challenges that corporations face when they perform strategic-planning exercises, it also provided evidence of benefits associated with planning. In fact, Armstrong (1991), and later Shea and Rothstein (2006), concluded that there was a positive correlation between firm performance and strategic planning. Perhaps the best advice the survey of literature provided for this paper was how to modify traditional strategic-planning exercises to improve corporate performance.

Perhaps strategic planning does not result in substantially better performance because management is so comfortable creating strategies within the limits of the official future—what Wack (1985) called planning within the predetermined future—that they often fail to recognize the seriousness of some threats, even though they may be apparent. Similarly, Courtney and Kirkland (1997) considered that planning often fails because management expects to operate in an environment of low uncertainty and thus believes a simple forecast could resolve market uncertainty, though in reality most businesses operate in environments plagued by high uncertainty. Courtney and Kirkland do not recommend traditional strategic-planning exercises, such as forecasting, when the range of potential outcomes is so wide, because forecasting methods are not best designed to manage environmental uncertainty. Stickel (2001) believes that the best way to manage the impact of environmental risks on strategic planning is a technique called scenario planning.

SCENARIO PLANNING

Scenario planning is a somewhat recent addition to strategic planning; in fact, Schoemaker (1995) credits its creation to Herman Kahn's work for the Department of Defense during the early 1960s. Kahn is often associated as the academician who developed nuclear war scenarios for the government, and his contribution led to a policy change during the Cold War years between the Soviet Union and the United States. Through his scenarios, which were sequences of what-if hypotheses, he showed how a nuclear war could not be won in real life—just in the planning room.

Aside from Kahn's strategic work, Schoemaker (1995) credited Wack (1985) as the foremost exponent in commercial applications of scenario planning. Wack (1985) described how he went about changing Shell Oil management's mind-set from a vision of stable, predictable futures into a perception of several potential realities. Burt (2006) notes that Wack's ability to shift management's strategic-planning process, which favored traditional forecasting methods, into a more uncertain view of reality helped Shell Oil's planning team foresee the oil crises in 1972, 1974, and 1980. Grant (2003) also substantiates Wack's claim that scenario planning was the tool Shell Oil's management used to uncover market opportunities, and therefore it is acceptable to say that scenario planning was very effective in bringing about better corporate performance. Grant (2003) richly described the competitive situation in the oil markets much the same way this paper has approached it. In his view, that market was characterized by hypercompetition, fast dynamics, and technological changes in oil extraction, yielding significant competitive advantages for first movers; in other words, the oil exploration market could be described as turbulent. Grant used the industry to explain exactly how the combination of these major sources of risks operated to upset strategic planners' views of a relatively predictable and unchanged competitive market, and he described how those organizations greatly benefited from the adoption of scenario-planning processes.

Wack (1985) advocated that scenario planning's greatest benefit was to change managers' mind-sets; in other words, Wack used scenario planning as a learning tool, and not as a substitute for traditional forecasting exercises. Nevertheless, the literature often associates other benefits with scenario-planning exercises.

Scenario Planning Benefits

Schwartz (1996) advocated that scenario planning was beneficial to organizations because it provided a context for management conversations outside of the predictable future. In fact, Schwartz's (1996) point addresses Mintzberg's (1994) main criticism of the traditional strategic-planning process: that it makes managers conform to a view of the official future. Scenario planning forces managers out of this intellectual prison because it requires planners to look outside the corporate environment to search for other environmental sources of uncertainty or potential disruptions to the planning process. Once the veil of the official future, often a product of traditional forecasting exercises (Wack 1985), is lifted, then managers are free to consider what other alternative realities could materialize in the future. This outward orientation of scenario-planning exercises is exactly the medicine that the literature (Wack 1985) recommended as a vehicle to combat some of the failures of traditional strategic planning, such as a focus on an internally generated view of the world.

Along the same lines, Van der Heijden (1996) advocated that organizations should pursue scenario-planning exercises if they believed the future would be different from the past; this is a direct criticism of traditional forecasting methods, which basically use extrapolations of the past and trend lines to create an image of the future. In Van der Heijden's (1996) view, scenario planning addresses the main weaknesses of strategic planning because it forces managers to look into the sources of demand uncertainty.

Schoemaker (1995) advocated that scenario planning addresses the weakness of traditional strategic-planning processes because one if its steps is to evaluate the level of technology, identify potential evolution paths, and imagine potential technological disruptions. In essence, Schoemaker provides a very good answer to Mintzberg's (1994) criticism that strategic planning often fails to address the environmental risks arising from technological change.

Wack (1985) saw scenario planning as a learning tool, and Ringland (1998) saw it as a perfect way to develop managers' skills. The learning process takes place because, once managers cannot fall back to the comfort of the official future and have to go into uncharted territory, they retrain their cognitive abilities to be more sensitive to potential disturbances in the environment. Once managers are more in tune with their surroundings, and are capable of identifying where potential disruptions could take place, they would be less likely to passively accept the traditional assumption of a predictable future; the resulting dialogue intensity would lead to more in-depth discussions with senior-level managers.

The combination of more freethinkers with improved communications results in a much more robust decision-making process (Wright 2005). In fact, Schwartz (1996) even argued that the increased level of debate led to managers becoming more proficient in processing vast amounts of information, increased their environmental awareness, increased their sensitivity toward social trends that might lead to increased regulatory pressures, and ultimately led to a more participative decision-making process. In his view, any sort of activity that produced such increased awareness should be a high priority in any corporation. Others, however, do not share the same opinion.

Scenario Planning Weaknesses

Although there is evidence (McCarthy and Mentzer, 2006) that strategic-planning processes based on traditional forecasting methods often failed to provide sufficient guidance for corporations trying to overcome environmental uncertainties, it is also true that scenario planning has its critics. Perhaps the most direct criticism of scenarios is that they might not be completely relevant to managers. Mason (2003) advocated that senior managers often cannot dedicate the amount of time necessary to perform a real scenario-planning exercise, and they delegate the function to mid-level managers. In turn, participants are not perfectly clear if their efforts will reach top managers or even if the product of the analysis is in line with top management's expectations. In essence, one of the pitfalls of scenario planning is that it requires a significant level of senior management commitment, and that might not always be possible; thus, planners are not absolutely sure if they are tending to top management dilemmas or not.

Other critics, chiefly Courtney (2003), argued that scenarios failed because managers often did not hold realistic expectations about the output of the process; some managers need to see immediate actionable results, whereas others are content with increasing organizational knowledge. Courtney (2003) proposed two distinct types of scenarios: one that emphasized higher-level objectives and corporate vision and another directed at immediate decisions. Vision-centric scenarios focus on the environment at large, on major trends, and are often associated with longer-horizon objectives that require decisions to take place in some defined range in the future. Decision-centric scenarios focus on a given environmental challenge, often associated with some decision in the very immediate time horizon. The key differentiators are the timing of the strategic-response need and the degree of association with corporate objectives. Since immediacy of need can be a subjective concept, some managers might be frustrated with the time it takes to produce a single actionable strategy.

A different type of criticism relates to timing and cost. Schoemaker (1991) advocated that there are some situations where the timing necessary to engage in full-blown scenario-planning activities, and the costs, cannot be justified. In some instances, there is no business need to engage several managers to address some market discontinuity; in other instances, the hierarchical structure is rigid, and there is no space for mid-level managers to play in vision setting. At other times, a simple forecast combined with some sensitivity analysis can provide sufficient information for managers to arrive at a well-informed decision, and therefore scenarios would just be wasteful. There apparently are pros and cons on the uses of scenarios.

EFFECTIVENESS OF SCENARIO PLANNING

The short answer about the impact of scenarios on corporate performance is that it is relatively limited. Wack (1985) undoubtedly provided the most resounding evidence of performance improvement, as Shell Oil would otherwise not have been able to capitalize on the environment without the benefit of scenarios. Phelps (2001) advocated that there was some weak but positive correlation between scenario usage and improved corporate performance for both information-technology consulting and water-bottling industries. Finally, Ahn (2002) advocated that scenarios were effective instruments in reducing market-driven uncertainties in the telecommunications industry.

The long answer about the impact of scenarios on corporate performance is that it depends on factors related to the internal nature of the firm and characteristics of the external market.

Proponents of the use of the internal nature of the firm as a gauge for better performance advocate that scenarios bring positive results and incremental value added in situations where the traditional strategic-planning process failed to help management pursue pressing corporate objectives. The process fails perhaps because managers are blinded by their own cognitive abilities or are not experienced enough to make out which environmental threats are important (Stahl and Grigsby 1992); or perhaps the communications process is so flawed that planners and managers are uncertain about the significance of their contributions (Pons-Novell 2003). Perhaps the current planning process is very inflexible and therefore creativity is lacking in the organization (Van der Heijden 1996). In such instances where internal characteristics are lacking, scenarios bring benefits because they are often associated as powerful learning tools (De Geus 1988).

Proponents of the use of external characteristics as ways to measure potential scenario benefits advocate that this technique helps the organization overcome serious environmental threats. Drejer (2004) argues that companies operating in markets where the pace of technological change is too fast benefit from scenarios, because the technique allows them some insight into potential disruptions, so that they are not taken completely by surprise. Fletcher (2006) argues that scenarios are beneficial in markets plagued by intense fragmentation, because the technique forces managers to be closer in line with consumer needs; in time, these managers learn to anticipate consumer wants, which translates into a significant competitive advantage. McCarthy and Mentzer (2006) argue that scenarios are beneficial to firms facing increased demand uncertainty, because the technique forces managers to think through uncertainty drivers and how those risk levers impact demand, as opposed to their relying on flawed assumptions of stable futures driven by traditional forecasting methods. Dreyer (2004) and Roney (2003) argue that scenarios improve corporate performance because they help managers anticipate and deal with potential changes in the regulatory environment. Schoemaker (1991) argues that scenarios improve corporate performance for firms operating in situations where their markets experience constant turmoil, or when some discontinuity is expected.

It appears from the survey of the literature that it is possible to identify one example, that of Shell Oil, where scenario planning can be directly traced to improved corporate performance. In some industries, such as bottling, consulting, and telecommunications, there is evidence of improved performance. It is even possible to infer that corporate performance improves in situations where either the internal operations need improvement or the external environment is so complex that it requires a scenario-planning intervention. The literature thus provides evidence that scenario planning yields better corporate performance; the literature also provides mechanisms for one to ascertain the combination of internal characteristics and external environment where scenarios would bring the most benefits.

It is also apparent that the greatest proof of scenario-planning effectiveness in yielding better performance came not from commercial applications, but rather from public policy. It was precisely Kahn's (Phelps 2001) pioneering work in the 1960s that allowed for the superpowers to move away from a collision course into a détente situation, which ensured a peaceful domestic environment for Western European and U.S.-based corporations to grow. The original national security application produced such an outstanding success that society today continues to reap the benefits of scenario planning, and corporations continue to leverage this powerful tool in pursuit of performance excellence.

SCENARIO PLANNING: PROFESSIONAL FUTURIST'S TOOL OF CHOICE

The case for scenario planning as an analytical tool to help professional futurists see the world with new eyes has always been strong, especially in light of strong evidence from recent World Future Society meetings. The *2006 State of the Future* report (Glenn and Gordon 2006) outlined several 2020 global energy scenarios where the technique was used to help one break away from old paradigms and, in a sense, see the world with new eyes. The technique also showed on the *2007 State of the Future report* (Glenn and Gordon 2007), when the objective was to envision the future of education and learning in 2030. Hines (2006) also made the case that futurists need to form alternative realities in order to understand uncertainties and develop strategic options to mitigate risks. And it is the opinion of this researcher that scenario planning presents itself as the most viable analytical instrument in the futurist's toolbox.

More recent literature (Gayoso 2007) demonstrated how futurists can apply scenario planning in order to create a better corporate future. Recently, Holtzman and Leeb (2008) demonstrated how scenario planning can be used as an effective tool to promote greater integration among competitive intelligence, market research, and strategy. In essence, futures and business literature continue to provide strong evidence that scenario planning is not just a tool of yesteryear, but rather an effective way to help futurists break apart from old stereotypes and see the world with new eyes.

CONCLUSION

The paper started with a working definition of strategic planning and how it is used to increase corporate performance. One central criticism of the planning process is that it often results in a situation where managers are overconfident about the future and unable to deal with environmental risks.

The literature demonstrated how nuances in the cognition process, pace of technology change, consumer market fragmentation, demand uncertainty, and lack of regulatory environment awareness combine to result in a resounding defeat of the planning process.

Scenario planning, a construct from the 1960s, first appeared in the public policy arena as a method to analyze potential strategic moves between the two superpowers of the time. Business analysts, namely those at Shell Oil, were quick to realize that this technique had potential in the business world. In fact, the Shell Oil planning team proceeded to develop the first commercial scenario-planning application with great success. This method was credited with helping planners uncover business opportunities and environmental threats previously not detected by traditional strategic-planning methods.

Even though scenario planning, due to its complexity and cost, is not recommended for situations characterized by low uncertainty, it worked well in the turbulent context of a Fortune 500 company. In fact, to this day, the Shell Oil case is regarded in the literature as the most outstanding scenario-planning success story. The literature is full of examples of how business futurists, academics, and other analysts use the tool in order to see the world with new eyes.

It is true that there is evidence scenario planning has been effective in increasing corporate performance in some contexts, but it is also true, perhaps, that the biggest benefit humankind ever realized from this technique came from the original public-policy application. Thanks to this analytical method, U.S. defense strategists arrived at the conclusion that a war against the Soviet Union did not yield any meaningful victory. The decades of peace resulting from this conclusion allowed corporations to exist and prosper in a tense but stable environment. In fact, the Cold War years ended without a direct confrontation between the two superpowers, which would have muted the discussion on corporate performance altogether.

REFERENCES

Ahn, J., and A. Skudlark. 2002. "Managing Risk in a New Telecommunications Service Development Process through a Scenario Planning Approach." *Journal of Information Technology* 17 (3): 103-118.

Akhter, S. 2003. "Strategic Planning, Hypercompetition, and Knowledge Management. *Business Horizons* 1:19-25.

Armstrong, J. 1991. "Strategic Planning Improves Manufacturing Performance." *Long Range Planning* 24 (4): 127-129.

Armstrong, J., and D. Reibstein. 1985. *Strategic Planning in Marketing.* New York: John Wiley & Sons.

Burt, G. 2006. "Pre-determined Elements in the Business Environment: Reflecting on the Legacy of Pierre Wack." *Futures* 38: 830-840.

Caldart, A. 2006. "A Formal Evaluation of the Performance of Different Corporate Styles in Stable and Turbulent Environments." Unpublished working paper. Navarra, Spain: IESE Business School, University of Navarra.

Courtney, H. 2003. "Decision-Driven Scenarios for Assessing Four Levels of Uncertainty." *Strategy and Leadership* 31 (1): 14-22.

Courtney, H., and J. Kirkland. 1997. "Strategy Under Uncertainty." *Harvard Business Review* (November) 67-79.

De Geus, A. 1988. "Planning as Learning." *Harvard Business Review* 66: 70-74.

Drejer, A. 2004. "Strategic Scanning and Learning the New Competitive Landscape—A Learning Approach." *Strategic Decision* 1: 3-32.

Dreyer, B. 2004. "Uncertainty, Flexibility, and Sustained Competitive Advantage." *Journal of Business Research* 57: 484-494.

Drucker, P. 1995. *Managing in a Time of Great Change.* New York: Truman-Talley Books.

Fletcher, W. 2006. "The Splintered Society." *Journal of Market Research* 48 (4).

Gayoso, R. 2007. "Using Future Trends and Vision to Create a Better Corporate Future." In *Hopes and Visions for the 21st Century,* ed. T. Mack, 235-49. Bethesda, MD: World Future Society.

Glenn, J., and T. Gordon. 2006. "2020 Global Energy Scenarios." In *2006 State of the Future,* 53-65. Washington, DC: The American Council for the United Nations University.

Glenn, J., and T. Gordon. 2007. "Future Possibilities for Education and Learning by the Year 2030." In *2007 State of the Future,* 53-56. Washington, DC: World Federation of United Nations Associations.

Grant, R. 2003. "Strategic Planning in a Turbulent Environment: Evidence from Oil Majors." *Strategic Management Journal,* 24: 491-517.

Gupta, M. 2004. "To Better Maps: A TOC Primer for Strategic Planning." *Business Horizons,* 47 (2): 15-26.

Hines, A. 2006. "The State of the Art in Strategic Foresight." In *Creating Global Strategies for Humanity's Future,* ed. T. Mack, 270-81. Bethesda, MD: World Future Society.

Holtzman, J., and S. Leeb. 2008. "Moving from Good to Great: Creating Linkage between CI, MT and Strategy. Workshop presented at the 15th Annual Competitive Intelligence Executive MindXchange. Clearwater, FL: Frost & Sullivan.

Hughes, S. 2005. "Competitive Intelligence as Competitive Advantage." *Journal of Competitive Intelligence and Management,* 3: 3-18.

Kotsialos, A. 2005. "Long Term Sales Forecasting Using Holt-Winters and Neural Network Methods." *Journal of Forecasting,* 24 (5): 353-68.

Mason, D. 2003. "Scenarios and Strategies: Making the Scenario about the Business." *Strategy and Leadership* 31(1): 23-31.

McCarthy, T., and T. Mentzer. 2006. "The Evolution of Sales Forecasting Management: A 20-Year Longitudinal Study of Forecasting Practices." *Journal of Forecasting,* 25 (5): 303-24.

Mintzberg, H. 1994. *The Rise and Fall of Strategic Planning.* New York: Free Press.

Phelps, R. 2001. "Does Scenario Planning Affect Performance? Two Exploratory Studies." *Journal of Business Research* 51(3): 223-32.

Pons-Novell, J. 2003. "Strategic Bias, Herding Behavior and Economic Forecasts." *Journal of Forecasting* 22: 67-77.

Porter, M. 1980. *Competitive Strategy.* New York: Free Press.

Ringland, G. 1998. *Scenario Planning: Managing for the Future.* New York: John Wiley & Sons.

Roney, C. 2003. "Planning for Strategic Contingencies." *Business Horizons* (February) 35-42.

Schoemaker, P. 1991. "When and How to Use Scenario Planning: A Heuristic Approach with Illustration." *Journal of Forecasting,* 10: 549-64.

Schoemaker, P. 1995." Scenario Planning: A Tool for Strategic Thinking." *Sloan Management Review* (April): 25-40.

Schwartz, P. 1996. *The Art of the Long View: Planning for the Future in an Uncertain World.* New York: Doubleday.

Shapiro, C. 1989. "The Theory of Business Strategy." *The RAND Journal of Economics* 20 (1): 125-137.

Shea, R., and H. Rothstein. 2006. "Thirty-Five Years of Strategic Planning and Firm Performance Research." *Academy of Management Proceedings.*

Stahl, M., and D. Grigsby. 1992. *Strategic Management for Decision Making.* New York: PWS Kent Publishing.

Stickel, E. 2001. "Uncertainty Reduction in a Competitive Environment." *Journal of Business Research,* 51: 169-77.

Strandholm, K. 2004. "Examining the Interrelationships among Perceived Environmental Change, Strategic Response, Managerial Characteristics, and Organizational Performance." *Journal of Business Research,* 57: 58-68.

Van der Heijden, K. 1996. *Scenarios: The Art of Strategic Conversation.* New York: John Wiley & Sons.

Wack, P. 1985. "Scenarios: Shooting the Rapids." *Harvard Business Review* (December): 139-50.

Wright, A. 2005. "Using Scenarios to Challenge and Change Management Thinking." *Total Quality Management* 16 (1): 87-103.

Visionary Concept

Combining Scenario Methodology with Concept Development

*Sami Leppimäki, Jukka Laitinen, Tarja Meristö,
and Hanna Tuohimaa*

Change factors like globalization, fast technological development, and energy and environmental issues are challenging the cus-
tomary ways of business thinking. The new challenges are crystallized in the form of new emerging economies of central and eastern
Europe, Asia and South America. When facing a continuously
changing operational environment, industries as a whole and companies individually need to be able to adapt and to renew themselves
accordingly. In a world of fast changes, new innovations have to be
technologically feasible and fulfill market needs, but they also have
to conform to the requirements (e.g., safety and environmental)
placed by society.

The challenges of the future could be incorporated into strate-

Sami Leppimäki is a researcher in economics at the Corporate Foresight
Group CoFi. E-mail sami.leppimaki@abo.fi.

Jukka Laitinen is a researcher at the Corporate Foresight Group CoFi.
E-mail jukka.laitinen@abo.fi.

Tarja Meristö is a research director and corporate futurist at Åbo
Akademi University. E-mail tarja.meristo@abo.fi.

Hanna Tuohimaa is a researcher at the Corporate Foresight Group CoFi.
E-mail hanna.tuohimaa@abo.fi.

gic considerations, the innovation process, R&D planning, and product development of companies by combining scenario thinking into concept development. This new approach enables companies to produce visionary concepts, which illustrate and give form to future challenges and opportunities, enhancing industries' and companies' possibilities to prepare themselves for the future.

In this paper the theoretical background of the method for creating visionary concepts is introduced. In addition, a set of general-level background scenarios of the operational environment are presented. Also, the characteristics of the actual visionary concepts created to fulfill the requirements of the scenarios are discussed. Finally, the tasks and benefits of visionary concept development are discussed.

This article is based on research conducted in the Systematic Product Concept Generation Initiative project. The project was carried out in 2002–2004 jointly by Åbo Akademi University, Helsinki University of Technology, and the University of Arts and Design Helsinki, and funded by the Finnish Funding Agency for Technology and Innovation (TEKES).

TWO WELL-ESTABLISHED METHODS IN THEIR OWN DOMAINS

The scenario method is a widely used tool in the field of futures research. In recent years, the scenario approach has been more and more utilized for foresight purposes in companies. Alternative future scenarios have been used, for example, to support the strategic planning and decision making of a company or to explore the relevant future market developments. In addition, scenario thinking has often been used to map technological development. Traditional scenario planning includes the creation of alternative futures; i.e., identifying driving forces and consequent development paths leading to different future outcomes.

In engineering and design, concept development usually refers to preliminary plans for a new product or service. Usually these plans or drafts are sketched in the front end of the product development process. However, these concept drafts are not necessarily directly used as plans for production as such. Concepts are seen more as a platform for investigating opportunities, and they thus function as decision-making tools. Concepts typically include information about the product's or service's function, specifications, target markets, technology to be used, and business potential. Some of the most promising concepts are maybe later developed further into production ready versions; others are intended to be used otherwise in the company's future product development efforts (Ulrich and Eppinger 2003).

WHY COMBINE SCENARIOS AND CONCEPT DEVELOPMENT

Concept development is a valuable method when companies are developing new offerings to the markets. Concept design is a valuable assistant for ideation and invention. It also makes it possible to thoroughly develop and compare different solutions in parallel before making final decisions about implementation and making heavy investments in production. Concept development activity is a well-established tool, especially in creating new products, but applicable also to new service- or business-model development. Usually concept development is a relatively short time range activity. Its aim is to either plan new products or services to accompany the company's existing ones or to sketch the main features for next-generation offerings. Longer time range concepts are rare, with the exception of some industries such as the car industry. In addition, future-oriented concepts have often been targeted into one base scenario, not linked to the set of alternative scenarios.

Truly wide-scale systematic utilization of futures research in concept-developing activity has been missing. The need for a longer view into the future is the main factor that brings scenarios together with concept-development methods. With scenarios it is possible to bring alternative developments of the future into the concept-development process.

Future product concepts belong to the latter group because they are used to develop company functions on a longer time scale.

METHOD DESCRIPTION

The method for creating visionary future product concepts consists of five main steps. The first step is the identification of change factors, which forms basis for the second step—i.e., scenario building. The third step is the identification of product needs in each scenario. The fourth step is the actual generation of future product concepts based on the market need identified in each scenario. The fifth and last step of the method is the timing of R&D activities and operations. This step also includes other considerations concerning the contribution the visionary concepts might have to the company's business planning or strategy.

1. Identification of Change Factors

The goal of recognizing change factors is to find the central driving forces that steer different future paths. Mapping change factors consists of going through different data sources. It's important to assure diversity of the change factors when collecting data. This can be done by using PESTE-analysis, in which the data is divided into five different categories: political, economic, social, technological, and ecological. Thus, PESTE analysis ensures a holistic approach, with different aspects to be included in the investigation. Recognizing the change factors enables us to find the starting points for different scenarios and then to build the scenarios.

2. Scenario Building

After the change factors are mapped, they can be used to build alternative scenarios. The scenario filter model is a formal method by which one can illustrate the scenarios comprehensively. It is based on the interaction of market, technology, and society in order to create innovations. With this approach, different aspects and different time frames in scenario building can be considered. The market dimension works in the shortest time frame because companies, investors, and consumers are reacting rapidly to market changes. Society's time frame is a bit longer; it's often considered to last for an electoral period. Technology works in the longest time frame; technological policy definitions can be made even for decades ahead. The scenario filter model combines underlying factors in a scenario and points out the driving forces and turning points in a scenario tube. Building scenarios with the filter model ensures that the scenarios describe the world as diversified as possible, since all scenarios can consider market, technology, and society points of views.

The alternative scenarios are constructed by using filters. One scenario consists of several filters (market, technology, and society). The first filter, which is the primary driving force, is called the driver filter. The scenarios are grouped according to different driver filters into scenario tubes. Thus, there can be market-driven, technology-driven, or society-driven scenarios. Within a scenario tube, there can be several scenario paths. Each scenario path can be completed with storylines that describe each scenario more precisely.

3. Identification of Product Needs

When identifying product needs, we first choose the theme we are interested in. Then theme-related future tables are constructed by utilizing information received from the two former phases. In the future table, we list variables related to the theme and then give alternative values to those variables. Thereafter, we inspect future tables in the case of each scenario and choose characteristic values for each variable. By combining all chosen values, we get a logical list of characteristics that can be utilized in further concept creation.

4. Generation of Future Product Concepts

The path from an idea to a product can be described as follows:

idea > concept draft > design concept > future product concept
application > product

The creation of ideas and the generation of future product concepts are useful to carry out within the same group that also builds the scenarios. Thus, the future-related mind-set is already stuck in the group members' minds. Usually, the ideation and the generation of product concepts are carried out in workshops. At first, a certain theme is chosen and discussed in each scenario's case. The ideas rising from discussion are written down, and those with the most potential are chosen for the next phase. Consequently, some of the chosen ideas are developed into concept drafts. The concept drafts with the most potential are evolved to design concepts and further to future product concept applications. When choosing future product concepts, it is important to take into consideration different features related to them, such as technical feasibility and market potential.

5. Timing of R&D: Activities and Operations

The fundamental goal of R&D activities is to ensure the success of the company. So when considering new ideas and concepts, it is essential to analyze their future business potential. For companies, the realization of future business potential is much related to the timing of R&D activities and operations. It's a matter of making correct investment decisions and allocating resources at the correct time. Timing is also related to the company's strategy in different scenarios and its risk profile. If the company chooses aggressive strategy and aims to realize product concepts with high business potential, it has to support this aim by investing in R&D activities early enough (Kokkonen et al. 2005).

ACTOR PERSPECTIVE FOR SCENARIOS AND CONCEPT DEVELOPMENT

External change factors build up the framework for the scenarios and also for the visionary concepts. However, the factors are interrelated with the actors, and that's why pure objective knowledge about factors is not enough. Different actors have different interests, aims, and needs. Furthermore, there may be discrepancies in actors' capability and will for risk taking and the actors' visions of the future. Therefore, it is important to take this actor-view into consideration when creating scenarios for visionary concepts. As mentioned in the method description, it is preferable that the same group of people who are generating future concepts are also building the scenarios for the basis of the concepts phase. When people have been involved in the process from the very beginning, they have time to assimilate the content of the scenarios. This boosts group members to create more and better ideas in the phase of concept generation.

SCENARIOS OF THE OPERATIONAL ENVIRONMENT

The scenarios described in this article are relatively general for concept development, but they could be used as a starting point for more detailed, company-specific scenario building. The general scenario descriptions are as follows (Sääskilahti et al. 2005).

- **Asia-led scenario.** In this society-driven scenario, the focus of global economy, markets, economic growth, and volume shifts to Asia. Although global integration continues, there are new players in the global economy. China is on its way to become the biggest economy in the world. In this scenario, Asian business practices dominate. This scenario highlights the challenges created by new emerging markets with their cultural characteristics and related consumer habits and values.

- **U.S.-led scenario.** In this society-driven scenario, there are growing tensions among economic blocs (European Union, United States, Asia). The United States is still the only superpower, but the focus of the global economy is gradually shifting to Asia. However, traditional Anglo Saxon business practices continue to dominate. This "business as usual" scenario extrapolates present trends into the future and illustrates the world of ever tightening competition and increasing efficiency and profit requirements.

- **EU-led scenario.** In this society-driven scenario, the European Union gains diplomatic dominance in forums like the UN and international organizations. Russia becomes an EU member and provides considerable resources of oil, gas, and raw materials for European industry. In addition, the European Union improves its positions in technology and science. Basically, this scenario describes the new bloom of Europe and its consequences to the global economy.

- **Epidemic and sabotage.** In this society-driven scenario, global development is characterized by discontinuities occurring one after another (for example World War III, Pakistan versus India conflict, terrorism, environmental disasters). Epidemics might also be something totally different from the much-discussed SARS, AIDS, Ebola, or smallpox. The development of this scenario is marked by uncommunicativeness, restrictions, and insecurity. This scenario highlights possible future threats that could jeopardize the overall positive development of the global economy.

- **Changing values.** In this market-driven scenario, consumer values change dramatically. The main theme of development is the people's transformation from consumers into citizens and the power shift from multinational corporations to nongovernmental organizations. Consequently, local brands may prevail over global ones. This scenario may lead to a so-called "no logo" development or even to eco-fascism as an extreme form. This scenario illustrates the rise of postmodern antimaterialistic values, which prioritize cultural and environmental issues over economic ones. This kind of development could impugn the whole economic system.

- **Bio boom.** In this technology-driven scenario, revolutionary developments in biotechnology change the world. Biotechnology supplements or even substitutes other technologies. Consequently, several new technologies emerge. In this scenario, biotechnology applications also achieve full consumer approval. This scenario describes a world where a full-scale technological revolution is taking place. It challenges us to think what kind of consequences the biotech revolution would have on society, markets, and other technologies (Kokkonen et al. 2005).

- **South-America scenario.** In this society-driven scenario, South American countries join forces and develop their education system to a model that provides equal opportunities to all children. The political situation in South American countries is relatively stable, and citizens trust the authorities. Due to a better-educated population, South America has more knowledge — and therefore more power — internationally. It will be an active player, developing its portfolio from mining and other primary products into more developed products. Overall, the people will be in better health and have more choices to decide over their lives, and the continent as a whole will be in a more powerful international position (Haanila et al. 2007).

CONSIDERATIONS REGARDING THE CONCEPT-DEVELOPMENT PHASE

One critical issue when entering from the scenarios to the concept-developing phase is the accurate identification of the market needs of each scenario, as this is a precondition for the creation of successful concepts. Without clearly stated market needs, there are no starting points for concept development.

Another important issue is the evaluation of the suitability of the concepts, not only for the scenario for which the concepts were developed, but also for other scenarios. It is possible for some concepts to be relatively generic and therefore viable in several scenarios. However, the existence of several generic concepts indicates that the scenarios are too similar with each other.

DIFFERENT TYPES AND LEVELS OF CONCEPTS

Regarding the time perspective, different levels of concept-developing activity can be identified. The main levels are the vision-

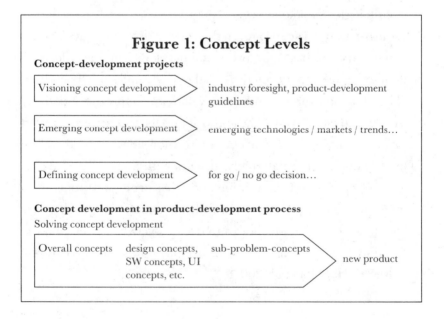

Figure 1: Concept Levels

Concept-development projects

Visioning concept development — industry foresight, product-development guidelines

Emerging concept development — emerging technologies / markets / trends…

Defining concept development — for go / no go decision…

Concept development in product-development process
Solving concept development

Overall concepts — design concepts, SW concepts, UI concepts, etc. — sub-problem-concepts — new product

ing, defining, and solving levels. Visioning concept development has the longest time perspective. Consequently, visionary concepts are utilized in activities such as industry foresight. Defining and solving concept development have shorter time perspectives and are therefore more common tools used for companies' everyday product and service development.

VISIONARY CONCEPTS IN ALTERNATIVE SCENARIOS

There are several ways to present and illustrate the visionary concepts. However, the concept description should include at least the main features of the concept, estimations on its market potential, and its technical feasibility. These are the main dimension of the concept by which a picture of the future operational environment is depicted. Also, illustrations, sketches, animations, or other visual presentation materials are excellent ways to communicate the concepts and related ideas.

The time perspective of visionary concepts is long. Therefore, they are targeted to the markets of the future, realized with the technology of the future, and guided by societal norms and legislation of the future. Consequently, some details and features of the concept are difficult to describe and are more or less a matter of imagination.

Visionary concepts highlight the opportunities and challenges of each scenario. They illustrate what the market needs are and what kind of new market segments could be found in each scenario. Also, technological development and its focus areas are clearly presented in the technical features of the visionary concepts. In addition, the societal characteristics of each scenario are portrayed in the visionary concepts.

THE TASKS OF VISIONARY CONCEPTS

Visionary concepts include multiple tasks. First of all, the process of creating visionary concepts strengthens the linkages between top management and the R&D staff because both groups are forced to better perceive each other's perspectives. It also helps to communicate the company's vision and mission from management to other personnel. In other words, scenarios and concepts can be considered as a means of communication. In addition, one task is to promote the creation of "common corporate awareness" concerning the future challenges, opportunities, and threats that are presented in the form of concepts. Visionary concepts also test the strategy of the company at the product level, bind strategic consideration and R&D tighter together, and impugn the chosen strategy from "down under" (i.e., from product level). Consequently, it enhances the directing and correct timing of the R&D projects in the long time range (e.g., skills, investments, resources, etc.).

THE BENEFITS OF VISIONARY CONCEPTS

The benefits of visionary concepts are closely related to the tasks mentioned above. Several benefits arise from the long time range that is an essential feature in visionary concepts. To begin with, visionary concepts enable systematic examination of alternative future developments because future scenarios are illustrations of the company's operational environment in the future. Visionary concepts also take into account the driving forces (e.g., changes in values, technological breakthroughs, and new markets), as well as market potential, uncertainty, and challenges related to the future in alternative scenarios. Moreover, visionary concepts enable product concept design and R&D for the future, while next-product generation visualizes the future as products corresponding to market needs.

VISIONARY CONCEPTS' LINKAGES TO INNOVATION MANAGEMENT

In many cases, innovations may occur due to serendipities. However, by systematic and high quality innovation management, it is possible to improve and strengthen the innovation process. Thus, for companies that are aiming to renew and/or grow in the future, it is essentially important to handle innovation management properly. Innovation management affects the innovation culture and innovation strategy of the company, as well as the recourses reserved for innovation operations.

Thus, there is a direct link between innovation management and visionary concepts: When the company is investing in innovation culture, it reserves enough resources for the visionary concepts. In that case, visionary concepts are an essential part of a company's innovation strategy. Similarly, visionary concepts have effects on the innovation management: Alternative scenarios, which are created in the visionary concepts procedure, enhance the knowledge concerning the company's futures options. In addition, the company may utilize the flexibility that scenarios create in its strategy work (Meristö et al. 2007; Meristö et al. 2006).

REFERENCES

Haanila, T., et al. 2007. *Research Report: South American Future Scenarios 2022*. Turku: Corporate Foresight Group CoFi/Åbo Akademi University.

Kokkonen, V., M. Kuuva, S. Leppimäki, V. Lähteinen, T. Meristö, S. Piira, and M. Sääskilahti. 2005. *Visioiva tuotekonseptointi (Visionary Concept Development)*. Hollola: Teknologiateollisuus ry, Salpausselän Kirjapaino Oy.

Meristö, T., J. Kettunen, S. Leppimäki, and J. Laitinen. 2007. "Competitive Advantage Through Market-Oriented Innovation Process — Applying the Scenario Approach to Create Radical Innovations." In *Proc. of The XVIII ISPIM Annual Conference Innovation for Growth: The Challenges for East & West*, M. Torkkeli, S. Conn, and I. Bitran, eds. Warsaw, Poland, June 17-20.

Meristö, T., J. Paasi, S. Leppimäki, P. Valkokari, J. Laitinen, P. Maijala, S. Toivonen, T. Luoma, and R. Molarius. 2006. *Managing the Uncertainty of the Future in the Business Driven Innovation Process* (in Finnish with English Summary). Turku: Corporate Foresight Group CoFi/Åbo Akademi University.

Sääskilahti, T., M. Kuuva, and S. Leppimäki. 2005. *A Method for Systematical Future Product Concept Generation*. International Conference on Engineering, ICED 05, Melbourne, August 15 – 18.

Ulrich, K., and S. Eppinger. 2003. *Product Design and Development*. New York: McGraw-Hill/Irwin.

A Scientific Approach to Collaborative Innovation and Strategic Foresight

Connecting the "Dots" Outside the "Box"

Howard S. Rasheed

THE INNOVATION IMPERATIVE

Dynamic changes in the global economy, technological advances, and the evolution in consumer and market demands have put great competitive pressures on businesses and organizations throughout the world. Economic systems are universally experiencing a paradigm shift in which knowledge resources such as information, human capital, and intellectual property are more critical than land, natural resources, and labor. The manipulation of knowledge resources affords new sources of wealth creation based upon innovative intellectual assets, collaborative learning networks, and effective infusion of advanced technology.

Identifying, creating, and distributing knowledge within an organizational knowledge network to stimulate awareness and learn-

Howard S. Rasheed is CEO and founder of Institute for Innovation and an associate professor of management at the University of North Carolina, Wilmington. E-mail hrasheed@ec.rr.com.

ing may be the most important competency of the future for creating and sustaining competitive advantages in the new global economy. The Internet and related computer networking capabilities have been the primary driving force responsible for knowledge workers growing to 80 percent of the North American workforce (Haag et al. 2006).

To create competitive advantage, organizations spend tremendous resources on perfecting systems throughout their value chain process—from production to customer service. In a knowledge-oriented value chain system, innovation and discovery transform insight and technology into novel products, processes, and services that create value for stakeholders and society. Although an innovation value chain should consist of formal processes that harness and exploit creativity, most organizations do not invest in developing a system for new idea creation, innovation, and strategic foresight.

Despite the challenges of systemization, innovation is clearly an important initiative. According to the Boston Consulting Group 2006 Senior Executive Innovation Survey, 72 percent of the U.S. executives surveyed ranked innovation in the top three of strategic priorities, up from 66 percent in 2005. Seventy-two percent of respondents said their companies will increase spending on innovation in 2006. However, nearly half of those surveyed remain unsatisfied with the financial returns on their companies' investments in innovation.

Considering the potential value of the "next big idea," leaving innovation to random and serendipitous flashes of brilliance is not a proactive approach befitting industry leaders. Great organizations find a way to focus the creative energy of their stakeholders through systematic ideation in their efforts to maintain industry leadership in innovation, new product development, breakthrough technology, and world-class core processes. Continually introducing new or improved products, technologies, and programs to their customers is required for growth. Companies and organizations must innovate and change just to survive in competitive, global markets with increasing customer sophistication and demands. In the final analysis, organizations must create value through perpetual innovation or lose their competitive advantage. In the short term, value can be achieved by satisfying a need in a market niche. Because of hyper-competitiveness of a transparent marketplace, any value creation based on a replicable product, service, or business model can quickly lose its rarity and any first-mover competitive advantage.

Sustainable competitive advantage is built on creating value from rare and inimitable resources. The challenge in a global economy is to keep those resources rare and inimitable. Knowledge has been a resource that has emerged in the knowledge-based economy as the key ingredient to that sustainability. The problem is that knowledge is becoming a commodity, with the globalization of quality education and the ubiquitous availability of knowledge.

Driving forces are leveling the playing field, such as the egalitarian impact of the Internet, the ease of movement between countries (particularly for study), and well-educated ex-patriates returning home to an improving quality of life. With the emergence of well-educated workforces and high-quality educational infrastructures in the former communist bloc and very large aggressively developing countries such as China, India, and Brazil into the global economy, having a knowledge-based economy is not a monopoly of the West or the developed Far East.

Considering the rampant U.S. consumer economy based on unrealistic standard-of-living expectations, most informed people realize the United States cannot continue to lose ground in its balance of payments. Additionally, the burden of being the world security force, particularly as the nation responds to real and perceived global threats, has drained domestic resources to adequately care for the basic needs of citizens, such as health care.

Discourse from government and corporate thought leaders usually convey a vague aspiration toward maintaining an advantage in innovation, without substantive solutions. According to the Task Force on the Future of American Innovation, which issued "The Knowledge Economy: Is the United States Losing Its Competitive Edge? Benchmarks of Our Innovation Future" (http://futureofinnovation.org/PDF/Benchmarks.pdf):

> The United States still leads the world in research and discovery, but our advantage is rapidly eroding, and our global competitors may soon overtake us.... It is essential that we act now; otherwise our global leadership will dwindle, and the talent pool required to support our high-tech economy will evaporate.... This is not just a question of economic progress. Not only do our economy and quality of life depend critically on a vibrant research and development (R&D) enterprise, but so too do our national and homeland security.

If we look at the value created by innovative products in America, and remove entertainment and adjust for piracy, we would have a much more realistic, yet pessimistic picture. American scientists are losing ground in terms of the percentage of academic articles being published globally, as well as the number of patents being filed. So if the United States is losing ground in its remaining source of competitive advantage, the nation needs to rethink its very superficial answer of more innovation. What's needed is a system to ensure effective and sustainable efforts toward innovation.

Many thought-leaders question whether a system of innovation is possible. Steve Jobs has been quoted as suggesting the answer is hiring bright people. Jobs's "system" supposedly consists of bright employees pitching their best ideas to Steve for a thumbs-up or down response. This is hardly a replicable system or culture that takes advantage of the creative energy throughout the organization.

Paradoxically, efficient organizations implement business process systems for every aspect of their value chain, input, process, and output. Yet, arguably the most important key to their sustainability — innovation — is left to serendipity and random chances of brilliance.

So how do we provide a systematic approach to innovation? That is the question this paper seeks to address. This is not to assume that there is one answer to this question, but this paper offers an approach that is scientifically supported and replicable in many organizations. We propose a methodology for a *collaborative innovation network,* a cyberteam of self-motivated people with a collective vision, who are enabled by the Web to collaborate in achieving a common goal by systematically stimulating ideation. The result is ideation that exceeds the value creation potential of traditional strategic-planning and knowledge-management paradigms.

COLLABORATIVE INNOVATION

Innovation can be both an art and a science. A purely artful approach to innovation is random and surreptitious. Traditional brainstorming sessions, where bright people gather in a room and throw thoughts and ideas around, have been the business world's traditional approach to collaborative innovation. According to research, there are a number of group and organizational factors that inhibit the efficiency of group creativity.

To overcome group barriers and achieve higher levels of innovation requires training, diverse perspectives, and integration of team members (Paulus and Brown 2003). A system of innovation that encourages creativity must create an environment that stimulates the use, or combination, of unique categories of knowledge (Paulus and Brown 2003). Innovative teams or organizations require loose structures, appropriate distribution of expertise, effective communication, and distribution of creative activities throughout the organization (Sawyer 2007). Artificial boundaries in organizations can inhibit knowledge transfer among groups or units.

A useful scientific approach to brainstorming must allow companies and organizations to harness the creative energies of their human resources by breaking down these artificial boundaries. It must be flexible enough to incorporate the effective elements of traditional brainstorming sessions. Additionally, it must have the structure and discipline to synthesize multidimensional elements in a dynamic environment to achieve true "out of the box" thinking.

A scientific approach should also contain the elasticity to be as simple or as complex as the project requires. And it must be circular enough to allow a systematic and interactive approach to finding the final actionable idea. This means that the "big idea" from one session can become the subject of innovation in another session, further refining the discovery in each collaborative cycle. This scientific approach to brainstorming must provide a reporting mechanism to profile the process followed and justify the final idea/innovation selected for action or development.

As many companies seek to implement globally diverse collaborative innovation networks, they must learn to create a knowledge system that is not constrained by time, distance, organizational boundaries, and culture. This paper suggests the framework for such a knowledge system that can provide a systematic approach to creating an innovation value chain. The benefit of defining and implementing such a system is that executives, leaders, and scientists will have a replicable methodology for harnessing the collective genius of the organization and its stakeholders and for creating a sustainable culture of innovation.

This approach to a collaborative innovation network is theoretically supported by what we refer to as *the science of visionary thinking*. By refining the best thinking models in the literature and promoted in commerce, we propose a scientifically based construct of visionary thinking and its unique value proposition.

The underlying knowledge system for visionary thinking is first presented in the context of a discovery continuum that articulates the range of ideation applications based on its potential for paradigmatic change and its temporal context. The traditional approaches to ideation are discussed in the context of brainstorming and brainwriting techniques. We further address the concept of dynamism in knowledge systems in terms analogous to changing states of energy in quantum physics and cognitive processes associated with insight from new research in neuroscience.

A significant contribution of this model is based on a unique ideation methodology entitled the *Six Steps to Collective Genius,* which we use as a framework for this science-based approach to visionary thinking. The first step is focused attention and visualization of expectations, based on cognitive psychology theory. Second, we define and justify the importance of *dynamic knowledge,* rather than tacit and explicit knowledge, when scanning for information in the macro- and microenvironments of the organization. Third, this dynamic knowledge is analyzed and prioritized using group collaborative evaluation metrics.

In the fourth step, we look at the infinite possibilities of opportunities and challenges discovered from the permutations of dynamic knowledge intersections. This new concept of dynamic knowledge convergence synthesizes theories from extant divergent and convergent thinking models. In the fifth step, new ideas evolve from systematic and focused attention on the most relevant and probable opportunities and challenges discovered in previous steps. The high-valued ideas are identified, refined, and shared, using a collaborative metric. We will then show how envisioning techniques such as impact analysis and scenario development can illuminate the long-term effects of visionary thinking. Finally, after establishing the basis for the "science of visionary thinking" model, we will discuss some applications and present case studies to support our concept.

THE INNOVATION PARADIGM

Innovation can occur at several points along a time and paradigmatic continuum. Emergent ideas fall along a time horizon from the present to the future and in degree of paradigmatic shift from paradigm preserving to paradigm breaking. Organizational-change constructs range from problem solving to strategic visioning, including continuous improvement, reengineering, and strategic planning. Ideas range in innovativeness from incremental improvement to breakthrough inventions and paradigm-shifting concepts. The ideation process can add value to the organization at any point along this continuum, depending on the scope of desired outcomes.

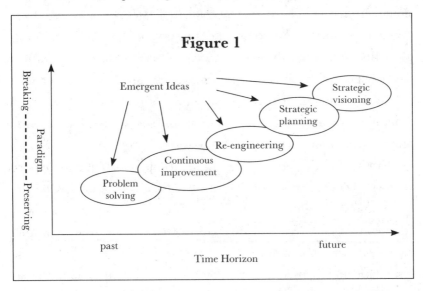

Figure 1

Emergent idea creation and sharing is accomplished through individual activities of creativity called brainwriting and group activities known as brainstorming. Brainstorming is a decision-making technique used to describe the verbal generation of ideas by a group (Brahm et al. 1996). A similar group technique, brainwriting, emphasizes the silent generation of ideas in writing, which are then shared, to invigorate new ideas. According to Osborn, brainstorming is 44 percent more effective than traditional problem-solving methods. Brahm et al. (1996) concluded that brainwriting will produce more ideas than brainstorming, although not necessarily ones that are more unique or of better quality. Paulus and Yang (2000) maintained that the quality of creative and innovative ideas produced through brainwriting depends on the idea exchange process, and are particularly enhanced with the use of computer-based systems.

Opportunity Recognition

As a subset of the emerging knowledge and innovation theme, opportunity recognition is central to the entrepreneur's ability to generate excessive rents necessary to justify the high risk of new venture development. Additionally, opportunity recognition skills allow managers and stakeholders to anticipate technological disruptions and discontinuities in existing markets.

Opportunity recognition is commonly defined as the perception of a potential to create a profitable new venture or to improve the strategic position of an existing business (Tesfaye 2004). Rather than a discrete random event, opportunity recognition is more often an emergent process driven by learning (DeTienne and Lyon 2004).

Knowledge System Dynamism

Historically, knowledge has been defined as tacit knowledge that resides in the minds of individuals and explicit knowledge that is articulated, codified, and stored in organization media. These definitions of knowledge only depict static information in dormant environments. In reality, knowledge systems are a dynamic and complex interaction of informational units within an environmental context. In the context of an industry, this information interacts via semipermeable organizational boundaries.

We define dynamic knowledge as information that is characterized by vigorous change; i.e., it has movement, in a direction, over a period of time. Its momentum is typically caused by a driving and energizing force or forces in an organization's external environment. This changing and chaotic behavior must be viewed from the perspective of the knowledge system's particular environmental frame of reference.

This concept of dynamism is analogous to the changing state of energy in physics. The amount of momentum that an object has depends on two physical qualities: the mass (energy or weight) and the velocity (speed of movement) within a frame of reference. Similarly, dynamic knowledge momentum can be measured in terms importance of the knowledge (i.e., mass) and in terms of relevance to an industry's competitive environment or an organization's strategic intent. Also, the rate of change is measured in terms of its probability of occurrence in the future (i.e., velocity). Dynamic knowledge can be therefore described in terms of rate of change over time (i.e., increase of X percent over Y period of time). The product of these variables (momentum) measures the implications of the dynamic knowledge for the future.

METHODOLOGY: SIX STEPS TO COLLECTIVE GENIUS

As mentioned before, the concept of an organization's value chain is central to its ability to create sustainable competitive advantage. Only recently (Hansen and Burkinsaw 2007) has the concept of value chain been applied to innovation. We extend the literature by presenting a methodology for creating a sustainable innovation value chain using a six-step process—Six Steps to Collective Genius—as described in Figure 2 and subsequently discussed.

Step 1: Focused Visualization

Focused visualization is based on the concept in cognitive psychology called focused attention, which is the process of selectively

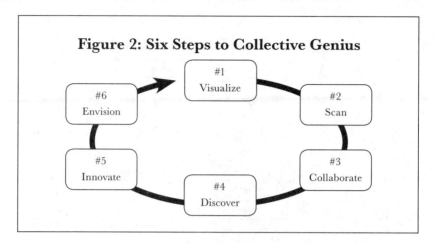

Figure 2: Six Steps to Collective Genius

concentrating on one thing while ignoring other things. Focused attention is the ability to respond discretely to specific visual, auditory, or tactile stimuli. Focused visualization builds task consensus using mind-mapping techniques to visualize the organization's environment, strategic goals, operational issues, and desired outcomes. This graphical presentation creates an infrastructure to focus research and organize database input.

Focused visualization facilitates the creation and communication of knowledge through the use of computer graphic representation techniques. The primary tool is a *mind map,* which is a diagram used to represent words, ideas, and tasks graphically linked to a central key word or idea. It is used to generate, visualize, structure, and classify concepts to facilitate a brainstorming effort for a given task by encouraging consensus on a conceptual framework.

In Figure 3, we present an example of the visualization stage of a project with the Center for Strategic Studies that was performed on behalf of the Brazilian Ministry of Science and Technology.

Step 2: Scan and Research

Scanning is the process of researching and sharing key information of an organization's macro- and industry-level environment.

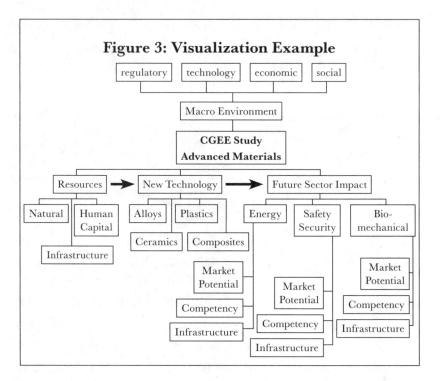

Figure 3: Visualization Example

Macroenvironmental knowledge is external variables typically categorized into four basic societal level factors:

- Economic.
- Political-legal-regulatory.
- Social-cultural-demographic.
- Technological.

Recent literature suggests ecological factors have become popular as a fifth category.

The secondary level of environmental knowledge is the industry level, which focuses on dynamic knowledge related to a particular industrial sector or industry. The tertiary level of the environment relates to changing dynamics in the organization.

A unique contribution of this brainstorming process is the focus of research and environmental scanning efforts on *dynamic knowledge.* This is in contrast with tacit and explicit knowledge, which are static observations of information in a historical context.

Focusing on converting or refining static (tacit and explicit) knowledge into dynamic knowledge emphasizes foresight rather than hindsight. At the macro level, dynamic knowledge can be in the form of prevailing trends, emerging issues, expert predictions, and alternate scenarios.

Trends are sustainable changes in a particular direction for moderate to long durations, usually based on historical data. On a time continuum, historical trends are patterns of phenomena that have occurred in the distant past. *Emerging trends* have occurred in the recent past and are expected to continue over into the near future. *Emerging issues* may not have historical data but have recently materialized as an important subject matter with relevance to the future. *Expert predictions* may not have historical data, but informed opinion predicts a strong possibility of occurrence in the future. *Alternative scenarios* are a description of future conditions based on sound information.

At the micro level, the research focuses on dynamic knowledge that depicts change momentum for the organization, such as changes in market share, primary and secondary levels of the value chain, and changes in human capital, production capacity, and support structures. Again, the emphasis is focusing on information that exhibits change momentum and relevance to the future of the industry or organization, depending on the particular context.

Step 3: Evaluation

The measurement of the dynamism of knowledge researched is a subjective process that relies on the collective wisdom of participants to provide a metric for evaluating momentum. Research focuses on a variety of societal, industrial, and organizational emerging issues, trends, and predictions that are pertinent to the firm's theme or topic. Issues are ranked by probability of occurrence in the future and relevance to industry. This metric allows the emerging issues database to be prioritized based on group average product scores of the evaluation variables. This provides a measurement of change momentum.

Step 4: Discovery—Dynamic Knowledge Convergence

As suggested by our discussion of knowledge dynamism, knowledge does not come in isolated bits of data, but in a holistic system of independent yet interrelated and infinite intersections of information. This characteristic of the system is analogous in quantum physics to a wave that is a disturbance which propagates through space, transferring energy and momentum.

Interference is the addition (superposition) of two or more waves that result in a new wave pattern. As most commonly used, the term interference usually refers to the interaction of waves that are correlated or coherent with each other, either because they come from the same source or because they have the same or nearly the same frequency.

Thomas Young's double-slit experiment showed interference phenomena where two beams of light, which are coherent, interfere to produce a pattern as shown in the following diagram.

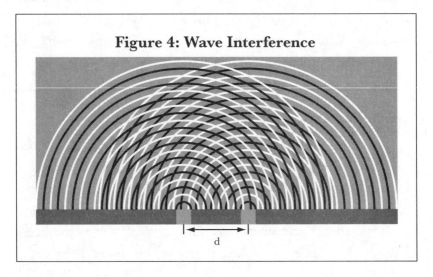

Figure 4: Wave Interference

d

In quantum physics, the outcome of even an ideal measurement of a system is not deterministic, but instead is characterized by a probability distribution. Consequently, the larger the associated standard deviation observed, the more uncertain the outcomes in the system.

In nuclear physics, new matter is produced from the collision of neutrons and protons. This high energy interaction produces quantum levels of energy and gamma rays as a byproduct.

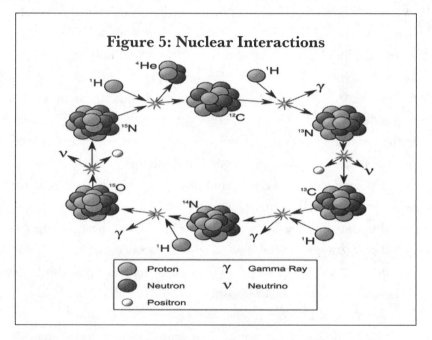

Figure 5: Nuclear Interactions

Similarly, in neuroscience, new research suggests that seldom-used regions of the brain are activated when neurons interact and create new pathways. Similar to quantum physics, in this high-energy process, gamma rays are produced at the moment of insight. To overcome the brain's natural resistance to change, repeated attention must be given to interconnecting new neuron paths. This process enhances mental capabilities, rewires the brain for insight, and encourages out-of-the-box thinking.

As in the case of a particle accelerator in nuclear physics, facilitating the interaction of dynamic knowledge accelerates the process of ideation. Although the subsequent energy caused by interference is characterized by uncertainty and chaos, within a controlled system of knowledge it could account for extraordinary breakthrough innovation. This visionary thinking model proposes a controlled system for accelerating the interaction of dynamic knowledge.

In this system, dynamic knowledge is converged using bisociative or multisociative thinking process to discover the infinite possibilities for opportunities, challenges, and new ideas. This value-added business process uses a proprietary methodology called *Dynamic Knowledge Convergence:* a perpetual process of multi-dimensional, higher-order, and analogical thinking; an iterative process of research, analysis, and out-of-the-box brainwriting and brainstorming techniques. It is based on a synthesis of extant research on divergent and convergent thinking models.

Divergent and *convergent* thinking are the two types of human response to a set problem, as identified by Guilford (1982). Convergent thinking usually generates orthodoxy, whereas divergent thinking always generates variability. Divergent production is the creative generation of multiple answers to a set problem. Divergent thinking is the ability to draw on ideas from across disciplines and fields of inquiry to reach a deeper level of knowledge.

Theoretically, divergent thinking is analogous to the often promoted concept of out-of-the-box thinking. The box is a metaphor for the domain boundaries of conventional knowledge, tacit and explicit. Out-of-the-box thinking can lack reliability when performed outside the boundaries of standard knowledge domains, due to the chaos and uncertainty of unsupported theories. Lateral thinking, an out-of-the-box approach popularized by de Bono (1967), uses a technique called provocative operations to look at a problem from a new perspective. It is used to propose an idea, which may not necessarily be the optimum solution but shifts thinking patterns away from predictable to unexpected thoughts, hopefully leading to ideas not otherwise obvious.

Convergent production uses deductive reasoning to generate one optimum answer to a problem, usually where there is a compelling inference. The use of inferential logic generally leads to a solution based on existing knowledge rather than knowledge creation. Typically, this approach obviously has limited application to innovation, since the convergent thinker focuses on the problem as stated and tries to synthesize information and knowledge to achieve a solution.

This paper suggests Dynamic Knowledge Convergence as a theoretical synthesis of divergent and convergent processes. Instead of a divergent thinking that can be chaotic and undisciplined, this approach uses input from divergent knowledge domains and a systematic and repeatable convergent ideation processes.

Dynamic Knowledge Convergence is partially based on the concept of bisociation, first introduced by Koestler (1964). He suggested that more interesting ideas in the arts come from relating two or more unrelated genres. Generally, bisociation refers to "the pattern of perceiving of a situation or idea in two self-consistent but habitually incompatible frames of reference." Bisociation incorporates the concept of intersecting ideas from two seemingly unrelated things to anticipate the convergence of major ideas.

Theoretically, the more dissimilar the concepts, the more unexpected and impressive the discoveries can be. This visionary thinking approach extends the bisociation concept into a multisociative brainstorming process that can incorporate more than two disparate variables.

Bisociation is a type of analogical and metaphoric thinking process that leads to the acts of great creativity from the more familiar and mundane associative (purely logical) thinking. *Bisociative thinking* is distinct from *associative thinking*. Association refers to previously established connections among ideas, while bisociation involves making entirely new connections among ideas.

The theory of bisociative thinking presumes that when two independent matrices of perception or reasoning interact with each other the result is their fusion in a new intellectual synthesis, which can produce intellectually challenging effects. These matrices articulate any ability, habit, skill, or any pattern of ordered behavior governed by a code of fixed rules. The more independent the matrices, the more unexpected and impressive the achievement and, subsequently, the more novel the discovery.

In contrast to organizational learning, which is the acquisition of a new skill, *bisociation* is the combination, reshuffling, and restructuring of skills. The term *bisociation* is meant to point to the independent, autonomous character of the matrices, which are brought into contact in the creative act, whereas *associative thought* operates among members of a single preexisting matrix.

Similar to the high energy produced by a particle accelerator in physics, focused attention on the infinite possible interactions of dynamic knowledge produces high-energy insights from the intersections of waves of energy in the form of knowledge possibility. If these waves of energy are directed in a systematic rather than random manner, orderly interference will produce more opportunities of insight and foresight.

Based on cognitive psychology theories, this divergent knowledge and convergence process stimulates the fusion of neurons in the brain by systematically focusing on the infinite permutations of dynamic knowledge, thereby increasing the likelihood of insightful discovery.

In this knowledge system, the output from the interaction of these waves of knowledge results in opportunities and challenges. Opportunities are favorable future outcomes for the industry or organization's task environment. Opportunities manifest as positive situations in which gains are likely and over which the organization

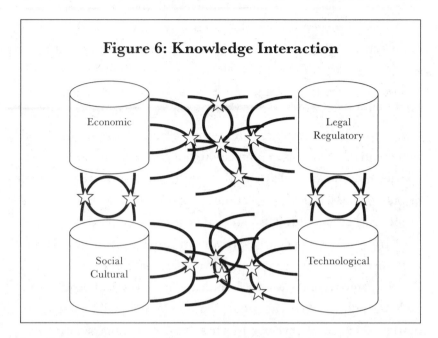

Figure 6: Knowledge Interaction

has limited control. Challenges are unfavorable future outcome, which manifest as negative situations in which losses are likely and over which one has relatively little control.

In general, strategists primarily focus environmental scanning efforts on searching for opportunities, whereas threats are of secondary interest. More specifically, firms engaged in proactive strategy implementation look for opportunities, whereas reactive managers will scan for challenges. Of course, a natural tendency for growth-oriented firms and new ventures is to focus on opportunities in the entrepreneurial planning process.

Step 5: New Idea Generation

As the process of building the previous four steps in this methodology shows, new idea creation is an iterative process of research, analysis, and out-of-the-box thinking. This contrasts with the traditional approach of having the brainstorm participants offer ideas without the benefit of collaborative visualization, research, or discovery as antecedents to ideation. In this systematic and disciplined approach, ideation evolves at each stage to intelligently consider the nearly infinite possibilities of opportunities and challenges to foster creation of new ideas. Furthermore, this systematic approach to creativity builds consensus at each stage because of the democratization of the ideation process. This approach improves the likelihood that creativity will lead to innovation, but only if it can be commercialized or implemented as a product, technology, strategy, program, or public policy. These innovations capitalize on new opportunities or minimize related threats and challenges.

Innovations can generate new markets, applications, and business models and new combinations of transaction architecture. Brainstorming efforts produce radical innovations of new value-added products or services that can be commercialized and new markets that can be developed. Incremental innovations of new processes, organizational structures, supply sources, and exchange mechanisms can be exploited. These new ideas are scored and ranked based on potential value and probability of success in the context of the organization's core competencies. Ideas are prioritized, and appended contributions are shared online using brainstorming and brainwriting techniques.

Step 6: Envisioning: Scenario Development and Impact Analysis

The process of envisioning facilitates the visualization of the future of desired outcomes. Visionaries develop scenarios for each prioritized idea that describes, in narrative format, the future impact of the new idea on the general society and any relevant industries. Participants analyze the potential impact of each idea at the organizational, departmental, or functional levels.

The system provides a virtual Delphi panel to evaluate ideas. The Delphi method is a systematic interactive method for obtaining forecasts from a panel of independent experts. The carefully selected experts are engaged at the end of the brainstorming process to provide an evaluation of the ideas presented, as well as the reasons for their judgments. It is believed that during this process the group will converge toward the best ideas.

INNOVATION VALUE CHAIN

Finally, we summarize this collaborative innovation methodology in the context of business process management, a field of knowledge at the intersection between management and information technology. This typically involves operational business processes rather than top-level strategic decision-making processes. An argument could be made that innovation systems don't exist because of top management's unwillingness to impose discipline on their task environment at the strategic level.

We present the results of this six-step process in the context of business process management model as an *innovation value chain,* consisting of the following components as presented in Figure 7:

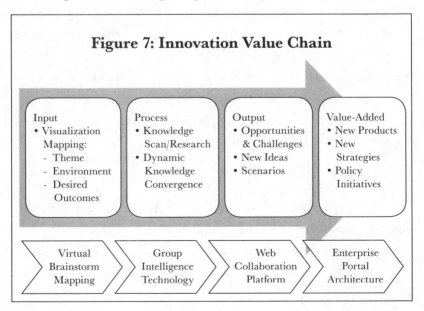

Figure 7: Innovation Value Chain

Input	Process	Output	Value-Added
• Visualization Mapping: - Theme - Environment - Desired Outcomes	• Knowledge Scan/Research • Dynamic Knowledge Convergence	• Opportunities & Challenges • New Ideas • Scenarios	• New Products • New Strategies • Policy Initiatives
Virtual Brainstorm Mapping	Group Intelligence Technology	Web Collaboration Platform	Enterprise Portal Architecture

- **Input.** *Focused visualization:* Focusing attention and building task consensus using mind-mapping techniques to visualize the organization's environment, strategic goals, and operational issues creates a knowledge-management infrastructure (knowledge inventory system) for research input. *Scan:* Researching the organization's macro- and microenvironment, focusing on converting knowledge from static (tacit and explicit) knowledge into dynamic knowledge (emerging issues, prevailing trends, expert predictions).

- **Process.** A proprietary business process using Dynamic Knowledge Convergence, a perpetual process of multidimensional, higher-order, and analogical thinking; an iterative process of divergent knowledge and convergent process, as well as brainwriting and brainstorming techniques, supported by a robust decision support system.

- **Output.** *Opportunity and challenge recognition* identifies favorable and unfavorable future outcomes. *New idea generation* for new products, services, and markets; invention and commercialization of technology; new public policy and program initiatives. *Scenario development* and *impact analysis* help to envision future of desired outcomes.

- **Value Added.** The value added to the organization can come in the form of new products, services, markets, or business models; new strategies; new policy and program initiatives; or incremental innovation or disruptive technology.

CONCLUSION

We have considered the importance of innovation in the global context, particularly from the American frame of reference. It is clear that dominance in the new economy will continue to shift toward the nations and organizations that respond to this innovation imperative.

We have provided a new approach to collaborative innovation by developing a new model for the knowledge system that is holistic and dynamic. Although many give lip service to the need for innovation, commitment to a value-added system has been generally neglected. By focusing attention on dynamic knowledge and the infinite possibilities created from its interactions in a disciplined system, we can learn to leverage the intellectual capital in our organization as well as our stakeholder environment.

Implementing such a collaborative innovation system using a robust information technology can help executives harness the collective genius throughout the organization, capitalizing on the advantages of hierarchical, cultural, and geographic diversity. The benefit of a participatory management style that feeds on consensus building at every level of the organization has been well documented. The results can have long-lasting impact on the organization and its industry, as well as improve the lives of the global society we all live in.

REFERENCES

Brahm, C., and B. Kleiner. 1996. "Advantages and Disadvantages of Group Decision-Making Approaches." *Team Performance Management,* 2 (1): 1-31.

de Bono, Edward. 1967. *The Use of Lateral Thinking.* North Pomfret, VT: Trafalgar Square.

DeTienne, S., and M. Lyon. 2004. "Grounded Theory Development and Empirical Testing of Opportunity Identification Processes." Presented at the 2004 Babson Entrepreneurial Conference.

Guilford, J. P. 1982. "Cognitive Psychology's Ambiguities: Some Suggested Remedies." *Psychological Review,* 89: 48-59.

Haag, S., M. Cummings, D. McCubbrey, A. Pinsonneault, and R. Donovan. 2006. *Management Information Systems For the Information Age* (3rd Canadian Ed.). Whitby, ON, Canada: McGraw-Hill Ryerson.

Hansen, M., and J. Burkinsaw. 2007. "The Innovation Value Chain." *Harvard Business Review* (June).

Koestler, A. 1964. *The Act of Creation.* New York: MacMillan Company.

Paulus, P. B., and V. R. Brown. 2003. "Enhancing Ideational Creativity in Groups: Lessons from Research on Brainstorming." In *Group Creativity: Innovation through Collaboration,* edited by P. B. Paulus and B. A. Nijstad. New York: Oxford University Press.

Paulus, P., and H. Yang. 2000. "Idea Generation in Groups: A Basis for Creativity in Organizations." *Organizational Behavior and Human Decision Processes.* 82 (1): 76.

Sawyer, K. 2007. *Group Genius: The Creative Power of Collaboration.* New York: Basic Books.

Tesfaye, S. 2004. "Entrepreneurial Capacity, Firm Characteristics, and Opportunity Recognition in Small Firms." Presented at the 2004 Babson Entrepreneurial Conference.

Part 3

Problems and Opportunities

The Globalization of Crime

Stephen Aguilar-Millan, Joan E. Foltz, John Jackson, and Amy Oberg

The nature of crime has changed significantly in a single generation. Just twenty years ago, crime was organized in a hierarchy of operations. It was "industrial" in that it contained the division of labor and the specialization of operations. This structure extended internationally, as organized crime mirrored the business world that it aped.

And then something changed. The vertical and horizontal hierarchies dissolved into a large number of loosely connected networks. Each node within a network would be involved in any number of licit and illicit operations. The span of the networked system became global. An event in one place might have a significant impact on the other side of the world. In a word, one thing happened to crime — globalization.

Organized crime is about the illicit flow of goods and services in one direction and the flow of the proceeds of crime in the other. Just as the business world has benefited from globalization, so has

Stephen Aguilar-Millan is the director of research for The European Futures Observatory. E-mail stephena@eufo.org.

Joan E. Foltz is a socio-economic researcher with Alsek Research. E-mail jfoltz@cox.net.

John Jackson is a sergeant with the Houston Police Department. E-mail johna.jackson@cityofhouston.net.

Amy Oberg is a corporate futurist with the Kimberly-Clark Corporation. E-mail amy.j.oberg@kcc.com.

organized crime. The purpose of this paper is to examine some of the aspects of the globalization of crime. We shall start with an overview of the globalization of crime, followed by a consideration of white-collar crime — the point at which the criminal world meets the mainstream world. We shall then examine two case studies — the U.S.–Mexico border and then the modern slave trade — before coming to some tentative conclusions.

THE GLOBALIZATION OF CRIME: AN OVERVIEW

A consideration of the globalization of crime has to start with the fall of the Berlin Wall and the *Washington Consensus* that followed from it. For most of the twentieth century, the two dominant and competing ideologies were those of Soviet communism and Western capitalism. By the 1990s, the internal tensions within Soviet communism were such that, as an ideology for government, it had collapsed. There then followed an international consensus — the *Washington Consensus* — that the way in which international affairs should be organized ought to be along the lines of Western capitalism.

In practice, Western capitalism consisted of a belief in free markets for the allocation of resources, free flows of goods and services across international borders, and the free movement of labor and capital to harness the demand created by the free market. This laid the basis for globalization, which was taken up in the development of international institutions, such as the World Trade Organization, to facilitate free trade across the globe. The *Washington Consensus*, however, was a necessary but not sufficient condition for the process of globalization to take hold.

For globalization to take hold across the world, two further revolutions were needed — the growth of low-cost mass transit facilities and the growth of international telecommunications, which we shall stylize as the development of the Internet. The transportation revolution facilitated the mass movement of goods and people across the globe. Falling freight rates, underpinned by cheap energy sources, led to a significant increase in the volume of world trade and facilitated the development of passenger routes as part of an integrated global network. The Internet revolution has allowed the development of global service infrastructures, such as banking and financial services, and has expanded the managerial span of control such that global operations can now be monitored and controlled remotely from anywhere in the world that has Internet access — which, using satellite communications, is pretty much anywhere in the world.

As these revolutions — the freeing of markets, the transportation revolution, and the Internet revolution — were taking place, the way in which the world works was also changing. An important, but subtle, shift in the *modus operandi* of global business was taking place. As the process of globalization started to take hold, the world shifted from being one of hierarchies to being one of networks. Within each network lay a number of autonomous and semiautonomous nodes, who connect with each other — through the market — when they wish to interact, and who have no connection with each other when the need does not arise. The rise of the networked organization laid the foundation for two features of modern life — outsourcing (where key roles are undertaken outside of the formal organizational structure) and offshoring (where, using the benefits of the transportation revolution and the Internet revolution, the key roles can be undertaken anywhere in the world). Needless to say, such encouragements of licit trade proved to be a boon for illicit trade as well.

In many ways, it is helpful to consider criminal activities as a form of business activity. Admittedly, it is a special form of business activity, but it can be instructive to start from this point. If we think of the flow of illicit goods — be they narcotics, people, counterfeits, human transplant organs — from the commercial perspective, the key to the operation is that of logistics — moving the goods from the point of origin to the point of consumption. The revolution in transportation has aided this considerably by lowering the cost of freight and increasing the number of routes available. The securing of these routes for illicit flows of goods has also led to the growth in the arms trade — especially of personal weapons of a relatively small caliber.

From the perspective of the law enforcement agencies, the problem with policing such activities is one of jurisdiction, which has led to the increase in the amount of cross-border police cooperation. In the interdiction of the flow of illicit goods, the key to success is to have good intelligence, which has led to the greater cooperation between the law enforcement agencies (usually the police and customs agencies) and the military services (particularly military intelligence and the naval arm). In this respect, the law enforcement agencies have globalized in order to respond to global criminal gangs.

This, however, is in the corporeal world. Some illicit activities have moved from the corporeal world to the virtual world. For example, the development of the Internet has allowed much pornographic activity to migrate to the virtual world. Initially, this was restricted to the transmission of images, but the development has taken on new forms with the rise of online worlds such as Second Life.

This has given rise to the problems associated with the confusion of legal jurisdictions. For example, in the case of online gambling, UK firms were engaged in the provision of gambling activities that were legal under EU law, but contrary to U.S. law. Alternatively, Second Life is alleged to host pedophile rings whose activities take protection from the First Amendment in the United States, but whose activities are contrary to EU law. There is a degree of harmonization in legal codes, but this process is far from complete. What is needed is the globalization of legal codes to complete the process.

The flow of illicit goods in both the corporeal and the virtual worlds are crucially underpinned by the provision of illicit services — particularly illicit banking and financial services. The development of the Internet has assisted greatly the use of money laundering by the global criminal networks. This is likely to become even harder to police as new forms of money and financial instruments emerge — can we imagine a Rotterdam cocaine futures market? — and as the existing payment networks extend their coverage across the globe. The nature of banking is also changing. As we see with the development of payments through cell-phone transfers, it will become harder for the monetary authorities to police the monetary system.

This may or may not bode well for the future. From a futures perspective, we can reasonably expect the flow of illicit goods to increase if the process of globalization continues to develop. Some of the flows will be diverted from the corporeal world to the virtual world. New crimes will develop within the virtual world as people exercise their inventiveness. All of this will be underpinned by the further development of illicit services to channel the proceeds of crime to licit investment assets. The response of the law enforcement agencies is likely to be toward greater cooperation among the national agencies and a greater involvement of military assets for law enforcement purposes. However, this is unlikely to be entirely successful unless there is a greater willingness at the political level toward the harmonization of legal codes and the deployment of international resources to where they have the greatest impact. This point is most ably demonstrated in the area of white-collar crime.

THE HIGH STAKES OF WHITE-COLLAR CRIME

The profile of white-collar criminals is changing as the high stakes of the game increases with the possibility of enormous pay outs. Not only organized groups, but individuals lured by the opportunities accessible through technologies that manage the globally integrated financial systems have fueled the $1-trillion illicit trade market. With the rapid advancement of wireless technology that enables financial transactions in every region in the world, those opportunities for white-collar crimes are proliferating as fast as the criminal landscape is changing.

Organized crime has long been involved in money laundering, fraud, and currency counterfeiting for self-benefit. More recent concerns for governmental agencies are how those activities and other white-collar crimes using financial networks are now of a magnitude that threatens national security and global financial markets. White-collar crime also includes intellectual property crime, payment card fraud, computer virus attacks, and cyberterrorism. But corporate fraud has become a priority of the FBI, which pursued cases that involved more than $1 billion in losses to individuals, as well as securities and commodities fraud that amounts to approximately $40 billion worth of corporate losses per year.

The sophistication of the schemes is growing, and the frequency of events is accelerating as the technology eases the transferring of money across international borders and provides access to identity. The amount of corporate and financial records that can be used for manipulation increases the size of the potential opportunity, which also and expands the threat to global proportions. The availability of these systems enabled some of the most significant cases to be carried out by individuals and not criminal organizations. The most recent case of securities fraud caused a loss of $7.21 billion for the French bank Société Générale and is suspected of precipitating a major drop in the global stock markets. The rogue trader, Jérôme Kerviel, allegedly misappropriated computer access codes and falsified documents to accumulate stock positions worth $73.5 billion.

Technology enables these growing trends. But the spread of capitalism that promotes open markets and has a goal to maximize opportunity blurs the line of what is considered criminal behavior or creative money management. Not only the presence of opportunity, but the amount of potential payoff is enticing to individuals who do not fit the typical criminal profile. In addition, creation of regulatory policies to control new open markets adopting capitalism challenges not only foreign economic and political policies, but also social attitudes toward money and finances worldwide.

Establishing a global definition of white-collar crime, particularly with activities involving corruption, corporate malfeasance, and stock manipulation, can be difficult due to cultural differences that may not consider certain sociological behaviors as criminal activity. White-collar crime is not always a clear-cut act of deviance and is often intermingled with legitimate behavior that is spread out over a number of incidents. Also, the attitudes and social environment supported by the goals of capitalism further blurs the categorization of behavior that should be rewarded or penalized, hence fueling its growth with limited barriers.

The interconnectivity of electronic funds transfer systems, which handle more than $6 trillion in wire transfers daily, coupled with the speed of those transactions, adds to the difficulty of tracing money transfers, particularly when funds cross borders into regions where regulations are not enforced. However, the threat from money laundering that funds terrorist activities poses to national securities and balancing of international trade systems is galvanizing more countries' participation in international organizations that are trying to regulate and control fraudulent financial activity. International agencies, such as Interpol, also work closely with technology providers to develop security controls for tracking and preventing financial and high-tech crimes. But even the most advanced security systems and coordinated enforcement cannot alleviate the risks of targeted international financial systems.

Daily international transfers of $2 trillion via computer communications pass through conventional banks, Internet banking, mobile banking, and e-commerce transactions. Many transactions cross borders without going through financial institutions, but through professional services, such as real estate agents and accountants facilitating transactions that exchange cash for purchases to mask ownership of originating funds. Offshore corporations and relatives also offer assistance transferring funds via mobile phones and Internet payment services such as PayPal.

The advanced security technology and anti-money-laundering measures in banks and other financial institutions are triggering cash movements across country borders. This is due to the changes in free movement among countries and trading blocs. Efforts to regulate financial transactions, investments, and reporting requirements for issues of transparency may be thwarted by threats to move commerce to another country that welcomes economic opportunities with fewer restrictions. This stance would be plausible in a competitive environment, supported by capitalistic goals, that prioritizes maximizing profitability. This fosters an environment that begets corruption. The forces that dominate capitalistic environments will also be those that contrarily self-regulate the manifestation.

The control mechanisms of the interconnected systems will be developed as the spread of threat propels cooperation among countries wanting to participate in the global economic markets. The expansion of globally integrated electronic fund transfer platforms that process financial transactions over the Internet and mobile handhelds, which provide the accessibility of criminal activities, also increases the transparency of cross-border e-commerce and investment transactions, thereby improving tracking and security. Rogue traders and terrorist groups may continue to manipulate currencies and stocks and threaten to infiltrate financial systems. But countries, companies, and individuals will have to increasingly weigh the opportunities for fast and easy money versus regulation and security.

As competition and opportunities are sought after by more players in a larger global market, more creative financial instruments and structured deals set up an environment where payoffs and fewest controls impel fraud and corruption. Without guidelines and a definitive identification of what constitutes punishable criminal activity, new business models will be created that stretch the systems and threaten economic stability, such as the subprime lending debacle.

As super-capitalism drives the engine of global economic growth, the push for new financial instruments and schemes will spread into other areas of corporate fraud. Creative methods for utilizing available financial and personal information are changing the landscape of the white-collar crimes, increasingly targeting banking and investment accounts through "computer intrusion" and manipulation of investments, such as stocks and commodities. "Pumping and dumping" stocks that set deceptive market prices, inflating commodities and foreign currencies, and Ponzi schemes that siphon money from investors in one venture to pay another venture are jeopardizing not only personal portfolios, but also the stability of the global investment community. In 2006, the FBI investigated 1,165 cases of securities and commodities fraud that amounted to $1.9 billion in restitutions and $62.7 million in seizures. But even with recognition and crackdown, the cases of fraud and corruption are expanding in scope and amount.

This shift in focus from traceable transactions and communications to unethical business practices that impact the free markets will dominate international regulatory bodies that acknowledge the need to define white-collar crime and establish globally supported tracking systems, and venues for prosecution. The challenge is to regulate criminal activities operating in a virtual space of global industries that are becoming more disconnected from country jurisdictions. This will require not only international cooperation, but also the sharing of information among law enforcement agencies and the ability to seize assets.

Implementing measures that prevent access to financial and communication systems, coupled with strengthened enforcement, will deter money laundering and terrorist activities that are constantly gaining international cooperation. However, corporate and securities fraud will require recognition and consistent definition to combat threats to global financial systems, which will likely not evolve until a significant disruption impacts all members of the global free market. Competition will be a continuing force that determines the direction of corporate crime, such as corruption, and the development of economic and trade regulations. Markets, systems, and money flow will go where the infrastructure provides the best opportunities for profit and market participation. Hence, there is a high probability that the number of elusive white-collar criminals and the frequency of fraud cases that threaten the economic balance will expand along with the breadth and depth of the global expansion of capitalism until all governments understand that weak systems and corruption are not conducive to economic regional development. One case in point is the U.S.–Mexico border.

CASE STUDY: THE U.S.–MEXICO BORDER

The border between the United States and Mexico is 1,954 miles long and the most heavily transited international border in the world. In 2004, there were 242 million crossings from Mexico into the United States. Mexico is the United States' second-largest trading partner and a party to the North American Free Trade Agreement. Yet, mixed among the legal trade and visitations are smuggled goods and the infiltration of illegal migrants. The problem is so substantial that it has inflamed passions and become a focal issue in the American presidential campaign. Crime, lawlessness, and death have come to describe public perceptions of the border. High-profile incidents involving the deaths of persons being smuggled into the United States, the deaths of Americans at the hands of illegal immigrants, infiltrations of armed paramilitary groups, attacks on border patrol agents, and concerns that terrorists could enter the United States have fed this perception. Amidst the turmoil, organized criminal enterprises operate from bases in Mexico and through networks in the United States.

Criminal enterprises are in business to make money. Most often, they do so through the smuggling of contraband. As a consequence, money and contraband are coupled in exchange loops. Along the U.S.–Mexico border, the contraband consists primarily of drugs and people. Criminal organizations are players in a coevolutionary system with government. The organizations present today are the products of a multi-decade evolutionary path that began with the Medellín and Cali cartels of Colombia. In a continuing engagement of action and reaction, governments have pursued strategies that have shaped the contemporary organizations. Because both criminal enterprises and governments have a need for secrecy, details about criminal activity are sketchy, at best. They are episodic, sporadic, and replete with hyperbole and rumor. Nevertheless, an experienced observer can make informed observations about the nature of criminal enterprises on the border.

During the *Miami Vice* days, drug contraband was shipped from Colombia to the United States through the Caribbean islands. As a result of successful enforcement actions by the United States, the drug cartels moved their transshipment avenues west. Successful aerial interdiction by the U.S. Customs Service made direct smuggling flights into the United States untenable. Consequently, Colombian traffickers began to contract with emerging organizations in northern Mexico. Initially, these organizations specialized in border transshipment, taking custody of the client's narcotics in Mexico and delivering them to the client's agents in the United States. In the process, the locus of power shifted from the Colombian cartels to the Mexican cartels. The Mexican cartels also developed sophisticated money-laundering operations to realize their profits. The demise of the Colombian cartels precipitated a transition in the shape of organizations to less vertically integrated models; the new system offered a network of criminal organizations with various specialties.

Today, there are five Mexican cartels: the Gulf, the Sinaloa, the Juarez, the Tijuana, and the Valencia. Three of the five — the Sinaloa, Juarez, and Valencia — cooperate in an alliance called the Federation. The Gulf and Tijuana cartels have also partnered against the Juarez cartel. In the midst, affiliated *coyote* organizations have arisen to smuggle human beings into the United States. They provide services to an international clientele.

Due to its recent violence, special attention should be paid to the Gulf Cartel. In March 2003, the head of the Gulf Cartel, Osiel Cardenas, was arrested by Mexican authorities. As so often happens when a cartel leader is removed from power, lieutenants within the organization violently clashed over succession. Further, the Sinaloa Cartel sought to exploit the opportunity to expand its area of control. During the resulting war between 2003 and 2006, politicians and police officials across the eastern border were targeted in intimidation killings. Reprisals and tactical attacks against rival groups also drove body counts upward. The bloodiest battlefront was in Nuevo Laredo. In 2005 alone, 105 executions occurred in that city. Between 2004 and 2005, 170 people disappeared, including forty-three Americans from Laredo, Texas. Alejandro Dominguez survived just six hours as police chief.

Most of the violence committed by the Gulf Cartel is attributed to the cartel's enforcers, *Los Zetas*. While all cartels employ enforcers, none can match the effectiveness of the Zetas. In 1998, Cardenas recruited the original thirty members of the Zetas, lieutenants and sub-lieutenants of the GAFES (Grupo Aeromovil de

Fuerzas Especiales), a special operations unit of the Mexican army. The deserters subsequently equipped and trained new recruits into a highly capable force estimated at upwards of 2,000 people. The group is alleged to have contracted with street gangs in the United States, particularly Texas. The Zetas have been linked to various killings in the United States, including a Dallas police officer. Reports of incursions by units of the Mexican army into the United States escorting drug shipments likely refer to the activities of the Zetas. Recent reports suggest the Zetas have split with Jorge Eduardo Costilla-Sanchez, Osiel Cardenas's reported successor. Some believe the Zetas are attempting to consolidate control of trafficking activities along the entire border and throughout Mexico.

What can we expect in the future? Much depends on how powerful the Zetas grow, whether the Mexican government can eradicate corruption and reestablish control over the largely lawless regions dominated by the cartels, and U.S. policy along the border. Policy regimes that simply maintain enough pressure to force the cartels to evolve will likely result in more efficient and sophisticated criminal enterprises. Policy regimes that eliminate or substantially constrain the cartels may force human and narcotic trafficking across other borders. So long as demand for illegal drugs and illegal labor remain high, traffickers will adjust and find new ways to move contraband. These flows, however, are occurring on a global scale, as the modern slave trade demonstrates.

CASE STUDY: THE MODERN SLAVE TRADE

If you were to ask someone today to talk about human slavery, they would think that you wanted to talk about history; in fact, you would be talking about current events. Human slavery is alive and prospering hundreds of years after wars were fought to abolish it. It is a growing part of the larger global problem of human trafficking.

Human trafficking involves the involuntary movement of people across and within borders and typically involves coercion, deception, and violence. Behind drugs and guns, human trafficking is the third largest illicit global trade and reportedly the fastest growing. While exact numbers associated with human trafficking are hard to generate, the United Nations estimates that global trafficking involves at least four million people each year and generates estimated annual revenues of $7 billion–$10 billion. By some accounts, however, the UN estimate is quite low. China reportedly generates $1 billion–$3 billion annually via trafficking while Mexico reportedly generates $6 billion–$9 billion each year from human trafficking activities.

Many trafficked victims fall into some form of human slavery — serving as sex, farm, factory, or domestic slaves. In many cases, the victims are young children who have been sold into slavery by family members desperately in need of money. As workers they are levied with a "debt" for the amount paid as well as costs for food, housing, and whatever else the enslaver may wish to include. The result is a debt they can never pay off and a life of bondage, often controlled by violence. Globally, it is estimated that some 27 million people worldwide are being held as slaves. According to the FBI, the global human slave trade generates about $9.5 billion per year. Compared with the International Labour Organization (ILO), the FBI estimate is quite conservative. The ILO estimates revenues to be around $32 billion annually.

The sex trade is one segment of human trafficking — and a segment in which at least 95 percent of the victims are female. Girls are easily deceived into the sex trade, believing they are going to jobs that will lead to a better life for themselves and their families. "Recruiters" who begin the initial deception can earn up to $500 for each girl, quite a significant amount of money in many areas of the world. They target young girls, preferably ages twelve to seventeen; traffickers pay higher prices for virgins and young girls because they have longer "shelf lives." Virgins can bring traffickers up to $500–$1,000, compared with other young girls who are trafficked and sold for as little as $50 each. For pimps, a virgin can bring in up to $750 for her "deflowering." Once "soiled" however, her value plummets; she'll bring in only $2.50 per "John."

Sex slavery, trafficking, and trade can be found all around the world: in China, Cambodia, Thailand, Russia, the Philippines, Colombia, Japan, Italy, the European Union and the United States, to name just a few. Southeast Asia is one of the world's largest exporters of sex slaves and a sex hot spot. Thanks to devastating and widespread poverty, there is an abundant supply of recruits available to meet the demands of wealthy customers in Japan, China, Australia, Europe, and the United States. In 2006, Cambodia was one of the busiest spots in the world for human trafficking, with a majority of victims from Cambodia being delivered into the sex trade in Southeast Asia. An estimated 30,000 of those Cambodians exploited in the sex trade were children.

The former Soviet Union states are hot spots for recruitment and trafficking, thanks to their poverty and social and political disarray. Girls desperate for something better are easy targets, and high corruption facilitates trafficking with little risk. These girls are often routed through Romania, Serbia, Montenegro, or Croatia to San Foca, Italy (one of the most trafficked sex slave routes), and onto final destinations in the European Union, United States, Middle East, or Asia Pacific.

Employing their financial resources to bribe officials, international networks to arrange swift transport, and new technologies to generate false documents, traffickers can complete the process of abduction in one hot spot to delivery in another within a forty-eight-hour to two-week time frame. Globalization has made human trafficking easier. Deregulation, open borders, entwined economies, and the ease of international banking have all facilitated the ability to market and traffic human beings. The complexity of networks, e-cash, and cross-border enforcement issues have also significantly decreased risk associated with this illicit trade.

There is direct correlation between economics, social conditions, and political stability and human trafficking and slavery. In essence, the higher the degree of poverty and the higher the social and political unrest, the higher the incidence of outward human trafficking. These conditions offer little hope for the future and consequently provide a lucrative pool from which to recruit victims who are desperate to improve their state. New wealth around the world is creating increasing demand, particularly for sex slaves. The combination of simultaneous high demand and high supply will keep the sex slave industry growing, at least over the short-term future.

Governments had been trying to curb human trafficking, but much of the policing focus and funding has shifted from trafficking and other such crimes to terrorism, so action has become limited. Human trafficking is also an international issue, complicated by politics, morality, and gender biases that collectively have also limited government activities.

Nongovernmental organizations (NGOs) are not so burdened. They can more easily work across borders and across organizations than can official government agencies. While they have been making progress against human trafficking and slavery, they, too, have been limited. NGOs suffer from lack of funding, and efforts to raise funds have been difficult. The phenomenon of human trafficking and slavery is evidently so abhorrent that it is hard to find those who will acknowledge its existence and fund efforts against it. How to rid the world of human trafficking and slavery is a question that, even after hundreds of years, continues to plague humanity.

CONCLUSION

It is easy to find the conclusions of this paper depressing. One of the flaws in market-based capitalism is that it is open to corrupt influences and encourages undesirable behavior in providing a profit from supplying a demand. As we have seen, as long as there is a demand for narcotics, as long as there is a demand for human servitude, there will be a market in human misery.

Interestingly enough, those who earn their livings in this way also desire to make their money respectable. They, in turn, are victims of the system that they exploit and are exploited by those operating in the financial world, for whom they provide commissions, fees, and retainers. The point at which dirty money is laundered clean is the point at which those who operate in the world of organized crime wish to enter the mainstream world. This is the Achilles' heel of global organized crime.

Given the global nature of the monetary system that is being used, one would expect an international effort to harmonize the regulation of the global monetary system. By and large, this is happening. We have not reached a harmonious point just yet, because a wide agreement will entail the sacrifice of some national interests; these are not readily conceded in international negotiations. However, progress is being made in this area.

When we look to the future, we can see a greater degree of international cooperation in dealing with globalized crime. We can also see the greater use of military assets in assisting the policing efforts, particularly in the roles of interdiction and intelligence gathering. Modern terrorism has blurred the boundary between war and peace, and modern organized crime has blurred the distinction between law enforcement activities and military operations. This is likely to continue into the future.

The process of globalization is not yet complete. As an integrated system of trade and finance, it has become very developed. The problems that we currently face with globalization as a process are because the system of trade and finance has developed faster than the regulatory framework in which that trade occurs. As we move into the future, we can expect to see the regulatory framework catch up with the new reality of trade and finance. We would hope that this is bad news for organized crime.

REFERENCES

Altman, Dennis. 2001. *Global Sex*. Chicago: University of Chicago.

Barchfield, Jenny, and John Leicester, "French Bank Says Trader Hacked Computers." Associated Press, January 27, 2008.

Batstone, David. 2007. *Not for Sale: The Return of the Global Slave Trade—and How We Can Fight It.* San Francisco: HarperOne.

Federal Bureau of Investigation. 2006. *Financial Crimes Report to the Public Fiscal Year 2006.* Washington, DC: Federal Bureau of Investigation.

Glenn, Jerome C., and Theodore J. Gordon. 2007. *2007 State of the Future.* New York: World Federation of United Nations Associations.

International Boundary and Water Commission, http://www.ibwc.state .gov/, as retrieved January 17, 2008.

International Labour Office. 2005. "A Global Alliance Against Forced Labour: Global Report under the Follow-up to the ILO Declaration on Fundamental Principles and Rights at Work." Geneva: International Labour Office.

Naim, Moises. 2005. *Illicit: How Smugglers, Traffickers, and Copycats Are Hijacking the Global Economy.* New York: Doubleday.

United States Department of Transportation. 2006. U.S. International Travel and Transportation Trends: 2006 Update. Washington, DC: United States Department of Transportation.

Winer, Jonathan. 1998. "Combating Money Laundering." Testimony before House Committee on Banking and Financial Services, Washington, DC.

Zhang, Sheldon X. 2007. *Smuggling and Trafficking in Human Beings: All Roads Lead to America.* Westport, CT: Praeger Publishers.

Seeing the Future through The Lens of Telegeography

Looking at New Ways to Address Global Warming, Clean Energy, and the 9/11 Attacks

Joseph N. Pelton and Christine Robinson

Telegeography is a concept first proposed by Greg Staples in his 1993 book. In essence, telegeography suggests we are entering a new era in human history where human enterprise focuses primarily on moving ideas and electronic messages rather than moving people and things. In the new world of telegeography, propinquity, or nearness, hinges on broadband electronic access rather than physical geographical access. In this new way of viewing the world, a global enterprise with offices linked together via fiber-optic cables, satellites, and wireless communications systems can achieve instant interconnectivity across the street or by spanning the oceans. In this new world, "nearness is measured in time and not distance." Cities halfway around the world are right next door in the world of tele-

Joseph N. Pelton is director of the Space and Advanced Communications Research Institute at George Washington University. E-mail joepelton@verizon.net.

Christine Robinson is an Enterprise Architect and Business Continuity and Disaster Recovery principal consultant with Computer Sciences Corporation. E-mail crobinson24@csc.com.

geography. Colleagues in the world of cyberspace are always milliseconds away. However, such details as human sleep cycles do need to be taken into account. North-South telegeography works easier than East-West. In this virtual world of telegeography, housing and offices can be cheaper, energy costs cut sharply, air and water pollution greatly reduced, and security enhanced.

Telework, for a "typical worker" for a single day, reduces gasoline consumption by 1.4 gallons, according to a study for the Consumer Electronics Association in September 2007 (www.CE.org).

In a year, millions of teleworkers (there are now tens of millions worldwide) could reduce carbon dioxide and other noxious gas emissions by many millions of tons. At the same time, they could also conserve energy, unclog highways, and boost productivity. A distributed network of workers is much more secure and is more productive since, for one thing, they are not spending one to three hours a day commuting to and from work. Further, if they choose, they can live in more affordable, enjoyable, or scenic housing. "Lone eagles" who are telecommuters living in places like Colorado, Crete, or the coast of Chile have enjoyed the benefits of telegeography for some time now. If the house and the office of the future were to be built around electronic efficiencies and cyberspace luxuries, they could also be smaller, more convenient, cleaner, and certainly "greener."

Slowly we have begun to realize the "inconvenient truth" that the release of greenhouse gases poses a grave threat to long-term human survival. Yet most measures do not even cope with global patterns of growth. Further, we need to recognize that more than Homo sapiens are at risk. Large mammals of all types, from aardvarks to polar bears to yaks, are now high on the imperiled list. Most politicians and economists have failed to recognize a basic fact: that our economic systems do not include preservation of the species in our pricing mechanisms. Current pricing systems for gasoline, automobiles, and most natural resources continue to render quite good corporate profits. At the same time, these archaic market-pricing systems, over time, can ultimately eliminate some of the basic commodities needed to run with reasonable efficiency a capitalist production and consumption system. We call these "commodities" in our capitalist pricing system *people* or *consumers*. Wipe out people and modern civilization, and you end up with a major recession every time.

An elegant example of a pricing system that failed is on the island of Nauru in the Pacific. The entire country, a source of nitrogen-rich farm fertilizers and phosphates has been literally mined away for years. Over much of the twentieth century the economics seemingly worked, but now the island's population is ill-equipped to cope with a rising sea level, and the survival of all Nauru's people is at risk. In short, if our current market pricing system does not adapt to environmental realities, there is likely to be a problem. Pricing does not include a component that focuses on survival of the species. If it did, gasoline that takes millions of years to produce would likely cost more than wine. If our current pricing and tax systems continue unabated and unreformed, we could, in a century or two, manage to wipe out most human consumers. Such a result could put a rather large dent in longer-term economic growth.

The first level of response to global warming has been modest energy savings through improved transportation systems with greater fuel efficiency. Hybrid cars are certainly not a bad place to start. But in the post-9/11 world we have ended up taking halfway measures in addressing both personal security and global warming. In short, our approach is simply too little and too late. Meanwhile, more and more animals are joining the endangered list, and the ocean levels are rising. Few people seem to have realized that an integrated systems approach is needed to address some of the most demanding of these environmental problems. The lessons that we did not learn from 9/11 about urban development and global conservation are staggering.

THE TELEWORK AND TELEGEOGRAPHY APPROACH TO THE FUTURE

The ironic thing is that there is a single, straightforward response to global warming, soaring energy costs, clogged transportation systems, high-cost housing, and increased terrorism. We have yet to implement on a systematic basis the leveraged advantages of both telework and telegeography. Although some local jurisdictions and some companies have moved in this direction, we are far short of the full potential that could be ours—and in many different ways:

- Eliminating the need for vast new expenditures on transportation systems.
- Reduced oil, gas, and coal prices.
- Significant reductions in air and water pollution and greater protection of the ozone layer, rain forests, polar caps, and oceans.
- Increased environmental protection of endangered species.
- More cost-efficient operation of business, with lowered costs of operation and enhanced recruitment from a much larger pool of employees.
- Faster response times.
- More energy-efficient and lower-cost housing that is "smarter," "greener," and cheaper to own and operate.

These still-overlooked strategies can also markedly help reduce rising energy costs spurred by soaring petroleum prices. This approach to the future might be called a "telegeography strategy" or even more simply a "systems strategy." Such a strategy, emphasizing telework, would powerfully leverage the potential of information and telecommunications systems to reduce the need for polluting energy and transportation systems. At the same time, it can also remove or reduce obvious terrorist targets, redefine urban development in a way that saves time, money, and energy and provide a new level of security to the collective community.

Daniel Walker Howe, in his recent book *What Hath God Wrought: The Transformation of America, 1815-1848,* suggests that after more than a century of opportunity we have still not "seen the future that could be." On the subject of the telegraph and electronic communications, Howe suggests, "In a broader sense ... the spread of the electric telegraph effectively decoupled communications from transportation, sending a message from sending a physical object." The potential of electronic communications to transform society and move electrons and photons rather than people, cars, trains, trucks, and airplanes has yet to be fully understood, appreciated, and reflected in modern economic and pricing systems.

For more than a millennium, we have been inventing ways to move people faster and packing them more densely in urban centers. Likewise, we have increasingly transformed economic systems with fewer and fewer people involved in farming, mining, and manufacturing while more and more people are engaged in some form of service industry. The opportunity to create a greener, smarter, cleaner, and cost-efficient society out of this industrial transformation has, up until now, been largely lost.

Is Taller Better? The Edifice Complex

One of the preoccupations of twenty-first-century society has been the ever-rising "edifice complex" to build the ever-taller tallest skyscraper in the world. The Sears Tower (1,450 feet) in Chicago has been supplanted by higher buildings in Kuala Lumpur, Shanghai, and Taiwan. Taiwan 101, the current record holder, will be topped by the Lotte Super Tower in Seoul (1,820 feet) in 2012. All of these attempts to reach to greater heights will be greatly outdistanced by the incredible new "spike in the sky," the Burj Dubai. This colossus will soar a distance somewhere in excess of 2,500 feet tall, or very close to a half mile into the sky. It will extend to twice the height of the Empire State Building. The taller the building, however, the more inefficient it can become due to the structural requirements and space needs defined by elevators, heating and ventilation systems, etc. Structural engineer Bill Baker of Skidmore, Owings & Merrill has with the Burj Dubai tower ingeniously found a fundamentally new type of design. Baker has hit upon using a concrete-buttressed core that realizes narrower floors, more window space, and much more usable space (Blum 2007, 214-25).

At one level, the greater concentration of people can be energy efficient, and in a mixed-use development where people can live, shop, and work in the same or adjacent buildings, the energy costs, especially for transportation, can be greatly reduced. But the energy, transportation, and environmental cost of building super-tall buildings is enormous, even those that use green systems. Further, these buildings clearly become likely terrorist targets that serve to make them armed and tightly sealed armed fortresses. Misguided architectural advocates from Paolo Solari to Bill Baker to Noriaka Korokawa have, over time, backed superdense phallic palaces that may have had relevance to the nineteenth and twentieth centuries, but are not only archaic but ultimately a dangerous concept for the twenty-first century. The wave of the future should be urban development based on a distributed and electronically interconnected telegeography. In such a world of telegeography, proximity is based not on physical proximity but on broadband telecommunications. Suburban sprawl can be checked by mid-rise buildings.

THE FORCES TOWARD TELEGEOGRAPHY AND TELEWORK

The twenty-first century requires a whole different approach to transportation, urban planning, and business workforce distribution. Telework will ultimately become the predominant workforce paradigm for businesses in the twenty-first century. This is currently a controversial and hotly debated conclusion, but its inevitability will be clearly seen some decades from now as we move to outposts on the Moon and even Mars. In such a world, telegeography will be supplanted by telepresence. Powerful economic and even political forces will drive us toward telework, telegeography, and systematic/ multidisciplinary tele-strategies. These forces include:

1. Energy and transportation costs.
2. Real-estate values.
3. Environmental factors and the need to reduce greenhouse gases and restore the protective ozone layers.
4. Competitive industrial factors and economic pricing systems in a global marketplace.
5. Antiterrorism security measures.
6. Information security.
7. Business and government continuity and disaster recovery.

The United States could provide leadership in the global community by embracing this new approach. In this regard, the United States may be able reclaim some amity among nations by becoming a positive rather than a negative force in the campaign to combat global warming.

Part of the reason we have made so little progress on this front is our educational systems. Economists work with economists, engineers work with engineers, architects work with architects, and sociologists work with sociologists, while businesspeople and capitalists look pretty much at short-term profits. The benefits of telework and telegeography become most clear in a multidisciplinary world where there is an opportunity for architects, engineers, IT and telecom designers, transportation planners, environmental scientists, economists, and sociologists to work together to plan integrated systems and also take a longer-term view of things.

Currently, multidisciplinary consulting and construction companies are designing and building "cities of the future" in places like Malaysia, Jordan, Saudi Arabia, and Dubai. So far, these efforts are largely aimed at adding the latest high-tech fashions to new urban designs. The potential to create environmentally sound, low-energy-consuming, nonpolluting, and affordable cities with efficient transportation and utility systems remains underachieved or totally neglected. This is, in part, because educational disciplines operating in their separate silos do not yet realize that systems planning for the twenty-first century requires colleges and universities that train interdisciplinary teams of students to work together on complex projects. Efforts such as the International Space University, which includes students from more than a dozen different disciplines who work together on complex design projects, show some hope for the future, but we seem to be going far too slowly.

THE ENERGY AND TRANSPORTATION CRUNCH

On a recent trip to Beijing, our group found the pollution was so bad that we did not see the sun from our hotel or almost a week until rain cleared the air. Today, over 1,000 cars a day join the streets of China's capital—some 400,000 each year. The numbers are even larger in Shanghai, and the pollution is even worse. Coal-fired electric power plants and a torrent of additional cars, trucks, and buses added to the streets of China's cities contribute to the pollution.

The experience in India is not much different. The limited amount of petroleum available on Planet Earth suggests that the paradigm of more and more automobiles, trucks, buses, rails, and jets carrying more and more people within and between urban centers can only be short lived. In a service-industry-driven world, the concept of people commuting to and from work each day (with four trips a day in countries with siestas) makes increasingly less sense. The advantages of telework in terms of energy conservation, reduced transportation costs, savings of worker time and energy, etc., are increasingly clear.

Real-Estate Values

Many companies, such as NEC and Hewlett Packard, that now have tens of thousands teleworkers widely distributed in satellite work centers (in the case of NEC) and in home work centers (in the case of Hewlett-Packard) have found many benefits and productivity gains from teleworking. One of the key benefits has been a significant reduction in building costs and the ability to shift business operations from some of the most expensive downtown urban locations to much lower cost suburban or exurban locations. NEC executives have noted that building new headquarter facilities in the heart of the Shinjuku area of Tokyo is simply not economical in a global competitive economy. Real estate valued at a $1,000 to $2,000 a square foot can now be traded via telegeography and telework systems for space costing a fraction of that amount.

Environmental Factors and the Need to Reduce Greenhouse Gases

In Arlington (Virginia) County, where the authors live and serve on its IT Commission, the government has won a series of national awards for its green policies. It has created a network of bike trails. County facilities have a portion of their energy supplied from wind turbine farms. County buildings are equipped with energy-efficient light bulbs, and commercial and residential buildings are actively encouraged to be constructed to new green standards to save energy. County car fleets are being transitioned to hybrid vehicles, and mobile workers are equipped with broadband wireless systems to reduce trips back to county offices. These and other steps are laudable and worthwhile, but even if all these steps are added together, they represent gains that are modest in comparison to converting a significant amount of the county workforce to teleworking operations. If county businesses were to convert to widespread telework operations, the energy savings, reduction in transportation miles traveled, and reduction in greenhouse gases would produce the most dramatic gains of all. Moving ideas and electrons instead of people is the single most significant way to reduce greenhouse gas emissions in cities where services represent nearly 80 percent of all economic activity.

Climate change and global warming affect not just the human race, but also plant and animal species. Images of polar bear cubs falling through the polar ice caps represent frightening and horrific harbingers of the effects of global warming on animal species. With water levels rising around the planet, air temperatures rising, and unusual and sometimes deadly weather patterns, global warming caused by greenhouse emissions put pressures not just on humanity but also on vast numbers of other species. Some species have already disappeared, and more species will disappear with increasing frequency. Global warming affects the entire food chain, not just humans. If we truly are the caretakers of the planet, don't we have a responsibility to effect change for our own as well as the greater good?

Competitive Industrial Factors in a Global Marketplace

The use of broadband systems to move information, news, and telework services is a powerful competitive tool. Enterprise networks can bring Singapore closer to Los Angeles than is Arkadelphia, Arkansas. Telegeography changes proximity. Broadband satellites, fiber-optic networks, and millimeter-wave mobile systems allow global businesses to be flexible, responsive, and highly competitive. Global consulting firms such as Booz Allen Hamilton, Deloitte and Touche, Bearing Point, etc., equip their staff with laptops, BlackBerrys, Wi-Fi connectivity, and satellite telephones that allow them to connective via virtual private networks to global databases. These telecom and information systems for road warriors cost a mere fraction of a high-rise office. Teams can be assembled from around the country and around the world. Broadband electronic connectivity provides proximity without burning mega barrels of fuel and releasing tons of greenhouse gases. The environmental and energy savings are almost a byproduct, since teleworking is key to achieving higher levels of productivity and an edge in a worldwide crucible of competitive companies. Equipping a teleconsultant with $5,000 in telecom and computer equipment versus spending $25,000 a year on a fully appointed office creates a whole different business model for service industries. This is a model that has been followed by companies such as Jet Blue, AT&T, Hewlett-Packard, Intel, and NEC, as well as much smaller service companies.

Telework and telegeography offer the United States significant benefits toward achieving competitiveness in a variety of ways. It increases the nation's ability in a global marketplace to attract and retain new and existing workers. Baby boomers who wish to retire from full-time employment or have more flexibility in their lifestyles often find telework has great appeal. Why live in crowded metropolitan areas when one could live in a small farming community or Vail with skiing at your doorstep, and telecommute or fly in for meetings when needed. On the other end of the spectrum, the newer workers entering the workforce often bring a very different work ethic and are accustomed to working under different conditions than those of previous generations. Both can find significant appeal to the telework model to foster increased competitiveness and benefit the planet's ecology and sustainability.

Antiterrorism Security Measures

Another byproduct of telegeography and telework is that there is no longer a need to create huge corporate headquarters as a fortified camp guarded by phalanx of armed guards and metal detectors. Distributed workforces that work from home, telework centers, or customer sites not only lowers costs but also eliminates the need to create elaborate physical security processes for these buildings (although this doesn't eliminate the need to strengthen information security fortifications through attracting and retaining the valuable resources needed to create them). Gigantic high-rise buildings that become virtual cities are hard to protect from explosives, poisoned air conditioning or plumbing systems, or even natural disasters such as fires and earthquakes. Ironically, internal security systems not only represent huge costs, but ultimately are useless against external attacks such as a jetliner flying into a building.

Assuming that the right security measures are in place, distributed systems, in short, are more cost effective, flexible, energy efficient, environmentally friendly, and physically secure. Instead, however, we are rather perversely and irrationally continuing an "arms race" to build higher and higher skyscrapers that are more "brown" than "green" and that represent human pride rather a rational response to twenty-first-century human and environmental needs. We are now developing better and better virtual capabilities that allow teleworkers to feel as though they are in the actual central hub of operations.

TELEPOWER FACTS AND INFORMATION SECURITY

The broad argument presented above may seem subjective and perhaps even emotionally argued, but there is hard evidence to back up these assertions. Let's examine the facts.

The United States needs information security specialists who can help protect us from cyberattack and other risks inherent in the cyberworld of today. We live in a world where virtually everything runs on IT, threatened every single moment of every single day and where a hacker can cause a security breach that can propagate around the world in seconds. Systems that maintain the environment in office buildings run on IT, and the bigger the building the greater the potential threat. Even dams and traffic lights depend on IT to run the increasingly complex systems that govern them.

Employers could use the telegeography approach to attract and retain valuable information security workers. Telegeography and telework can help to provide the ever-increasing numbers of information security workers needed to protect us in our increasing complex world. If these systems are properly designed, they can also help provide a greater quality of life and aid in providing access to any piece of information that workers might need to perform their jobs remotely rather than sitting on the highway in traffic. Telework could serve as a valuable enticement to attract information security workers; they would be less physically at risk if their employers would encourage distributed workplaces and not concentrate them and others in huge edifices. Physically handicapped people would only need to move from one room in their house to another.

BUSINESS CONTINUITY AND DISASTER RECOVERY, OR CONTINUITY OF GOVERNMENT

So far in the United States, mainly the financial and the health-care communities have some level of understanding about how important maintaining their mission and mitigating risk is to their mission survival. So far, some do a good job, but most lack the depth of understanding and the skills to address this area sufficiently to provide the degree of protection required. Most seem to think about the obvious disasters, such as 2005 Hurricane Katrina and the 2007 San Diego wildfires. Many don't realize that a power outage could potentially cause equally as much damage to an organization's ability to sustain its mission and recover its systems as a major one caused by a fire or earthquake. Outages cost businesses money and prevent government from serving the public as intended.

This new approach further encourages telework and telegeography to also increase emergency preparedness. Telegeography makes people and organizations safer from many perspectives and offers so many substantial benefits toward reducing climate change and global warming.

THE ENVIRONMENTAL AND "DOLLAR AND SENSE" BENEFITS

A new national study commissioned by the Consumer Electronics Association (CEA) shows that using electronics to telecommute currently saves the equivalent of 9 billion to 14 billion kilowatt-hours of electricity in the United States each year — the same amount of energy used by roughly 1 million U.S. households every year. *(Authors' note:* It should be further noted that the TIAX LLC study took a limited definition of teleworkers. Some other studies that have included workers who telework on one or two days a week and other types of employment have placed the numbers teleworkers and the energy savings more than twice as high.)

The CEA study, conducted by TIAX LLC of Cambridge, Massachusetts, found that just one day of telecommuting saves the equivalent of up to twelve hours of an average household's electricity use, 1.4 gallons of gasoline, and reduces CO_2 emissions by seventeen to twenty-three kilograms per day (TIAX LLC 2007).

According to this same study, if a worker with a forty-four-mile round trip telecommuted five days per week, that worker would save, per year, approximately 320 gallons of gasoline and reduce carbon-dioxide emissions by 4.5 to 6 tons per year, which is comparable to the electricity consumed by an average household in four to six months according to TIAX researchers (TIAX LLC 2007).

IBM has achieved great success with telework and promoting a mobile workforce. It instituted a telecommuting program in 1995 and encourages a mobile workforce to attract, retain, and motivate its workers. This approach has now grown to include about 40 percent of its 128,000 U.S. employees who do not have dedicated company office space, an increase from 30 percent in 2001. Roughly 25 percent work from home, and others are mobile or on customer assignment (Alterio 2007).

The nonprofit Telework Coalition reports that employers achieve an average savings of $3,000 to $10,000 by reducing office space for workers who telecommute (Alterio 2007).

The Dieringer Research Group performed a study in which it found a 65 percent increase in workers telecommuting from home within the last two years (Alterio 2007). Figure 1 shows some of the major multinational corporate users of telework. It also indicates that smaller companies within the Telework Coalition, for instance, are effectively using telework to extend productivity, cut costs, and help create a greener environment.

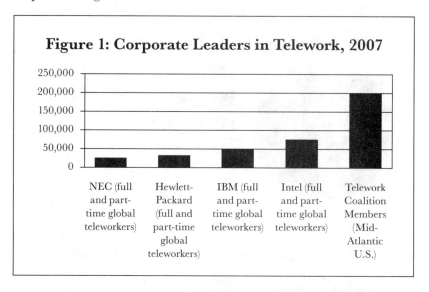

Figure 1: Corporate Leaders in Telework, 2007

U.S. AND OTHER NATIONS CAN PROVIDE LEADERSHIP IN THE GLOBAL COMMUNITY

The United States, as well as other nations, stands to gain significantly by using telework and telegeography to reduce the danger inherent in concentrating large numbers of people and functions. A shift to implement telegeography strategies in a significant way can help to slow climate change and global warming, not to mention the benefits it could bring to workers and employers. We can both become better caretakers of the planet and pave the way for a better way of life for workers and their families, as well as employers.

Today, the United States is one of the worst contributors toward global warming. The surging growth and industrialization of China has now made this rising giant the second-largest contributor. The United States has not won friends for its role in withdrawing from the Kyoto Treaty agreements to limit greenhouse emissions. The rather obstructive stances by U.S. officials at the recent world summit on the environment has only served to diminish U.S. popularity further.

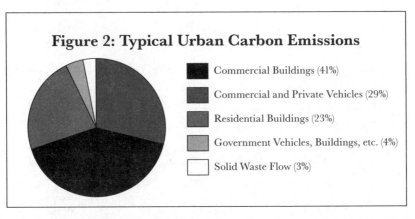

Figure 2: Typical Urban Carbon Emissions

- Commercial Buildings (41%)
- Commercial and Private Vehicles (29%)
- Residential Buildings (23%)
- Government Vehicles, Buildings, etc. (4%)
- Solid Waste Flow (3%)

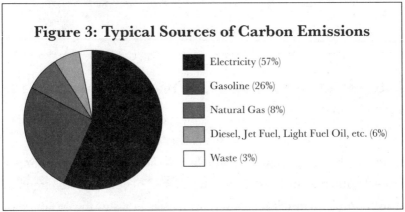

Figure 3: Typical Sources of Carbon Emissions

- Electricity (57%)
- Gasoline (26%)
- Natural Gas (8%)
- Diesel, Jet Fuel, Light Fuel Oil, etc. (6%)
- Waste (3%)

The United States could potentially regain some goodwill if it were to actively advocate new IT approaches to combat global warming and offer such an approach forward on the part of economically advanced countries. The current profile for harmful emissions for economically advanced communities can be seen in Figures 2 and 3. An active shift to telework and telegeography strategies can lead to significant reductions in gasoline and electricity consumption, and this in turn would significantly reduce carbon emissions.

The findings from the CEA study also indicate that telecommuters in the United States reduced gasoline consumption by about 840 million gallons, while curbing CO_2 emissions by nearly 14 million tons. This level of CO_2 reduction is equal to removing 2 million vehicles from the road every year (TIAX LLC 2007).

RECOGNIZING THAT TELEWORK AND TELEGEOGRAPHY IS NOT A PANACEA

At the turn of the twentieth century, the London City Council faced an environmental crisis and the possibility of financial bankruptcy. The problem was the removal of tens of thousands of tons of horse manure from city streets each year. The solution to the environmental crisis that the London City Council embraced was the horseless carriage. The clean automobile that would not drop manure all over the streets was seen as protecting the city from ruin.

The key to the future can sometimes be to recognize the mistakes of the past and implement proactive policies to avoid past errors. The truth is that information and communications technology (ICT) is not entirely clean; it does lead to carbon emissions and a variety of environmental problems. Steps are needed to manage and clean up these technologies, and these actions are needed sooner rather than later.

It is rather surprising to some to learn that ICT, in some economically developed cities at least, contributes up to 2 percent of the carbon emissions. The sources of these carbon emissions are shown in Figure 4. Efforts need to be taken now to make ICT systems cleaner and greener.

Figure 4: ICT Equipment Is Not "Green"

PCs and Monitors: 39% of ICT's carbon contributions

Servers including Cooling: 23%

Fixed-Line Telecommunications: 15%

Mobile Telecoms: 9%

LAN and Office Telecoms: 7%

Printers: 6%

The truth of the matter is that ICT—once seen as the way forward to a greener and cleaner society—has often been rather indifferent to its contributions to carbon emission and e-waste. Figure 5 shows the growing amount of e-waste in the United States and around the world.

Figure 5: Global E-Waste

In 2007:
- 160 million PC disposals (460,000 per day)
- 550 million cell phone disposals
- Only 5 percent to 10 percent of the above will be reused

What's in E-Waste from Technology:
- Plastics (including PVC)
- Chromium
- Lead
- Brominated flame retardants
- Cadmium
- Beryllium
- Mercury

By 2012:
40 million servers and 800 million PCs will be shipped

Clearly these rather startling and even depressing numbers, as seen in Figures 5 and 6, suggest that an e-based business world does not automatically create a green world. Strategies for coping are clearly needed. The approaches outlined in Figure 6 are clearly only a beginning.

Figure 6: Strategies for Diminishing E-Waste

- **Reduce Consumption**
  - Consume fewer servers, printers through server virtualization, intelligent distribution of printers (does everyone need a printer?)
  - Stop over-provisioning; improve capacity planning
  - Turn equipment off, turn power management on (1-watt limits on power management systems)
  - Go from always on to always available
  - Print less, and when you print, duplex
  - Average worker consumes 1,000 pages, or forty pounds of paper a month
  - It's not the printing, it's the environmental cost of creating the paper
  - Benchmark today's power consumption (electrical bill) and set targets to reduce

- **Reuse**
  - Extend the life of assets; it's the creation of the asset, not the use, that constitutes the real environmental cost
  - Use recycled paper

- **Recycle**
  - Ensure and validate the correct disposition of e-waste
  - Buy recyclable products

WHAT NEXT?

If one accepts this vision of what could be, then what? How can we best see the future in terms of a clean, smart, and green world of telegeography? Specific actions should proceed at the local, national, and global levels. These are outlined below:

Local Objectives

- Adopt telework targets for local government to achieve participation by at least 20 percent of the workforce. Even police forces and fire-fighting personnel can achieve these figures because of administrative support requirements.
- Create incentives for private workforce to achieve similar telework targets.
- Adapt offices to telework levels so that occupied space and associated heating, lighting, and air-conditioning is reduced as appropriate.
- Redistribute workforce so that it is less vulnerable to disasters or terrorist attack.
- Create opportunities for people to interact socially (in person or online electronic teams).
- Explore longer-range targets as the above goals are met.

State, Provincial, and National Objectives

- Adopt telework targets for state or national governments to achieve participation by at least 20 percent of the workforce.
- Create national incentives for private-sector workforce.
- Integrate telework objectives into environmental, energy, transportation, land-use legislations with five-, ten-, fifteen-, and twenty-year target goals.
- Establish goals to for cleaner IT and telecom equipment and paperwork reduction.
- Create database to compare state, provincial, and national standards.

International Goals and Objectives

- Create international goals for telework among OECD countries and develop treaty-based goals to provide progress in all the areas being pursued at local, state, and national levels.

- Create a global database reporting on various telegeography programs that allows easy access to comparative information in categories such as demographics, transportation, energy consumption, pollution reduction, housing, and land use.

- Create international prizes for the countries achieving the most progress on objectives and the most inventive use of telegeography in various key areas (equivalent to Nobel Peace Prize in prestige).

Education and Training

- Develop new college, university, and educational programs around the world that create multidisciplinary and systems planning programs to address complex problems such as transportation, energy efficiency, pollution reduction, housing, and land use.

- Create study and research centers to investigate not only telegeography, telework and integrated systems analysis and planning, but also economic and pricing systems designed to reward sustainability and other practices needed to sustain humans, wildlife, rain forests, wetlands, agricultural systems, clean energy, and nonrenewable resources or to create tax or other penalties to discourage practices that threaten human, wildlife, and agricultural ecosystems that sustain life.

- Create new study centers to examine new technologies to sustain human life, create clean energy, clean transportation systems, and sustainable living, recreation, and work units.

The above suggestions are only a few ways to start "seeing the future through new eyes." Others can contribute perhaps much better and clearer ideas about how the new world of telegeography can be created—both sooner and more effectively. Perhaps the World Future Society could create an interactive Web log to allow a discussion of such initiatives. The sky is no longer the limit, and physical transport need not be either. The world of telegeography is nearer than you think, in several senses of the word.

REFERENCES

Alterio, Julie Moran. 2007. *Westchester Journal News,* reprinted in HonoluluAdvertiser.com.

Belcher, Jack. 2007. "Greening IT," presented at Department of Technology, Arlington County (November).

Blum, Andrew. 2007. "The Ultrabuilder." *Wired* (December): 214-25.

Hardy, Michael. 2006. "Telework Mandates Open Doors to New Business: Seizing on Government Requirements Can Bring Success to Federal Contractors." *FCW* (March): http://www.fcw.com/print/12_5/news/92472-1.html.

Howe, Daniel Walker. 2007. *What Hath God Wrought: The Transformation of America, 1815-1848.* New York: Oxford University Press.

Laitner, John A. "Skip," and Karen Ehrhardt-Martinez. 2008. "Information and Communications Technologies: The Power of Productivity," Report No. E081 (February), American Council for an Energy-Efficient Economy.

Pelton, Joseph N. 2004. "The Rise of Telecities: Decentralizing the Global Society." *The Futurist* (January-February): 28-33.

Staple, Gregory. 1993. *TeleGeography.* Washington, D.C.: TeleGeography Inc.

TIAX LLC. 2007. *The Energy and Greenhouse Gas Emissions Impact of Telecommuting and E-Commerce. A Study for the Consumer Electronics Association* (September).

Wilsker, Chuck. The Telework Coalition, http://www.telcoa.org/id310.htm.

Viewing Economics Through the Prism of Sustainable Development and Self-Sufficiency

Bruce E. Tonn

> Our rational minds tell us that a sustainable world has to be
> one in which renewable resources are used no faster than they
> regenerate; in which pollution is emitted no faster than it can
> be recycled or rendered harmless; in which population is at
> least stable, maybe decreasing; in which prices internalize all
> costs; in which there is no hunger or poverty; in which there is
> true enduring democracy. But what else? (Meadows 1996)

SUSTAINABLE DEVELOPMENT

There is no one universally accepted definition of sustainability. Probably the most famous and recognizable definition of sustainability was offered by the Brundtland Commission in 1987,
which defined sustainable development as: "Development that
would meet the needs of the present without compromising the ability of future generations to meet their own needs" (WCED 1987).
Most definitions suggest that sustainability involves balancing envi-

Bruce E. Tonn is a full professor in the Department of Political Science,
University of Tennessee, Knoxville, and a consulting editor for the journal
Futures. E-mail btonn@utk.edu.

ronmental, social, and economic factors. Judicious use of resources and reduction of waste are other important factors. These are the central themes of Herman Daly's three principles of sustainability:

1. Nonrenewable resources should not be depleted at rates higher than the development rate of renewable resources.
2. Renewable resources should not be exploited at a rate higher than their regeneration level.
3. The absorption and regeneration capacity of the natural environment should not be exceeded (Daly 1990).

The Next Step's four principles of sustainability also combine the materials and social equity viewpoints:

1. Substances extracted from the lithosphere must not systematically accumulate in the ecosphere (this principle mainly refers to toxic substances that damage living cells).
2. Society-produced substances must not systematically accumulate in the ecosphere (this principle refers to materials that cannot be recycled and do not quickly and/or safely decompose when placed in waste disposal sites).
3. The physical conditions for production and diversity within the ecosphere must not be systematically deteriorated.
4. The use of resources must be effective and just with respect to meeting human needs (Holmberg et al. 1996).

The Second World Conservation Strategy of the International Union for Conservation of Nature and Natural Resources, the United Nations Environment Program, and the World Wildlife Fund state that society is ecologically sustainable when it:

1. Conserves ecological life-support systems and biodiversity.
2. Ensures that uses of renewable resources are sustainable and minimizes the depletion of nonrenewable resources.
3. Keeps within the carrying capacity of supporting ecosystems (IUCN 1991).

Other definitions of sustainability more explicitly express the integration of environmental, economic, and equity issues. For example, Maureen Hart views the economy as existing within the larger sphere of society, and society as existing within the larger sphere of the environment. In this view, "sustainability requires managing all households—individual, community, national and global—in ways that ensure that our economy and society can continue to exist without destroying the natural environment on which we all depend" (Hart 1999).

Sustainability is often viewed in terms of self-sufficiency. Self-sufficiency can be viewed at a world scale. The Ecological Footprint methodology developed by Wackernagel and Rees (1996) translates economic consumption of all sorts into demand for land. If demand for land exceeds the land available to support consumption, then an unsustainable situation exists. By their calculations, it would take nearly six Earths to support the current human population if everyone on Earth consumed at the same rate as Americans. Clearly, this is not a self-sufficient condition.

Lastly, sustainability can also be viewed through the lens of long-term survival. To be sure, the litany of catastrophe-scale problems facing humanity is long and well known. Such risks include nuclear war, catastrophic global warming (Yin et al. 2006), global cooling in the very long term (Cocks 1993), massive volcanic eruptions (Bryson 2003), and collisions with near-Earth objects (Ahrens and Harris 1994; Rabinowitz et al. 2000). We also face myriad other risks that, when aggregated, can equal or possibly even surpass such catastrophic risks. These include terrorism, energy shortages, flu pandemics, HIV/AIDS, air and water pollution, water shortages, soil erosion, species extinction, and fire (Tonn 2006). In general, overutilization of natural resources can lead to collapse (Diamond 2005; Tainter 1998). Many are worried about more exotic risks such as those related to out-of-control nanotechnologies (Joy 2000), the emergence of super computer intelligences (Vinge 1993), and the creation of Earth-destroying tears in the fabric of space-time within new high-energy physics devices (Rees 2003). Lastly, some argue that the threat of human extinction is real (Leslie 1996) and that we need to invest heavily in survival research (Seidel 2003) and integrated 1,000-year planning (Tonn 2004a).

Three major implications can be distilled from these writings on sustainability that have implications for economics. First, consumption must be reduced. Nonrenewable resources, such as fossil fuels and primary metals like copper and platinum, need to be conserved. Certainly, there are innumerable opportunities to reduce waste and energy use (Hawken et al.1999). However, over the long term, it can be argued that society needs to dematerialize. In other words, the material throughput of developed economies needs to be substantially reduced (Daly 1996).

Second, an attractive strategy to achieve these economic goals is to think small (Schumacher 1973), with a decided emphasis on self-sufficiency. New technologies in energy, nanotech, information, and biology have the potential to promote self-sufficiency at the household and community level while potentially increasing the quality of life. Thus, one can imagine communities that are energy independent, grow substantial portions of their own food, and produce carbon-based nanomaterials (at first crudely and in the future with the help of intelligent fabricators), with which people could make everything from clothes to roofing to utensils to light-emitting diodes. If the system could extract carbon from the air, using solar energy to break down carbon dioxide, then the system could both reduce the amount of greenhouse gases in the atmosphere and produce materials in which the carbon would be permanently sequestered in our built environment. Information technologies for education, medical care, entertainment, and the production of other goods and services would be heavily used. As Nicholas Negroponte (1995) envisions, we need to move bits and not atoms as much as possible.

Presumably, these local systems would also recycle most wastes and conserve land and water.

The lowest-energy-use scenario entails advanced technologies to support local self-sufficiency. Thus, extremely efficient photovoltaics, probably based on advances in nanotechnology, must be developed. Photovoltaic systems can be augmented by micro-hydro turbines, non-platinum based hydrogen fuel cells where hydrogen is produced using algae or other bio-based processes (and not derived from nonrenewable fossil fuels), biomass, wind, geothermal, and even ocean tides and currents. Self-sufficient systems can require their owners to devote substantial amounts of their working time to operate and maintain. Information technology and self-sufficiency could reduce the movement of people and goods to almost preindustrial levels. Clothes, dishes, and other household items can be designed to reduce the energy to clean these items. Water should also be conserved, reused, and husbanded. This new economy would be low throughput and local but very advanced technologically.

Third, a concerted effort is needed to protect life on Earth into the distant future. The major policy implication is that a much higher portion of economic activity must be devoted to sustainability concerns. The research and development requirements needed to deal with the problems listed above are numerous. Significant resources will need to be devoted to carbon management, space defense, and space exploration. Concomitantly, it can be argued that even more resources should be devoted to energy efficiency and renewable and fusion energy, human health research, nanotechnology, and biotechnology. Even more powerful computer systems (e.g., quantum computers) will be needed to support climate modeling, drug and materials research, and science and technology development in general. To support all these activities, science and technology education will need to be improved, not only at our universities and colleges, but through K-12, too.

Economic Implications

There are at least five major economic implications of a world characterized by lower material throughput, increased levels of self-sufficiency, and increases in resources devoted to survival. They are:

1. Gross domestic product will naturally decrease.
2. Money needed in the economy will likely decrease.
3. The share of the government's portion of the economy will likely increase.
4. The role of the nonprofit sector in the economy is likely to increase.
5. The share of the private sector's portion of the economy will likely decrease.

Gross domestic product will decrease for two reasons. First, fewer goods will be purchased as the economy dematerializes and moves toward local self-sufficiency. Second, as self-sufficiency increases, people will need less income to meet their economic needs. They will spend more time working on local self-sufficient production and less time in salaried positions. In this new economy, less money will be exchanged, which will be measured by economists as a decline in gross domestic product.

It would not take a huge decrease in personal consumption to result in a reduction of GDP. For instance, in a sustainable world, it could be assumed that households will purchase less food, fewer clothes and appliances, less energy and water, and less entertainment and personal-care products and services. It can also be assumed that households will purchase fewer personal vehicles and associated goods and services (e.g., gasoline and motor oil, automobile insurance). In 2005, 70 percent of U.S. GDP was attributable to personal consumption. Thus, if there was a 10 percent drop in household consumption, a reasonable estimate for an economy transitioning to sustainability, then GDP would drop by at least 7 percent (not counting second- and third-order impacts on gross domestic private investment).

Of course, a decrease in GNP given this scenario does not mean that the national economy will suffer. We will need to move "beyond growth," in the words of Herman Daly (1996), as the paradigm for economic policies. While classical economic growth, as measured by GNP, may not continue to increase, economic development will increase and benefit from the use of a combination of advanced technologies. Life-spans will continue to increase, environmental quality will improve, people will have access to less- expensive energy resources, and they will have access to more and better information. Fewer pressures at work may have positive impacts on personal, family, and community lives.

Since less money will be exchanged within the economy, less money is needed in the economy. Technically, the money supply as measured by demand deposits, other checkable deposits (the two components of M1), savings deposits, small-denomination time deposits, and retail money funds (the three components of M2) would need to decrease. If the money supply is not reduced, then inflation will ensue because more dollars will be available to purchase less goods and services. On the other hand, currency might have to increase to better support local economies (currency is a component of M0). [Note: On September 30, 2004, in the United States, M0 was measured to be $720 billion, the two components of M1 to be $640 billion, and the three components of M2 to be $4.996 trillion (Wikipedia 2006).]

In the late twentieth century, approximately 6 percent of the U.S. workforce was employed in the general area of science and engineering. Of this number, a relatively few actually worked in areas directly related to sustainability, as defined above. Most either worked on defense-related R&D (50 percent of federally supported R&D) projects or in the private sector on product-related projects (two-thirds of R&D nationally). The effort devoted to energy research, space defense and exploration, climate change, carbon management, and many other areas listed previously probably did not exceed 10 percent of the science and engineering workforce. Thus, one can argue that less than 1 percent of the U.S. workforce was devoted to sustainability concerns.

It is very conceivable that, if the United States were to seriously address sustainability, at least 20 percent of the workforce would be directly engaged in sustainability research, development, and associated programs. Many millions of people would work in the space programs, designing, prototyping, testing, implementing, and administering a plethora of space-based systems, from tens of new telescopes to numerous space stations to thousands of deep-space probes sent to find new homes for Earth-life. Many millions more would be working to protect the Earth's environment, managing the climate, controlling invasive species and devastating pathogens, and building the supporting technologies required for these grand efforts. Currently in the United States, there are approximately 7.3 million people whose occupation is education, training, and library administration. This number would probably need to double to meet the demand for more and higher quality science and technology education, which ought to also include serious class work in ethics, the humanities, and social science. It could be argued that even 30 percent of the workforce would probably be severely insufficient to meet the goals set out above. However, it should be expected that the millions engaged in such activities in the United States would be joined by many millions more from around the world to create research societies (Tonn 2004b).

The nonprofit sector of the U.S. economy has grown tremendously in recent years. The total number of charitable organizations grew from about 1 million in 1996 to almost 1.4 million in 2004, a 29 percent increase. The number of grant-making foundations increased from 56,000 to 99,000 during this time period. In 1995, nonprofit organizations composed 12.4 percent of GDP (Mechstroth and Arnsberger 1998). Among the largest nonprofit organizations in assets in the year 2003 were Harvard College ($63 billion), the Smithsonian Institution ($1.3 billion), the Nature Conservancy ($3.7 billion), Howard Hughes Medical Institute ($13.7 billion), and the Red Cross ($3.3 billion).

Nonprofit organizations provide a very long list of services. These include education and medical care. Many nonprofits focus on environmental, community, and social issues. Also, many are being formed to promote local economic collaboration, usually in the form of cooperatives. The cooperatives distribute food, provide new forms of housing, and help people grow food cooperatively. It can be strongly argued that, in a world moving toward local self-sufficiency, the need for local cooperatives will increase, thereby further increasing the nonprofit sector of the United States.

The discussion above suggests that approximately 30 percent of the U.S. workforce could be directly engaged in publicly supported sustainability programs and expanded educational efforts. Other governmental activities would need to be continued. Currently, all government employment in the United States represents about 16 percent of the workforce. Allowing some overlaps between current government programs and publicly supported sustainability programs, let's assume that 45 percent of the U.S. economy could be engaged in sustainability and other governmental efforts. Let's also assume that in sum sustainability efforts result in reduction in demand for energy and in demand for national and international markets to provide a wide range of materials and products. The movement toward a low-throughput, self-sufficient economy could result in a loss of 35 percent or more of the private-sector jobs. The resulting economy could look like this: 50 percent devoted to sustainability and other government programs, 25 percent to nonmarket self-sustainability and nonprofit activities, and 25 percent to private-sector activities.

Is it possible for a developed country to redeploy 35 percent of its private-sector workforce? A cursory review of the current workforce suggests that there is a tremendous amount of slack in the system. Millions of people in the United States are employed in "nonessential" occupations and industries. For example, in 1999, more than 22 million people reported working in office and administrative support occupations, almost 13 million in sales and related occupations, nearly 10 million in food preparation and services, about 2.5 million in personal care and service occupations, and about 1.5 million in arts, design, entertainment, sports, and media. The eating and drinking places industry employs very close to 8 million people; real estate about 1.5 million; hotels, rooming houses, and other lodging places almost 2 million people; apparel and accessory stores just over 1 million; amusement and recreational services about 1.7 million; motion pictures nearly 600,000; and advertising almost 300,000. The total employment in just these occupations is more than 64 million people, almost 50 percent of the workforce. It is not being argued that each and every person in these occupations and industries has the potential to be rocket scientists. It is being argued that most of the people in most of these jobs could be employed in ways that enhance rather than threaten sustainability.

Thus, the new economy would probably not be dominated by markets and firms. The private sector would produce and sell nanotechnological, biotechnological, and new energy systems and will extract and sell virgin materials needed to manufacture these systems and as inputs to the systems. The private sector would continue to offer services, such as insurance, and probably continue to produce enormous amounts of entertainment products. However, the world described above would see major declines in the centralized manufacture of many items and substantial decreases in the retail sector.

How Would Economic Theory and Policy Respond?

Let's approach this question from the perspective of a central bank, like the U.S. Federal Reserve Bank (The Fed). The Fed has several goals with respect to managing the economy. Controlling inflation is a key goal. Managing economic expansion so as not to stoke inflation is another goal. Thus, the Fed will act at times to cool down a rapidly expanding economy so as to reduce the risks of rampant inflation (which could result, for example, from increasing wages due to labor shortages in an expanding economy). The Fed would also like to see as many people employed as possible, given that there is always a level of natural unemployment.

The Fed manages the economy through management of the money supply, for which it has several tools. For instance, the Fed can buy and sell securities on the open market, which can increase or decrease the money supply, respectively. The Fed can also change how much money banks need to keep in reserve to help cover bad loans, for instance. However, the most important tool currently used by the Fed is to increase or decrease interest rates that banks must pay for short-term loans from Federal Reserve banks. This interest rate is known as the federal funds rate. Increasing this interest rate, which then increases other interest rates in the economy, tends to decrease loan activity, which then decreases the money supply, economic activity and inflation. Decreasing the interest rate helps to increase the money supply and spur economic growth. The Fed tends to raise the federal funds rate as the economy heats up (i.e., as the percentage increase in GDP increases from one year to the next) and as the inflation rate increases. The Fed tends to lower the federal funds rate as the opposite happens.

In the beginning stages of a transition to a sustainable economy characterized by lower throughput and more self-sufficiency, GDP would decrease. Without realizing that this GDP decrease was related to sustainability achievements, the Fed could interpret this decline as a true decline in economic activity. The Fed would then move to increase the money supply to increase economic activity. Through its various policy tools, the Fed's actions would increase the money that banks would have to loan. Given the logic of the current economy, these loans would primarily be to spur increased consumption of goods and services (e.g., through more consumer loans, more loans to companies to expand production, etc.). Thus, this normal response from the Fed would act directly against programs designed to reduce throughput in the economy.

Additionally, the Fed's actions may inadvertently help to increase inflation. This is because less money is actually needed in the system to support fewer purchases of goods and services. Decreasing the federal funds rate, for example, would actually increase the money supply. The result would be more dollars in the economy chasing fewer goods and services. An inflationary economy could turn out to be just unstable enough to stall the transition to a more sustainable economy. As reported in the Wikipedia entry for *money supply*, "In [macroeconomic] theory, money supply would expand when well-being is improving, and contract when well-being is decreasing, giving all parties in the economy a direct interest in improving well-being" (Wikipedia 2006). Unfortunately, in an economy transitioning to sustainability, this assumption is completely wrong. Money supply could be decreasing when well-being is improving, and an increase in money supply could reduce well-being.

TOWARD SUSTAINABLE ECONOMIC THEORY AND POLICY

It needs to be emphasized that even a highly sustainable economy will require some management. Money will still be used. People will still need to be employed, even if the notion of employment were to be expanded to include self-sufficiency. Goods and services will still need to be produced, probably in an environment characterized by scarcity for many years into the future. Thus, it should not be concluded that a sustainable economy does not need macroeconomic theory and policy or even a central banking system. It should be concluded that macroeconomic theory and policy need to change. So, how can macroeconomic theory and policy change to more appropriately service an economy transitioning to sustainability?

Two suggestions are offered to start with. First, a better signal for sustainable economic activity needs to be developed. The GDP signal cannot distinguish true economic decline from an increase in sustainability. A better signal could do so. Numerous proposals have been made to replace GDP with better economic indicators, many of which incorporate sustainability concerns. These include the Index of Sustainable Economic Welfare (ISEW) or Genuine Progress Indicator, Genuine Savings, Sustainable Net Domestic Product (SNDP), Human Development Indicator, and Ecological Footprint, among others (Henderson 1996). A benefit of these indicators is that they highlight how fast we might be drawing down nonrenewable resources, to what degree current economic activities are unsustainable, and changes in other important aspects of life (such as life span, health, etc.).

Unfortunately, these indicators are more useful for government policy makers and the development and implementation of government policies and programs (fiscal policy) than they are to help guide macroeconomic policy as implemented by the Fed (monetary policy). While economic activity is an important foundation for well-being, the Fed's tools to control the money supply and economic growth have no direct relationship to reducing ecological footprints or improving human health. Yet another indicator needs to be developed that is meaningful to macroeconomists and accurately captures movements toward sustainability.

This new indicator needs to encompass nonmarket economic activities. Specifically, the new indicator needs to capture economic activities associated with self-sufficiency. The value for products produced for one's own use can be estimated by the prices for similar products sold in the marketplace (e.g., by using the same methodology used by producers of the Consumer Price Index to determine whether a product priced in one month is similar to a product priced the previous month). Theoretically, it can be assumed for the sake of accounting that a transaction occurred from oneself to oneself (or from a community to that community in the same manner as transactions between firms or governments are accounted for). Let's call this new indicator the Complete Gross Domestic Product (CGDP).

The CGDP can increase when more products are produced self-sufficiently by more people. Also, as self-sufficiency productivity increases (e.g., when a household produces more products for itself using the same amount of human labor), then CGDP would increase as self-transactions increase.

The CGDP concept is not entirely new. Proposals have been made in the past to include women's unpaid work and child-care activities in GDP (Landefeld and McCulla 2000). Traditionally, women spend more time raising children, keeping house, and caring for the elderly than do men. Including this work in GDP is seen as one way for society to signal its value of this work. Placing monetary value on these types of activities would be fairly straightforward; it would just require estimating how much money it would cost to buy child care, housekeeping services, and elder-care services from the private sector. Research by Sousa-Poza et al. (2001) suggests that these types of nonmarket activities already compose a large part of the Swiss economy, from 27 percent to 39 percent with respect to housework and 5 percent to 8 percent with respect to child care.

It is suggested that, to estimate CGDP, these types of activities should be included even though it is unlikely that there will ever be significant productivity increases associated with child care or elder care. Additionally, to be complete, black market activities also need to be measured and included in CGDP. After all, people are still producing goods and services even if the monetary and/or in-kind transactions are off the books.

The second suggestion has to do with the tools available to economists to manage the economy through managing the money supply. The set of tools needs to be expanded. For example, to spur economic activity, the Fed could benefit from using a tool to increase the money supply without necessarily increasing unsustainable consumption. This tool could work through the nonprofit sector instead of through the profit-driven banking sector (Tonn 2000). How could this tool work? One way would be for grant-making foundations to have special accounts at Federal Reserve banks. The size of the accounts would depend upon the size of their endowments. When the Fed wishes to increase economic activity (broadly defined), the foundations' lending accounts could be increased. Similarly, when the Fed wishes to decrease the money supply, the accounts could be decreased and/or the ratio of grants to endowment activity could be temporarily dropped. Other arrangements could be devised to include a broader array of nonprofit organizations.

These two suggestions — for CGDP and to control money supply partly through the nonprofit sector — should help support the transition to a sustainable economy. However, in the longer term, a more fundamental theory of economics is needed. This is because, in the long term, sustainable economies may become much less dependent upon money, national and international markets, and people working for wages. Current economic theory is often characterized as flowing from market capitalism, but it is really money-based. A self-sufficient, sustainable economy will still have capital, and markets will still exist, albeit both much more local and decentralized than now. It just will not be as dependent upon the exchange of large sums of money.

Thus, this theory needs to be based on a more fundamental notion of economic transaction than simply the exchange of money.

The theory needs a broader definition of unemployment and even employment. Is a person who works 20 hours a week to self-produce all needed products, but who does not have a salaried job, unemployed? Probably not. Is a person who works 20 hours a week to self-produce products, but who does not produce enough to feed himself or his family and does not have a salaried job, unemployed? Again, probably not, but there is a problem here. That person needs a salaried job to supplement his self-production and/or needs better self-production technology, better training on existing technology, or more opportunities to obligate this time to more productive self-producing activities.

The concept of obligation is probably a central one for a new, more fundamental economics. In our traditional, money-based economy, people obligate their time and talents to employers. In exchange, employers are obligated to provide employees certain things, including money. Money can be seen as reservoirs of potential, unspecified obligations payable upon presentation of the money. What the Fed is doing when it increases money supply is increasing the supply of unspecified obligations, increasing the potential stuff people will do for other people. As people do more stuff for other people, then this impact has a multiplier effect throughout the economy, thereby increasing the impacts of a small increase in unspecified obligations on overall economic activity. If there is obligational slack in the economy (e.g., unemployment), then the Fed could increase the amount of obligational expectations (e.g., increase the money supply). If people are over-obligated (e.g., if unemployment is very low), then, in order to decrease inflationary pressures, the Fed could reduce the obligational potential of the economy.

In a self-sufficient, sustainable economy, the Fed should be able to manage levels of obligations, not strictly measured by money but as measured by something more fundamental. A measure for economic obligation needs the attention of future research. However obligations are measured, the Fed or some other entity needs to know when people are under-obligated in terms of meeting their basic needs. The Fed needs tools to help increase the obligations made throughout the economy (e.g., by injecting carbon feedstock into the economy instead of money to spur local nano-fabrication). The Fed needs tools to help people meet their needs more effectively and efficiently but in sustainable ways. The Fed needs to be able to understand if and how the economy continues to develop (and not just grow). It would be good if the measurement approach was time invariant. Currently, growth is good. Policy makers expect to report positive percentage growth rates to their constituents, even though over a period of hundreds or even thousands of years these percentage increases mean absolutely nothing except that we have completely lost our minds!

OTHER MAJOR ECONOMIC CONSEQUENCES

It needs to be pointed out that a sustainable economy that is largely self-sufficient will have many other economic policy issues to deal with. For example, several traditional sources of government revenue would most certainly shrink in this new economy. Currently, the flow of money between market actors is taxed in various ways to fund the operation of government. As the exchange of money decreases, so will the receipt of sales and income taxes, at the very least. This is very problematic, since it was suggested above that the share of government in the economy should increase to help satisfy sustainability goals.

One response might be to increase tax rates on the remaining monetary transactions. This seems unreasonable, as the tax rates could be extremely high — so high as to further reduce the market demand for such products. A better approach might be to draw upon the nascent theory of obligations mentioned above. Maybe instead of money people will be expected to meet their obligations to gov-

ernment through their time and in-kind contributions. A self-sufficient person could work part time for the government (for no salary)
to meet her obligations. That person or that person's household or
community could also contribute in-kinds goods and services to help
those who must work more time for the government. Determining
all the different ways that people could meet their obligations to
government requires a very sound theory of obligations as well as
the application of sophisticated computer technology to keep track
of everything.

As people move from a paradigm of forty-hour weeks and salaried employment to permanent part-time employment, nonsalaried
work, and self-sufficiency, the basis for pay-as-you-go the Social Security system begins to breakdown. What is it other than money that
people could contribute to Social Security over their working lives to
help them in retirement? What does "retirement" mean in a world
dominated by nonsalaried work, permanent part-time employment,
and self-sufficiency?

This is a particularly intriguing question. One might be
tempted to argue that, in a self-sufficient world, your family and
community will take care of you in your old age. This solution is
inconsistent with modern society (at least in the United States), which
finds high rates of moving, smaller household sizes, and large increases in the number of single-person households. Family and community ties, even in a utopian sounding self-sufficient society, are
unlikely to increase.

Thus, some innovation is needed. Maybe people can build up
stocks of materials that can be drawn down and/or traded later in life.
Maybe they could save excess amounts of carbon-based nanomaterials, water, and even energy (e.g., chemical batteries or as potential
energy in water towers or as hydrogen). As part of one's obligations to
the government, people would also be obligated to build up their savings in the same way that people are currently obligated to contribute

to their Social Security. Unemployment payments, pensions, health benefits, and disability insurance and benefits are also tied to full-time salaried work and would also need to be rethought.

The last issue to be dealt with here is wealth. Much of people's wealth is in the form of market-based instruments, such as stocks and bonds. In the new economy, the role of traditional firms will decrease and the wealth generated by this part of the private sector will decrease. Many people rely on such wealth to help supplement Social Security and pensions after retirement. If people cannot build wealth as easily in the traditional sense but still have the need to build wealth to ensure their personal economic security, how will wealth be built in the new economy? How should these types of issues be handled in a new economy? Maybe wealth needs to be replaced with personal economic and heath security in the new sustainable economy.

In any case, answering these types of questions will require new economic theories that are more general than are today's economic theories. Government financing cannot be based almost solely on taxing the exchange of money. Societies should not have to rely on the sale and consumption of toilet paper to provide funds for public schools; one is not necessarily related to the other. In this new sustainable world, this link between economic consumption and provision of essential services can be broken.

CONCLUSIONS

In summary, to attain sustainability requires a sea change in economic thought and substantial changes in the world's developed economies. It is very likely that some economic changes will take place with or without government intervention. Technological trends in the areas of nanotechnology, biotechnology, energy technologies, and information technologies in combination with depletion of fossil fuels and efforts to buffer communities from the random impacts of economic globalization all favor movement toward self-sufficient production. Too many people will benefit from self-sufficiency to prevent this from taking place. The only question is whether economists and governments will facilitate a smooth and efficient transition toward this new economic regime or instead support and implement policies that will make the transition more painful than it needs to be.

REFERENCES

Ahrens, T., and A. Harris. 1994. "Deflection and Fragmentation of Near-Earth Asteroids." In *Hazards Due to Comets & Asteroids,* ed. Tom Gehrels, 897-927. Tucson: University of Arizona Press.

Bryson, B. 2003. *A Short History of Nearly Everything.* New York: Broadway Books.

Cockes, Doug. 2003. *Deep Futures: Our Prospects for Survival.* Montreal: McGill-Queens's University Press.

Daly, H. 1996. *Beyond Growth: The Economics of Sustainable Development.* Boston: Beacon Press.

Daly, H. 1990. "Toward Some Operational Principles of Sustainable Development." In *Ecological Economics,* Vol. 2, 1-6.

Diamond, J. 2005. *Collapse: How Societies Choose to Fail or Succeed.* New York: Penguin Group.

Hart, M.1999. *Guide to Sustainable Community Indicators,* 2nd ed. North Andover, MA: Hart Environmental Data.

Hawken, P., A. Lovins, and H. L. Lovins. 1999. *Natural Capitalism: Creating the Next Industrial Revolution.* Boston: Back Bay Books/Little, Brown and Company.

Henderson, H. 1996. *Building a Win-Win World: Life Beyond Global Economic Warfare.* San Francisco: Berrett-Koehler Publishers.

Holmberg, J., K. Robert, and K. Eriksson, 1996. "Socio-ecological Principles for a Sustainable Society." In *Getting Down to Earth: Practical Applications of Ecological Economics,* eds. R. Constanza, O. Segura, and J. Martinez-Alier, 17-48. Washington, DC: Island Press.

International Union for Conservation of Nature and Natural Resources, United Nations Environmental Programme, and World Wildlife Fund. 1991. *Caring for the Earth — A Strategy for Sustainable Living.*

Joy, B. 2000. "Why the Future Doesn't Need Us." In *Wired,* Issue 8.04.

Landefeld, J., and S. McCulla. 2000. "Accounting for Nonmarket Household Production Within a National Accounts Framework." In *Review of Income and Wealth,* Vol. 46, Issue 3, 289-307.

Leslie, J. 1996. *The End of the World: The Science and Ethics of Human Extinction.* New York: Routledge.

Meadows, D. 1996. "Envisioning a Sustainable World." In *Getting Down to Earth: Practical Applications of Ecological Economics,* eds. R. Constanza, O. Segura, and J. Martinez-Alier, 117-126. Washington, DC: Island Press.

Meckstroth, A., and P. Arnsberger. 1998. "A 20-Year Review of the Non-Profit Sector 1975-1995." *SOI Bulletin,* Fall, http://www.irs.gov/pub/irs-soi/20yreo.pdf (accessed May 16, 2008).

Negroponte, N. 1995. *Being Digital.* New York: Knopf.

Rabinowitz, D., E. Helin, K. Lawrence, and S. Pravdo. 2000. "A Reduced Estimate of the Number of Kilometre-Sized Near-Earth Asteroids." In *Nature,* 403, 165-166.

Rees, M. 2003. *Our Final Hour.* New York: Basic Books.

Schumacher, E. F. 1973. *Small Is Beautiful: Economics as if People Mattered.* New York: Harper & Row.

Seidel, P. 2003. "Survival Research: A New Discipline Needed Now." In *World Futures,* 59 (3/4), 129-133.

Sousa-Poza, A., H. Schmid, and R. Widmer. 2001. "The Allocation and Value of Time Assigned to Housework and Childcare: An Analysis for Switzerland." In *Journal of Population Economics,* 14 (4), 599-618.

Tainter, J. 1998. *The Collapse of Complex Societies.* Cambridge: Cambridge University Press.

Tonn, B. 2006. "Futures Sustainability." In *Futures* (in press).

Tonn, B. 2004a. "Integrated 1000-Year Planning." In *Futures,* Vol. 36, 91-108.

Tonn, B. 2004b. "Research Society: Science and Technology for the Ages." In *Futures,* Vol. 36, 335-346.

Tonn, B. 2000. "Monetary Policy and the Non-Profit Sector," opinion piece. In *Chronicle of Philanthropy,* October 19.

Vinge, V. 1993. "The Technological Singularity." VISION-21 Symposium sponsored by NASA Lewis Research Center and the Ohio Aerospace Institute, March 30-31, 1993. Available January 28, 2006, at http://www.ugcs.caltech.edu/~phoenix/Lit/vinge-sing.html.

Wackernagel, M., and W. Rees. 1996. *Our Ecological Footprint: Reducing Human Impact on the Earth.* Gabriorla Island, BC, Canada: New Society Publishers.

Wikipedia, 2006. "Money Supply." http://en.wikipedia.org/wiki/Money_supply (accessed September 30, 2006).

World Commission on Environment and Development. 1987. *Our Common Future.* New York: United Nations.

Yin, J., M. Schlesinger, N. Andronova, S. Malyshev, and B. Li. 2006. "Is a Shutdown of the Thermohaline Circulation Irreversible?" In *Journal of Geophysical Research—Atmospheres,* 111 (D12): Art. No. D12104.

Faster, Larger, Riskier

Investing in the Future Global Stock Exchange

Joan E. Foltz

Prognostication of a market-based governance system, one where global development is driven by free-market forces, is supported with the accelerating globalization within the financial industries, particularly the stock exchanges. Emerging as a leader toward a unified global system is the projection of what could soon become a Global Stock Exchange made up of either one dominant exchange or two primary exchanges that are restructuring the global stock, commodities, and currency markets.

The brisk merger activity among stock exchanges is forming interdependent, global financial markets and creating shifts in the forces within financial systems, most importantly the power structures. These long-term structural changes bring new characteristics and powerful implications that impact not only the global economies, but also corporate strategies and individual investors' decisions, requiring a different way to eye the new landscape emerging in the trading environment.

The current phase of rapid consolidation of exchanges was propelled by the New York Stock Exchange when it became a public corporation in 2007. At that time, the purpose of the exchange shifted

Joan E. Foltz is a principal at Alsek Research. E-mail jfoltz@alsekresearch.com.

away from providing an organization supporting its members to maximizing business profitability by horizontally expanding with the immediate acquisition of the Euronext, the European exchange. This propelled a merger and deal mania among competing exchanges and related infrastructure companies scrambling to capture international territory.

With the spread of the adoption of capitalism and free-market economic systems, countries with nationalized exchanges will be unable to compete against the behemoths created by the mergers and acquisitions (M&A) that are forming a globally interconnected trading system of powerful networked partners. The vertical and horizontal depth of the M&A activity spreading into other segments of the investment industry advances the efficient infrastructure, which opens a myriad of opportunities for new financial product innovations. However, it also creates structural changes that will alter the future of equities' market behavior. These opportunities attract new entities, which in turn will create new challenges as different major factors surface.

GLOBAL REACH: THE CHANGING LANDSCAPE

M&A activity is forming a global financial landscape layered with intertwined, networked exchanges and affiliated stakeholders servicing the different subsets of companies from large multinationals to small firms, all seeking exposure to international investors. This phase of consolidation, led by the two largest exchanges—the NYSE/Euronext and NASDAQ—is shaping into a few predominant transregional systems. The rate of expansion follows the rate of change made in emerging regions' regulatory policies as they allow foreign ownership of national exchanges, open to free markets, and form strategic alliances to share trading platforms or other transaction-processing systems.

Distinct financial centers are arising within the regionally cen-

tered, interdependent systems, as the competitive race to capture
markets in equities and other financial products repositions national
players. Since many of the major markets (e.g., the BRICs — Brazil,
Russia, India, and China) still restrict foreign ownership, the final

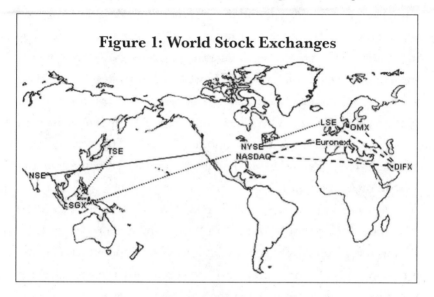

Figure 1: World Stock Exchanges

alignments culminating into power centers remain unforeseen.

In 2004, NASDAQ started competing for the listing business
by offering dual NYSE-NASDAQ listings for companies. New accounting standards that allowed companies to cross-list on foreign
exchanges significantly expanded their access to foreign investors
and larger markets. Now, U.S. investors can access more than 420
non-U.S. companies listed on the NYSE and approximately 335 on
the NASDAQ exchanges and through American Depository Re-
ceipts (ADRs). Companies registering initial public offerings that
want the benefits offered by the NYSE, but do not want to pay the
costs incurred when registering as a U.S. offering, can go through
Euronext, a branch of the NYSE.

In the future, as the exchanges continue to merge and share
infrastructure, the trading landscape will likely morph into one in-

terconnected exchange, where trades will be accessible to any investor on a centralized trading platform. The listing exchange and regulations will be transparent to the trader. Until then, the primary driver of the industry's consolidation will be competition for the potential surge of liquidity found in new emerging markets.

Both regulatory changes and advancements in electronic trading systems have enabled exchanges to go global. NASDAQ, which started as an electronic exchange, always had a strategy to build an international trading service based on an online-trading system. Since the 1990s, NASDAQ has built a foreign presence through various alliances, starting with a joint Internet information service with the Hong Kong Stock Exchange and its launching of the NASDAQ Canada in 1999.

On the European front, the Paris, Brussels, and Amsterdam exchanges formed the Euronext in 2000, which also acquired the Portuguese Lisbon exchange. In 2007, as soon as the NYSE became a public corporation, it proposed a merger with Euronext, which was finalized in 2008 to form the world's largest stock exchange, valued at more than $20 trillion.

The NYSE takeover of Euronext triggered a rush for stake claiming. However, bidding wars emerged when the NASDAQ, a 15 percent stakeowner in the London Stock Exchange, made a bid to acquire the remaining LSE shares in 2006. The offer was rejected. Moreover, the aggressive move to take over the third-most-active exchange pulled Borse Dubai, a United Arab Emirates exchange, into negotiations, which caused a significant change in the landscape of global financial centers.

The ongoing fight to acquire the LSE ended with a shuffle of convoluted ownership structure. Borse Dubai settled with a 28 percent stake of the LSE purchased from NASDAQ's shares. NASDAQ became the principal commercial partner of Dubai International Financial Exchange in exchange for the Borse Dubai taking 19.99

Table 1: Top 10 Stock Exchanges

Stock Exchange	Market Value (US$ trillions)	Total Share Turnover (US$ trillions)
NYSE Euronext	$20.70	$28.70
Tokyo	4.63	5.45
NASDAQ	4.39	12.40
London	4.21	9.14
Shanghai	3.02	3.56
Hong Kong	2.97	1.70
Toronto	2.29	1.36
Frankfurt	2.12	3.64
Madrid	1.83	2.49
Bombay	1.61	0.26

Source: Wikipedia.

percent stake in the NASDAQ. And Borse Dubai took the NASDAQ branding name.

While the LSE fights to maintain its independence and ward off takeovers, the NYSE and NASDAQ continue to build their global networks. In 2008, NASDAQ and the OMX (agglomeration of Stockholm, Helsinki, Copenhagen, Latvia, Lithuania, and Estonia exchanges) will merge into the NASDAQ/OMX, pending approval by Sweden and other Nordic and Baltic jurisdictions. The agglomeration of the various NASDAQ mergers and alliances will cultivate the first exchange that will span the United States, Europe, and the Middle East regions.

The emergent organizations do not clearly define territories or differentiating regulations. Dubai has plans to become a major financial center servicing the Asian region between East Asia and Europe. Singapore, already an established financial center for the

Asian-Pacific region, is a prime target for M&A activity as that region develops. In 2007, Tokyo purchased 5 percent of the Singapore Exchange, SGX. Rumors say the Tokyo Stock Exchange (TSE) plans to take a major stake or acquire SGX. That could expand the products and technology the TSE already shares with the LSE. However, targeting the Asian region is already part of the NYSE Euronext and NASDAQ expansion strategies.

Aggressive-deal making activity is not limited to any city or country, but surfaces in all areas that enable foreign participation. NASDAQ long ago established an office in India, and NYSE Euronext already purchased the maximum allowed foreign ownership of 5 percent in India's Mumbai exchange, the National Stock Exchange. The NYSE also made headway into China with the first registered representative foreign exchange office. However, the advantage of any leading exchange may change as restrictions on foreign ownership are lifted in the emerging regions.

As globalization of the industry opens opportunities, the pressures to perform as a publicly traded company will fuel further consolidation necessary to achieve efficiencies of the integrated technologies and to exploit the massive global market. Small, regional, and single-platform exchanges will be unable to compete.

New Forces in the Global Exchange System's Structure

As a revolutionary exchange structure emanates, new powerful forces will impact directions of the global economy and wield enough power to influence regulatory policies governing regional economics and foreign trade. Electronic trading systems, coupled with a new massive market composed of different players, could create significant shifts in the distribution of global capital formation. Also, both infuse different behaviors into trading systems.

Information technology has leveled the playing field by providing access to information and electronic trading to individual retail traders with the same detail as professional traders and institutions. However, the expanded base of traders also introduces new investment strategies, trading styles, and intentions, often with conflicting goals. Many new traders and investors making the market are from regions that only recently adopted open markets and capitalist economic structures, where individuals may not be protected from market fluctuations. The dynamics of matured trader groups intermingled with novice entrants, whose understanding of market behavior is based only on current market conditions, could incite volatility both in the trading arena and in the economies of specific regions—if shifts of fast money constitute instability. Conversely, a more risk-averse group of global players could add stability or induce new agents that would balance short-term speculative progression.

Spread of Risk and Governance

The expansion of the market adds liquidity, which fuels more economic opportunities. The diversity of players that comes with an international market also changes along with the shift in large holdings. Institutions, such as insurance companies, pension funds, and corporations, utilize different avenues to invest large pools of capital with minimal impact to any particular stock or market. However, foreign institutions are now composed of large sovereign funds that often trade on the open markets and impact certain sectors and individual stocks. Concerns regarding their intentions, or at least their ability to have control over stocks, industrial sectors, and regional economies, are heightened by the lack of regulation, accounting standards, and transparency of the foreign entities.

Escalating numbers of pension funds spread across the world, along with economic growth in the emerging regions, should mitigate any intent to manipulate a targeted stock or economy by a sovereign entity. As the dispersion of foreign investments widens, the sovereign fund could expose its own country's downturn risks through the fund's other investments. Any sovereign fund concentrating financial activity to a specific target will likely trigger intervention before any significant event occurred.

The integrated connectivity of the pan-global exchanges, as mapped in the NYSE and NASDAQ expansion, provides the means to spread risk and leverage accumulated wealth, which is likely to be of more value to any fund in a global economy than begets a countervailing force. Intentionally threatening a global imbalance would provoke protectionist policies that could reduce capital flow to that country. Hence, impacting capital formation would likely be avoided. However, capital infusion could be used to influence countries' and corporations' decisions that indirectly impact the trading environment.

The trading environment is a large, interdependent system, so the emerging structure will likely develop into a self-correcting, balanced system that is less overpowered by waves of momentum and speculative trading. However, the probability of forces threatening the system's performance rises if foreign markets overadjust with regulatory policies that impact the integrated global market as these countries learn market-based economics.

The formation of regional financial centers, such as New York, London, Dubai, and Singapore, plays a key role in global stability. This is a step forward in the globalization transition, which leads to international regulation and has the potential to undermine the powers of nation-states.

Eventually, the global exchanges will have to agree to a set of international standards. Without those, the practices of all players may not be in the best interests of any particular country. An example is speculative commodity prices driving up inflation, which could hurt economies that cannot absorb the costs. Another example is the 2007 subprime mortgage crisis, which started in the United

States and rippled throughout the foreign exchanges due to foreign participation in the derivatives, yet alleviated some of the risk to the United States. Risk will increase as countries deregulate to participate in the global market. Competing financial instruments will propagate new investment opportunities, which will continue until creative financing is exhausted or the ramifications from regional regulatory regimes pose predatory or protectionist repudiation. The most significant benefit of a global market is that risk is spread across the world.

The decoupling of investment banking from commercial banking regulations has opened the doors for developers of creative securitization that has embedded unregulated financial instruments in the complex integrated systems; such moves expose innocent recipients to unknown high levels of risk and insecurity. Without a set of international accounting standards, the exploitation of unregulated securities by passing them through regulated funds will become harder to track as the portfolio of investment products inflates choices.

The geographic diffusion of shocks no longer depends on the epicenter of the shock or the periphery. The spatial dislocations are now more dependent on the linkage between the participants in the arbitrage. Episodes that cause economic crisis to a particular country will receive pressure from agents in the trading system. The correcting mechanism will come from the periphery (countries) that will impart controls on the market, which is more prone to organization based on human behavior. The free-for-all speculative trading that some fear could lead to a gambling market should evolve into a global institution with universal ideologies. Decision making will shift from the financial institutions, broker/dealers, and traders as the center of gravity to a universal world order. Organization will not be based on ideologies, but on risk management of an integrated economy.

Globalization has shifted traders' awareness from regional centers to the core of financial centers. Economic concerns that impact overall exchange performance arise from adverse shocks to asset sectors. Political or economic instability at the periphery usually remains insignificant, discounted with little impact on markets. This global mind-set versus a regional mind-set will prevail in a pan-regional marketplace.

Capital Formations and Shifts in Distribution

A global stock exchange platform makes the opportunity for asset accumulation available to more people. Inequalities in capital formation can accrue in open markets if governments are left out of the distribution architecture. As countries adopt market-driven governance, more people will be pushed toward participating in pension funds and other types of private investing in a system that used to be exclusive to the wealthy and countries with stable exchanges. The self-organizing system will increasingly expose retail traders to a complex array of investment choices and schemes. "Smart money" and institutional traders moving into assets that require an understanding of sophisticated asset management to yield the higher rates of return will leave individual investors to lower-return assets, thus perpetuating the increasing gap between wealthy capitalists and investors attempting to generate pensions.

Investments maximizing returns by chasing emerging regions and innovations can infuse significant amounts of capital into a region or sector without having a long-term commitment. The risk of oscillating and massive withdrawals exposes regional development to the vulnerabilities of market sentiments. Any increase in volatility or instability created by the diversified pool of investors could cause governments to change policies regulating foreign ownership and investments.

If systemic problems in the global exchange become unpredictably chaotic, investors and institutions will decouple from the public exchange and migrate to alternative trading platforms, such as the emerging private exchanges, to invest among a more efficient market in a lower-risk environment. These exchanges could draw the liquidity, often called "dark liquidity," from the private equity firms and major markets as companies look for some regulation, plus the necessary liquidity to facilitate large transactions.

These alternative trading platforms could disrupt the financial landscape and the structured network of exchanges by aligning with partners from other segments of the financial industry, such as banks, service, and technology providers. Depending on the formation and allocated resources and alignments, each exchange offers differentiating services suitable to the goals of large block traders.

In 2007, NASDAQ announced its PORTAL Market, a closed trading system available to brokers and institutions trading 144A securities (unregulated securities restricted to qualified institutional buyers worth more than $100 million). The trading platform increases the liquidity by enabling foreign investors and other qualified parties to conveniently participate in private sales of 144A securities through an efficient execution network.

Private exchanges operate not only with minimal regulation, but also with no transparency. Qualified investors that can absorb risk are invited to trade large blocks in Project SmartPool, an electronic block trading market accessible to European sell-side firms, a partnership between the NYSE Euronext and investment bankers NP Paribas and HSBC. Parties will be able to trade without disclosing their identity or the bid/ask prices or size of trade. Minimal information will be required pre-trade, and information will only be posted after settlement.

Alternative exchanges are outcomes of regulations, such as MiFID in Europe and Reg NMS in the United States, which take the investing environment from a highly controlled regulatory structure to a free-market system. The flood of new products and platforms for trading and investing that comes from deregulating the industry will continue to change the landscape as interacting participants produce a collective structure. These dark-liquidity trading platforms are estimated to already process more than 5 percent of the trading volume in the United States.

CHANGES IN INVESTMENT STRATEGIES

The evolving exchanges present dynamic and fluid options to the individual trader, brokers, and corporations. The changes in the trading environment's system structure will likely require adjustments in strategies to include more risk assessment and more sophisticated methods to identify opportunities to generate capital gains. As integrated pan-global exchanges open foreign markets to more investors, the systemic complexity will only grow.

Analysis of any market will require an international mind-set, a global view, and a whole-system understanding. Investors — corporate, institutional, and individual — will have to be able to assess opportunities throughout the world, not necessarily by regions, but by individual stocks. With an interconnected system, a company of any size need not depend on its economic success being linked to a country or region, but rather on its competitive position in the world market.

The complexity of understanding the expansive landscape saturated with a myriad of financial products and equities could have a residual effect that slows down the capital distributions while the system finds stability. Likewise, the risk and volatility from an open-market system could push private investors to seek stability in funds or drive out players from the market, which will reduce liquidity and cause further downturn.

Corporations may opt to list with exchanges that are less regulated to avoid stringent reporting rules such as Sarbanes-Oxley requirements. Likewise, other companies may seek a regulated environment for stability. In a global financial system, companies have the option to choose the best match for their strategies, whether it is a foreign listing or a cross-listing. This makes a market of conflicting goals.

A corporation that wants a market with the liquidity and ability to handle large IPOs, which would typically seek to be listed on the New York Stock Exchange, could list on a European exchange if the terms are more beneficial. The interdependent exchanges provide the option to raise capital and receive the securitization in multiple locations without dislocating the company's central operations. Threats from listed companies to move to another country will limit the ability of the SEC and other regulators to impose their will. These threats could be mitigated if investors prefer to keep their trading within a regulated framework for increased protection.

Overall, the structural changes in the globalization of exchange systems bring advantages such as an expanded market and opportunities for corporations. However, challenges could become disadvantageous for individual traders.

A rise of private exchanges could leave the NYSE and NASDAQ to be the aftermarket for individuals, which would result in these exchanges becoming a gambling system functioning more on behavior and computerized algorithms than on investments. Those characteristics could become more pronounced than the skeptics already perceive. Individual traders could be shut out of the lucrative IPO market if initial offerings migrate toward private exchanges or other instruments where there is less volatility. This could lead to only high-risk IPOs that are more likely to fail or be insignificant to debut on one of the major exchanges (NYSE, NASDAQ, LSE).

The decoupling of the large block institutional traders from the public exchanges would grossly affect stock market performance. Left to individual players, the market would become more of a behavior and sentiment indicator than an economic barometer. Fads, bubbles, and momentum could dominate strategies. Timing the market would become a prevalent tactic rather than short- and long-term investing. This would leave less-active traders disadvantaged in a constantly fluctuating market.

Protection will be needed for individual investors who have to rely on investments for retirement, particularly if Social Security becomes privatized or there are other disruptions in pension assets. However, the massive aging population could force alternative safe havens to be offered. Demand is expected only to increase with the growing aging population around the world. But it is the role of the industry to provide options for security. The conflict will be between a global exchange, which has a purpose to maximize opportunities fueled by liquidity, or secure programs for asset protection and sub-scribed payout.

FUTURE OUTLOOK

Globalization of exchanges will continue to evolve and revolu-tionize the financial industry as new economic theories are explored. Products for creative securitization will be tested. And the role of global exchanges will be scrutinized as they struggle to improve their competitive position versus providing options that are in the best interest of investors.

The solidity of the entire global financial system will likely re-quire somewhat of a regulated architecture. Else, national econo-mies run a risk from potential spillover effects resulting from events in other regions. Being on the periphery of an interconnected system does not provide any safeguards from the core's behavior.

In an open market, government policies will be less influential than traders' behavior. Exchanges will become more representative of a gambling environment than an investment platform. And even though the stock market has been long compared to a casino, that strategy will dominate until an event disrupts the fundamental structure created by a shift in electronic trading systems' methods.

As with globalization of any industry, continuing deregulation in the financial sector will nurture more creative products, more competition, and more consolidation until a chaotic environment stresses the current trajectory and causes a sharp reversal. In this industry, there would be no reversal of a global exchange, but the force of an international regulatory body would prevail. Fragmentation of the major exchanges will result when the rise of private exchanges draws liquidity from the major markets to the point of reducing performance and functionality. Other alternative collective structures could emerge from restructuring alliances in multiple sectors, such as technology companies.

As with all systems, the trading exchanges will continue on an evolutionary path. And while in the era of globalization, they will continue to go through stages and phases of consolidation and fragmentation, just as other industries do. However, since the stakes can be high when dealing with huge sources of capital and economic control of companies, industries, and countries, wild cards are a possibility, although unlikely due to sophisticated monitoring. The advantage of an interdependent exchange is that it is based on an electronic platform that tracks all transactions.

A wild card that would disrupt the trading revolution might be, for example, a sovereign fund with enough wealth to overpower or threaten a major economy by successfully manipulating a market, which would lead to financial wars. However, evolution of a global economy makes most countries participating in it interdependent, with a high probability that spillovers of any cataclysmic event would carry significant economic damage to the perpetrator.

A more likely scenario is the rapid shift between dominant regional financial centers that would lead to a significant global imbalance of major economies and threaten a global economic collapse. This is in line more with the emergence stage of a self-organizing structure. At that point, controls would be put in place to stop economic destruction and reverse course. Success of these controls depends on the governing bodies to implement appropriate measures and acknowledgement by the global community of the inferences.

The trajectory building by the consolidation of exchanges, overall, produces benefits that far outweigh risks. Cycles and instability can slow down the evolutionary process, but they will be corrected. Alternative exchanges and complexity may drive traders out as players, but capital will remain in the system by means of one of the integrated options. Complexity could also create opportunities for those who have different skill sets and strategies to work within the new systems.

REFERENCES

Berger, Suzanne. 2003. *The First Globalization: Lessons from the French.* MIT, http://web.mit.edu/polisci/research/berger/lessons-latest_English_version.pdf.

Forbes, Kristin. 2007. "Global Imbalances: A Source of Strength or Weakness?" *Federal Reserve Policy in the Face of Crises.* Cato Institute (April 11).

Forrester, Jay. 2003. "Economic Theory for the New Millennium," Plenary Address at the International System Dynamics Conference, New York (July 21).

Kaminski, Graciela L., and Carmen Reinhart. 2002. "The Center and the Periphery: The Globalization of Financial Turmoil." International Monetary Fund (November).

Knowledge@Wharton. 2002. "Global Securities Markets Present Tough Challenges for Investors and Regulators." http://knowledge.wharton.upenn.edu (January 16).

Knowledge@Wharton. 2006. "LSE, NYSE, OMX, Nasdaq, Euronext ... Why Stock Exchanges Are Scrambling to Consolidate," http://knowledge .wharton.upenn.edu (March 22).

Knowledge@Wharton. 2000. "Stock Exchanges in the Market for Partners," http://knowledge.wharton.upenn.edu (June 7).

Mosley, Layna, and David Andres Singer. 2006. "Taking Stock Seriously: Equity Market Performance, Government Policy, and Financial Globalization." MIT, http://web.mit.edu/dasinger/www/ MosleySingerNov14.pdf (May).

Moyer, Liz. 2007. "Barely Private Exchanges," *Forbes* (August14).

NASDAQ corporate, http://www.nasdaq.com.

NYSE Euronext corporate, http://www.nyse.com.

Shaw, Richard. 2007. "A Unified, Global Stock Exchange May Be Approaching," http://seekingalpha.com (November 21).

Thurow, Lester. 1997. *The Future of Capitalism*. New York: Penguin Press.

Veon, Joan. 2006. "The New York Stock Exchange Goes Global: The Cherry on Top of World Government," http://rense.com (March 8).

In Praise of Academic Disengagement

Michael Bugeja

Fifteen years ago, you couldn't sell college students anything. First, you couldn't find them. They would have one address at a residence hall or off-campus rental, but were seldom there. Second, if you found them, typically they had no money after paying rent and buying beer. Third, they had weird consumer habits, like eating peanut butter for a month to afford a spring break trip to Acapulco.

Nonetheless, students were important because their demographics placed them in the eighteen- to twenty-four-year-old bracket during which they would make brand decisions to last a lifetime. If parents had bought Colgate toothpaste, then children might show their rebellion by purchasing Crest.

So basically, to reach students, media companies distributed magazines or direct mail to places where they might turn up eventually—in the lobbies of residence halls and apartment complexes, in entrances of campus and city buildings, in the student newspaper, or at the local post office.

All that has changed. Now we know where students are at any minute of any day because of global positioning satellite software. Moreover, we have since outsourced the student loan industry, with scandals to show for it, providing disbursement amounts far surpassing tuition and fees. Third, we have given students credit cards.

Michael Bugeja is director of the Greenlee School of Journalism at Iowa State University. E-mail bugeja@iastate.edu.

It is no coincidence that students are apt to own three digital devices: a laptop, an iPod, and a cell phone. They pay to purchase the device, to accessorize the device, to gain access for the device, to use credit cards via the device, and to amass credit card debt because of the device.

As if this were not bad enough, educators have introduced these devices, platforms, and applications into the classroom in the name of "engagement," a barometer of just how distracted our learners are, blurring boundaries between learning and amusement on residential campuses, just as their parents have blurred boundaries between work and home using e-mail, BlackBerrys, and pagers.

So, on top of paying bills for each of three digital devices, students must also dole out tuition and fees that have risen dramatically each year at high-tech private and public institutions.

This is why I am advocating "academic *dis*engagement." Typically, the notion of teachers disengaging from students and the devices that distract them seems hopelessly aloof and elite, especially as futurists advocate new learning technologies and innovative teaching methods.

This essay aims to reevaluate new learning technologies and question innovative teaching methods utilizing those technologies because, in addition to undermining academic values, these approaches generally have curtailed knowledge, hindered critical thinking, and blurred the boundaries between learning and entertainment in an era that requires commitment rather than engagement.

According to my unabridged *Random House Dictionary*, the generic meaning of *engagement* is "to occupy the attention or efforts of (a person or persons)." When applied to education, the word conjures a high-tech classroom with serious students typing on laptops and glancing up occasionally at a peripatetic professor as the words *technology, knowledge*, and *innovation* scroll across the screen. Note that I didn't use the word *commercial*, although you may have envisioned one, only now returning to the previous sentence to reread the word *screen*. This is how commercial our future has become. We think like a commercial. We act like a commercial. And we engage learners using the same techniques as marketing agencies, clustering students into affinity groups (read: *psychographics*) in social networks or virtual worlds.

My *Random House Dictionary* has a more specific meaning of *engagement* as it relates to business, as in "to secure for aid, use, or employment, etc., hire" and "to bind, as by pledge, promise, contract, or oath; make liable." Perhaps you may be envisioning a legal agreement now with fine print.

The fine print, as it relates to technology, is in the service terms, such as this one from the virtual-life video game Second Life:

> **5.1 You release Linden Lab from your claims relating to other users of Second Life. Linden Lab has the right but not the obligation to resolve disputes between users of Second Life.**
>
> As a condition of access to the Service, you release Linden Lab (and Linden Lab's shareholders, partners, affiliates, directors, officers, subsidiaries, employees, agents, suppliers, licensees, distributors) from claims, demands and damages (actual and consequential) of every kind and nature, known and unknown, suspected and unsuspected, disclosed and undisclosed, arising out of or in any way connected with any dispute you have or claim to have with one or more users of the Service (http://secondlife.com/corporate/tos.php).

For the record, this specific clause goes on for another 182 engaging words in an application that bestows anonymity on users, including thousands of professors and students on hundreds of digital "islands" bought and sold daily with "Linden dollars" in Second Life. The statement disavows liability from anything one avatar can do to another, which is about everything people can do to each other behind the virtual curtain.

In *The Chronicle of Higher Education* (Bugeja 2007), I explored the potential for lawsuits and public-record violations involving the use of Second Life as a learning platform. The first essay, "Second Thoughts about Second Life," concerned who would be held accountable for incidents of harassment and assault in virtual worlds with restrictive service terms. I recommended legal and curricular analyses as well as research and assessment augmented by discussion in public forums.

In a follow-up essay, "Second Life Revisited," I explored Linden Lab's service terms in relation to Freedom of Information Act requirements at public institutions. Paul N. Tanaka, general counsel at Iowa State University, has said that most university materials posted to Second Life would likely fall under the definition of a public record, while others that did not might still be important in any violation of our faculty handbook or student codes.

Subsequently, it was the legal consensus at ISU that professors generally do not have the right to negotiate contracts on behalf of the institution by agreeing to service terms that bestow anonymity and disavow liability. These are legal opinions. A test case has not yet been litigated. When it is, you can count on the news media putting the focus on educators who have introduced these consumer applications into the classroom at the expense of taxpayers and benefactors. You also can anticipate legislators, regents, or benefactors making inquiries or holding meetings in the wake of such incidents and learning, among other things, about the vulgarity of griefer (i.e., causing grief) attacks, as well as concerns about harassment and assault in virtual environs.

That is why educators who want to invest in Second Life should demand from Linden Lab an educational grid with service terms that yield to academic rules to ensure that code violations apply in virtual worlds with access to records and identities of avatars.

These issues also apply to social networks such as Facebook or educational blogs, increasingly popular with librarians, recruiters, and administrators attempting to engage the interactive student.

In January 2008 I was invited to participate in an online debate hosted by *The Economist* about use of such networks as learning platforms. I noted that advocates presume applications are free because somebody else is paying for them. Often, I argued, it is the teacher and librarian who fail to realize that funds may come out of salaries, facilities, and pockets of students whose debt rises with each new digital ploy to engage them.

I also make the point that many institutions, including my own, are pondering whether to cease supporting e-mail and contract with commercial venders. According to *The Chronicle of Higher Education*, Google and Microsoft "can provide better e-mail service at a price that's hard to beat—free" (January 16, 2008).

How generous of Google and Microsoft! With AOL and Yahoo!, they control large shares of all online advertising revenue in the United States. Nothing they do is for free.

If academic institutions realize that they cannot underwrite the cost of e-mail, how are we going to keep underwriting as learning platforms social networks, virtual worlds, and classroom use of consumer gadgets like Twitter—an insidious cell-phone application that asks, "What are you doing now?"—exposing students to more credit-card debt?

Chances are, the tweeting students in the digital classroom are glancing furtively at their professor with a Bluetooth in his ear because they are not listening to the lecture, but rather texting friends on social networks, downloading music or videos, or purchasing products on eBay or Amazon. I should know. In 2007, we surveyed students in the Greenlee School of Journalism and Communication, which I direct at Iowa State, with these startling results:

Question: Have you done the following during class:

1. Taken or made a cell phone call (or sent/read text messages)?
    Yes: 163 (74.8%), No: 54 (24.8%), Abstaining: 1 (0.4%)

2. Instant messaged on your laptop?
    Yes: 100 (45.9%), No: 117 (53.7%), Abstaining: 1 (0.4%)

3. Social networked (Facebook, MySpace)?
    Yes: 129 (59.2%), No: 86 (39.4%), Abstaining: 3 (1.4%)

4. Checked, read, and/or sent e-mail?
    Yes: 162 (74.3%), No: 55 (25.2%), Abstaining: 1 (0.4%)

5. Listened to music or watched movies?
    Yes: 60 (27.5%), No: 157 (72.0%), Abstaining: 1 (0.4%)

6. Played a computer game?
    Yes: 74 (33.9%), No: 141 (64.7%), Abstaining: 3 (1.4%)

7. Used a laptop to surf a non-assigned Internet site?
    Yes: 138 (63.3%), No: 78 (35.8%), Abstaining: 2 (0.9%)

8. Made an online purchase (Amazon, eBay, etc.)?
    Yes: 40 (18.3%), No: 176 (80.7%), Abstaining: 2 (0.9%)

9. Which is greater (click one)?
    ISU: 154 (70.6%), Other: 60 (27.5%), Abstaining: 4 (1.8%)

10. Done everything at one time or another in 1-8 above?
    Yes: 79 (36.2%), No: 138 (63.3%), Abstaining: 1 (0.4%)

11. Been so bored you just had to do any of 1-8 above?
    Yes: 167 (76.7%), No: 49 (22.5%), Abstaining: 2 (0.9%)

12. Been annoyed by others doing any of 1-8 above?
    Yes: 154 (70.6%), No: 61 (28.0%), Abstaining: 3 (1.4%)

Extra Credit: Are you taking this quiz during class right now?
    Yes: 55 (25.2%), No: 158 (72.5%), Abstaining: 5 (2.3%)

Since the dissemination of this survey, about one-half of the professors in our school have inserted clauses into syllabi forbidding use of digital devices. Here is a sampling:

• Use of a computer, cell phone, pager, or other electronic device is distracting to other students. Use of any electronic device during class time will result in a grade of "F" for the course. Students must take notes using a paper and pen or pencil. *(Mass Media and Society)*

- Cell phones, pagers, etc., are to be placed on silent or vibrate during class and are NOT to be answered. If during the course of a taping a cell phone, pager, etc., rings that student will lose participation grade points. *(Electronic Media Production)*
- Please turn off your cell phone before class. If your cell phone rings during class, the instructor will answer it for you and will return your phone to you at the end of class.... The Internet should be used for class purposes. *(Public Relations Techniques)*
- No computers, phones or other electronic devices are allowed in this class. This is a journalism school and students are trained to listen and to take notes with a pen or a pencil. The urge to browse with a laptop or text with a cell phone is too distracting.... Unauthorized use of electronic devices during class time will result in the lowering of your final grade by one full letter for each occurrence. *(Publicity Methods)*
- *Cell Phone Rule:* If your cellular phone is heard by the class (including ring/tone/beep/vibration) during official class period you are responsible for completing one of two options: 1. before the end of the class period you will sing a verse and chorus of any song of your choice or, 2. you will lead the next class period through a 10-minute discussion on a topic to be determined by the end of the class. (To the extent that there are multiple individuals in violation, duets will be accepted). *(Technology, International, Social and Human Aspects)*

As you can see, students, taxpayers, parents, and benefactors are paying for wireless technology, and many professors are forbidding use thereof because of the level of distraction that accompanies the blurring of place and occasion. I call this digital displacement. Although the circumstances of such displacement vary, all scenarios will have in common:

- Clash of environments, virtual and real.
- Blurring of physical and social boundaries.
- Blurring of role and identity.
- Influence on values and priorities.
- Impact of all of the above on relationships.

Digital displacement is especially associated with the video gaming phenomenon. Children used to play in parks or neighborhoods before migrating to malls where video games could be found in arcades. Children had to wait their turns to play the most popular games, interacting with attendants, patrons, peers, other parents, and strangers. They played games according to parental and arcade schedules rather than their own. From an interpersonal perspective, this required persuasion and patience—valuable learning skills. That soon changed. Home consoles put arcades out of business, and video games moved from malls to living rooms. Yet, children still had to interact with each other face to face. *What game to play? What level of difficulty? Who gets what controller?* They also had to interact with parents about when play began and ended—again requiring tact, persuasion, and negotiation.

But when gaming went digital so that children could access it on demand, they no longer had to gather with friends or interact with them and parents. They hopped off the school bus or bed and rushed to computers and consoles to play each other online in a place that was not really there.

Now, thanks to "engagement," we have brought displacement to residential campuses, creating a clash of environments, virtual and real, by deploying as learning platforms social networks like Facebook and virtual worlds like Second Life. In doing so, we have further eroded interpersonal skills by blurring physical and social boundaries legally, ethically, and pedagogically. We have blurred identity, too, as person or as avatar, with default virtual names and different body types and physical abilities. That affects values, priorities, and relationships because we put more emphasis on someone somewhere else rather than the place we are or the person we are with.

More important, use of such platforms adds to debt, especially in virtual-life gaming programmed for revenue generation with buying, selling, and vending all manner of phantom objects, from digital genitalia to palatial estates. Only in America and parts of Europe, where living standards are abundant compared with the rest of the world, can we invest educational funds in a game that bestows a second fantasy life on top of our first magnificently privileged one. Didn't the inventors of these technologies foresee a future of enfranchisement, if only we could provide access to the "second" and "third" worlds of the planet? One ambassador of that concept was Nicholas Negroponte in his 1995 book *Being Digital* and who remains hopelessly lost in his own brand of technostalgia, continuing to develop his One Laptop Per Child in geographic areas that require nets for malaria infestations rather than corporate ones on the Net.

That is why educators have been focusing on access to Internet, concerned about the digital divide; now that the divide has been bridged, we're concerned about access to education. Tuition at most institutions has risen on average about 6 percent annually, with room and board rates rising about 5 percent. If tuition continues to rise, fewer students from the middle and lower classes will be able to afford college.

Access to education was a revolutionary concept in the United States. John Jay, first chief justice of the United States, believed education to be the soul of the republic, "and nothing should be left undone to afford all ranks of people the means of obtaining a proper degree of it at a cheap and easy rate."

Those famous words appeared in a March 24, 1785, letter to

Benjamin Rush, congratulating him upon securing the charter for Dickinson College. Dickinson's current president, William G. Durden, has written powerfully about rising costs at his own institution.

In a co-authored essay in *Inside Higher Ed,* Durden notes that higher education is running on a broken financial model. There is little correlation, he states, between cost and tuition, with both escalating rapidly (Durden and Massa 2008). One of his arguments has been that colleges and universities are already cost-conscious, perhaps more than other social organizations. However, he has observed, any savings are rapidly consumed by such demands as more financial aid, new programs, research support, employee benefits, and technology.

Higher education continues to invest in technology not because administrators are convinced that learning outcomes improve because of "new learning technologies" and "innovative teaching methods" utilizing those systems. They invest in the belief that engagement improves retention, so that students do not drop out of college or transfer to another more affordable one. Enrollment remains the chief factor of budget.

In academe, any use of the word "engagement" suggests an endorsement by the National Survey on Student Engagement, whose philosophy gauges the quality of institutions by activities that give meaning and value to collegiate life.

In a recent speech, I contended that these activities have proliferated technologically beyond the intent but nevertheless in the name of NSSE, whose 100-question survey contains only four questions related to technology or, once again, more technostalgia:

- [Have you] used an electronic medium (listserv, chat group, Internet, instant messaging, etc.) to discuss or complete an assignment?
- [Have you] used e-mail to communicate with an instructor?
- [To what extent does your institution emphasize] using comput-

ers in academic work?

- [To what extent has your experience at this institution contributed to your knowledge, skills, and personal development in] using computer and information technology?

Students not only use electronic media to discuss or complete an assignment, but they have *become* the assignment in virtual worlds as avatars and have checked e-mail out of boredom; they also text each other, download music, visit social networks, and make online purchases in wireless classrooms during lectures.

Attempting to engage today's students, we have embraced consumer technologies on the flawed assumption that students want to learn through the same devices that amuse and distract them.

Case in point: A University of Michigan study found that students generally do not want to communicate with librarians on Facebook or MySpace. According to one library blogger commenting on the study, one question "found that by and large the respondents use social networking sites, but the majority (76%) *would not* respond to a library presence on Facebook or MySpace, either because existing methods of contact were sufficient or because these tools are social networks and not places for library invaders" (January 14, 2008).

When contemplating the future, I have become increasingly concerned about the long-term effect of virtual realities. Today's students have been reared on simulated experience since childhood, and we continue to perpetuate that phenomenon in the academy without assessing whether it leads to real-world interaction or commitment. My belief is that it does not. If students want to learn what it feels to be a rock star, they don't have to dedicate years playing guitar or drums before live audiences; they buy "Rock Band" for Xbox and then go on to other things.

This is why I have recommended that administrators and professors ask these basic questions before investing any further in technology:

- **The Motive.** What is the motive embedded in the interface or application, and how can we adjust for or sanction that, especially if it involves corporate revenue generation involving credit cards?

- **The Debt.** What new costs will students incur via credit cards in addition to tech fees and textbooks if we require use of the device, application, or platform?

- **The Risks.** What are the perils—privacy invasion, copyright infringement, online harassment, etc.—that might trigger controversy or undermine faculty handbook compliance or student code investigations?

- **The Budget.** What will the technology drain from the IT system by way of bandwidth or upgrades and support to existing computers, devices, and services?

- **The Terms.** How will service terms of the technology vendor hinder or alter academic values such as transparency, disclosure, and shared governance?

- **The Pedagogy.** How will instructional methodology change if we incorporate the technology into the curricula?

- **The Demand.** Has the high-tech course or curriculum been evaluated in terms of student interest in existing modules such as a seminars, workshops, or independent studies already in the course catalog?

- **The Time.** What type of learning curve is required to use the device, application, or platform, and what will we lose by way of content during class because of it?

- **The Assessment.** How will this device or application enhance or detract from learning objectives or otherwise contribute or detract from departmental mission?

- **The Workload.** How will semester course assignments and scheduling change for colleagues if new technology initiatives are added to the existing curriculum, requiring new preparations and extended computer laboratory access?

- **The Sacrifice.** What are professors and librarians willing to sacrifice, if anything, to help underwrite the increasing cost of technology?
- **The Netiquette.** When, where, and for what purpose is use of the technology (especially mobile devices) appropriate or inappropriate?

At many institutions, falling retention rates are associated as much with financial burden as classroom engagement. In addition to learning curves required to master new applications and platforms, as well as higher operational budgets for IT support, maintenance, and staff hires, we are introducing students to applications programmed for corporate revenue generation, increasing student debt.

That debt will rise again when students graduate and encounter real-life problems that promise to tax their pocketbooks as much as their intellect, ranging from oil depletion to global pandemics. Rather than preparing them to face these challenges, we continue to emphasize engagement rather than *commitment*, without which we cannot resolve environmental, health, water, fuel, and food issues in the next decade.

Administrators and professors would do well to embrace commitment, too. That means helping institutions cut tuition by cutting curricula, which has been expanding on autopilot since the 1980s (Bugeja 2008) and often is associated with "new learning technologies" and "innovative [virtual] teaching methods." Or, if they believe in those technologies and methods, they should describe what sacrifices they would make in the name of lower tuition, from sparser facilities to fewer trips to academic conventions. Educators can also counteract digital displacement by emphasizing the importance of real rather than virtual environments, establishing clear boundaries between learning and entertainment, reminding students of their real identities and societal obligations as citizens, and helping them develop lifelong learning habits that nurture critical thinking rather than inspire rampant consumerism, which is at the core of global problems threatening the planet and our future.

REFERENCES

Bugeja, Michael. 2007. "How to Fight the High Cost of Curricular Glut." *The Chronicle of Higher Education* (February 1) 54 (21): A33.

Durden, William G., and Robert J. Massa. 2008. *Inside Higher Ed* (February 5), available from http://www.insidehighered.com/views/2008/02/05/durden.

Librarian in Black. 2008. "Social Networking for Libraries a Bust?" (January 14), available from http://librarianinblack.typepad.com/librarianinblack/2008/01/social-networki.html.

The Wired Campus (e-mail service of *The Chronicle of Higher Education*). January 16, 2008.

Part 4

Inspiration and Action: Moving Forward

The Future Is All Around Us

Clifton Anderson

Environmentalists study the maze of interrelationships connecting humans with all other living beings, and they also investigate nature's extensive life-support systems. They are, necessarily, futurists. Forward-looking and imaginative, environmentalists envision a world set free from the perils of global warming, resource depletion, and poisoned air, water, and soil. Their big question is, How do we get there from here?

In speeches, articles, and books, environmentalists were busily discussing the environmental movement's future just as the new century approached. Two years into the 2000s, Ted Nordhaus and Michael Schellenberger stimulated ongoing discussion and debate with an essay entitled "The Death of Environmentalism." They later expanded their views in a book, *Break Through: From the Death of Environmentalism to the Politics of Possibilities*. Their book calls for creation of a viable, politically attractive environmental movement.

Doom-and-gloom predictions lack popular appeal, according to Schellenberger. "We need a politics that is positive and that inspires people around an exciting and inspiring vision," he says.

Any effort to widen environmentalism's appeal would require good supporting evidence — positive, logical ideas that are more substantial than mere political slogans would be. Strong, meaningful support for the environmental movement is readily available

Clifton Anderson is a University of Idaho professor emeritus in the field of agricultural communications. E-mail clifa@verizon.net.

from a variety of sources. People with exceptional qualifications have powerful ideas that environmentalists can use as they try to change the world (a task they have struggled with for years).

In this essay, attention is spotlighted on eight individuals. They are representative of perceptive thinkers all over the world, persons who show concern for Planet Earth and its inhabitants. The eight include a globe-trotting community development specialist; a designer who learns from nature; a founder of the communitarian movement; a leading bioregionalist; an eminent professional in the field of global development; a Good Samaritan intent on helping humans (and nonhumans) who need help; a political psychologist who studies people's attitudes, their political thinking, and their involvement in politics; and a scholar who sees signs that a new global cultural transformation is now in progress.

Ideas formulated by sensitive, caring people today may avert serious situations tomorrow. Our unsolved problems are not a suitable gift for the future, but solutions that work should be welcome there. The future is all around us, waiting for our input. Good ideas for achieving a better future will be examined shortly. First, at this point, it is suitable to mention the genesis of our environmental problems.

AFTER NEGLECT, RENEWAL?

Saving the environment should be our number-one priority in the twenty-first century. Up to the present, we have neglected basic environmental needs. Century by century, we disfigured nature with our ugly ecological footprints, and we have never invested the time and effort that an adequate cleanup would require.

Through the quiet, slow-paced years of prehistory, human society treated the environment with benign neglect. Nature pretty well took care of itself.

After humans became busy plowing fields, felling forests, and damming streams, the age of environmental exploitation had begun. It continues in our day. Through their involvement in the environment, humans created conditions that have resulted in global warming, pollution, erosion, environment-related diseases, and a host of other serious problems.

Not long after the dawn of the Industrial Revolution, the environment began issuing distress signals. Pollution occurred — mostly on a local scale — but carbon-laden discharges rising from smokestacks and toxic sludge oozing into rivers were major problems conveniently ignored. As time went by, the environment continued to call for help, and the response from human society was timidly tentative.

Positive actions for environmental renewal were happening a century ago. President Theodore Roosevelt summoned state governors to the 1908 Conservation Conference, held in the White House. Roosevelt emphasized conservation of soil, water, forest, and mineral resources. Under his leadership, the National Park Service was created.

During the 1930s, the need for vigorous programs to save soil and tame rivers became apparent as rivers flooded their banks and huge dust clouds moved across the Great Plains region. President Franklin Roosevelt initiated far-reaching soil and water conservation programs. In his 1936 classic, *Rich Land, Poor Land,* writer Stuart Chase said America was just beginning to repay the environment for damage caused over many years by destructive loggers, farmers, miners, and developers.

Agricultural chemicals' ecological damage became widely discussed after Rachel Carson's *Silent Spring* was published in 1945. Carson proposed strict control over use of DDT, and that approach was tried. Finally, in 1972, the dangerous, long-persisting insecticide was banned by the Environmental Protection Agency.

The initial DDT ban had interesting loopholes. American

firms could continue manufacturing DDT; their export sales were not limited in any way. Inside the United States, DDT could still be applied to a few minor crops.

Time and again, U.S. environmental regulations have been riddled with exemptions and exceptions. To protect the nation's health, the Clean Air Act of 1970 required coal-fired power plants to sharply reduce harmful smokestack emissions. An exception was made for older plants (presumed to be near the end of their service); they were not required to comply with the cleanup rules. Today, thirty-eight years later, exempted plants remain in operation, poisoning the atmosphere with mercury, lead, and other pollutants. Air pollution remains a major unsolved problem, with attempted solutions always falling short of the mark.

The crippled environment requires careful rehab — not just an occasional aspirin or Band-Aid. Strangely, as William Shutkin points out, "environmental laws are intended merely to control pollution, not prevent it." He continues:

> Emission standards and permits are by definition allowances to pollute. Accordingly, the key regulatory issue is how much, not whether pollution is safe and tolerable. Environmental law thus treats pollution as a necessary evil, to be controlled as opposed to eradicated (Shutkin 2001, 102).

THINKING CHANGES THE WORLD

While struggling to save the world, environmentalists need the help of reflective activists — people who are both dreamers and doers. The eight individuals featured in the following pages are non-stop thinkers who are seeking answers to difficult questions. Here, in brief, are some of their ideas on timely topics.

Don Harter: Targeting Hunger and Poverty

Don Harter, a specialist in community development, applauds the short sleeves and informal diplomacy of Peace Corps workers. "They are excellent ambassadors," he says. "They go abroad to help people and are pleased to live in villages where they can gain the friendship and cooperation of local people."

On his foreign visits, Harter avoids tourist hotels and stays in local residents' homes whenever possible. Helping solve hunger and poverty problems has occupied a good share of his time for years. It began with a study trip to Mexico in 1972. Since then, as a volunteer, he has completed community development assignments in twenty-one countries.

After retiring from the University of Idaho faculty in 1996, Harter has contributed more than five years of voluntary service abroad.

Solving community problems must be the responsibility of community members, Harter believes. He sees his role as that of an initiator, encouraging local people to recognize a particularly troublesome situation and then helping them to consider workable solutions. He wants them to have ownership of the action program that develops.

On one voluntary assignment with a social-service organization, Harter spent a year at the project site. Usually, a project develops over several months, and then he moves on. Harter will stay in touch, checking on the project's progress by e-mail. He will be ready to make a personally financed return visit to the project site, if necessary.

"Maintaining project continuity is essential," Harter says. "Leadership takes a long time to develop, and I want to be called on whenever I can give help or encouragement."

When asked why he volunteers for service overseas, Harter says people in developing areas urgently need help. "Besides," he adds, "when you give something and get nothing monetary in return, you gain a special satisfaction."

The world's needy people are getting assistance from various national governments and international agencies, as well as charities and nongovernmental organizations. Against great difficulties, progress is being made. At the same time, some economic initiatives from the developed world have been negative. Efforts to globalize the developing nations' economies have been particularly harmful.

Foreign corporations promoting globalization have been able to cancel developing nations' laws establishing environmental protections, workers' rights to bargain collectively, and workplace safety regulations. The World Trade Organization has ruled that laws protecting workers and the environment are invalid if they impede the free conduct of trade.

Social and environmental progress in the developing world would benefit the entire planet. Economic globalization will not be a positive influence until it recognizes all peoples' political, social and environmental rights. From India, activist Vandana Shiva says a growing anti-globalization movement is now challenging "the idea that you need to destroy the planet before you save it" (Shiva 2003, 154).

Janine M. Benyus: Taking Nature Seriously

Designing products that will be kind to the environment is the mission of Janine M. Benyus. She says good product design is urgently needed in our wasteful, polluting society. For examples of commendable, no-nonsense design, she suggests looking around in the world of nature.

Microscopic algae use a natural crystallization process to assemble their shells. By bringing this process into factories, designers will make it possible for computer chips to assemble themselves, Benyus says.

Also, she points out that the sure-footed gecko lizard has equipment that industry is copying. The gecko's feet have pads that allow it to cling to rocks and other surfaces. The gecko's pads are providing inspiration for a new type of adhesive tape.

After 3.8 billion years of experimentation, nature has learned many lessons that can be helpful to us today. Benyus and other biologists are pioneering in a new science called biomimicry. Their goal is to observe Earth's living systems and find out what works, what lasts, and what is appropriate for humans to adapt.

As a design consultant, Benyus advises business executives how to develop products that will contribute to environmental health and well-being. She helped found the Biomimicry Guild, which offers educational opportunities, and the Biomimicry Institute, an environmental justice organization.

The present environmental crisis is complicated, and Benyus expects relief will come from a variety of sources. Biomimicry research in these subject areas might help:

- **Energy.** We need to know more about the hummingbird's ability to cross the Gulf of Mexico on less than three grams of fuel.
- **Heating and air-conditioning.** In the heating and air-conditioning they install in their dwellings, termites are far ahead of us in regard to efficiency.
- **Survivability.** Whales and penguins live long periods of time underwater without scuba gear.
- **Navigation.** Bees, turtles, and birds are excellent navigators, and they need no maps.
- **Maneuvering.** The best helicopter cannot match the dragonfly's maneuverability.

Production practices of agriculture and industry fall far behind the no-pollution standards set by nature, Benyus believes. She says usage of chemicals in agriculture is excessively high. Nitrogen fertilizer, applied to boost crop yields, causes severe pollution, poisoning lakes, rivers, and drinking-water sources.

Herbicides are major pollutants also, Benyus says, and the problem magnified after crop breeders developed new varieties that have built-in resistance to powerful herbicides. When growing the new crops, farmers often increase herbicide dosage and, as a result, herbicide pollution problems increase.

Designing the tools and processes needed by a world seeking improved environmental health will be a major undertaking. We also have to adjust personally, getting used to necessary lifestyle changes. Can we learn to feel good about giving up things we never really needed? Are we able to surmount the inhibitions that have prevented our society from facing the environmental implications of continued population growth?

The environment-related problems confronting us are of tremendous magnitude. Benyus cites some details:

> Each month, 8 million people (the population of New York City) join an Earth already groaning. In the United States, we generate 12 billion tons of solid waste a year—that's twenty times the total amount of ash released by the 1980 eruption of Mount Saint Helens. Over 200 million tons of airborne wastes are added to the atmosphere each year, joining the 90,000 tons of known nuclear waste, most of which will be poisonous for another 100,000 years (Benyus 1997, 240-41).

Amitai Etzioni: Building Community Power

Too much power in a few hands will endanger freedom, says Amitai Etzioni, George Washington University sociologist and a founder of the communitarian movement. He believes local communities need to exercise their strong moral authority, thereby checking the government's growth of power and also limiting the political strength of corporate interests.

Members of a community develop a shared moral culture that unifies them and adds bedrock strength to democratic institutions, according to Etzioni.

Government has important duties, and the market economy has necessary functions to perform. However, Etzioni insists, people should be able to protect themselves from improvident actions of the government and the economy.

In the communitarians' view of the future, what is the role of government? Etzioni wants a "lean but active" government offering a high level of social services. Everyone is entitled to "shelter, clothing, food, and necessary health care." Many government services could be handled most efficiently at a local, grassroots level, he says, and communities should be able to appraise their own problems and work out appropriate solutions.

What is the role of the market economy? Again, Etzioni proposes to protect people within a community from excessive interference by powerful outsiders.

The people's right to rule themselves is violated, Etzioni suggests, whenever corporations contribute campaign funds to politicians who are running for office. The solution could be laws prohibiting non-individuals from participating in politics. Another possible solution is public financing of political campaigns.

As a sociologist, Etzioni has had a distinguished career. He has written more than a dozen books and more than 200 scholarly articles and book chapters. He served as president of the American Sociological Association. He is a founder of the Communitarian Network, which supports the growth of grassroots democracy.

Searching for ways to help democracy thrive in our complex society, many social scientists are examining the possibilities for strengthening face-to-face democracy in local communities. Etzioni believes communities with keen and kindly moral perspectives are well suited for key roles in a campaign to revivify American democracy.

Community can serve a central purpose in an individual's life, Etzioni says. He explains:

It is not merely a place that is warm and supportive, but also a group that draws on the affection members have for one another—to make them nobler than they would otherwise be. People are especially mindful about the admonitions and gentle chiding of those close to them (Etzioni 2003, 237-38).

Our goal should be a fair society, Etzioni says. He envisions "a society in which everyone is treated with full respect, recognizing that we are all God's children. A society in which no one—adult or child—is left behind" (Etzioni 2005, 211).

Peter Berg: Reinhabiting the Planet

Gaining awareness of one's linkage to the environment is the first step toward becoming a responsible, caring human being, according to Peter Berg. A former environmentalist who is now a leading bioregionalist, Berg says many people drift through life in a trancelike state, never thinking deeply about the origin of everyday things—the water they drink, the food they eat, the homes they inhabit, as well as fuels and other gifts from nature that they prodigiously squander.

Everyone in the world has a home-place, a base of operations, and people who are unsure of their home area's resources, geography, history, problems, and possibilities are very much out of touch with reality, bioregionalists say.

For Berg, the process of learning about one's area (and then resolving to help improve local and regional conditions) is a phenomenon he calls "reinhabitation."

Other species necessarily adjust to the environment's requirements, but humans have been less adaptive. Berg asks people to "reconceptualize your relationships with the elements of the planetary biosphere, people, society, and the exigencies of contemporary life."

In the early 1970s, a group of activists who were concerned about the environment's continuing degradation decided that environmental work needed to be approached from a cultural perspective. People were the principal actors here. How well informed were they? Was there widespread readiness for positive action to restore the environment? How did people visualize the environment and their relationships to it?

The name for the new movement, bioregionalism, was coined by Berg. He wanted people to consider the region in which they resided as having central importance in their lives. He thought each person should be deeply aware of "a life-place, the natural place around you that's alive and contains your life as well as the lives of other species." For Berg, bioregionalism has a clarity of purpose that environmentalism sometimes seems to lack.

Among bioregionalists, a geographical area that has distinctive natural characteristics is considered a bioregion. One bioregion may have prairie land, another may display mountainous terrain, and a third may include row crops and orange groves. Within a bioregion, there could be a diversity of ecosystems, including farms, urban areas, suburbs, and wilderness.

Through a process of acculturation, a resident of a bioregion may become a reinhabitant, an appreciative partner in the life-sustaining functions of the region and its constituent ecosystems.

Each bioregion should attain a high degree of self-sufficiency, bioregionalists say. Local food production could satisfy most local needs. With transportation costs rising, new manufacturing plants in the region might have a competitive advantage over distant suppliers. Instead of importing energy from suppliers in other areas, a bioregion should develop pollution-free energy systems utilizing wind, water, sunshine, and other renewable sources. Residents should seek to improve ecological efficiency in the region's existing agricultural, domestic, and industrial technologies.

Face-to-face democratic decision making in the proposed bioregions would occur in community meetings as well as on the job in offices, shops, and factories. What is envisaged here is truly grass-roots democracy.

A primary objective of the bioregionalism movement is to promote a caring-and-sharing attitude among all members of a community. With this ethos in place, the people making decisions would carefully take into consideration the needs of others plus the bioregion's environmental requirements.

Berg was one of the founders of The Planet Drum Foundation, a San Francisco–based organization promoting bioregional ideas. It maintains a directory listing 250 bioregional groups around the world. Berg travels extensively to take part in projects such as the reconstruction of a city in Ecuador badly damaged in an El Niño storm in 1998.

Urban sustainability is a major challenge, Berg says. Urban renewal in the twenty-first century involves many difficult issues. For example:

- Faced with the threat of global warming, will industrial countries make rapid progress in reducing their urban smokestacks' release of carbon dioxide and other greenhouse gases?
- Will bioregionalists be able to convince people living in condominiums that recycling bathwater has become an environmental necessity?
- Will city dwellers utilize safe, efficient methods for recycling the mountains of organic wastes that urban living generates?
- As green space continues to disappear, will urban dwellers be able to maintain close affiliation with their bioregions' natural assets?

Confident that a caring-sharing attitude can surmount serious difficulties, bioregionalists expect to see great environmental and social progress occur in and around big cities.

Coralie Bryant: Making Social Systems Inclusive

In an increasingly interdependent world, people everywhere are sharing common problems. It is no longer accurate to describe one nation as "developed" and another as "developing." There are rich nations and poor nations, says Coralie Bryant, but all countries need to develop greater problem-solving capabilities.

"Are we not all developing nations?" Bryant and co-author Christina Kappaz ask in *Reducing Poverty, Building Peace* (Bryant and Kappaz 2005). Poverty is a universal blight, and ending it is a responsibility of communities, nations, and international agencies, the authors say.

Poverty is disruptive, dividing society into privileged upper classes and an unfortunate lower class made up of people who lack access to assets widely available to the majority. Denied access to loans and other financial resources, the poor are not able to progress through their own ventures. Lacking access to important educational resources, poor people remain locked into poverty, generation after generation.

Bryant is a researcher and consultant whose extensive experience in global development includes service with the World Bank and Columbia University's Economic and Political Development Program. She offers an encouraging assurance: The war against poverty is winnable. She is concerned with effectiveness, and she sees participatory styles of development yielding good results whenever communities, institutions, and poor people stay involved and work together.

How are violence and poverty intertwined? Martin Luther King Jr. said, "Violence is everything that denies dignity and leads to a sense of hopelessness and helplessness." The unfair exclusionary practices still persisting in society are causing widespread hopelessness and helplessness among poor people, Bryant says.

Finding the appropriate road to a superior future is no easy task. In this new century, our vision of what lies ahead is becoming more clear as informed people volunteer their ideas. Environmentalists remind us that continued wastefulness and pollution will lead to environmental disaster. They offer instead attractive pictures of a transformed, sustainable future.

Bryant and other development specialists urge us to remodel global societies (including our own) so that they will no longer exclude poor people from real participation in the rich opportunities that life is currently offering. Thanks to these good-spirited visionaries, blueprints are now becoming available to help us construct a better, more humane world.

Julia Butterfly Hill: When Actions Have Impact

In the lifetime of every dedicated environmentalist, there has occurred at least one special time — one golden moment of truth — when the individual's commitment to the greening of the earth becomes absolute, fixed, and irrevocable. In some cases, the truth-knowing experience recurs time and again.

For Julia Butterfly Hill, encounters with truth took place repeatedly during more than two years when she lived in a tree, protecting the thousand-year-old California redwood from a crew of loggers.

She had expected to stay in the tree only briefly, protesting the planned assault on the old tree, but her mission proved to be of long duration. Her thoughts during that period are included in her book, *The Legacy of Luna* (Hill 2001).

After prolonged negotiations with the Pacific Lumber division of Maxxam Corporation, Hill succeeded in saving the tree Luna from destruction. Because the news media had reported her persistent effort to save the ancient tree, a large segment of the public cheered Hill on when she began her tree-sit in December 1997.

Two years later, people hailed her victory as proof that one person fighting for a good cause could triumph over great odds. Hill always amended that claim, insisting that her numerous supporters had made her stay in the tree possible.

Thinking about ways to save the environment, Hill came to realize that the environment can be affected—positively or negatively—by small, incremental changes. She explains:

> It's all about cumulative impact. Every action we take on this planet affects so much more than our personal lives. If we recognized and accepted responsibility for the compounding impact of our actions, the streams and rivers where the fish spawn would not be loaded with sedimentation. The people looking to the salmon for food would take enough for sustenance and would not take for profit. If we accepted our responsibility for the cumulative impact, there would be plenty of fish for all, including the seals (Hill 2001, 142).

Responsible, caring individuals can make the world a better place, Hill insists. She has worked on civic improvement projects in the United States and abroad. Recently she helped create The Engage Network, an organization linking people interested in community organizing and civic engagement. The network provides information-sharing assistance for community organizations.

Jon Krosnick: Examining Global Warming

Is global warming a bona fide problem? After pondering this question for years, the American public has finally decided that ongoing climate change is a serious problem requiring immediate attention.

Jon Krosnick, Stanford University professor of communication, political science, and psychology, has observed public opinion shedding its uncertainties and thus becoming more decisive. Since 2006, he says, the American public has moved "from wondering whether global warming is happening to, 'O.K., it's happening; what are we going to do about it?'"

In 1995, the news media reported global warming forecasts made by the scientific community. The print media's reports also contained statements from a few skeptics who saw no serious threat in global warming. Who was most believable? The American public hesitated, with many individuals not ready to commit themselves, but further climate change evidence has helped clarify public opinion on global warming.

Investigating shifts and changes in public opinion is an important phase of Krosnick's research work. He has found that, on the global warming issue, people who distrusted scientists could still accept scientists' views on climate change — if those views corresponded with their own personal observations of changes in temperature and air pollution levels in recent years.

Measurement of public opinion provides insights into problems of America's democratic political system (which is supposed to represent the will of the people). Prompt worldwide action will be needed to check the greenhouse gases that are accelerating global warming. The U.S. public seems ready to confront the challenge of climate change, but government leaders are not ready. The United States has failed to live up to its international greenhouse gas emission requirements, and it has resisted UN efforts to make compliance with the emission requirements mandatory.

Special-interest groups seeking to defeat, delay, or modify proposed environmental reforms have been active through the years. Their strategies include efforts to control public opinion. In her book *Global Spin,* Sharon Beder examines "the way that corporations have used their financial resources and power to counter gains made by the environmentalists, to reshape public opinion, and to persuade politicians against increased environmental regulation" (Beder 1998, 15).

To be effective, public opinion must be heard. However, Douglas E. Booth says, "The process of public discussion and debate that could lead society down the path to more extensive environmental rights is unrealizable in a world of powerful corporations capable of dominating public discourse and public decision-making.... The only final answer to this dilemma is a transformation of existing economic arrangements that would bring corporations themselves under the influence of democratic decision-making" (Booth 2004, 233).

Democratic decision making may, in time, become embedded in the business community. For now, it is important to bar corporations from making political contributions and thereby maintaining dominance in state and national politics. Without doubt, public support of political campaigns would reduce the political thrust of special interests.

According to reputable public opinion polls, fully 84 percent of the U.S. public consider themselves to be environmentalists. This major segment of the public wants to protect the environment for their children and future generations.

Are members of this numerically significant group ready to take steps to improve environmental sustainability? Are they dissatisfied with the manner in which governmental decision making on environmental policies has been conducted in the past? Do they believe substantial progress is being made in the campaign against global warming? Although public opinion seems to favor environmental reform, any successful reform drive will have to be supported by a knowledgeable, politically active citizenry.

Thomas Berry: Reinventing Ourselves

Will global society be able to get off the perilous path that may be leading us to extinction? Thomas Berry, a perceptive student of human history, is optimistic. Although he blames humans for damaging the environment severely, Berry expects the world to experience a new age of redemption and renewal.

A brand-new chapter in human history — a positive, decisive advance forward for the entire environment — can come into being whenever people have gained intellectual vision, spiritual insight, and physical resources sufficient to make good things happen, Berry says. Instead of their continuing to be "a disruptive force on the Planet Earth," he expects people to become a world-saving force of goodness and kindness.

Berry believes humans need to reinvent themselves, first by examining themselves critically, and then by deciding how to improve their performance as menders and protectors of Planet Earth.

Here are some of the steps that Berry suggests for individuals seeking a new identity as productive, creative environmentalists:

- Make sure that the problem-solving sciences and technologies you depend upon are coherent with the technologies of the natural world. "Our knowledge needs to be in harmony with the natural world rather than a domination of the natural world" (Berry 1999, 162).

- Recognize the world's community of life systems and understand the crucial importance of human participation in that community. To build a workable future, we need to consider "the Earth as a single community with ethical relations determined primarily by the well-being of the total Earth community" (Berry 1999, 163).

- Expect environmental progress to flourish in bioregions (identifiable geographic regions that contain interactive life systems). Through regional development, we can obtain productive agricultural and industrial systems that are well suited to the environmental needs of their host regions.

- Realize this is a time for powerful, positive dreams. Unfortunately, the governing dream of our society today appears as a kind of ultimate manifestation of "a deep inner rage of Western society against its earthly condition as a vital member of the life community" (Berry 1999, 165). To escape this negative frame of mind, society must have a new revelatory experience.

- Everyone should become more conscious, more deeply aware that our society's involvement in the life community qualifies us to participate in an inspiring Earth-generated dream of the future. "We probably have not had such participation in the dream of Earth since earlier shamanic times, but therein lies our hope for the future for ourselves and for the entire Earth community" (Berry 1999, 165).

Humans' perceptions of the realities they encounter within the environment have changed over time. Since the Industrial Revolution, people have tended to manipulate the environment in order to achieve results they themselves desired. Confident in their own superiority, many have disregarded whatever "rules of nature" others had tried to formulate.

Is the "me-first" attitude changing? Berry, a Catholic monk, sees a genuine transformation in progress. He says:

> We are now experiencing a moment of significance far beyond what any of us can imagine. What can be said is that the foundations of a new historical period, the Ecozoic Era, have been established in every realm of human affairs.
>
> The mythic view has been set in place. The distorted dream of an industrial technological paradise is being replaced by the more viable dream of a mutually enhancing human presence within an ever-renewing organic-based Earth community.
>
> The dream drives the action. In the larger cultural context the dream becomes the myth that both guides and drives

the action (Berry 1999, 201).

Together with Harter, Benyus, Etzioni, Berg, Bryant, Hill, and Krosnick, Berry expects society to experience positive changes as people become more perceptive regarding the world and the social forces that shape our history. Berry is optimistic, confident that we can rectify our past errors — our prolonged misuse of the environment and our callous disregard of poor people who have needed our help. When we change our behavior, he says, we will then be able to look out and see a transformed world.

GETTING READY FOR CHANGE

A group of people meeting to discuss environmental problems may pose a clear and present danger. That is the message I received on April 22, 1970, the first Earth Day. Along with six fellow faculty members at a college in mid-America, I attended an outdoor meeting on the campus. Twelve students also attended.

We sat down on well-manicured grass, elected a chairman (by acclamation) and proceeded to discuss environmental problems affecting our campus, the town, and the nearby countryside.

All at once, we were surrounded by a horde of noisy, exhaust-belching lawnmowers. They kept crisscrossing the area where we sat, never intruding on our immediate space, but their noise level was high. We tried to ignore them and continued our meeting.

Twenty-two minutes later, the lawn-mower brigade was gone, but someone had turned on the sprinklers. Slightly damp but still undaunted, we retreated to a friendly off-campus pub.

Often, people who have behaved negatively do change. It is possible the groundskeepers I encountered on Earth Day 1970 now recycle their trash, contribute to environmental organizations, and worry about global warming. Or maybe not.

Everyone need not become an environmentalist, but it is reasonable to assume that almost everyone is aware of two spine-tingling facts: (1) the era of cheap petroleum is over, and (2) the threat of global warming becomes more real each day.

Cheap oil made possible many useful extras in our lives — things like heating fuel, motor fuel, fuel for electric power generators, non-rubber tires, many pharmaceuticals, easy-care clothing, new building materials, and a multitude of plastic gadgets. We will miss the past, but we cannot retrieve it. We are obliged to go ahead with designing and constructing a workable future less dependent on oil.

Global warming is approaching but is still at the stage where we can take steps to slow it down. We must act before Greenland's vast ice sheets melt, raising oceanic levels higher and higher, causing floods to inundate coastal areas.

For institutions and individuals, this is a time for change. People are exploring ways in which social systems could become more inclusive, more democratic. In the environmental movement, new emphasis is being placed on solving nasty problems, not just making do with partial fixes.

SOLUTIONS THAT DON'T WORK

New problem-solving technologies are always welcome. However, it is important to recognize the inadequacies of some new ideas and new systems. It is wrong to pretend that our growing energy crisis can be solved by shifting from fossil fuels to nuclear energy or gasohol.

At this time, nuclear energy is extremely risky, potentially a major environmental hazard. There is no safe place in which to dispose of radioactive wastes. Years ago, nuclear waste was to be disposed of in holes drilled deeply into the earth. This unsafe idea was shelved, but nothing better took its place. Dangerous wastes continue to pile up in "temporary" storage.

Gasohol is gasoline blended with ethanol manufactured from food crops. Too expensive to compete with gasoline on the open market, gasohol is heavily subsidized by the federal government. Production of ethanol is energy-intensive. Crops must be grown, harvested, and converted into ethanol in factories, with much energy expended at each stage of production.

As a source of ethanol, corn actually yields less energy than the total amount of energy expended in its production. Ethanol is a loser, and its deficiencies should be obvious in any diligent search for new energy. Right now, politicians seem ready to do anything to deal with the energy crisis, completely undeterred by the hard facts of *energy in* versus *energy out*.

Weeds, wastes, and low-value agricultural byproducts may become valuable energy sources in the future. First, extensive research will be needed. In nature, other energy sources may be useful. At present, solar energy offers promising possibilities. Other sustainable energy sources under review include wind power, tidal energy, smaller-scale hydropower, and geothermal power.

DEMOCRACY'S GREAT IMPACT

Democracy has contagious ideas. The belief that everyone's welfare is important has become standard doctrine in the environmental movement. Opinions have changed. Not long ago, indignant urban residents displayed "Not in My Backyard" signs as they protested plans for construction of toxic waste incinerators near their homes. Now, environmentalists generally understand that dangerous, polluting installations should not be allowed near any residential neighborhood.

Environmental injustices that result in health problems need to be corrected. For instance:

- Millions of Americans have respiratory problems and other ailments that are aggravated by pollution. U.S. industry discharges 11.4 billion tons of toxic wastes into the environment each year.
- The majority (three out of five) of African Americans and Latinos

nationwide live in communities that have illegal or abandoned toxic dumps.

- More than 313,000 farm workers (mostly undocumented immigrants) suffer from pesticide poisoning each year.
- Native Americans suffer a disproportionate environmental risk of illness and other health problems caused by industrial pollutants.
- More than 43 million people live within four miles of at least one of the nation's most dangerous toxic waste sites (places included on the National Priority List of the Environmental Protection Agency).

Seeking Environmental Justice

A society plagued by injustices and inequities is unhealthy; it is lacking in the compassion and the resolve one would expect of thriving democratic societies. Recognizing that ecological ills are symptomatic of deeper ills in society, many environmentalists are building alliances with other citizen activists, hoping to form a broadly based reform movement.

Daniel Faber says the "movements for environmental justice are increasingly embracing the principles of ecological democracy. Of these principles, the most fundamental is the claim that those communities of people suffering ecological injustices must be afforded greater participation in the decision-making processes of capitalist industry and the state (at all levels), as well as the environmental movement itself, if the social and ecological problems plaguing *all* Americans are ever to be resolved" (Faber 1998, 1).

Every so often, business owners have volunteered to extend decision-making powers to their employees. Sometimes, in gratitude for their workers' loyalty through the years, owners have converted their firms into employee-owned businesses. In another arrangement, the owner cedes some important decision-making powers to the firm's employees.

Successful in many lines of business, cooperatives may be owned by either patrons of a business or its workers. Various styles of decision making have evolved in co-ops.

If many workers participated in business decision making, this would help democratize the economy. It would give workers a voice in deciding environment-related questions affecting the health and welfare of large numbers of people. Some decisions that a business will make could have special relevance for local residents and the surrounding environment. Shared decision making would be a great gain for grassroots democracy.

RESTORING COMMUNITY

A strong, cooperative community spirit develops in an area in which residents decide to communicate with each other about their common problems and then work together for satisfactory solutions. In urban and rural areas, people are discovering they can achieve worthwhile goals through community solidarity.

Many difficult problems merit community consideration. In recent years, environmental issues have been of pressing importance. In Detroit, two years of protests by local residents resulted in a hospital closing down a medical waste incinerator that had been linked to the high rate of asthma among local children. When local people protested the presence of a new hazardous waste site in North Carolina, their action triggered similar protests (and site closures) in several states.

Sociologists anticipate severe urban-centered environmental problems in the years to come. Worldwide, cities are growing at a fabulous rate—faster than at any previous time in human history. Pollutants and toxic wastes could become critical problems. Due to the energy crisis, supplies of water, heat, and inexpensive transportation might be limited.

Quality of life might show substantial improvements, however.

Viewed from the perspective of someone living fifty years from now, the ads in today's news media could be confusing. Why all the emphasis on consuming without taking into consideration the primary need for a sustainable environment?

Life as it is lived by a member of a community consists to a great degree of caring and sharing. You care for other community members and you share each other's lives, knowing your life goals are very similar. Of course, each member is unique, a separate person. If two members disagree, they find a way to agree on many particulars, thereby reaching an amicable conclusion — an authentic win – win situation.

Time spent caring and sharing will be enjoyed by the people sojourning together down life's highway. Will the entire world benefit? Noam Chomsky seems to suggest that the caring-sharing pilgrims' example may convince others that the light of hope still shines in this dark world. Chomsky says:

> At this stage in history, one of two things is possible. Either the general population will take care of its own destiny and will concern itself with community interests guided by values of solidarity, sympathy and concern for others or, alternatively, there will be no destiny for anyone to control.

REFERENCES

Beder, Sharon. 1998. *Global Spin: The Corporate Assault on Environmentalism.* White River Junction, VT: Chelsea Green Publishing.

Benyus, Janine M. 1997. *Biomimicry: Innovation Inspired by Nature.* New York: William Morrow.

Berry, Thomas M. 1999. *The Great Work: Our Way into the Future.* New York: Bell Tower.

Booth, Douglas E. 2004. *Hooked on Growth: Economic Addictions and the Environment.* Lanham, MD: Rowman & Littlefield.

Bryant, Coralie, and Christina Kappaz. 2005. *Reducing Poverty, Building Peace.* Bloomfield, VT: Kumarian Press.

Etzioni, Amitai. 2003. *My Brother's Keeper: A Memoir and a Message.* Lanham, MD: Rowman & Littlefield.

Etzioni, Amitai. 2005. "The Fair Society." In *Uniting America: Restoring the Vital Center to American Democracy,* edited by Norton Garfinkle and David Yankelovich. New Haven, CT: Yale University Press.

Faber, Daniel. 1998. "Introduction." In *The Struggle for Ecological Democracy and Environmental Justice: Movements in the United States,* edited by Daniel Faber. New York: Guilford Press.

Gottlieb, Robert. 2001. *Environmentalism Unbound: Exploring New Pathways for Change.* Cambridge, MA: MIT Press.

Hill, Julia Butterfly. 2001. *The Legacy of Luna: The Story of a Tree, a Woman, and the Struggle to Save the Redwoods.* San Francisco: Harper.

Klein, Naomi. 2007. *The Shock Doctrine: The Rise of Disaster Capitalism.* New York: Henry Holt.

Liotta, P. H., and Allan W. Shearer. 2007. *Gaia's Revenge: Climate Change and Humanity's Loss.* Westport, CT: Praeger.

Moran, Emilio F. 2006. *People and Nature: An Introduction to Human Ecological Relations.* Malden, MA: Blackwell.

Sale, Kirkpatrick. 1985. *Dwellers in the Land: The Bioregional Vision.* San Francisco: Sierra Club Books.

Shiva, Vandana. 2003. "The Myths of Globalization Exposed: Advancing toward Global Democracy." In *Worlds Apart: Globalization and the Environment,* edited by James Gustave Speth. Washington, DC: Island Press.

Shutkin, William A. 2001. *The Land That Could Be: Environmentalism and Democracy in the Twenty-First Century.* Cambridge, MA: MIT Press.

Leadership as Legacy Work

Les Wallace and James Trinka

Our greatest responsibility is to be good ancestors. (Jonas Salk)

The twenty-first century has signaled a need to think differently about leadership, developing leaders, and leadership impact. The last two decades of research and teaching have provided valuable clarity as to how leadership is learned and, therefore, how to help us learn to become better leaders. *Fortune* magazine went so far as to lead their story on "What it Takes to Be Great" by announcing: "Research now shows that the lack of natural talent is irrelevant to great success. The secret? Painful and demanding practice and hard work" (Colvin 2006). We're not certain that talent is irrelevant, but the point about learning is crucial to effective leadership and leadership development.

We use legacy as a means of helping people see leadership through new eyes. This line of sight to legacy emanates from our career work in leadership development in the government and the private sector, where we have been privileged to serve thousands of learners by facilitating discovery of lessons on leadership. We acknowledge researcher and author Marcus Buckingham's caution

Les Wallace is president of Signature Resources Inc. and co-author of *A Legacy of 21st Century Leadership* (iUniverse, 2007). E-mail les@signatureresources.com.

Jim Trinka is the technical training director for the Federal Aviation Administration (FAA) and co-author of *A Legacy of 21st Century Leadership*. E-mail jim.trinka@faa.gov.

that corporate America has overcomplicated the role of leader. We believe it is possible to uncomplicate leadership by focusing on fundamental and meaningful outcomes—legacy—and carefully considering your strategies for creating a leadership climate (Wallace and Trinka 2007).

Elements of what we will identify as twenty-first-century leadership were indeed percolating earlier in the literature than December 31, 1999. Most certainly Peter Drucker's early work (1967), Donald Schon's seminal work on learning societies and learning organizations (1973), Warren Bennis and Burt Nanus's discourse on a search for new leadership (1985), Charles Handy's reflection on discontinuous change (1990), and Peter Senge's perspectives on leading learning organizations (1990) all predated the turn of this century by many years. Yet today, as "leadership" has become a lightning rod for what's right and wrong with global business and government, it's possible to discern a set of challenges and principles that, to us, clearly converge to suggest what twenty-first-century leadership should look like.

We do not claim rights to the topics of leadership and legacy, nor is it our intent to pronounce our perspective any better than those of others who have written eloquently on the topic. We do suggest that the demands on organizational leadership have shifted significantly in the last couple of decades, and great leaders keep recalibrating their talent and strategy. It is our purpose to challenge the reader with several fundamental thoughts, one of which is that you're leaving a legacy whether you're thinking about it or not. We believe that thinking about legacy and making legacy intentional will help us see our leadership potential through a new prism.

A LEGACY PERSPECTIVE

Effective leaders make a difference, and they leave legacies. Whether you assume a leadership role in a crisis situation or serve as a leader in an organization for an extended period of time, you leave behind an imprint of your leadership. Some imprints are healthy, some less so. Simply remember the climate of leadership and performance you may have inherited throughout your career to validate our case.

In the last decade, research emanating from case studies, surveys, focus groups, and twenty-first-century leadership theory share a common finding: Effective leaders never stop learning. That is, they never reach a final destination in their leadership journey. They continue learning, adapting, and seeking impact as they come into contact with new people, organizations, opportunities, and dilemmas. While core values may remain steadfast and their leadership competencies may mature, great leaders seek ongoing opportunities to enhance their own leadership impact and the imprint they leave on an organization — legacy. Organizations and/or specific work groups may have different needs and challenges that require a leader to focus his or her attention on particular values and competencies. A leader may leave a legacy of integrity, transparency, and a commitment to learning in one situation and may find different priorities in another. In fact, great leaders know that a textbook approach to leadership will not yield the kind of legacy they seek not only with the people they lead, but also with the organizations they serve.

How does a leader approach this difficult task? To explore the landscape of potential legacies, a leader might begin by focusing on some recognized best-practice leadership competencies (e.g., leading change, collaboration, leveraging diversity, and developing others). Numerous researchers have closely examined successful organizations and leaders and suggested a list of common competencies possessed by the best. Typically, the research identifies a core of ten to twenty competencies and/or characteristics that differentiate great leaders and organizations from the rest (Zenger and Folkman 2002). Supposedly, if you as a leader focus your attention on some or all of these items, you can move from good to great and can ensure that you leave a positive legacy. However, from most of this competency research, you may gain very little insight into which of these characteristics and/or competencies is more important than the others and may wonder where to start on this daunting challenge. Does your organization require ongoing transformation and flexibility right now, or should you focus more on developing others or on embedding a new era of collaboration in the organizational culture? The point is that great leaders learn the solutions to these leadership dilemmas day-to-day in organizations worldwide. The key resides in the learning process—i.e., continuing to see leadership as a learning process—and not necessarily in the competencies and characteristics themselves.

We think of leadership as a portfolio of characteristics and competencies that we grow over time as we learn to see and deal with dilemmas with a greater field of vision Thus, a growing portfolio helps determine a leader's legacy as does the business situations in which they find themselves.

A Twenty-First-Century Leadership Perspective

The age of heroic leadership is over. The myth of the "great man" or "great woman"—leading larger than life and rescuing powerless organizational associates—has been dispelled. Great leadership occurs in a culture of leadership that is expected, developed, and distributed at all levels of the organization where people can display their natural ability to learn, adapt, and—yes—lead. Leaders don't create followers. They create other leaders.

Transform Rather than Rescue

While periodic exigencies hit the desks of leaders, today's leadership is more about ongoing transformation than seasonal rescue. Quite possibly, it's more about revolution than evolution. Not only is the world more chaotic and complex, but also the velocity of growing complexity is accelerating. Donald Sull of the London Business School captures this intense pressure not only to change reactively but also to transform proactively. He notes, "Uncertain markets exert an unforgiving selection pressure on companies by churning out an unrelenting series of opportunities and threats. New companies emerge to pursue novel opportunities, while established companies that cannot adapt fail. The only way to avoid this harsh Darwinian pressure is to adapt to changing circumstances before market pressures select against your company" (Sull 2006). In their own way, governments and nongovernmental organizations around the globe experience similar pressures.

The pace of growing complexity demands that twenty-first-century organizations listen more closely to external trends and business environment shifts, believe in ongoing change, and set the bar high for revolutionizing themselves regularly. Hamel and Valikangas (2003) remind us: "In the past, executives had the luxury of assuming that business models were more or less immortal. Companies always had to work to get better, of course, but they seldom had to get different—not at their core, not in their essence. Today, getting different is the imperative." In *Leading the Revolution*, Gary Hamel is even more passionate about the need for organizational transformation in the twenty-first century by declaring, "Evolution keeps us alive; revolution keeps us relevant" (Hamel 2000).

The status quo is slow death, and transformational leaders help people let go of old models that worked in the past for new models that better fit the developing environment. We all become limited by comfort and reliance on established mental models of how enterprises should behave. As numerous authors have pointed out over the last couple of decades, leadership in a postmodern world requires that we challenge traditional mental models (Wind et al. 2004). Leaders tend to be able to create a sense of excitement about where the organization can go rather than a sense of remorse for the models they must leave behind. Rather than annual strategy sessions, twenty-first-century leaders create ongoing conversations about the future, help the organization think more strategically and challenge assumptions about their models.

Leveraging Diversity, or Just Like Me

If it's up to the individual leader to create the organizational values and then hold people accountable, there will always be a top-down mantra to them rather than a community of ownership. Yes, leaders stand up for values and model personal responsibility. They even demand that values shift when the internal and external environments require it. However, lasting greatness comes from broad ownership rather than the single-minded will of one leader.

In today's organization, the diverse backgrounds and perspectives require that organizational values be shaped by leveraging that diversity. In *Authentic Leadership*, Bill George talks about this cultural quality as "not a question of achieving affirmative action quotas, but rather of building breadth of thought and opinion into the decision making process" (George 2003). David Thomas and Robin Ely's observations on this aspect of diversity reminds us that "diversity should be understood as the varied perspectives and approaches to work that members of different identity groups bring" (Thomas and Ely 1996). This diversity is more than respecting differences; it is about strategically using differences as an organizational resource for seeing new avenues to effectiveness.

Distributed Leadership vs. Top Down

When the members of a team all look to a single source or hero for rescue or guidance, they're playing a risky game. Twenty-first-century leadership requires a different model built upon a phalanx of leaders, all capable, confident, and prepared for the villains and threats to their organization: leaders at all levels. Yes, employees and staff also step up to leadership.

Where the heroic leader may only see other leaders around them, the transformational leader seeks out, develops, and rewards leadership at all levels. Transformational leaders believe in distributing leadership. They can be seen mentoring, coaching, and ensuring that development resources are invested in all managers and staff in the organization. The self-confidence based upon competency development, clear objectives, and interdependent collaboration built by transformational leaders permeates the organization. Resiliency and resolve are built deeper into the bench rather than with only a few power hitters. Twenty-first-century leadership commits to developing successors so that, when one generation of leaders moves on, a legacy of leadership is maintained.

"Our" vs. "My" Vision, Mission, and Values

The age of heroic leadership gave great credit to the dynamic leader bringing his or her personal version of nirvana to the huddled organizational masses. The age of transformational leadership finds stronger power in the facilitation of a common, energizing, long-term vision owned by architects organization-wide. Yes, this is more difficult. Yet, we all care for a product we help build and fight for a goal we help set with greater vigilance than one given to us by others. Simon Cooper, president of Ritz-Carlton, captured it best when he observed, "No one is more apathetic than in pursuit of someone else's goal" (Cooper 2005). Senge (1990) contrasts the generic "vision statement" so popular in this era with "genuine vision." Genuine vision consists of pictures of the future commonly shared across the organization—shared, not because the leader said so, but because people have been involved in shaping this powerful view of their future.

Heroes certainly have that fiery speech and energizing "rah rah" that can send teams into frenzied short-term effort. Transformational leaders, however, imbue a sense of quiet community "can do," and we stay on the bus long term because we all feel ownership.

Critical Thinking vs. Linear, Hierarchical Thinking

"Promise to disagree with me" may be the mantra of the transformational leader. When we all think alike, no one seems to really think much. Last century's model of looking to the top for answers or, worse yet, following a tried and true multilayer linear process to reach decisions, fails to keep organizations relevant to rapidly shifting problems, values, and models. A less symmetrical input and thought structure helps create a climate of creativity and critical breakthrough thinking throughout the entire organization. Critical thinking explores challenges from nontraditional as well as traditional perspectives. While law enforcement and war strategies are all adapting to asymmetrical thinking by our enemies, an organization must also leverage the power of asymmetrical critical thinking. Teaching people to think for themselves in different ways does not mean dismantling organizational authority or values. It does mean twenty-first-century leaders recognize that they don't have all the answers, and if they place boundaries on ideas, or require ideas to navigate a thick, bureaucratic, suggestion-box-like maze, they limit their leadership effectiveness.

Dialogue vs. Command-and-Control

How do transformational leaders build the capacity and resolve so people accept their own leadership, think critically, and step up when needed? Through ongoing dialogue about how the organization is doing, where it is going, and what might be expected. It is not debate, not discussion, but true dialogue where value conflicts are uncovered, new opportunities are discovered, and an informed and strategic perspective is embedded (Yankelovitch 1999). Dialogue applies "both/and" thinking rather than "either/or" thinking. The power of command is great and the dynamism of heroism is electric; however, the perspective, confidence, and capabilities built through transformational leadership dialogue live in the organization beyond any heroics.

Engaging the intellectual capital of your organization requires a commitment to lots of listening, appreciative questioning, and a deeper understanding of the motives and perspectives driving your workforce. Twenty-first-century leaders find the time to enlarge both the circle of dialogue and investment in real dialogue as a means of keeping fresh, connected, and alert to those they lead.

Ask vs. Tell

Transformational leaders facilitate mutual success by asking vs. telling. They look for "both/and" unity rather than "either/or" answers. This requires a patient, facilitative, and interest-based competency. Within a culture of transformational leadership, a greater number of people are better prepared for decisions and problem solving because they are led to explore new and diverse pathways rather than directed to the easy path. Michael Marquardt has written an entire book on the value of a leader's questions and suggests a "question does more than convey respect for the person to whom it's posed. It actually encourages that person's development as a thinker and problem solver, thereby delivering both the short-term value of generating a solution to the issue at hand and the long-term value of giving subordinates the tools to handle similar issues in the future independently" (Marquardt 2005). In *Funky Business*, the authors encourage leaders to learn to ask questions in unique ways and before others even think of asking (Ridderstrale and Nordstrom 2000). In this way, leaders help teach others to always be questioning and therefore help their organization potentially stay ahead of the need for reactive change.

Collaboration vs. Cooperation

Preschoolers are taught to cooperate. Adult success requires collaboration — sharing effort and resources as partners, not simply as good neighbors lending their tools across the fence. In the landscape of transformational leadership, a feeling of "teamness" exists where interdependent collaboration takes place regularly, not simply when the emergency siren sounds. Because silos and territoriality occur naturally from the intensive attention to executing tasks at the department and division level, the leader has to work harder to set a standard of collaboration across the enterprise and the value to be derived from our important mission. Silos need to merge into a cross-functional footprint in all that they do. Functional units need to think in terms of "all of us" rather than just themselves as they make decisions and plans. Human networks must anticipate the ripple effects of their efforts and alert their collaborative partners. Seamless collaborative efforts in planning and execution outperform short rallies of cooperation over the long term.

Territoriality is not only caused by believing your area might be the most important one. Territoriality may also be caused by conflict felt between work units. In their article "Want Collaboration?" Weiss and Hughes challenge leaders to think differently and focus on the conflicts, not the nice-nice, "kumbaya" initiatives. "Most companies respond to the challenge of improving collaboration in entirely the wrong way. They focus on the symptoms ('sales and delivery do not work together') rather than on the root cause of failures in cooperation: conflict. The fact is, you can't improve collaboration until you've addressed the issue of conflict" (Weiss and Hughes 2005). Powerful insight, we think, into diagnosing why we may not be getting the interdependency necessary for great outcomes.

Passion 24/7 vs. a Job

Twenty-first-century leaders believe they are in the job to do something rather than to have something to do. Heroic passion may well spike to great heights in time of need. However, passionate leadership can also be a choice for steady, resilient, and relentless effort. Passionate leadership can be a commitment to grow others, innovate, and create a quality work life. In *Good to Great*, Jim Collins refers to this type of leadership as "Level 5" leadership. It's neither sensational nor heroic. It is a determined, steady, and humble resolve. Twenty-first-century leaders don't decide at the heroic moment to "go"; they decided long ago and demonstrated an unrelenting commitment to new models that keep the organization viable, valuable, and vibrant.

Life is too short to work in a climate under pressure for which you have no love. We don't have to love everything we do, but we believe an element of twenty-first-century leadership is having a passion for leading and helping others find a similar passion. Don't mistake this as 1950s "rah rah." We speak here of valuing what you do and helping others see value for them. While a great speech maker may rile our emotion on occasion, we refer here to the leader able to use mission connectedness, a common energizing vision, and an appreciation for the contributions of others to build passion.

Leading *and* Following

It is not an either/or choice. Transformational leaders know when to lead and when to follow. If individuals cannot learn to subordinate themselves to a shared purpose, then no one will follow, and selfishness and anarchy may rule. Followership means we rely on each other, set aside personal agendas, and collaborate for the good of the organization. It also means being coachable and accepting the feedback and ideas of others. The tension between leading and following is acute in many organizations clinging to hierarchical leadership. The tension between leading and following is challenging to any organization that has not clearly defined its leadership model and the climate of leadership expected throughout. Where do your associates see you modeling good followership?

TRANSFORMATIONAL RATHER THAN TRANSACTIONAL

You may recognize the prior leadership elements as characteristic of transformational leadership as contrasted with transactional leadership. Transactional leadership — most characteristic of what we refer to as twentieth-century leadership — revolves around transactions between leader and followers based on self-interest and managing and controlling the enterprise. The source of influence in a transactional model is position or command authority. Put in traditional management jargon, it is planning, organizing, coordinating, directing, and controlling. Organizations need these transactional functions adequately fulfilled.

Transformational leadership engages people beyond self-interest based on moving the enterprise to new strategic positions, accomplishments, and innovations. The source of influence is not positional or hierarchical, but expertise, credibility, interpersonal competence, and role modeling. Put in traditional leadership jargon — it is developing others, culture building, strategic thinking, and marked change (transformation).

Another way to conceptualize the differences between transactional and transformational leadership may be to contrast the leadership focus. In Figure 1, we've exaggerated the differences in order to provide a clearer sense of transformational or twenty-first-century leadership.

FIVE LEGACIES WORTHY OF THE TWENTY-FIRST CENTURY

Many of you reading this heading probably thought, who are these guys to be nominating what my legacy should be? You would be right. Any prescriptive approach to your legacy would be arrogant and audacious, because we don't live in your leadership culture with your challenges and your competency sets.

Figure 1: Transactional vs. Transformational Leadership Focus

Some simple directional differences:

Heroic	Transformational
I	We
Boss	Coach
Tell	Ask
Independent	Interdependent
Exclusive	Inclusive
Push	Pull
Secretive	Transparent
Business Results	Balanced Measures
Limited Input	Lots of Input
Control	Facilitate
Stability	Change
Either/Or	Both/And
Operational	Strategic

However, we have lived in contact each year for more than thirty years with a multitude of organizations, leadership climates, and enterprise challenges. Those have been our work, our consulting, and our passion. From those contacts and our observations about the new challenges facing leadership in the twenty-first century, we will risk stretching your thinking around what we do believe are five crucial aspects of organizational leadership worthy of leadership legacy reflection. In an earlier publication we offered ten legacies worthy of consideration (Wallace and Trinka 2007). Are these the only ones? Of course not. One size cannot possibly fit all. However, we believe you will be able to see yourself in some small way in each of the categories discussed below. It is that reflection we seek as outcome.

1. Developing Leaders at All Levels

We believe leadership in the twenty-first century is less about you as a leader and more about the climate of leadership you are able to create. Such a climate is distinguished by believing that everyone has leadership in him or her and by a commitment to develop leaders at all levels. In their book by the same name, Spreitzer and Quinn call this focus *A Company of Leaders* (2001). During his GE years, Jack Welch modeled this commitment by personally teaching at GE's Executive Development Center every two weeks, and he didn't miss a session in sixteen years. David Novak, head of Yum! Brands, committed to leading ten weeks of leadership workshops around the world and understood how important it was for growing the business (Tichy 1997). Remember, the average manager spends 15 to 20 percent of his or her time on employee development activities, which implies the great ones commit even more (Corporate Executive Board 2003). Look for the teachable moments that present themselves every day.

In *The Leadership Pipeline* (2001), Charan, Droteer, and Noel write about making a commitment to helping each employee with leadership transitions, from individual leadership through enterprise-level leadership, for those who have the will to take on that challenge. The organizations demonstrating this commitment to leaders at all levels find traditional succession-planning tactics to be less critical, because they always have a ready pool of capable people already leading and ready to step in when positional openings appear (Benest and Wallace 2007).

2. Thinking Differently

What's not working? What are your challenges? What are our weaknesses? Chances are, these are the first questions you were taught to ask when you became a manager or took over a new work unit. Even if you were taught to use a full-spectrum set of questions like those in a SWOT (strengths, weaknesses, opportunities, threats) analysis, most likely you zeroed right in on the problems and weaknesses. This is not evil, nor is it bad advice.

However, we propose that a twenty-first-century leadership climate would benefit from looking more closely at what works and finding ways to do more or leverage that success even more. This approach is neither new nor less developed as leadership theory than other approaches. Well articulated by Cooperrider and Srivastva (1987), its premise is that an organization that keeps focusing on problems will find more and more things that don't work well. An organization looking to discover what it's best at will continue to find more and more that is good. Leaders use appreciative inquiry as a process for engaging people across the organization around what works. This approach enhances a climate of acknowledgement of contributions and success and builds an even greater energy for success and real innovation (Whitney and Trosten-Bloom 2003).

We're not suggesting you abandon a problem-solving approach. We are suggesting that you may leave your associates an even greater legacy of leadership by asking first "What's working well?" or "What are our greatest successes?" This approach makes traditional managers and leaders nervous. We are so ingrained to study the problems that it feels disingenuous to start the other way around. It's not either/or!

3. Transparency

While it may be harder to keep a secret in the modern-day organization teeming with e-mail, Internet, curious unions, customer groups, and the press, it's not a good idea anyway. People have always wanted to know the ins and outs of what's happening in their place of work—both strategic and tactical—and the reasons why. It's not easy, and it does take time to inform and provide rationale. However, trust, commitment, and better overall decision making at the lowest levels occur when the climate of leadership is open rather than closed. Why is this so hard? Many reasons, but we can think of several to ponder in the context of a leadership discussion. First, too many organizations model leadership that's more secretive than open because their leaders don't trust the associates with full disclosure. Additionally, ask yourself how many leaders you've known who could share openly and were capable of managing the predictably tense dialogue that goes with communicating clearly while respecting the views of all organizational associates. Not many, we would venture.

Transparency is not simply about being open; it's also about the communication competencies to navigate the organizational discussion that follows in a manner that creates common energy, trust, and resiliency. Consider the transparency proposition from where you sit in your organization. To us, it feels worthy of a leadership legacy to leave a culture capable of handling transparency.

4. Innovation

A climate of creativity results in novel approaches being taken to traditional processes and products. However, a climate of innovation results in dramatic shifts in the entire model of why processes and products exist and how they should be delivered. Creativity happens much more naturally as employees and customers tinker, out of a sense of efficiency and effectiveness, with the elements of process and products. Innovation happens less naturally and requires a climate that allows organizational associates and customers to challenge the very nature of the process or product itself. As Day and Schoemaker suggest in their book about strategic vigilance, leaders must give people permission and "the ability to always question and provide room for disproving conventional wisdom" (Day and Schoemaker 2006).

Because innovation requires significant permission, energy,

and collaboration, the bigger innovation paradigm shifts are rarer than creative slants resulting in incremental changes. Permission, energy, and collaboration are the result of leadership. Think about your own organization: What big innovation has occurred in the last several years? Does your organization welcome the voices of those who think far beyond the horizon about your basic models of service and product? The contemporary organizational literature would tell us that innovation is rare and that it takes significant leadership to bring it to fruition. Because innovation is so rare, it certainly stands in our eyes as a critical nominee as a leadership legacy worthy of the twenty-first century.

5. Commitment to Learning

Leaders are learners. They never consider themselves to have already arrived and seem always to be seeking new perspectives, investigating what makes others successful, and reflecting on how they are leading. This is beyond simple curiosity for hobby topics or literature of interest. This is about leaders challenging themselves and teaching the organization to challenge itself to continue reflecting, learning, and growing. When Peter Senge introduced "learning organization" into common organizational language in 1990, he recognized a commitment to learning as an organization-wide legacy worthy of effort (Senge 1990). Is there an open climate of learning, dialogue about successes and failures, and non-finger-pointing autopsies of less than optimal outcomes? Are regular critical reflection sessions (Ernst and Martin 2006) commonplace in the learning structure of your organization?

LEAVING LEGACY IMPRINTS: FIVE POWERFUL LEADERSHIP BEHAVIORS

Leaders leave legacies. They impact an organization, work team, or individuals in ways that have lasting marks on culture and values, how people work together, and the growth of individuals. As a leader, your time is finite and shouldn't be squandered. Whether measured in years or shorter cycles, leaders always leave legacies: some huge, some small, some healthy, some less so. But they always leave a legacy.

We ask you to consider the primary channels through which leaders leave their fingerprints on organizations and people. This list is not exhaustive; it's merely suggestive of how leaders can cause positive leadership climates to take roots. We suggest you ask yourself, what is the context of 90 percent of your day? How much attention do you, can you, pay to these critical leadership legacy pressure points?

The Individuals Whom You Select

An impact-rich opportunity exists with every appointment, hire, and most certainly every promotion. Each new voice and behavioral model becomes a chorus for the legacy you wish to leave. Have you ensured a commitment to diversity, a system that puts the right people in the right roles at the right time? Does your organization accurately evaluate and develop employee potential? Are you deputizing the right people? Are your leadership expectations clearly at work in promotion decisions?

What do you do if the personnel system with which you work poses constraints upon you selecting the exact person you believe is the right match? Many of us have them—those systems where test scores or seniority might dictate the slate of candidates from which you must choose (or worse, the candidate you must take). This can be frustrating as well as damaging to the leadership culture you wish to build. Years of experience, high test scores, or bureaucratic ability to navigate a personnel system are not customarily the evidence of leadership we look for. If indeed your personnel system restricts your ability to select the candidates you consider right for leadership, then it's important to begin ensuring that the pipeline creating candidates is preparing leaders, not senior bureaucrats. By working hard to redesign leadership development from the ground up, including having those leaders with the right leadership competencies teaching and coaching in the developmental curriculum, you begin impacting the leadership quality of candidates choosing to advance. The higher the leadership quality in the pipeline, the less retarding the selection process will be on your legacy.

- Recall the last selection you made. How will that enhance your legacy focus?
- What are the upcoming opportunities to impact your leadership legacy by a personnel selection?

How You Offer Recognition and Appreciation

What gets noticed gets repeated. What gets repeated gets embedded. Recognition and reinforcement need to be matched to the style and sensitivities of the organization. Personal comments, thank yous, and notes of appreciation help sustain the effort. More prominent organization-wide awards become a clear message to everyone about what you believe is important. Professionals and macho organization types need this as much as anybody. While mission connectedness may be sufficient for most people to give you great performance, personal recognition is required to seal in leadership behavior. The more difficult the new behavior, the more counter to the old culture it is, then the greater the volume of recognition and appreciation is needed from you.

- What strategies are you using to reinforce, recognize, and appreciate the new behaviors and actions that support the legacy important to you?
- What management/leadership action have you recently recognized that is supportive of the climate of leadership/leadership legacy you desire?

The Coalitions You Form

Influence is not linear. Command is not simply hierarchical. And leadership is certainly not an individual sport. In addition to surrounding yourself with folks who complement and enhance your own leadership impact, whom have you recruited from the less obvious sectors of the organization to help give consistent voice to your legacy? Opinion leaders don't always occupy an official seat of power. They do, however, have the power to influence. Ensuring you have a coalition and that they feel the impact of your teaching, modeling, and communication simply distributes your legacy deeper and deeper into all the nooks and crannies of the organization. These coalitions allow you to leverage the leadership strengths that others possess, demonstrate openness to influence (followership), and distribute leadership even deeper into the organization.

- What broad-based coalition can you count on to support your leadership legacy objective?
- Can you name ten nonmanagement personnel who can be counted on to be vocal as your coalition?

Teachable Points of View

Influencing values and leading with impact requires that we be clear on our own points of view and how to teach what we've learned. Teachable moments happen every day in large and small venues. If you're clear on the impact you desire to make, then you most likely can tell instructive stories, ask questions that lead others to consider implications and values, and nurture others to develop strong ideas of their own. A good storyteller tells a good story; a great storyteller helps us see ourselves in the story (Wacker and Taylor 2000).

Are you teaching? Are you purposely spending the time to explore, explain, and have others engage you about your values, style, and approaches? While it's nice to be prominent in the leadership development program in your organization, also stay aware of the teachable moments that approach us every day. Are you also cognizant and openly appreciative of what others are teaching you? If you're approaching leadership as it's written about here, you're learning enormously as you go. You can also teach by letting others see how you learn. Leading is teaching and learning.

How we handle crisis/failure also offers incredible teaching moments. The Army War College reminds us that no battle plan ever survived the first shot intact. Bad things happen to great plans, and how you handle crisis when it happens leaves a deep impression on those keeping close tabs on how leaders lead. If you want people to react with the right instincts in hostile, confusing, and unpredictable moments, you have to demonstrate it yourself. These are moments and situations rich with influence potential: People are alert, seeking responsive leadership, and receptive. Ernst and Andre (2006) remind us that people learn best when they learn in the moment, and that critical reflections and dialogue as we go through challenging periods help keep the focus on improvement rather than fingerpointing.

- What formal and informal opportunities are you finding to teach?
- When's the last time you thanked someone for helping you learn by giving you a teachable moment?

Mentoring and Coaching

All winners have good coaches. You had natural talent, but others helped you focus, refine, and polish that talent into the leader you are today. Choose those you believe have the values you wish to promulgate and the talent to learn the leadership behaviors you believe important to the future of your organization, and then give them personal developmental attention. It's possible to handle three or four at a time. Yes, it takes time. However, remember your leadership mission: legacy. Great leaders have "teachable points of view" that accelerate the development of others and the organization at the same time. They also understand the two-way nature of teaching. By teaching and coaching others, leaders also become learners and grow their own ability to see the field of play and the pathways to success. Noel Tichy labels this the "virtuous teaching cycle" that winning organizations apply to continually generate more and more learning (Tichy 1997). Helping create a few more role models and several more voices for leadership will maximize the potential for your gift to take root.

- How do leaders in your organization learn to mentor/coach?
- Are mentoring and coaching commitments rewarded? How?

THINKING DIFFERENTLY ABOUT LEADERSHIP IN THE TWENTY-FIRST CENTURY

Most agree that demands for leadership have shifted in this century. Both the velocity and the mass of change drive new ways to learn and distribute leadership. A fresh perspective may be to see all leadership as legacy work: We are leaving those we are privileged to lead either more or less capable to lead themselves. Making this impact intentional and purposeful—legacy—helps leaders focus both their learning and their behavior.

Thinking about legacy requires us to move beyond short-term definitions of success and consider a journey from success to significance. We conclude by suggesting we should all reflect on the following two questions:

- What three legacy impacts will be the most important for where we currently lead?
- How are we preparing people to better lead their organizations because of our leadership legacy efforts?

REFERENCES

Benest, Frank, and Les Wallace. 2007. "Ten Pressure Points for Leadership Succession." *A Legacy of 21st Century Leadership*. New York: iUniverse.

Bennis, Warren, and Burt Nanus. 1985. *Leaders: The Strategies for Taking Charge*. New York: Harper & Row.

Charan, Ram, Stephen Drotter, and James Noel. 2001. *The Leadership Pipeline: How to Build the Leadership Powered Company*. San Francisco: Jossey-Bass.

Collins, Jim. 2001. *Good to Great*. New York. HarperCollins Publishers.

Colvin, Geoffrey. 2006. "What It Takes to Be Great." *Fortune Magazine* (October).

Cooper, Simon. 2005. "He Who Says It, Does It." *Business 2.0* (December).

Cooperrider David, and Suresh Srivastva. 1987. "Appreciative Inquiry in Organizational Life." In *Research in Organizational Change and Development*, W. Pashmore and R. Woodman, eds. Greenwich, CT: JAI Press.

Corporate Executive Board. 2003. *"Engaging Managers as Agents of Employee Development."* Catalog No. TD11IMXNC.

Dahle, Cheryl. 2007. "The Fast Company/Monitor Group Social Capitalist Awards: A More Powerful Path." *Fast Company* (January).

Day, George, and Paul Schoemaker. 2006. *Peripheral Vision: Detecting the Weak Signals That Will Make or Break Your Company*. Boston: Harvard Business School Press.

Drucker, Peter. 1967. *The Effective Executive*. New York: Harper & Row.

Engardio, Pete. 2007. "Beyond the Green Corporation." *BusinessWeek* (January 29).

Ernst, Chris, and Andre Martin. 2006. *Critical Reflections: How Groups*

Can Learn from Success and Failure. Greensboro, NC: Center for Creative Leadership.

George, Bill. 2003. *Authentic Leadership: Rediscovering the Secretes to Creating Lasting Value.* San Francisco: Jossey-Bass.

Hamel, Gary. 2000. *Leading the Revolution.* Boston: Harvard Business School Press.

Hamel, Gary, and Liisa Valikangas. 2008. "The Quest for Resilience." *Harvard Business Review* (September).

Handy, Charles. 1990. *The Age of Unreason.* Boston: Harvard Business School Press.

Laurie, Donald. 2000. *The Real Work of Leaders.* Cambridge: Perseus Publishing.

Leider, Richard, and David Shapiro. 2004. *Claiming Your Place at the Fire: Living the Second Half of Your Life on Purpose.* San Francisco: Berrett-Koehler Publishers.

Marquardt, Michael. 2005. *Leading with Questions: How Leaders Find the Right Solutions by Knowing What to Ask.* San Francisco: Jossey-Bass.

Ridderstrale, Jonas, and Kjeell Nordstrom. 2000. *Funky Business.* London: BookHouse Publishing.

Schon, Donald. 1973. *Beyond the Stable State: Public and Private Learning in a Changing Society.* New York: W. W. Norton and Company.

Senge, Peter. 1990. *The Fifth Discipline: The Art and Practice of The Learning Organization.* New York: Doubleday.

Spreitzer, Gretchen, and Robert Quinn. 2001. *A Company of Leaders: Five Disciplines for Unleashing the Power in Your Workforce.* San Francisco: Jossey-Bass.

Sull, Donald. 2006. "Difficult Decisions for an Uncertain World." *Finan-*

cial Times (March).

Thomas, David, and Robin Ely. 2003 "Making Differences Matter: A New Paradigm for Managing Diversity." *Harvard Business Review* (September/October).

Tichy, Noel, and Eli Cohen. 1997. *The Leadership Engine.* New York: HarperCollins Publishers.

Wacker, Watts, and Jim Taylor. 2000. *Visionary's Handbook.* New York: Harper Business.

Wallace, Les, and James Trinka. 2007. *A Legacy of 21st Century Leadership.* New York: iUniverse.

Weiss, Jeff, and Jonathan Hughes. 2005."Want Collaboration? Accept and Actively Manage Conflict." *Harvard Business Review* (March).

Whitney, Diana, and A. Trosten-Bloom. 2003. *The Power of Appreciate Inquiry: A Practical Guide to Positive Change.* San Francisco: Berrett-Koehler.

Wind, Jerry, et al. 2004. *The Power of Impossible Thinking: Transform the Business of Your Life and the Life of Your Business.* Upper Saddle River, NJ: Wharton School Publishing.

Yankelovitch, Daniel. 1999. *The Magic of Dialogue.* New York: Simon and Schuster.

Zenger, Jack, and Joe Folkman. 2002. *The Extraordinary Leader.* New York: McGraw-Hill.

High Schools of the Future

"Boot Camp"

Arthur Shostak

The only thing we have to fear is when, as a species, we don't believe in the future anymore. (Yves Behar, *Brandjam*, 2007)

Imagine the calendar reads September 1, 2015, and Elena, a teenage daughter of yours, is off with a smile and an air of high expectation to her magnet public High School of the Future. A learning community that takes tomorrow to heart, it resembles other schools devoted to the performing arts, the sciences, international affairs, the health sciences, and so on—but this time the focus is on the creative study of possibilities, perils, and policies. As well, it offers an opportunity for teenagers to test out whether they want to become career forecasters. As future futurists, they get to try out the role and resolve whether this is their calling.

Elena prepared for this special experience in a nationwide public school system that reoriented around 2010 to emphasize futuristics. By 2015, youngsters could identify future-shaping lessons from the past, uncover their own hidden assumptions about the future, draw insights into the future from the arts, appreciate the place of futuristics in every school subject, recognize progress being made

---

Arthur Shostak is a futurist and professor emeritus of sociology at Drexel University. He is the author of *Anticipate the School You Want: Futurizing K-12 Education* (forthcoming). E-mail shostaka@drexel.edu.

in shaping a finer future at home and abroad, understand the dy-namics of future job creation, understand globalization, and draw on ideas from one another and from concerned adults (their teachers and parents, relatives, neighbors, etc.).

Coming up to a revamped school building—spacious, airy, light, and distinctly modern-looking—Elena smiles at architecture that helps raise ambition and morale—architecture with clues to preferable futures. The school grounds host an operating windmill that is busy generating electricity. At its base, signage explains its cost, its rewards, and when, with savings from reduced consump-tion, the school expects to make back its investment in a wind sys-tem. The names of area venders are noted.

A Buckminster Fuller dome serves as a portable classroom or a large greenhouse. Administrative offices have glass walls so students can look in and staffers look out. An expansive open-space floor plan boasts many live plants. Rooftops are covered with sod and plants to help influence inside temperatures. Creative outdoor art signed by the maker—a teacher or a student—enlivens the setting. And a small fleet of official school cars, many (or even all) of them advanced hy-brids, electronic cars, or high-tech diesels, are parked outside.

Anyone stepping inside knows he or she is in a very imagina-tive place. The lobby contains a giant replica of our planet, with the ceiling indicating distances to the Sun and other planets. A video system circles the space, making available streaming electronic news of the moment. Dynamic electronic display cases feature colorful accounts of current and proposed future-shaping educational proj-ects at the school or around the world—displays rich in photos of current teachers and students.

Building hallways sparkle with student art on futures subjects, along with artwork from the covers of science-fiction magazines and from brilliant illustrators (such as Florida's Jacque Fresco and Roxanne Meadows). Photos—perhaps taken by students themselves—highlight newly constructed area buildings that are getting wilder all the time, as bold architects design buildings that are "whimsical, sensual, and possessed of a substantial wow factor."[1]

Elena's classrooms have the architecture, furniture, coloration, and "feel" of a base on Mars or the Moon, or an ocean-floor domed colony, or an interstellar starship, or any other such simulation, provided it stretches the imagination, intrigues the mind, and augments one's education. (As schools should be places students wanted to be, these gee-whiz settings have much to recommend them.)

Green-oriented students like Elena raise edible fish such as tilapia in tanks in the school basement. A campus greenhouse features cutting-edge experiments with plants that might prove to be new food sources. The school's workshops (computer repair, graphic arts, robotics, space technology, etc.) explore the use of experimental materials, such as those created from nanotechnology and biotechnology. Rain and soiled water from the lunchroom kitchen (or even the toilets) is recycled and made ready again for use by groundskeepers and building cleaners.

A decided effort is made to employ cutting-edge learning aids and even serve as beta test sites for technologies still not ready for the market. Clicker technology, for example, tickles Elena as it sets students against one another in a good-natured competition: They respond to a quiz by pressing the right key on a handheld clicker. A projection screen at the room's front tracks their responses in real time, then displays their responses with eye-catching graphics—anonymously, of course.

Teachers appreciate their ability to record data from individual students and transfer it through wireless technology in real time to a classroom computer program. They learn what is or is not getting across, and to which learner, especially those who do not dominate discussion.[2]

Elena also likes using an advanced pen-computer that uses

micro-dot reading technology to enable her to draw a calculator on a piece of paper, for example, and then tap on it to perform everything from additions to square roots.[3] She also employs a headset that lets her control simple actions, as within computer games, by using her thoughts. The device measures electrical activity in the brain and works with software to let users record a particular pattern they associate with a command used in the game, such as *move right,* or *lift that object.* To execute the command, the helmet wearer need only think the thought.[4]

Naturally, attention goes to computer-based gaming and simulations. The very popular series such as *The Sims, Civilization IV, Rise of Nations*, and other games help players take prudent risks in pursuit of objectives, make ethical and moral decisions, work in teams, and employ scientific deduction—all important matters in futuristics. Elena especially likes Internet-based massively multiplayer operations.[5] For example, *Tabula Rosa*, a science-fiction game, is complete with ethical parables and problems.[6]

Fifteen of Elena's high-school courses are required, and many electives add more spice to her high-school years. Listed below in alphabetical order, they share one characteristic in common: They are "tough fun" experiences, in that they are demanding, but also fascinating.

1. Assessment Processes

Students gain familiarity with major techniques for assessing large-scale social programs. The background, formulas, strengths, and limitations of social impact assessment, social indicators, and technological assessment warrant close study, as these tools are critical in taking the measure of an organization or social system that purports to help change our future.

A useful cogent model here, the U.S. Army's "After Action Review," asks, What was supposed to happen? What happened? And what accounts for the differences?[7] Student futurists might want to also ask, And what can be done to bring intent and results closer together?

2. Claims

Social impact and technology assessment methodologies operate at a fairly high level of generalization. These tools commonly look at large matters, such as entire social systems, or major components thereof, or entire technologies. It is vital to also get experience in testing claims for far smaller, more conventional products or services that are promoted as significant future-aiding items.

The market, for example, is now being flooded with new "green" products (and old repackaged ones) hyped as good for the environment. Foods are labeled not only as good for your health, but also as capable of preventing illness. Similarly, new coiled light bulbs are hailed as better for countering climate change, and so on. The student futurists learn to ask, Are they?

3. Collapses

Students profit from a clearer understanding of why plans to stay on top of the future often fail; that is, why the problem-solving abilities of societies often give out, why large social systems are inherently unstable, and why "complacent oligarchies, like soft cheese, turn rancid in the sun."[8] Unless high-schoolers clarify their thoughts in this vexing matter, they are unlikely to help prevent repeat tragedies.

Attention goes to the decline and fall of Greece and Rome, the disappearance of the Aztec and Mayan civilizations, the ancient African kingdoms, the Chinese "Middle Kingdom" empire, and other classic cases about which a good deal is known (and more is always being learned).

Here, as throughout a future-oriented curriculum, attention

goes to lessons bearing on future making, lessons that teenagers find inspiring, despite their origins in disillusionment, despair, and ruin. While large systems, like the United States, are difficult to keep on course, their capacity for adaptation or even renewal remains considerable.

4. Community Service

Student futurists spend considerable after-school time helping, but also studying organizations trying to make a difference. They are encouraged to go to a site likely to initially prove somewhat uncomfortable for them, crossing racial, ethnic, or sexual-orientation boundaries; these will likely prove to be, in time, rewarding socialization experiences.

As helpers, they should be available for almost any role thought valuable by the organization, as learning is possible almost everywhere (e.g., dishing out meals in a food kitchen for the homeless, or washing floors in a center for abused women). Students should seek goals beyond securing only clean office work.

After having settled in, the student should be charged with diplomatically seeking answers to a bevy of questions that deal with future-shaping matters; e.g., Does the organization have a long-range plan for its future? If so, when was it drafted, how, and why? What controversies did it resolve, and with what effect? What controversies did it leave unresolved, why, and with what effect? How much use does the plan actually get, why, and with what effect? How is it kept fresh? And, above all, how might explicit use of futuristics help improve the organization's plan and thus significantly aid the organization? A written report covering these matters is a large part of the course requirements.

5. Disputes

Likewise, controversies in forecasting warrant close attention.

It is vital that student futurists learn to adopt a healthy sort of skepticism where high-profile disputes and disputants are concerned. A case study, for example, is made of a clash between glaciologists who, looking at the same melting phenomena, do or do not forecast a rise in world sea levels during this century. Some expect a three-foot rise, thereby threatening extraordinary coastal damage and the relocation of hundreds of millions of people, with much ensuing hardship. Others, however, warn of six feet, and a few scoffers warn of only six inches.[9] How is a high-school student to find and adopt a position — so as to not feel paralyzed — when the experts are in sharp disagreement?

Coming closer to home, student futurists could ask whether or not the school lunch program should offer milk or meat from cloned animals (cows, goats, and pigs) and their offspring. (FDA approval, after more than six years of study, came early in 2008.) Some parents can be expected to hail related cost-savings and product upgrades (leaner and larger cuts of meat). They note cloning "has the potential to produce products that are safer, healthier, and tastier — bacon that has heart-protective Omega 3s, say, or milk produced by cows that are stronger and thus need fewer antibiotics."[10] Opponents, however, are likely to charge that cloning causes suffering to animals, citing a 2008 EU Study Group finding.[11] They may also warn darkly of imagined safety risks from what they call "Frankenfood."

After patiently studying both sides, and considering the material offered by such companies as Cyagra, Trans Ove Genetics, and ViaGen, students might ponder why, "like abortion and capital punishment, biotechnology inspires knee-jerk rhetorical passion rather than rational debate."[12] In due course, they might urge school buy-in, or explain why this is not their recommendation.

Students learn some people will cheer future-shaping products or trends that others fear or jeer; e.g., "Does a world of a million video channels on your iPhone sound exciting to you, or like a living hell of mindless dreck? Do you think stem-cell therapies will lead to better lives, or just prolong a painful and expensive process of aging and dying?"[13] They learn how to take sides—or find a way between extreme positions—and how to disagree without becoming disagreeable.

6. Limitations

Student futurists need to understand why forecasts have often been off the mark. They need to appreciate the toll taken on futuristics by today's weak theoretical models of change, dependent as they are on the social sciences, the youngest and least reliable of the sciences. The aspiring futurists need to understand why our mathematics and statistics are only as good as data entered, and that this data often has critical gaps, can be outdated, and sometimes even is false. Students need to be reminded that correlation does not necessarily imply cause.

Once limitations have been studied, energizing attention is paid to the many ways that forecasting tools are stronger now than five or ten years ago. Futurists work hard at remedying obvious faults, propping up weak links, inventing fresh tools, and, in a hundred and one other ways, trying to pass along a finer art than the one they inherited. The more that student futurists learn about these efforts—and the limitations that are their source—the better.

7. Love and Human Sexuality

Called elsewhere "Sex Education," this course enables teenagers to upgrade what most have learned primarily from peers or very uneven sources in our sexually saturated culture. Better still, attention is paid to the enriching place of caring, dedication, intimacy, and love in such matters.

The school's model relies on well-trained volunteer juniors and seniors who join their teachers in conducting outreach educational sessions for new students. Skits and interactive activities deal with abstinence, alcohol and drugs, dating violence, HIV/AIDS, sexual decision making, sexual harassment, and talking with parents. Additional topics include alternative sexual preferences, contraception choices, and insights from the art of love (à la Erich Fromm's classic book).

As well, classroom discussion considers the future of culture's saturation with sexual matters, the possible impacts of a male "fail-safe" contraception pill, guidelines for sexual relations among the first residents of a Moon or Mars colony, and the impact of reproductive technologies that makes childbirth by a female human an option (normal fetuses could be conceived outside the body, and brought far along by equipment originally developed to keep premature babies alive).

Course materials are available online 24/7 via a teacher-assigned password, and it has hypertext features to allow for advanced learning, the better to help a teenager develop informed, sound, and healthy feelings and views about love and human sexuality.

8. Methods

An energizing course focuses on the "how to" mechanics that set this art form apart and above fortune-telling, mysticism, and pop-culture nonsense. Youngsters should make hands-on, age-appropriate use (à la John Dewey) of such challenging tools as:

- Chaos and complexity theory
- Computer modeling
- Cross-impact analysis
- Delphi poll techniques
- Environmental scanning
- Expert interviews
- Futures wheels
- Games

- Relevance trees
- Scanning
- Scenario writing
- Science fiction
- Simulations
- Technological forecasting
- Trend analysis
- Trend extrapolation
- Visualization

Embedded in the methods course are exercises in use of the specialized language of futurists, such as *ambient energy, androids, biogenesis, biointeractive materials, brain-enhancing cognitronics, "black" biology* (e.g., germ warfare), *cybergenesis, cyborgs, digital platforms, genomic profiling, holography, molecular manufacturing, ocean-current power, species coalescence and dominionization,* and so on. More, of course, are added all the time. While admittedly odd on first contact, the concepts can and should be mastered, as they merit a place in a student's mental tool kit.

9. Perils

An especially challenging course assesses trends that pose vertigo-inducing glimpses of a perilous future that warrant proactive concern. For example, democracy is increasingly imperiled, as there is a systematic effort to weaken or even eliminate counterparts of the Bill of Rights in many countries, such as states of the former Soviet Union and Middle Eastern countries. Edicts, laws, and religious proclamations diminish freedom of assembly, smother civic society, and silence critics. Student futurists study high probability/high impact threats and ongoing responses.

10. Possibilities

This course explores imaginative ideas capable of radically altering the future—ideas yet to win implementation, but no less important for that. Students learn how to get past knee-jerk disbelief, suspend judgment, do research, and reach judicious estimates of the desirability, plausibility, and overall merits of proposals that some hail as brilliant but others dismiss as far-fetched.

Typical of a "wild idea" that gets attention is the American Solar Plan. It proposes a massive solar energy infrastructure theoretically capable, by 2050, of providing 69 percent of America's electricity and 34 percent of the nation's total energy needs. A vast area of photovoltaic cells (30,000 square miles) would be erected on otherwise barren land in the Southwest. Excess daytime energy would be stored as compressed air in massive underground caverns, to be tapped during nighttime hours. Large solar concentrator power plants would also be built. A new direct current high-voltage power transmission backbone would deliver solar electricity everywhere.

This project would displace 300 large coal-fired power plants and 300 more large natural gas plants and all the fuels they consume. It would help make the United States independent of overseas oil (dependence would be cut from 60 percent to none). It would drop U.S. carbon-dioxide emissions by 62 percent of the 2005 figure. As well, this grand plan would fundamentally cut U.S. trade deficits, ease political tensions in the Middle East, lower military costs, and increase domestic jobs.

Relying on only incremental improvements in solar technology, the project could cost as much as $420 billion in subsidies from 2011 to 2050, but proponents insist that this is a bargain in terms of energy and environmental gains.[14] They contend that the climate change crisis requires "all of us to think boldly about what should be done, and not be intimidated by the problem's large scope.... We can't be afraid to think big."[15]

Critics, however, note that as of 2008 solar power cost three to five times as much as coal (depending on the technology used). They doubt it will be cost-worthy soon, especially as it only represents less than one-tenth of one percent of the global energy market.[16] The American Solar Plan, they conclude, gets way ahead of itself—a damning judgment that student futurists could well evaluate.

Independent of the specifics of any reform scheme, students should take away from this course an appreciation of the indispensability of bold risk taking: "We can advantage only when we embrace risky breakout ideas. Our survival depends not on sticking to what works, but on making leaps that let us predict new challenges and seize on new opportunities."[17]

11. Reforms

This exciting course focuses on actual reform campaigns, as they are arguably second only to methods in importance in the entire futuristic curriculum. Students learn how to assess reform ideas that are put forward as future-shaping tools. They would assess and help improve or dispute the best of them.

Typical is an effort under way in 2008 in Hudson, New York, to "import" ideas based on the derelict shantytowns of Tijuana, Mexico, as a template for redevelopment of its own low-income area. The plan would feature creating a co-op grocery, communal gardens, playgrounds, an outdoor amphitheater, and "incubator spaces" for arts or job training. Proponents see here "the seeds of a vibrant social and architectural model, one that could be harnessed to invigorate numbingly uniform suburban communities."[18]

Naturally, overseas reforms—especially those seemingly transferable—warrant special attention. Israel, for example, announced early in 2008 that it has decided to make the country a laboratory to test the practicality of an environmentally clean electric car. Purchasers will get a subsidized car and pay a monthly fee for expected mileage, eliminating concerns about the fluctuating price of gasoline.

While only a few thousand are expected on the road in 2009, more than 100,000 electric cars should be there by the end of 2010, and 10 percent of all now being driven should be replaced annually. Promoters maintain that "the beauty of [the test] is that you have a real place where you can get real human reactions. In Israel they can control the externalities and give it a chance to flourish or fail. It needs to be tested ... and the Israeli government is to be commended for trying it."[19]

After studying such future-shaping reform ideas, native or foreign, students come up with their own tentative answers, then take these via the Internet to knowledgeable parties around the world, the better to learn the strengths and weaknesses of their ideas, and revise them. If students who at first rejected the reform later admit to a twinge of belief, and if those who rushed to embrace it later admit to a twinge of doubt, much sound learning is likely to have been achieved.

12. Science Fiction

The special world of science-fiction literature can barely be introduced in only one course, but an attempt is made nevertheless. Its extrapolations can serve as a "lens through which to examine the human condition in all of its ramifications."[20] Dedicated to conceiving the inconceivable, the genre is "more than just entertainment. It's a crash course in using your imagination, in sharpening your ability to speculate.... Its ability to encourage that streak of curiosity in kids and even adults is enormous."[21]

13. Slighted Futures

Teenagers learn about the future of overlooked peoples in the Adriatic countries, Africa, the Baltic nations, Central America, the Pacific Isles, and South America. As schooling in America was primarily Euro-centric, China and the Middle East only recently began to get overdue attention: "We're moving into a very new world, one in which countries from Brazil to South Africa to India and China are getting richer, stronger, and prouder. For America to thrive, we will have to develop a much deeper, richer, more intuitive understanding of them and their peoples."[22]

14. Social Competencies

Because all too many teenagers are naïve about behaviors that many adults have learned the hard way, a required course would promote the arts of conversation, diplomacy, etiquette, and related life management and social skills. To effectively and efficiently share forecasts is to first be able to raise confidence in one's person.

Accordingly, to enlarge a behavioral repertoire, student futurists first discuss the desirability of cultivated taste, a talent for listening, politeness, wit, and the like. Once this is clear, they gain practice in these matters through sophisticated role-plays; e.g., skits that explore how to ask or respond to unsettling questions, employ sophisticated language with flair, apologize for an unintended faux pas, defend oneself against a sharp-tongued critic, and come to appreciate the sagacity of the anonymous aphorism, "Do something every day you are afraid of."

To promote self-assurance and savoir-faire, students learn how to order a meal in either an upscale restaurant or a hoi polloi dive. They learn to "go native" as part of a global assignment without going overboard, and to read social cues in foreign settings. As well, they are introduced to the right and wrong ways of banking, using credit cards, arranging for loans, signing business agreements (co-signing, purchase, rental, etc.), and investing in the stock and futures markets. And, in a hundred and one other demanding situations, do themselves proud.

15. Utopian Ideas

Young people need help appreciating historic musings about

ideal societies and how to create and maintain them. This sort of poetic yet utilitarian thinking can serve as a welcome antidote to the enervating notion that this world is as good as it can get. Rather, a utopian blueprint can be turned into a real-world project, be embodied in measured achievements, and help produce a successor ideology capable of stimulating and justifying still further gains (along with testy diversity and vexing contradictions).

Utopian writers contend, "The age of imagination is not over. Utopias are not opposed to reality; on the contrary, they are one of the elements on which it is built, ... one of its essential components."[23] They insist the enormous scale of the challenges today — climate change, terrorism, looming food and water shortages, etc. — "may require quantum leaps [in reforms],... more utopians proposing 'dreams to live by,' more public intellectuals issuing impassioned wake-up calls, and more public citizens hungry to foresee and act."[24]

Naturally, classroom time includes the thoughts of critics, and of recently failed ventures ("New Utopia, an intended sea-based libertarian micro-nation in the Caribbean,... degenerated with breathtaking predictability into nonexistence and scandal." [25])

Attention should go as well to examples of successful modern applied utopian thinking, such as The Farm (Tennessee) and other communes around the world, as well as the entire Scandinavian nation complex and the small Kingdom of Bhutan, where a "Gross National Happiness" Index helps a democratizing monarch measure progress and minimize the toll that modernization can take. As well, of course, the worldwide environmental movement fits in here, especially as key members are busy promoting what they call "Greenopia."[26]

Key to assuring success here is informed, passionate, and unfettered public debate. The sooner that young minds, especially those of student futurists, wrestle with the ideas of outstanding utopians—Plato, Rousseau, More, Saint-Simon, and, coming closer to date, Ernest Callenbach, Paul Goodman, Jacque Fresco, R. Buckminster Fuller, Ivan Illich, Paolo Solari, Jim Wallis, and the inspiring like—the more likely their minds and spirit are to become as creative and nuanced as they wish.

PRIMACY OF ASKING

Whatever the subject matter is at the High School of the Future, emphasis is more on ratcheting up the quality of questions than on taking satisfaction from any tentative answers. The goal is to establish a cycle of inquiry. Student futurists like Elena learn to appreciate why a high school physics teacher very deliberately told his students, "At our present level of ignorance, we think we know...."[27] Accordingly, the courses emphasize taking eclectic inquiry strategies. Students are encouraged to keep noodling away at a problem, the better to arrive at tentative answers superior to any first good-enough ones.

SUMMARY

For far too long, the United States has lacked a place in the K-12 world where futurism is center stage, where it is the "second profession" of the adult staff, and the preoccupation of a self-selected body of tomorrow's forecasters. For too long, young people like Elena—curious about the gains and limitations of spending a career as a long-range forecaster—have had no place to go to test it out. With high schools of the future, we set this right.

Such schools are colorful, cutting-edge, and unapologetically demanding; their required courses can add much to the tool kit that graduates take with them. As well, they should whet the appetite for a post–high school education in advanced futuristics, and thereby produce a first-rate feeder source for well-schooled forecasters, such as talented teenagers like Elena, who over her lifetime will enjoy the cachet of a degree from the world's first public "boot camp" for future futurists.

Ed. note: Ideas in this essay will be expanded upon in the author's book *Anticipate the School You Want: Futurizing K-12 Education* (Rowman and Littlefield, forthcoming: September 2008).

NOTES

1. Richard Lacayo, "Curveballs Are in Play," *Time*, March 20, 2006, 98.

2. Winnie Hu, "Students Click Answers, and a Routine Quiz Becomes a Game," *New York Times*, January 28, 2008, A-22.

3. Miguel Helft, "LeapFrog Hopes for Next Hit With Interactive Reading Toy," *New York Times*, January 28, 2008, C-3.

4. Nick Wingfield, "Wii Fit, Other Innovations Unveiled," *Wall Street Journal*, February 20, 2008, D-6.

5. Paul Boutin, "A Sense of the Future," *Wall Street Journal*, January 26-27, 2008, W-8.

6. Nicholas Carr, quoted in Spencer Reiss, "Do You Trust Google?" *Wired*, January 2008, 42.

7. "Conceiving the Future," *The Economist*, February 9, 2008, 89.

8. James E. McWilliams, "Food Politics, Half-Baked," *New York Times*, February 5, 2008, A-23.

9. Eric Rignot, a longtime student of ice sheets at both poles for NASA's Jet Propulsion Laboratory, as quoted in Andrew C. Revkin, "In Greenland, Ice and Instability," *New York Times*, January 8, 2008, E-4 (1, 4).

10. McWilliams, "Food Politics," *New York Times*, op. cit. Cloning "deserves a fair hearing, one in which impassioned language yields the

floor to responsible discourse."

11. James Kanter, "Europe's Ethics Panel Says Cloning Harms Animals," *New York Times*, January 18, 2008, C-4.

12. Ken Zweibel et al., "A Solar Grand Plan," *Scientific American*, January 2008, 64-74.

13. John Rennie, "Big and Small Solutions," *Scientific American*, January 2008, 8.

14. Matt Richtel and John Markoff, "A Green Industry Takes Root Under the California Sun," *New York Times*, February 1, 2008, C-9 (C-1, 9).

15. Marshall Monroe, as quoted in Keith H. Hammond, "Do You Believe in Magic?" *Fast Company*, November 2006, 43.

16. Richtel and Markoff, op. cit.

17. Monroe, op. cit.

18. Nicolai Ouroussoff, "Learning from Tijuana: Hudson, N.Y., Considers Different Housing Model," *New York Times*, February 19, 2008, E-5 (1, 5).

19. James D. Wolfensohn, the former World Bank president and a modest investor in the project, as quoted in Steven Erlanger, "Oil-Free Israel Is Set to Embrace Broad Project to Promote the Use of Electric Cars," *New York Times*, January 21, 2008, A-7.

20. Lou Anders, ed., *FutureShocks* (New York: ROC Book / New American Library, 2006), 2.

21. Frank M. Robinson, *Science Fiction of the 20th Century: An Illustrated History*, Portland, OR: Collectors Press, 1999, 246.

22. Fareed Zakaria, "The Power of Personality," *Newsweek*, December 24, 2007, 41.

23. Patrice Flichy (trans. Liz Carey-Libbrecht), *The Internet Imaginaire* (Cambridge, MA.: The MIT Press, 2007 ed.), 207-8.

24. Warren Belasco, *Meals to Come: A History of the Future of Food* (Berkeley, CA: University of California Press, 2006), 266. "I doubt very much such problems can be overcome through pragmatism alone."

25. China Mieville, "Floating Utopias," *In These Times*, October 2007, 25 (24-28).

26. Eric Corey Freed, "Building in Sustainability," in *Greenopia: The Urban Dweller's Guide to Green Living* (Santa Monica, CA: The Green Media Group, 2007).

27. Anonymous teacher quoted in John R. Christy, "My Nobel Movement," *Wall Street Journal*, November 1, 2007, A-19.

Paid Volunteerism

Is There an Oxymoron in Our Future?

Jay Herson

The lead article in a special section on retirement of the *New York Times* last year had the headline "For Love and a Little Money — Retirees discover that being paid something for volunteer work can be good for the organization and for themselves" (Deutsch 2007). The article went on to describe the attitudes and experience of several volunteers and nonprofit organizations (hereafter referred to as "dot-orgs" as opposed to dot-coms) in the New York City metropolitan area. The article indicates a trend that baby boomers now entering retirement want to be paid some nominal amount ($10–$15 per hour) as volunteers to dot-orgs. The term *paid volunteer* refers to people working for this nominal wage in organizations that typically have unpaid volunteers with a part-time work schedule that requires weekly commitment and, perhaps, more hours than an unpaid volunteer. It is the impression of many, and the firsthand experience of some, that volunteer efforts are not taken seriously when there is no compensation. This new wave of volunteers feels that their time is better planned for and used more intelligently by the dot-orgs if they are paid. This attitude is shared by dot-com

Jay Herson is a senior associate at the Institute for Alternative Futures and managing editor of *FUTUREtakes*. E-mail jay.herson@earthlink.net.

executives. They are finding that the paid volunteer works harder and is more committed than the nonpaid volunteer. A dot-com manager may hesitate to ask a nonpaid volunteer to stay late to finish a project, but this kind of commitment would be understood by a paid volunteer.

It is important to distinguish between two types of volunteer jobs — the traditional and the professional. Traditional volunteers worked typing letters, cooking meals, painting walls, etc. — household skills. The professional volunteer may be doing computer programming, Web site design, writing a marketing plan, providing legal or financial advice, etc. — i.e., drawing on skills developed during working years. The baby boomers' preference for paid volunteerism was formed as they considered professional volunteer opportunities. However, there is evidence that this attitude is spreading to the larger volunteer community and affecting traditional volunteer jobs as well. This begs the question whether, if some volunteers are paid, a stigma might be placed on those who are not paid. Can both paid and unpaid volunteerism exist within the same dot-org? Will the "thousand points of light" give way to the "thousand W-2 forms"? Is it a dot-org labor market or an idealistic attitude to pay back society that will determine how the skills and knowledge of the baby boomers will be deployed in their later years? What is the future of volunteerism?

DRIVERS — MACRO ENVIRONMENT

The first step in assessing the future of volunteerism is to consider drivers of change. We first consider those at the macro level — those that affect all industries and organizations.

Demographic/Economic

Volunteering is increasingly becoming an activity for older people. The younger generations are in two-income families with childrearing responsibilities; many are immigrants in low-paying jobs. Volunteering is not an option.

The U.S. population is getting older; baby boomers (born 1946–1964) are beginning to reach retirement age, but they are working longer. This reduces the size of the pool of potential volunteers, thus increasing the demand for those interested in volunteering. The baby boomers are a very educated workforce and, if they are to volunteer, are likely to prefer professional volunteer opportunities over traditional volunteer opportunities. This may be true of the many professional career women who would want to distance themselves from traditional volunteerism, which many consider women's work.

Several family financial factors are involved. Many baby boomers started families late due to their need to acquire advanced degrees. Their parents are living longer. Even as retirees, the baby boomers may be financially responsible for children (college) and parents (health care) and are facing an increased cost of living, especially for their own health care while on fixed incomes. Baby boomers do not want to depend on Social Security.

Generation X, born 1964–1979, and also known as Generation 13 (Strauss and Howe 2001), is the next cohort to consider for the future of volunteerism. They will enter retirement age in the 2020s and 2030s. Many in this generation have already been observed to have distrust in traditional organizations like dot-orgs (examples would be recent problems at the Smithsonian Institution administration, the American Indian Museum, and the American Red Cross). They also will have had several careers, in response to rapidly accelerating technologies and societal change, and may have had long periods of underemployment and earned less money than their parents in real dollars (Pew 2007). Thus, Generation X will bring professional skills to volunteerism, may also push retirement to a late age, and have motivation to be paid as volunteers.

Societal Values

In terms of spiral dynamics (Beck and Cowan 1996), society is between "blue" (the more educated people earn the rewards) and "green" (all should benefit equally). In the middle is "orange" (each person acts on his or her own behalf to prosper). The paid volunteerism movement is sitting on orange. Political leaders are needed to push American society closer to green for the greater good of society. There is evidence that this type of leader, missing for several decades, is reemerging on the political scene.

Corporate values have pervaded society. Everything has its price. During their working careers, people have become used to being paid for performance, not for just showing up. People expect there to be consequences if they do not show up for their job. Therefore, there is every expectation for payment for work, however small. A once-a-year volunteer luncheon is not considered adequate compensation for work done well and performed with expertise that has taken a lifetime to learn. Retirees see many of their contemporaries working longer. Working as a paid volunteer is seen as a compromise from complete retirement and working longer while allowing the retiree to maintain a social network and identity that come from working. For many retirees, the ideal volunteer position is to do serious, substantive work for a worthy cause on a part-time basis. Many people among potential volunteers and dot-org executives feel that this kind of dream volunteer position can only exist if there is some form of payment. Besides payment, another aspect of the dream volunteer position is to be able to do all of it or most of it from home. The Internet allows paid volunteers to provide their professional skills without having to be at a physical location. However, paid volunteers must make a commitment to "show up" on a regular basis and to continue to use skills they developed during their working lives, rather than learning new skills. The nonpaid volunteer would have more flexibility. Retirees in the future may not be able to choose the latter if dot-org managers feel that the flexibility inherent in non-paid volunteerism is of little value to the dot-org.

DRIVERS — OPERATING ENVIRONMENT

We now consider those trends that affect the dot-org industry.

New museums and hospitals are being built, and the old ones are expanding with ultramodern wings. These dot-orgs need help with information technologies, Web design, safety, foreign-language skills, law (copyright, stolen art, rights of handicapped), marketing, retail, etc. There is no longer a need for people to address envelopes or to prepare food (most museum and hospital food services are contracted).

The types of services that come under the heading of professional volunteering had previously been delivered to dot-orgs through short-term contracts with individuals or consulting firms. However, the dot-orgs have found it much less expensive to pay a volunteer $10–$15 per hour for these services than a consulting firm. Also, some of the professional services require having people on site to supplement the full-time paid staff, such as for language translation or computer network administration. Dot-orgs prefer to have the "hook" of payment for these types of volunteers to make sure that people show up and can stay overtime if needed.

Baby boomers who are already retired have contributed non-paid services like writing a marketing plan for a dot-org, only to find that the plan was never used. There is a feeling that if this report were paid for it would more likely be taken seriously.

Some retirees may be well-off financially and may be very idealistic, but they feel there is nothing wrong in accepting the hourly wage to help defray their out-of-pocket costs of transportation and lunch.

A new fee-based industry is emerging to match up volunteer skills with dot-org requirements for paid volunteerism. ReServe is placing baby boomers in nonprofit organizations and government agencies. Experience Corps is providing similar placements on a nationwide basis, especially in public schools.

Law firms have long performed pro bono work for individuals and dot-orgs. Initially, these services were performed by their full-time staff. There is a trend for law firms to use their retired staff for pro bono work, with minimal hourly compensation. The law firm wants its retirees to take this work seriously and to be committed. It wants to ensure that both the lawyer and the job have a certain level of dignity. This pro bono initiative allows the retired staff to continue to use their legal skills and to work on issues they may have never encountered in their careers. It also enables them to still put on the dark suit a few days a week and interact with their former co-workers. Nonpaid volunteerism will find it hard to compete with this arrangement, and this law firm trend would likely set an example for pro bono work in related fields, such as public accounting and management consulting.

We now turn to three scenarios for the future of volunteerism.

SCENARIO 1: EXTRAPOLATIVE; STATUS QUO CONTINUES

The current trend toward paid volunteerism for professional volunteer jobs continues. However, many dot-orgs begin to treat paid volunteers just as they would any $10–$15 per hour employee. Paid volunteers begin to realize that they are willing to make only so much of a commitment for only $15 an hour. Negotiations take place, and paid volunteer salaries increase to a point the market can bear, around 40 percent of the volunteer's last hourly wage when employed. This comes with specific hours-per-week commitments from the volunteers.

This is acceptable to most of the volunteers, but not all. The upward volunteer salaries create budget problems for the dot-orgs, but market equilibrium is reached as dot-orgs reduce the number of paid volunteer positions using contractors, less-expensive retirees, and college students as interns for the responsibilities previously handled by paid volunteers. The dot-orgs experience a net loss in modernization due to limited budgets for supporting the contractors and paid volunteers. However, the equilibrium prevents a significant effect on society as a whole, except for a continued drift away from idealism (i.e., society moves toward spiral dynamics "blue").

As time moves on, Generation Xers replace the baby boomers as potential volunteers. Traditional volunteerism is marginalized in the United States at this point but is found on a larger scale in the new economies of Brazil, Russia, India, China, and South Korea, where a larger middle class tends to take hold. This results in improvement of conditions in these countries and creates an idealism that presents advantages on the world stage.

SCENARIO 2: CHALLENGING TIMES AHEAD

This era is characterized by a sharp decrease in people interested in nonpaid volunteer positions whether traditional or professional. Those nonpaid volunteers who do exist have low skill levels and come from lower-income groups. They work in traditional volunteer jobs that serve their communities, but they find it hard to keep a regular schedule due to personal crises in child care, housing, health, and so on.

The need to pay volunteers puts a demand on public budgets. Governments respond by creating incentives for nonpaid volunteers, such as tax deductions and free public transportation to and from volunteer job sites. However, a bureaucracy soon emerges to administer and enforce this program, as cheating abounds. The stigma of nonpaid volunteerism remains strong.

Private industry is asked to help the dot-orgs in their budget crises. They do make contributions, but the travel-related industries respond instead by providing frequent flyer miles and free hotel stays to legitimate nonpaid volunteers. In exchange for further financial support from industry, we might see the appearance of a MetLife installation gallery at the Museum of Modern Art and a United Airlines Theater at the Chicago Art Institute.

Monetary contributions to many charities decrease as society moves further toward spiral dynamics "blue" (less idealistic). Most middle-class people are seeking a return on investment for their contributions instead of an annual calendar or sheet of address labels. A shakeout occurs, squeezing out dot-orgs that cannot cope with increased expenses. Many of these dot-orgs are inefficient disease- or environment-related foundations that spent more than 20 percent of their operating expenses on administration, especially salaries. Such organizations have been classified as being especially inefficient by organizations such as Charity Navigator.

Many labor issues arise. Mid-sized law firms have long been squeezed by large firms with offices in principal cities of the world and solo lawyers in niche practices. In desperation, some of these mid-sized firms extend their pro bono policies, using retired partners from the large law firms as paid volunteers to work fifteen hours per week on regular cases. Three of these paid volunteers take a job away from a younger career lawyer. This causes recent law school graduates to boycott any firm employing the older paid volunteers. Museums hire retired art teachers as paid volunteers to serve as uniformed museum guards. This causes disputes from unions representing the people who formerly had these full-time paid positions.

The paid volunteer positions now experience high turnover because there are many to choose from, and a more mature market causes dot-orgs to increase the hourly compensation to meet competition. The paid volunteers changing jobs solely for higher hourly wages are those who probably had little commitment to the mission of the dot-org in the first place but were just looking to earn money. This is a subgroup of volunteers that emerges with the concept of paid volunteerism.

People are now working in their regular jobs longer, and many people with technical and customer service skills now live in China and India, making fewer people available for those professional-type jobs that must be anchored on site.

The placement of retirees into paid volunteer positions becomes a growing industry. Matchups between retired workers and dot-orgs now take place on an international basis. Companies performing these matchups are now part of large Internet service organizations like monster.com and careerbuilder.com.

Political campaigns, museums, hospitals, parks, and environmental causes all suffer from the budget crunch caused by this rush to paid volunteerism and the labor shortage. Private industry is able to eliminate a total collapse but cannot take care of all of the problems. The continued shrinkage of the United States in the world economy and domestic competition in industries that are often the largest public benefactors do not help this situation.

SCENARIO 3: PARADIGM SHIFT

The above scenario cannot last forever. Eventually, leaders emerge to swing the pendulum back to some form of idealism, where people are willing to be nonpaid volunteers in order to pay back society for the benefits they have received. These leaders will emerge because of the increased feminine and Asian cultural values introduced to society by elected officials and business leaders who are women, Asian, or members of other family-oriented minority groups. Late members of Generation X and the newly emerging Generation Y react to the spiral dynamics "blue" shift of their parents and move toward the more idealistic greater good of "orange" and "green." People work longer in jobs, with older workers opting to a four-day workweek. Those no longer working prefer to pursue hobbies and family activities. These people may be happy to volunteer for half a day per week in nonpaid positions, some of which may be professional in nature. Paid volunteerism begins to decrease.

The emerging software nations (Brazil, Russia, India, China, South Korea) have created low-cost software for dot-orgs supported from their own countries. The software requires skills that are common among Generation Xers, so the need for paid volunteers doing computer-related activities decreases. Museums are now more interactive, reducing the need for volunteer docents, and the legal profession is using paid licensed paralegals for most routine pro bono and mainstream activities. In fact, much legal, financial, and tax advice is given via the Internet and telephone from lawyers, paralegals, and accountants living in India. Language translation technologies reduce the need for paid volunteers to do these kinds of services and allow professional services to be delivered from countries whose principal language is not English.

MOST LIKELY SCENARIO

As Weiner and Brown (2005) have indicated, the pendulum never swings completely back. The future will be about 70 percent in Scenario 1 and 30 percent in Scenario 2. There will be increased incentives for nonpaid volunteering coming from both government and business. There will be a touch of idealism but not to the extent described in Scenario 3. In the end, it will be markets, not government, that will strike the needed balance between nonpaid and paid volunteerism. It will be a tightrope tethered by financial and labor issues within the dot-org community.

SIGNPOSTS

Signposts to watch for in the paid volunteerism trend would include the volume and content of traditional volunteer Web sites like volunteermatch.org and volunteersolutions.org and the newly emerging paid volunteer resources such as reserveinc.org and experiencecorps.org. Web sites for museums, hospitals, and environmental organizations would generally have sections on their volunteer requirements and policies. AARP is likely to be making surveys on how members of the age fifty and older cohort prefer to spend their time. Lifestyle patterns and values of people in their fifties would be a good indicator of the retirement patterns of the next retirement cohort.

REFERENCES

Beck, D. E., and C. Cowan. 1996. *Spiral Dynamics — Mastering Values, Leadership and Change.* Oxford: Blackwell.

Deutch, C. 2007. "For Love and a Little Money — Retirees discover that being paid something for volunteer work can be good for the organization, and for themselves." *The New York Times,* special section on retirement (October 23).

Pew Charitable Trusts Economic Mobility Project. 2007. Economic Mobility of Families Across Generations, http://www.economicmobility.org/reports_and_research/?id=0005.

Strauss, W., and N. Howe. 1991. *Generations: The History of America's Future 1584-2069.* New York: William Morrow.

Weiner, E., and A. Brown. 2005. *FutureThink: How to Think Clearly in a Time of Change.* Upper Saddle River, NJ: Prentice Hall.

Expansion for the Good of Humanity

Francis R. Stabler

WHY WE MUST GO

Humans started their exploration of space with the first Russian satellite in 1957. The space age was only twelve years old when the first humans walked on the Moon. In 1969, it appeared that humans were poised to quickly move out into the solar system. There was a widespread sense of excitement generated by the adventurers who were exploring the new world that man had gazed at since his early beginnings, long before it was known that the Moon was anything other than a light in the sky. On the education level, the United States was producing a higher proportion of scientists and engineers than at any time before or since, many attracted by man's push into space. This peak in science and engineering education was a major enabler of the technological leadership the United States enjoyed over the past several decades.

Then, for political and economic reasons, we lost our focus and did not continue with this exploration. Now, almost forty years later, we have achieved considerable advances in robotic exploration of the solar system, but we are currently only sending a few humans into orbit to work on the space station, with no plans to venture back to the Moon within the next decade. There is limited excitement for

Francis R. Stabler, retired from General Motors, is a consultant on automotive propulsion and energy. E-mail frstabler@cs.com.

the math and science education needed to maintain our technological advancement. The drop in scientific and engineering degrees in the United States since the end of the Apollo program is a concern for the future of U.S. technical leadership. Other nations, notably China and India, are doing a much better job of producing an educated workforce ready for the space age. An active manned space program to Mars could lead to a new wave of technically educated people ready to invigorate the economy of the nation with the vision to take this bold step. At the same time, this would provide needed support for humanity's move into space.

Many people are saying that it is a waste of resources to explore space when we have so many problems unsolved right here on Earth. Let's consider a few similar examples to see if this is a valid position.

About 80,000 years ago, a few humans migrated from Africa to what is now the Middle East. From there, they expanded east and west and eventually populated all of Asia and Europe. They may have been looking for better hunting, fleeing another tribe, or just curious about what was over the horizon. What they achieved is an expansion of the human race so that a single disaster in Africa would not wipe out the entire species. The expansion was not because the new lands were the most inviting on the planet. Asia and Europe were in the grip of an ice age and presented many challenges that humans did not face in Africa. Over the following millennium, humans advanced stone tool making, domesticated animals, and developed agriculture, which rapidly expanded around the known world. One thing that these first modern humans in Europe and Asia did not wait for was to fix all of the problems in Africa before they left. Human civilization was advanced and humanity was more secure because of this migration.

Fifty thousand years ago, a small group of humans left Southeast Asia by boat or raft and went on to settle the vacant continent of Australia. At this time, the Ice Age had much of the sea's water locked up in vast ice sheets. With the sea level around 300 feet lower than now, the chain of islands that now make up Indonesia were then connected by dry land, and it was possible to walk almost to Australia. Although the new continent would have been over the horizon, people watching flights of land birds would have known that land was near. Probably a few explorers ventured across the strait, found new land with good hunting, then returned for their families or the rest of their tribe. They had not solved all of the problems of Asia before they left, but they advanced humanity by making the trip. For most of them, it was a one-way trip, and Australia became their new home. This initial settlement of Australia contributed a new, isolated pocket of humanity that made the long-term survival of humans more secure.

It is estimated that, 20,000 to 30,000 years ago, humans in boats traveled along the edge of the sea ice in the Pacific and possibly the Atlantic to reach the Americas. A variety of cultures developed across the Americas. Towns and cities ranging from wood shelters to advanced stone monuments and buildings were constructed. They eventually built cities larger than those of Europe at the time. Humanity was then spread over much larger areas and fairly well isolated in ways that made survival more likely in event of major disease outbreaks, asteroid impacts, earthquake, or other natural disaster. Again, these migrations and new settlements were made without first solving all of the problems of Europe and Asia. Their one-way trips led to the establishment of several new branches of civilization. Humanity advanced and was better for this new diversity of culture.

In more recent times, without having first resolved all of the problems of Europe (or even of Spain), Spain funded Columbus's expedition to the Indies and, in 1492, opened a path for a new migration into the Americas. A wealth of gold and silver was found and returned to Europe. A more lasting impact on Europe was from the new plants from the Americas that today feed millions. Potatoes, tomatoes, and corn quickly became staples for many around the world, and all ate better because of this unplanned export from the new lands. Many people came to the Americas searching for wealth. Some found this wealth, but all found the challenge of hard work and, for many, the start of a new life of independence. Others came to escape persecution, for freedom of various kinds, or to build a new life based on their own hard work.

This opportunity to develop land or trades on their own was a powerful incentive for new settlers. Even with all of its advantages, the new American frontier was a challenge to the people arriving from around the world. Most came on what they knew were one-way trips. In wagons, on horseback, and on foot, they spread out across the continent to establish new lives for themselves and their children. A major side effect of this migration was the spread of democracy around the world, which improved the lives of millions. The descendents of this migration brought the world major contributions of the Industrial Revolution, such as the assembly line, and new transportation systems, such as trains and aircraft. They also made medical advances, such as vaccinations against and cures for diseases that had ravaged much of humanity. The new cultures that developed made major contributions to the people of Europe. On three occasions, the migrants to America were a major factor in averting attempts to oppress the people of Europe: World War I, World War II, and the Cold War. With the migration to the Americas, humans had again expanded their frontiers and were better for the effort.

All migrations have a window of opportunity when they can occur. The first modern humans left Africa at a time when North Africa and the Middle East were lush areas. The trip was easier than it would be in more recent times when both areas became largely desert. Lower sea levels due to the Ice Age made it much easier for humans to make the short trip to Australia — a much more difficult trip for small boats today and with fewer land birds crossing to give an indication of land over the horizon. Vast ice sheets spanning the northern oceans gave early humans a fertile sea to harvest on their travels along the edge of the sea ice to North America and on to South America. As the world warmed starting 17,000 years ago, the trip would have been much more difficult if not impossible with the available technology. Columbus's "discovery" of the Americas and the subsequent new wave of migrations was a fortunate confluence of a visionary explorer and a monarch with the wealth and vision to finance the initial trip. Without this combination, it could have been several centuries before the New World was identified and opened for European migration. The world today would be very different if Columbus had not made his trip in 1492.

Now we are on the brink of the biggest new frontier that humanity has ever had the opportunity to explore. We have orbited the Earth and walked on the Moon. We have sent probes to Mars and beyond to the very edge of our solar system. We are ready to put settlements on the Moon and Mars. It will not be easy. People will suffer great hardship, and some will die in the effort to establish these new homes for themselves and for humanity as a species. Even with the advantages of "modern" technology, life will be difficult. The migration will cost billions of dollars, yuan, euros, yen, rubles, or other forms of exchange. Some efforts will fail and many will not show a profit. What we are sure to gain are things that no one can foresee at this time. The major gain from this new migration into space will not be a profit, but the additional security for the survival of the human species. Once a settlement is made on Mars, humanity can survive even if disease, natural disaster, or war were to destroy life on Earth. Humans would still be vulnerable to natural events that endanger the solar system (gamma ray bursts, black holes, nearby novas, etc.), but we need to solve one problem at a time — quickly. There will still be a lot of things that need to be done on Earth to improve the lives of people, but all will gain from the new industries, services, and knowledge gained by humanity's venture into space. All of the money spent for exploration, new industries, and even the migration effort will be spent right here on Earth. It will create millions of new jobs, both directly involved in the effort and indirectly in the support and service industries.

It is important to take these initial steps to ensure that the human species survives. The window of opportunity could be small. A major economic collapse, a worldwide epidemic, or a major natural disaster could create a situation where humanity would not be capable of launching a space migration effort for many centuries — or possibly ever. Humanity could be destined to live out its limited future on this one planet instead of spreading through the unlimited space of the universe. Major climate changes could drastically reduce the size of the human population and its technical capability. As an example, the next ice age could be near, since warm interglacial periods have historically lasted only 10,000 to 20,000 years and the current one has covered about 17,000 years. If the next ice age were to begin before humans established an independent presence beyond Earth, there may not be a technical civilization capable of the trip for at least 80,000 years, when we have another warm interglacial period. All of the effort would have to be directed toward the survival of a relatively limited number of people during the ice age.

Why We Will Go

Maintaining a viable human species is a noble undertaking, but not likely to be sufficient to lead to the establishment of new settlements beyond the Earth. Vast resources are needed to start a settlement on the Moon, Mars, the asteroids, or beyond. Profit is the most likely incentive for exploration and settlement beyond Earth orbit. Freedom to pursue a desired lifestyle that is restricted here is another powerful incentive that has driven many previous migrations and could again.

Space exploration is an expensive and dangerous program, and the space frontier is far vaster than anything that humans have ever had the opportunity to settle. Space is a place where the human species can expand indefinitely and where great new human civilizations can be developed. It is where new concepts, new technologies, and new forms of human interaction and cooperation will emerge.

Where are the profits in this hostile environment? We frequently hear that the Earth is running out of resources, out of space, and out of energy. The universe beyond Earth's atmosphere offers virtually unlimited quantities of all of these. At the same time, these resources would also appear to offer almost unlimited opportunity for profit. If we have a shortage of metals, one or two medium-size asteroids hold enough metals to supply the Earth's needs for centuries. Solar energy can be concentrated relatively easily and used to refine metals on an asteroid. Pollution of the Earth by mining, refining, and processing of metals and other raw materials could be avoided if these operations take place in space.

Civilization on Earth has an increasing demand for energy, and the resources of space could offer pollution-free sources. Solar energy captured by orbital stations or lunar facilities and beamed to Earth could meet all of humanity's electrical energy needs. Terrestrial solar power is attenuated by the atmosphere and requires expensive, inefficient storage systems to provide power at night and in times of bad weather. Space solar energy can be available with full intensity for twenty-four hours a day, not just from sunrise to sunset on non-cloudy days. Space solar power would require major engineering projects but would not require new invention.

Another very promising energy source is nuclear fusion using helium-3. Helium-3 mined from the lunar surface could provide a reliable fuel for huge numbers of nuclear fusion power plants on Earth that would be carbon-dioxide free. China has already announced plans to move in this direction to gain the energy needed to keep growing their economy. They plan to place a prototype helium-3 mining robot on the Moon in the next few years to validate the presence of helium-3 and the ability to collect it. Construction of solar power facilities, whether in orbit or on the Moon, would require development of new launch systems and living facilities for construction crews. Helium-3 mining would require mining facilities and crews on the Moon. These mining facilities are likely to grow into towns and new settlements.

These projects would make it easier for settlers who want to move to the Moon or Mars, just as railroad construction towns and mining towns became the future cities of the American West. The lives of people of Earth would also be better because abundant pollution-free energy is the key for providing clean air and water, low or zero-pollution fuel for transportation, reliable heat and cooling, and numerous other things that many do without today.

Based on current knowledge and transportation cost, recovering resources from Mars is more problematic. This could change once the first explorers and settlers walk on the red sands. Mars does offer scientific information and land with the basic resources for survival. The British India Company and the American railroad land grant models are examples of ways to involve private resources in the exploration and settlement of Mars and potentially the asteroids. There is also the potential that Martian settlements could be founded by the same type of migration that brought the Pilgrims to New England, Quakers to Pennsylvania, or Mormons to Utah. People looking for freedom to practice their religion or social preferences will spend a great deal and commit themselves and their offspring to a hard life to achieve their goal. This could give us the first settlements of Mars, as well as give humanity a new way to ensure long-term survival.

To avoid limits of growth for the people of Earth, we need to reach outward for the harvest of materials and energy that are there for the taking. A major benefit of this harvest will be to reduce pollution on Earth while increasing the standard of living for humanity. People everywhere and at all levels of society will live better because of the knowledge gained in the exploration, the money spent for new jobs, and new materials or energy provided from off-Earth sources. This same effort will open the trail to the stars for human migration. Our species will gain new frontiers and greater chance of long-term survival.

HOW CAN WE GO?

NASA is promoting the invention of new propulsion systems, and this may be the way to launch new efforts to harvest the resources of near space. It is also possible that the invention of new propulsion systems is not required. Much of the work for gathering resources or developing solar energy could be done with existing expendable rocket systems in the United States, Russia, China, India, or other countries with launch capability. For heavy lifting, vehicles like the Saturn V rocket that took men to the Moon could be used. Even the shuttle launch system could be a major heavy lifter if the shuttle were replaced with a nonreturnable payload, with shuttle engines attached for the launch (reference Robert Zubin's *Mars Direct*).

Numerous new ways to get material and people into space have been studied but not yet built. The potential of a space tourist industry is driving the development of several new launch systems. Air launch of a suborbital or orbital craft seems to be the most likely method to carry the first privately launched tourists into space. Electric rail gun and high velocity gas gun technologies have a strong potential for delivering cargo to low Earth orbit for projects such as construction of solar power satellites. These technologies are not suitable for launch of humans or fragile cargo because of the very high launch acceleration. An even cheaper and more exotic way to reach orbit would be a space elevator. This is essentially a very long satellite in equatorial synchronous orbit, similar to existing communication satellites. While the space elevator is a sound theoretical way to reach space, it would require invention because at this time we do not have a material strong enough to serve as the elevator cable.

The cost of putting people and material into space must be reduced to enable effective harvesting of resources beyond Earth. I have faith in the ingenuity of mankind to develop the transportation needed to give access to the vast riches beyond our atmosphere. This same development will give humans a way to begin migration to new homes off this planet. It will be the first steps in the long-term survival of the human species independent of possible major disasters on Earth.

SUMMARY

We have a window of opportunity to avoid the limits of growth for humanity on Earth. Numerous natural and man-made disasters could close this window for centuries, millennia, or forever. A developing space tourist industry can generate interest in space, new launch capabilities, and space habitat knowledge. Energy and resources from space can improve the quality of life on Earth and produce the wealth to allow continued growth on Earth and in the solar system. Gathering these resources will simultaneously develop the systems needed to allow the migration of humans to the Moon, Mars, and beyond. These efforts will inspire new generations of young people to pursue education and opportunities in all of the sciences and in engineering. This, in turn, will drive the countries involved in these endeavors to new heights of technology innovation, wealth, and improved environment. The general growth in total wealth will help all people. More nations will have the wealth needed to move beyond investment in basic infrastructure development and work to clean and protect Earth's environment.

In the very long term, migration to the stars is needed to ensure the survival of humans. It is one step at a time, but the voyage that started with those early humans walking out of Africa into Europe needs to continue with manned ships to Mars. We are explorers who want to see what is over the next mountain or on the next planet. We also have many people who follow the explorers and create new settlements that extend human civilization. A choice faces humanity. Will we stay in place and accept limits to growth (and standards of living) or will we venture into new frontiers as our ancestors did to expand human civilization?

Ad astra.

Contributors

Stephen Aguilar-Millan is the director of research at the European Futures Observatory, an independent not-for-profit organization based in the United Kingdom, and a director of The Greenways Partnership, a firm of consulting futurists based in the UK. He consults widely for a range of clients based across the globe. He is a member of the Royal Economics Society, a fellow of the RSA, and a member of a number of other professional bodies in the UK. He is currently directing an international team of futurists engaged on a variety of issues ranging from "The Globalization of Crime" to "The Future of Male Lifestyles to 2020."

Clifton Anderson is a University of Idaho professor emeritus in the field of agricultural communications.

Denis L. Balaguer is a technology intelligence analyst at Embraer, where he is responsible for the elaboration of technology-development strategy. He is a PhD candidate in science and technology policy at State University of Campinas (Brazil). He also holds a master of science degree in aeronautical and mechanical engineering, a graduate degree in science journalism, and a bachelor's degree in mechanical engineering. He has published papers and book chapters in his research areas, especially futures studies and technological prospective, science and technology policy, and innovation and R&D management. He has taught strategic management and innovation management at the Vale do Paraiba University.

Jitendra G. Borpujari is currently consultant and temporary alternate to executive director for Saudi Arabia on the World Bank executive board. He served earlier as advisor and temporary alternate to executive director for Saudi Arabia on the International Monetary Fund executive board (1996-2005) and in various staff positions at the World Bank (1991-1996) and IMF (1969-1990). He was also Simon Chair senior associate at the Center for Strategic and International Studies (CSIS). He graduated from the universities of Gauhati (IA), Madras (BA), and Delhi (MA) and received his PhD in economics from Cambridge University. He has published articles on economic policy and social history issues in academic books and journals as well as newspapers in English and Assamese.

Irving H. Buchen earned his PhD at Johns Hopkins University. He has taught and been an academic administrator at Cal State, University of Wisconsin, and Penn State. He is currently on the doctoral business faculty of Capella and IMPAC universities. He is the author of more than 150 scholarly articles and eight books, most recently *Partnership HR* (Davies-Black, 2007), a series of profiles of the American workforce.

Michael Bugeja is director of the Greenlee School of Journalism and Communication at Iowa State University. Specializing in media ethics and new technologies, he writes frequently for *Teacher's College Record, Education Digest, Inside Higher Ed*, and the *Chronicle of Higher Education*. His research on new media has been cited in *The New York Times, Washington Post, USA Today, Christian Science Monitor,* and *The Economist,* among others. His award-winning *Interpersonal Divide: The Search for Community in a Technological Age* (Oxford, 2005) prophesied the negative effect of ubiquitous technology on neighborhoods and relationships. His most recent book, *Living Ethics: Across Media Platforms* (Oxford University Press, 2008), advocates for new media standards based on universal principles.

Alexandra Chciuk-Celt ("Sandra Celt") has been translating, interpreting, training translators, and editing language-related publications for over forty years. She has lived in many countries, traveled extensively, and is fluent in German, Spanish, French, and Polish in addition to her native English; since she learned most of these languages before the age of seven, she realized very early on that there is no single correct way to do or say anything and that attitudes can be molded. Before earning a PhD in comparative literature (CUNY Graduate Center, 1984), she majored in communications and almost double-majored in cultural anthropology at Hunter College in New York City.

José Luis Cordeiro (www.cordeiro.org) is founder of the World Future Society's Venezuela Chapter, co-founder of the Venezuelan Transhumanist Association, chair of the Venezuela Node of the Millennium Project, and former director of the World Transhumanist Association and the Extropy Institute.

Paul Crabtree has both government and industry technology-related analytical and managerial experience. This includes staff support for U.S. congressional transportation hearings and legislation, work on environmental and habitat standards for water resources projects, benefit-cost and environmental review of hydroelectric and other construction projects, management of a large information technology organization, and nuclear plant cost analysis.

Joan E. Foltz is a principal of Alsek Research, a socio-economic analyst of global economic development and publisher of *Alsek's Not-So-Daily Update,* unbiased mapping of market behavior.

Romulo Werran Gayoso is an economist and staff finance engineer at Intel Corporation, where he also serves in various volunteer, mentoring, and teaching capacities. He also teaches economics at the University of Phoenix, both on campus and online. He holds master's degrees in business administration and economics from Arizona State University, and is a PhD candidate in organization and management at Capella University, Minneapolis.

Jay Herson is a senior associate at the Institute of Alternative Futures in Alexandria, Virginia, and at Johns Hopkins University in Baltimore, Maryland. He is also managing editor of *FUTUREtakes*, an electronic newsletter (www.futuretakes.org).

John Jackson is a sergeant with the Houston Police Department.

Seth Kaufman currently works at Barnes & Noble.com in New York, where he is a vice president of merchandising. His fascination with William Tyndale began, strangely enough, while on assignment for TV Guide Online. Taking a break from a press junket, he visited the Huntington Library in Pasadena and stumbled on an exhibition devoted to Tyndale and the Bible. He recently completed a screenplay about Tyndale, *The Translator.* He is a former reporter and was on the staff of the *New York Post*'s Page Six. He lives in Brooklyn with his wife and two children.

Barton Kunstler, PhD, is a futurist specializing in systems and strategies that organizations can apply to produce creative, efficient, and high-performing approaches to innovation and communication. He is the author of *The Hothouse Effect* (Amacom, 2003), an internationally acclaimed book that explains the dynamics of highly creative organizations and communities. He has published journal articles and book chapters on a wide range of issues, including intelligence analysis, leadership, communication, technology, ancient myth and history, creativity, and education, and has presented on these topics at numerous conferences. His poetry has been published in several leading journals, and he has been featured on TV and written a regular column (1999-2002, 2004) about future-oriented issues for *The Metrowest Daily News*. He is a Fellow of the Proteus Management Group, a member of the World Future Society and of the Association for Strategic Planning, and formerly a full professor of management and program director at Lesley University in Cambridge, Massachusetts, for many years. He is also involved in several educational and community initiatives.

Jukka Laitinen, MSc (Econ.), graduated from the Turku School of Economics in 2004. Currently he works as a researcher in the Corporate Foresight Group CoFi in Åbo Akademi University. His current research areas include innovation management, scenario analysis, and other foresight methods.

Sami Leppimäki graduated from the University of Turku in 1999. Since February 2000 he has worked in CoFi as a researcher. His main areas of interest in the field of economics have been banking and finance (especially "bank crises") and the monetary system. Through his work in CoFi, the properties and characteristics of the new so-called digital economy as well as visionary concept development have risen to being his main area of interest.

Jeanne Belisle Lombardo holds a BA in Spanish and Latin American Studies from Arizona State University and is in the final candidacy stage in the interdisciplinary MA program in humanities from California State University. Currently, she works as a facilitator in employee and organizational learning at Rio Salado College in Tempe, Arizona. From 1998 to 2006, she was the coordinator of the successful Transition Program at Rio Salado College in Phoenix, Arizona. She has been a national paid consultant on college transition for adult education, a poet, editor, published writer, and international English language teacher. Over the last six years, she has been a regular attendee of WFS annual conventions and has actively contributed, with her husband, Tom, to the development of the Phoenix Future Salon, the *Odyssey of the Future* Web site, the Center for Future Consciousness, and various publications and workshops related to the future.

Tom Lombardo, PhD, is the resident futurist faculty and faculty chair of psychology and philosophy at Rio Salado College in Tempe, Arizona. He is a graduate of the universities of Connecticut and Minnesota and a graduate fellow of Cornell University. He has served as the chief psychologist and educational director at John Madden Mental Health Center and the dean of Forest Institute of Professional Psychology. He is an active member of and frequent writer for the World Future Society and the World Futures Studies Federation, an editorial board member of the *Journal of Futures Studies,* an advisory board member of Communities for the Future, and a member of the Educational/Consulting Board of the Acceleration Studies Foundation. His first book, *The Reciprocity of Perceiver and Environment*, is the best-selling volume in Lawrence Erlbaum's *Resources in Ecological Psychology* and has been translated into Japanese. He recently published two highly praised books: *The Evolution of Future Consciousness* and *Contemporary Futurist Thought*. His Web site *The Odyssey of the Future* (www.odysseyofthefuture.net) contains a wealth of informational and educational resources on the study of the future.

Tarja Meristö works as a research director and a corporate futurist at Åbo Akademi University. Her research area is future studies and scenario planning as part of the corporate strategy process as well as foresight studies in different fields. She has specialized in corporate futurology, especially in scenario planning and visionary leadership.

Don Mizaur is a senior consultant with Karl Albrecht International (KAI). He is a consultant, speaker, and author. His professional career has included being a vice president with Motorola, senior vice president with the American Productivity and Quality Center, and director of the U.S. government's Federal Quality Institute. Among the clients with whom KAI has conducted backcasting sessions are the U.S. Air Force, Nuclear Regulatory Commission, California Department of Corrections, San Diego Country Estates, and Midwest Employers Insurance Corporation.

Amy Oberg is a futurist and strategist who specializes in helping organizations better understand the emerging competitive environment and respond with effective, proactive strategies. With more than twenty-five years of cumulative experience in competitive, management, and market analyses, her insights regarding emerging trends, threats and opportunities, market conditions, and technology disruptions have been sought out by organizations in a wide variety of industries, including aerospace, energy, telecommunications, transportation, consumer goods, bio/pharma, real estate, and finance. She now serves as corporate futurist for Kimberly-Clark Corporation. She has been the invited keynote speaker at professional conferences, a guest lecturer at universities, and a quoted source for national and international media. She has provided input for international television programming and served as the creator and writer of the Boston radio program *Speaking of the Future.* She currently serves as a technology forecasting expert for TechCast and an advisor to Lifeboat Foundation. She is a member of the Association of Professional Futurists, World Future Society, and World Affairs Council. She holds a master's degree in studies of the future, a bachelor's degree in communications, and has completed the Program for Managers at Rice University's Jones Graduate School of Management.

Joseph N. Pelton is director of the Space and Advanced Communications Research Institute (SACRI) at George Washington University. He is the founder and vice chairman of the Arthur C. Clarke Foundation and also the founding president of the Society of Satellite Professionals. He played a key role in the founding of the International Space University, where he has served as dean as well as chairman of the Board of Trustees. He is the author of twenty-five books, including the Pulitzer Prize–nominated book *Global Talk*. Pelton has also been director of the ITP at the University of Colorado at Boulder and director of Strategic Policy at Intelsat. He is the former executive editor of the *Journal of International Space Communications*. He has been elected an associate fellow of the AIAA and as well as a full member of the International Academy of Astronautics. His awards include the Outstanding Educator award of the International Communications Association, the H. Rex Lee Award of the Public Service Satellite Consortium, the ISCe Award for Outstanding Educational Achievement, and the Arthur C. Clarke Lifetime Achievement Award. Pelton holds BS, MA, and PhD degrees from the University of Tulsa, New York University, and Georgetown University respectively.

Howard Rasheed is chief executive officer and founder of Institute for Innovation, a company specializing in strategic visioning concepts for innovation and creative thinking. He is the inventor of the Internet-based Idea Accelerator® Software based on the Bisociation Brainstorming™ process. He is also an associate professor of business strategy at the University of North Carolina, Wilmington, and holds a PhD from Florida State University in strategic, international, and entrepreneurial management. He has written more than twenty-five academic publications in the areas of innovation, e-commerce, business strategy, and entrepreneurship. He currently teaches courses in strategic management, entrepreneurship, and managing innovation and technology. He also has owned a consulting firm for more than thirty years that provides consultative services to small and mid-size entrepreneurial firms. The firm has written and competitively won more than $16 million in public and private contracts and grants.

Christine Robinson is an Enterprise Architect and Business Continuity and Disaster Recovery principal consultant at Computer Sciences Corporation, with system engineering experience with the U.S. government and the Verizon Corporation. She has presented to the U.S. Congress new security system concepts for government agencies and the Department of Defense. She is a member of the IT Advisory Commission of Arlington, Virginia.

Arthur Shostak, PhD, is a futurist and professor emeritus of sociology at Drexel University, where for thirty-seven years he taught and introduced courses in futurism, race and ethnic relations, social implications of twentieth-century technology, and urban sociology. Previously, he was on the faculty of the Wharton School of Finance and Commerce, University of Pennsylvania. He is the author of *Anticipate the School You Want: Futurizing K-12 Education* (forthcoming). He is a longtime member of the World Future Society and co-organizer of its Philadelphia chapter, which he headed from 1972 through 2004, and has been a futurist consultant for Fortune 500 companies, government, labor unions, and education at all levels. He served for twenty-five years as an adjunct sociologist with the National Labor College degree program at the AFL-CIO George Meany Center for Labor Studies. In 2006, he was designated Outstanding Applied Sociologist by the American Sociological Association, a lifetime achievement award. He is author, co-author, or editor of more than 150 articles and thirty-one books on a wide variety of topics that are outlined on his Web site www.futureshaping.com/shostak.

Francis R. Stabler is a consultant on automotive propulsion and energy, retired from General Motors. He has worked on projects such as military fire control systems, automotive engine control systems, advanced automotive technology development, and automotive competitive assessment. He holds electrical engineering degrees from the University of South Carolina and the University of Wisconsin.

Dave Stein is a physicist, operations research analyst, and retired military officer. He has also served as a defense analyst and as an adjunct college faculty member. Originally a U.S. Army officer, he transferred to the Air Force early in his career, where his tours of duty with the Air Force Scientific Advisory Board, the Air Force Studies and Analyses Agency, and Headquarters Air Force Materiel Command gave him extensive experience in defense technology investment planning, long-range force structure planning, and geostrategic analysis. A graduate of both the Naval War College and the Air War College, executive development courses for senior-level defense decision makers, he served as a key advisor to the Air Force Requirements Oversight Council (AFROC) and co-authored a key section of the Defense Critical Technologies Plan for the Executive Office of the President. His diverse interests range from next-generation physics to geostrategic issues, comparative cultures and religions, and cross-cutting future-related issues. He is the current editor-in-chief of *FUTUREtakes*.

Bruce Tonn, PhD, is a tenured, full professor in the Department of Political Science at the University of Tennessee, Knoxville (UT). He also directs UT's Masters of Science in Planning Program and is the Environmental Sustainability Program Leader for UT's Institute for a Secure and Sustainable Environment (ISSE). He is also a part-time senior researcher in the Environmental Sciences Division of Oak Ridge National Laboratory (ORNL), where he began his professional career in 1983. An active scholar, he has published more than 175 refereed journal articles, refereed conference papers, book chapters, and book reviews. In addition, he has authored/co-authored more than eighty technical reports, mostly peer-reviewed reports for ORNL. He is a consulting editor for the journal *Futures* and is on the editorial board of *Social Science Computing Review.* He received a BS in civil engineering from Stanford University, a master's in city and regional planning from Harvard University, and a PhD in urban and regional planning from Northwestern University.

Jim Trinka, PhD, is the technical training director for the Federal Aviation Administration. He is charged with establishing a career learning and development strategy for critical occupations in the Air Traffic Organization and developing a workforce plan to hire and train 12,000 new air traffic controllers over the next several years. He holds a doctorate degree in international politics from The George Washington University. With Les Wallace, he is co-author of *A Legacy of 21st Century Leadership* (iUniverse, 2007).

Hanna Tuohimaa finished her studies at the University of Turku in 2002 having her master's degree in sociology. She has been working at CoFi since September 2006, first as a research assistant and then from January 2007 onwards as a researcher. She has taken part in various projects focusing especially on Internet-based surveys.

Les Wallace, PhD, is president of Signature Resources Inc., an international leadership and strategy firm based in Colorado, with offices in Europe and Asia. Active in the World Future Society and the World Business Academy, Wallace also serves on the board of directors of Counterpart International, a global economic development and relief organization, and on the faculty of the Institute for Global Chinese Affairs at the University of Maryland, College Park. With Jim Trinka, he is co-author of *A Legacy of 21st Century Leadership* (iUniverse 2007).

WorldFuture 2009

Chicago Hilton & Towers • Chicago, Illinois • July 17-19, 2009

WHEN: Friday evening, July 17, 2009, through Sunday, July 19, 2009. Preconference courses on Thursday and Friday, July 16-17, 2009, and Professional Members' Forum on Monday, July 20, 2009.

WHERE: Chicago Hilton & Towers, Chicago, Illinois.

WHO: More than 1,000 futurists from around the world.

THE THEME: "WorldFuture 2009."

TOPICS: Technology, education, health, business issues, families and communities, work trends, social change, the environment, global perspectives, futures research, government and politics, and much, much more.

SPECIAL EVENTS: Table-top displays, free career counseling by professionals, a bookstore with a large selection of future-oriented titles, and meet-the-author sessions. Professional preconference courses on a wide variety of subjects.

NETWORKING OPPORTUNITIES: A complimentary welcoming reception, two keynote luncheons, group business meetings, reserved networking areas throughout the meeting, and more.

PRESENTATIONS: Proposal deadline is November 15, 2008.

HOTEL: Ideally located on Michigan Avenue, virtually everything to see and do in Chicago is a short walk or cab ride away. The Chicago Hilton has achieved an unprecedented fusion of historic luxury and contemporary amenities. Spacious guestrooms provide unrivaled comfort. All rooms are richly appointed with classic cherry furnishings, gleaming brass fixtures, and exquisite Italian marble.

ORGANIZERS: Susan Echard, vice president for conference operations, is creating a worldwide network of volunteers to structure the program and recruit speakers for the meeting.

FOR MORE INFORMATION CONTACT: World Future Society, 7910 Woodmont Avenue, Suite 450, Bethesda, Maryland 20814. Telephone: 800-989-8274 or 301-656-8274; Fax: 301-951-0394; E-mail: info@wfs.org; Web site: www.wfs.org.

About the World Future Society

The World Future Society is an association of people interested in how social and technological developments are shaping the future. It endeavors to help individuals, organizations, and communities see, understand, and respond appropriately and effectively to change. Through publications, online media, meetings, and dialogue among its members, it raises awareness of change and encourages development of creative solutions.

The Society takes no official position on what the future will or should be like. Instead, it acts as a neutral forum for exploring possible, probable, and preferable futures.

Founded in 1966 as a nonprofit, nonpartisan educational and scientific organization in Washington, D.C., the Society has some 25,000 members in more than eighty countries around the world. Individuals and groups from all nations are eligible to join the Society and participate in its programs and activities.

The Society holds a two-day, international conference once a year, where participants discuss foresight techniques and global trends that are influencing the future.

Chapters of the World Future Society are active in cities around the globe. Chapters offer lectures with well-known speakers, educational courses, seminars, and other opportunities for members in local areas to meet and work together. These local chapters give members a chance to meet other forward-looking people and to discuss various topics of the future.

The Society's Web site (www.wfs.org) features unique resources such as the online Futurist Bookshelf—brief summaries of new and noteworthy books, reviews, and links to order—and Web Forums on a variety of areas of interest to members. Also included are links to a range of resources such as futures blogs, educational programs and related organizations.

The World Future Society has published numerous books, including *Futuring: The Exploration of the Future* by Society founder Edward Cornish, as well as several print and electronic journals, including *The Futurist,* a bimonthly magazine focused on innovation, creative thinking, and emerging social, economic, and technological trends. *The Futurist* is available in newsstands throughout the United States.

For more information about the World Future Society and all of its programs, visit www.wfs.org.